LEGION OF SUPER-HEROES VOL. 2
THE TRIAL OF
THE LEGION

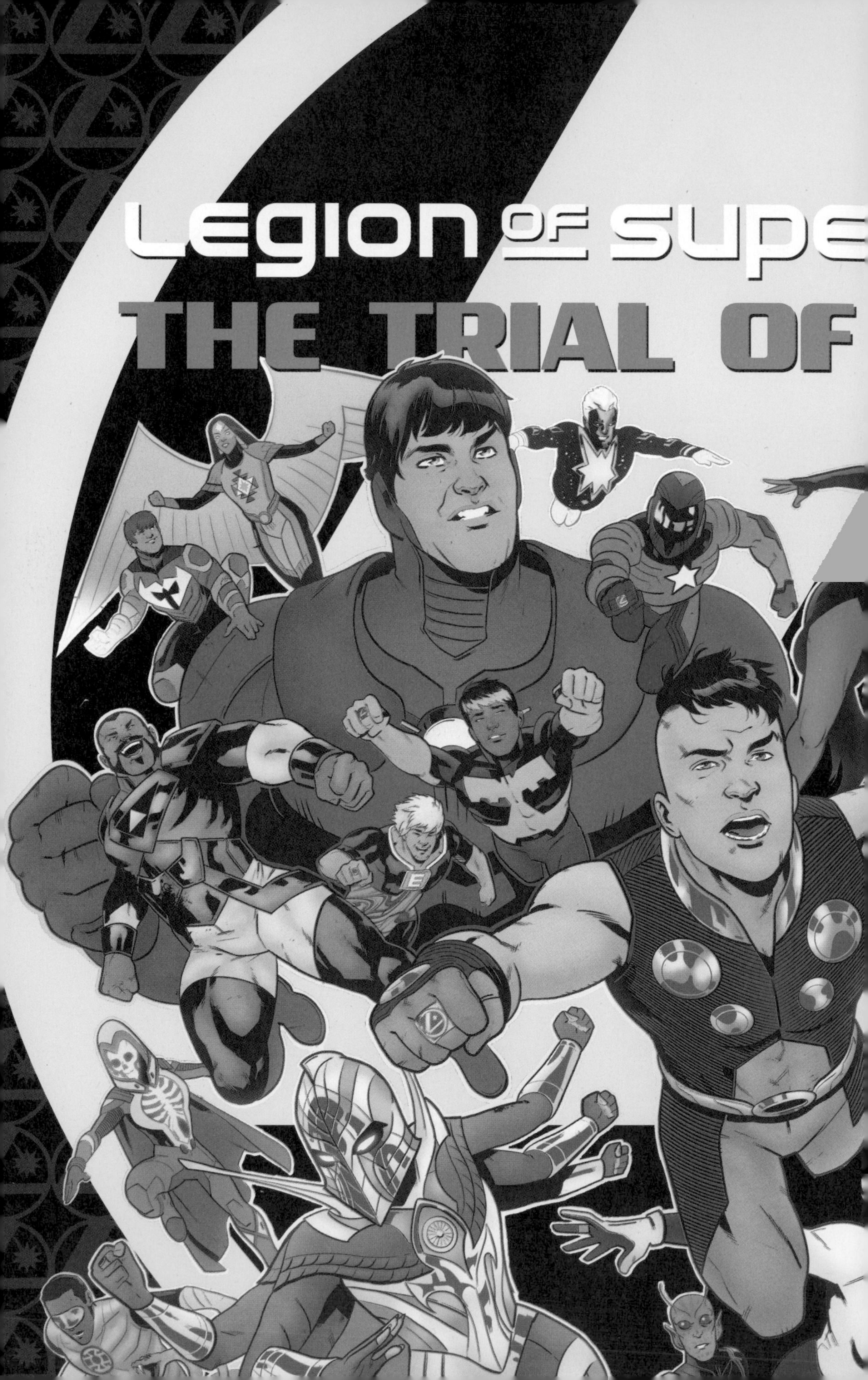
LEGION OF SUPE
THE TRIAL OF

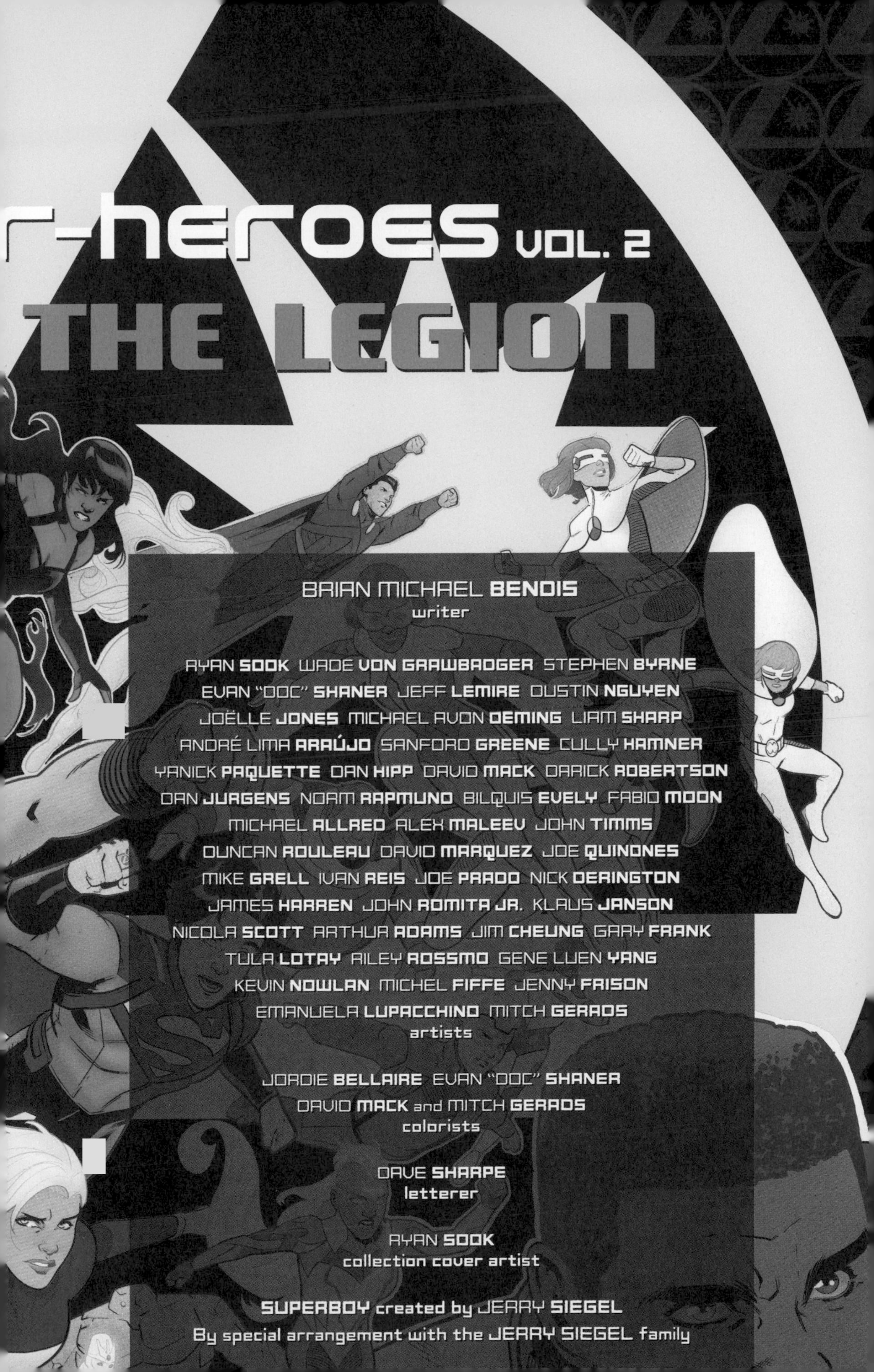

r-heroes VOL. 2

THE LEGION

BRIAN MICHAEL **BENDIS**
writer

RYAN **SOOK** WADE **VON GRAWBADGER** STEPHEN **BYRNE**
EVAN "DOC" **SHANER** JEFF **LEMIRE** DUSTIN **NGUYEN**
JOËLLE **JONES** MICHAEL AVON **OEMING** LIAM **SHARP**
ANDRÉ LIMA **ARAÚJO** SANFORD **GREENE** CULLY **HAMNER**
YANICK **PAQUETTE** DAN **HIPP** DAVID **MACK** DARICK **ROBERTSON**
DAN **JURGENS** NORM **RAPMUND** BILQUIS **EVELY** FABIO **MOON**
MICHAEL **ALLRED** ALEX **MALEEV** JOHN **TIMMS**
DUNCAN **ROULEAU** DAVID **MARQUEZ** JOE **QUINONES**
MIKE **GRELL** IVAN **REIS** JOE **PRADO** NICK **DERINGTON**
JAMES **HARREN** JOHN **ROMITA JR.** KLAUS **JANSON**
NICOLA **SCOTT** ARTHUR **ADAMS** JIM **CHEUNG** GARY **FRANK**
TULA **LOTAY** RILEY **ROSSMO** GENE LUEN **YANG**
KEVIN **NOWLAN** MICHEL **FIFFE** JENNY **FRISON**
EMANUELA **LUPACCHINO** MITCH **GERADS**
artists

JORDIE **BELLAIRE** EVAN "DOC" **SHANER**
DAVID **MACK** and MITCH **GERADS**
colorists

DAVE **SHARPE**
letterer

RYAN **SOOK**
collection cover artist

SUPERBOY created by JERRY **SIEGEL**
By special arrangement with the **JERRY SIEGEL** family

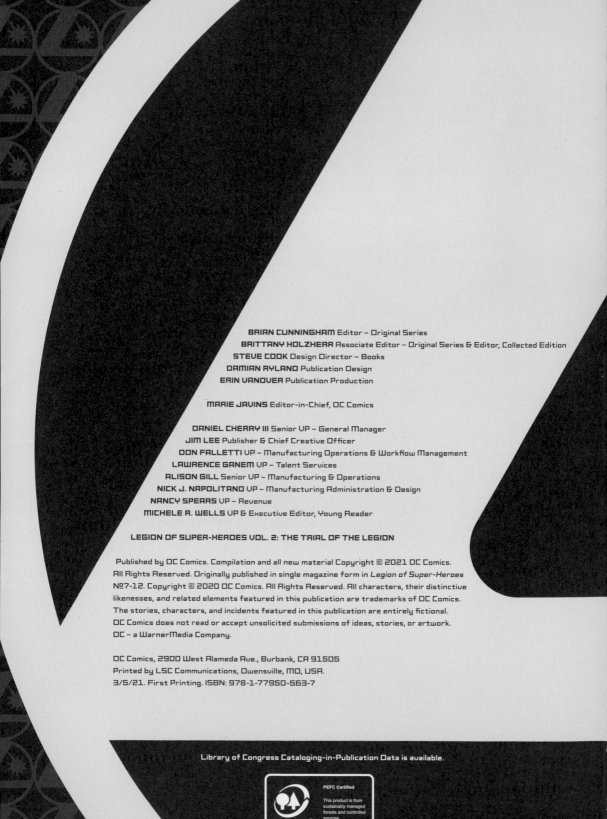

BRIAN CUNNINGHAM Editor – Original Series
BRITTANY HOLZHERR Associate Editor – Original Series & Editor, Collected Edition
STEVE COOK Design Director – Books
DAMIAN RYLAND Publication Design
ERIN VANOVER Publication Production

MARIE JAVINS Editor-in-Chief, DC Comics

DANIEL CHERRY III Senior VP – General Manager
JIM LEE Publisher & Chief Creative Officer
DON FALLETTI VP – Manufacturing Operations & Workflow Management
LAWRENCE GANEM VP – Talent Services
ALISON GILL Senior VP – Manufacturing & Operations
NICK J. NAPOLITANO VP – Manufacturing Administration & Design
NANCY SPEARS VP – Revenue
MICHELE R. WELLS VP & Executive Editor, Young Reader

LEGION OF SUPER-HEROES VOL. 2: THE TRIAL OF THE LEGION

DC Comics, 2900 West Alameda Ave., Burbank, CA 91505
Printed by LSC Communications, Owensville, MO, USA.
3/5/21. First Printing. ISBN: 978-1-77950-563-7

Library of Congress Cataloging-in-Publication Data is available.

PEFC Certified
This product is from
sustainably managed
forests and controlled
sources
PEFC/29-31-337   www.pefc.org

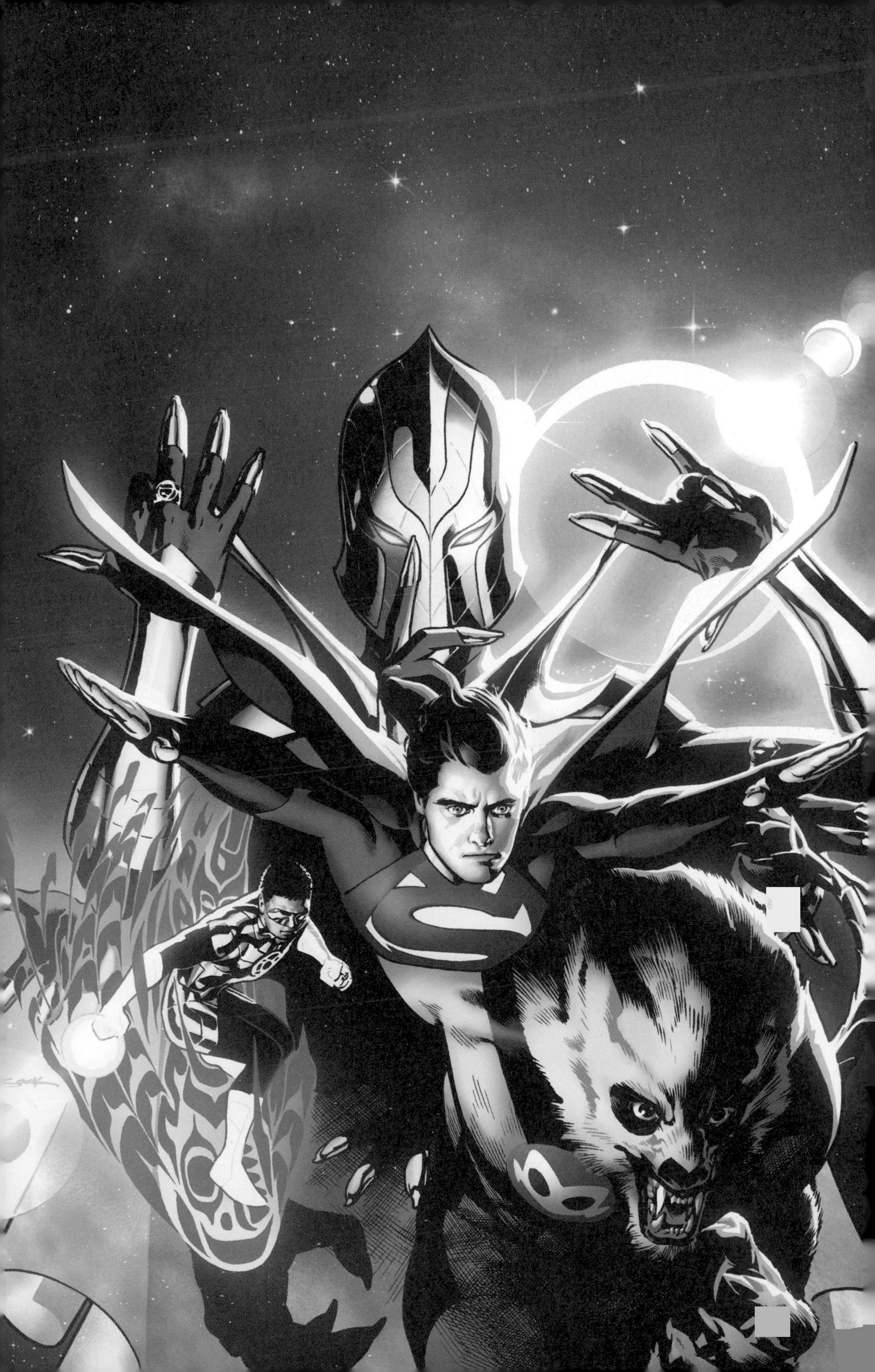

RYAN **SOOK**
Cover Artist

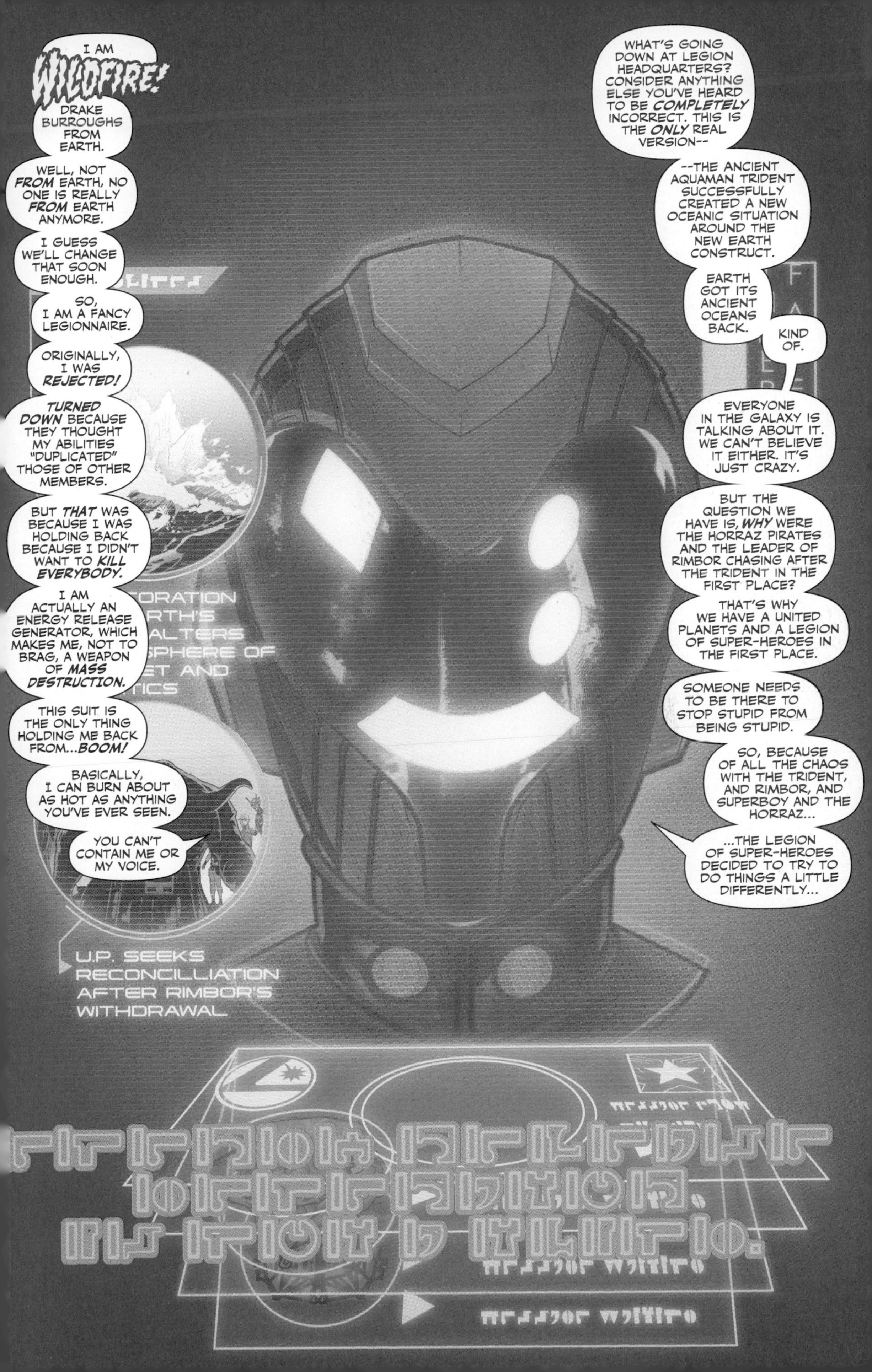
I AM WILDFIRE!
DRAKE BURROUGHS FROM EARTH.
WELL, NOT FROM EARTH, NO ONE IS REALLY FROM EARTH ANYMORE.
I GUESS WE'LL CHANGE THAT SOON ENOUGH.
SO, I AM A FANCY LEGIONNAIRE.
ORIGINALLY, I WAS REJECTED!
TURNED DOWN BECAUSE THEY THOUGHT MY ABILITIES "DUPLICATED" THOSE OF OTHER MEMBERS.
BUT THAT WAS BECAUSE I WAS HOLDING BACK BECAUSE I DIDN'T WANT TO KILL EVERYBODY.
I AM ACTUALLY AN ENERGY RELEASE GENERATOR, WHICH MAKES ME, NOT TO BRAG, A WEAPON OF MASS DESTRUCTION.
THIS SUIT IS THE ONLY THING HOLDING ME BACK FROM...BOOM!
BASICALLY, I CAN BURN ABOUT AS HOT AS ANYTHING YOU'VE EVER SEEN.
YOU CAN'T CONTAIN ME OR MY VOICE.
WHAT'S GOING DOWN AT LEGION HEADQUARTERS? CONSIDER ANYTHING ELSE YOU'VE HEARD TO BE COMPLETELY INCORRECT. THIS IS THE ONLY REAL VERSION--
--THE ANCIENT AQUAMAN TRIDENT SUCCESSFULLY CREATED A NEW OCEANIC SITUATION AROUND THE NEW EARTH CONSTRUCT.
EARTH GOT ITS ANCIENT OCEANS BACK.
KIND OF.
EVERYONE IN THE GALAXY IS TALKING ABOUT IT. WE CAN'T BELIEVE IT EITHER. IT'S JUST CRAZY.
BUT THE QUESTION WE HAVE IS, WHY WERE THE HORRAZ PIRATES AND THE LEADER OF RIMBOR CHASING AFTER THE TRIDENT IN THE FIRST PLACE?
THAT'S WHY WE HAVE A UNITED PLANETS AND A LEGION OF SUPER-HEROES IN THE FIRST PLACE.
SOMEONE NEEDS TO BE THERE TO STOP STUPID FROM BEING STUPID.
SO, BECAUSE OF ALL THE CHAOS WITH THE TRIDENT, AND RIMBOR, AND SUPERBOY AND THE HORRAZ...
...THE LEGION OF SUPER-HEROES DECIDED TO TRY TO DO THINGS A LITTLE DIFFERENTLY...
U.P. SEEKS RECONCILLIATION AFTER RIMBOR'S WITHDRAWAL

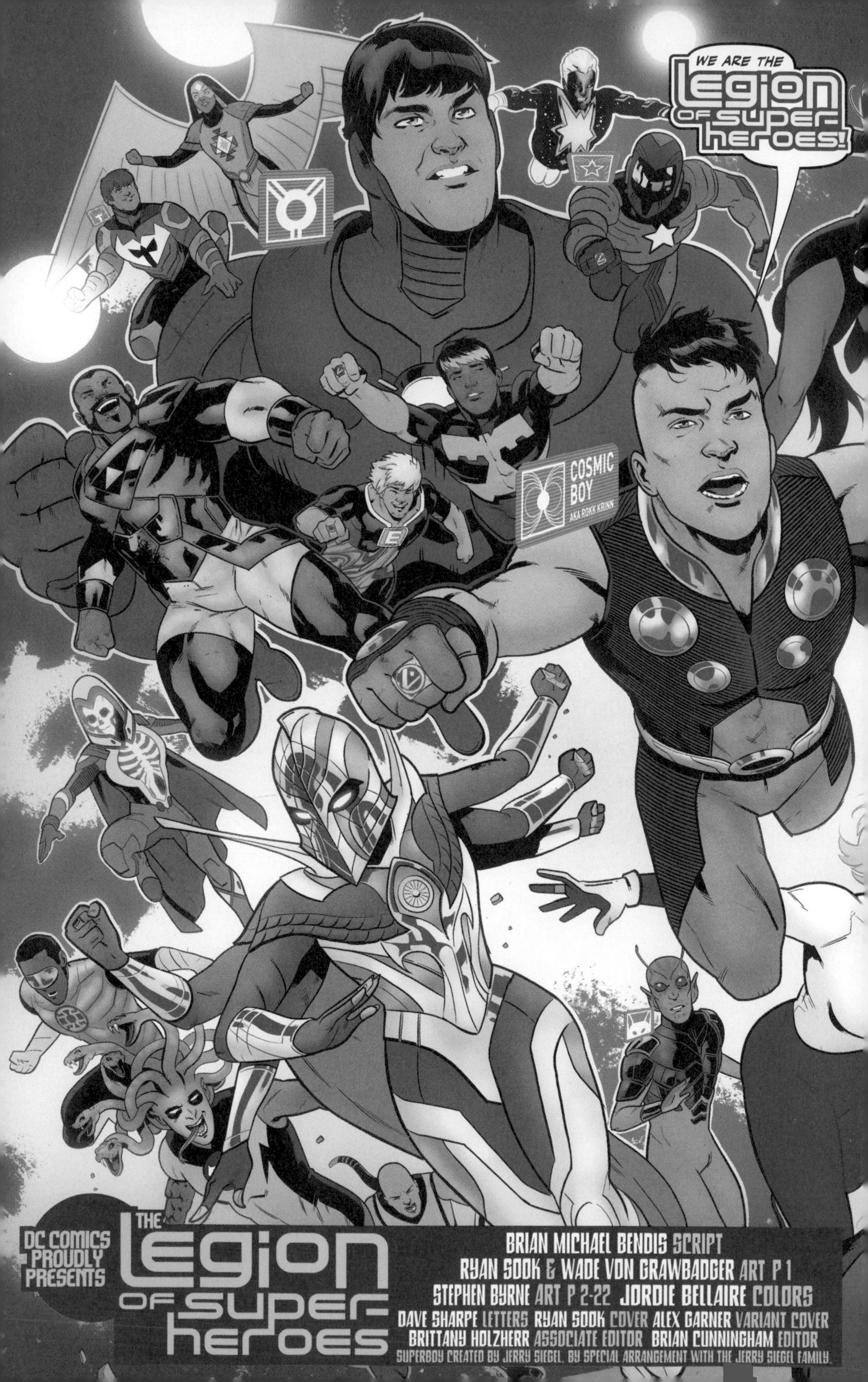
WE ARE THE LEGION OF SUPER-HEROES!
COSMIC BOY
AKA ROKK KRINN
DC COMICS PROUDLY PRESENTS
THE LEGION OF SUPER-HEROES
BRIAN MICHAEL BENDIS SCRIPT
RYAN SOOK & WADE VON GRAWBADGER ART P 1
STEPHEN BYRNE ART P 2-22 JORDIE BELLAIRE COLORS
DAVE SHARPE LETTERS RYAN SOOK COVER ALEX GARNER VARIANT COVER
BRITTANY HOLZHERR ASSOCIATE EDITOR BRIAN CUNNINGHAM EDITOR
SUPERBOY CREATED BY JERRY SIEGEL. BY SPECIAL ARRANGEMENT WITH THE JERRY SIEGEL FAMILY.

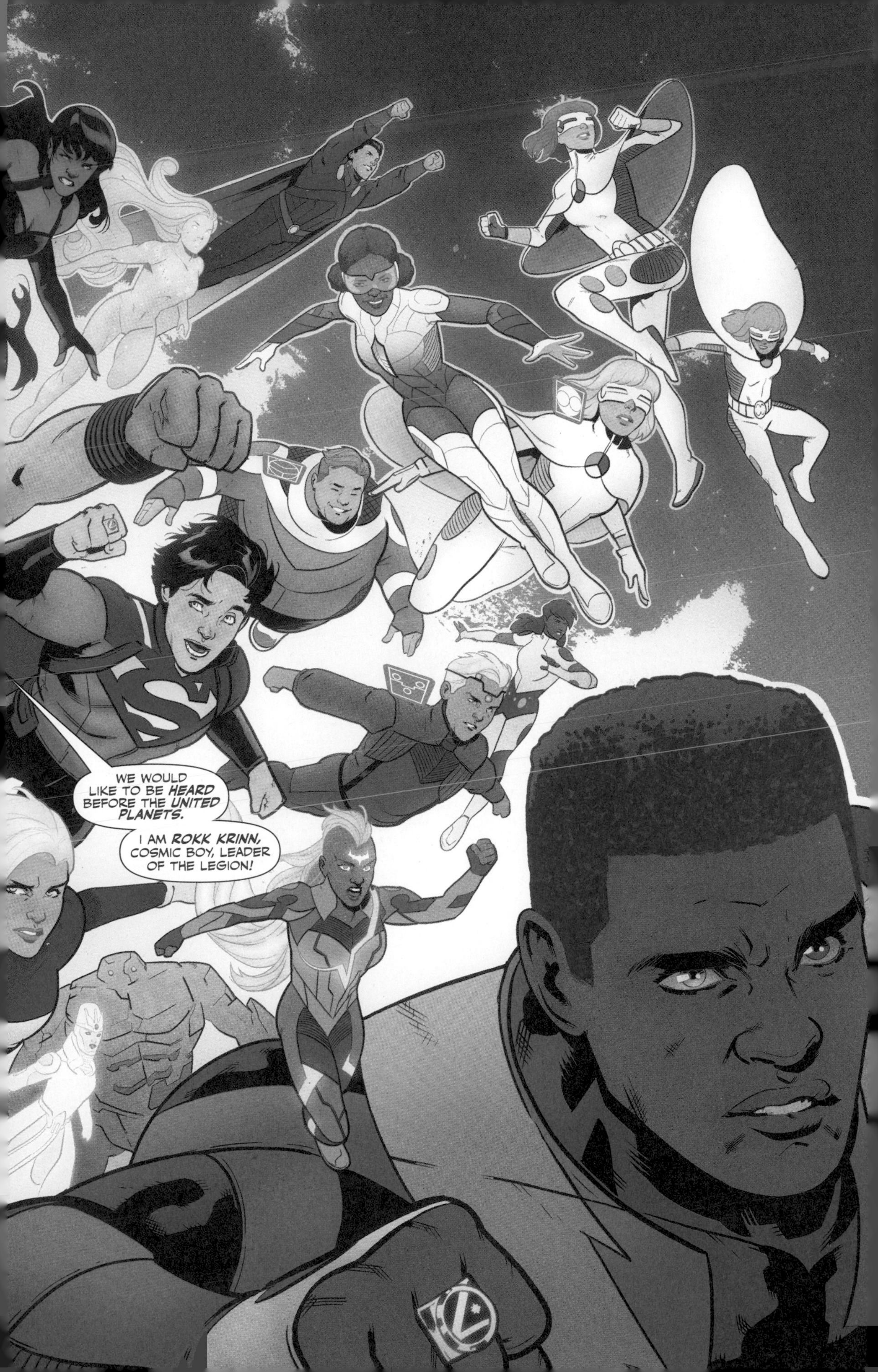
WE WOULD LIKE TO BE *HEARD* BEFORE THE *UNITED PLANETS.*
I AM ***ROKK KRINN,*** COSMIC BOY, LEADER OF THE LEGION!

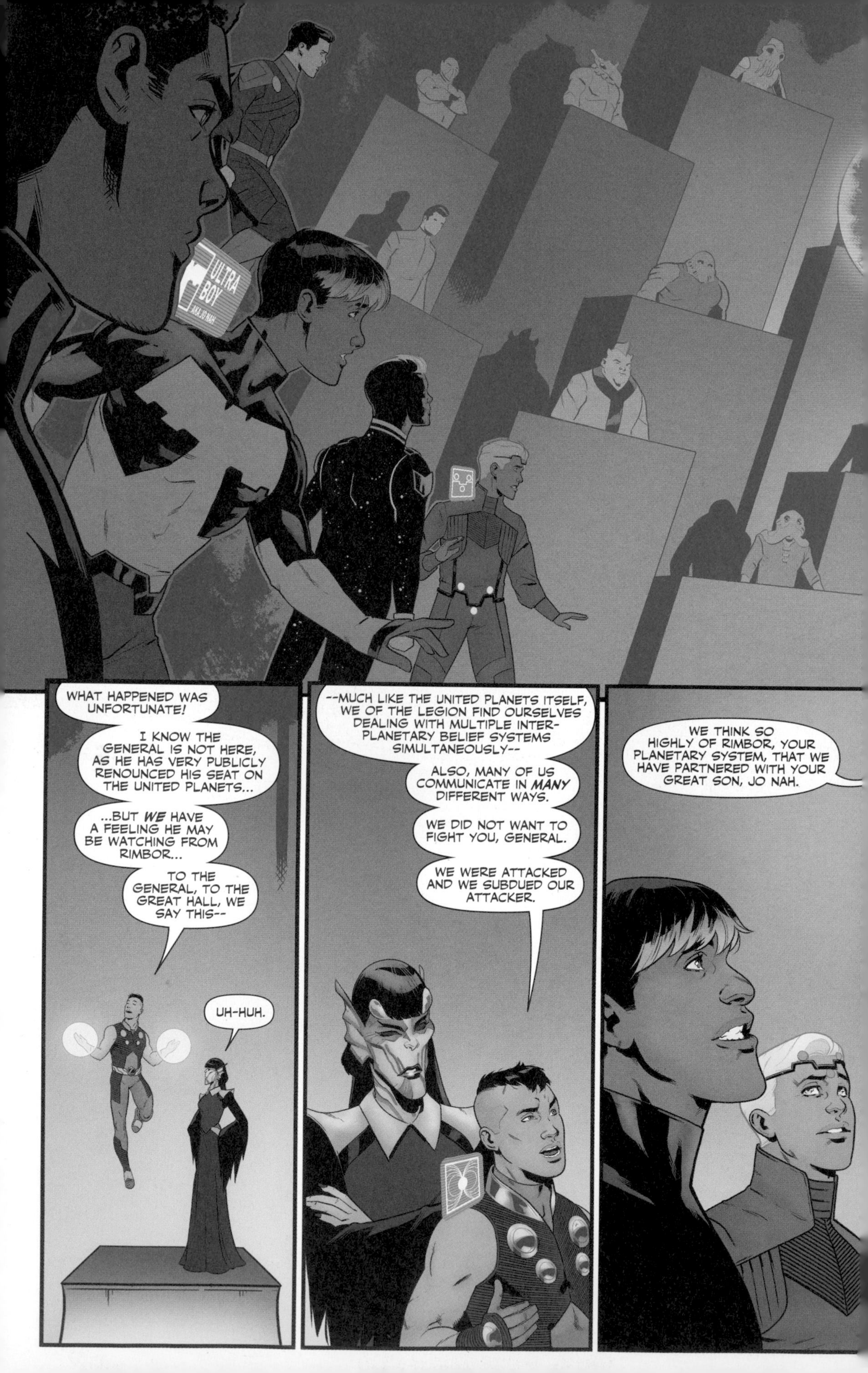
ULTRA BOY
AKA JO NAH
WHAT HAPPENED WAS UNFORTUNATE!
I KNOW THE GENERAL IS NOT HERE, AS HE HAS VERY PUBLICLY RENOUNCED HIS SEAT ON THE UNITED PLANETS...
...BUT WE HAVE A FEELING HE MAY BE WATCHING FROM RIMBOR...
TO THE GENERAL, TO THE GREAT HALL, WE SAY THIS--
UH-HUH.
--MUCH LIKE THE UNITED PLANETS ITSELF, WE OF THE LEGION FIND OURSELVES DEALING WITH MULTIPLE INTER-PLANETARY BELIEF SYSTEMS SIMULTANEOUSLY--
ALSO, MANY OF US COMMUNICATE IN MANY DIFFERENT WAYS.
WE DID NOT WANT TO FIGHT YOU, GENERAL.
WE WERE ATTACKED AND WE SUBDUED OUR ATTACKER.
WE THINK SO HIGHLY OF RIMBOR, YOUR PLANETARY SYSTEM, THAT WE HAVE PARTNERED WITH YOUR GREAT SON, JO NAH.

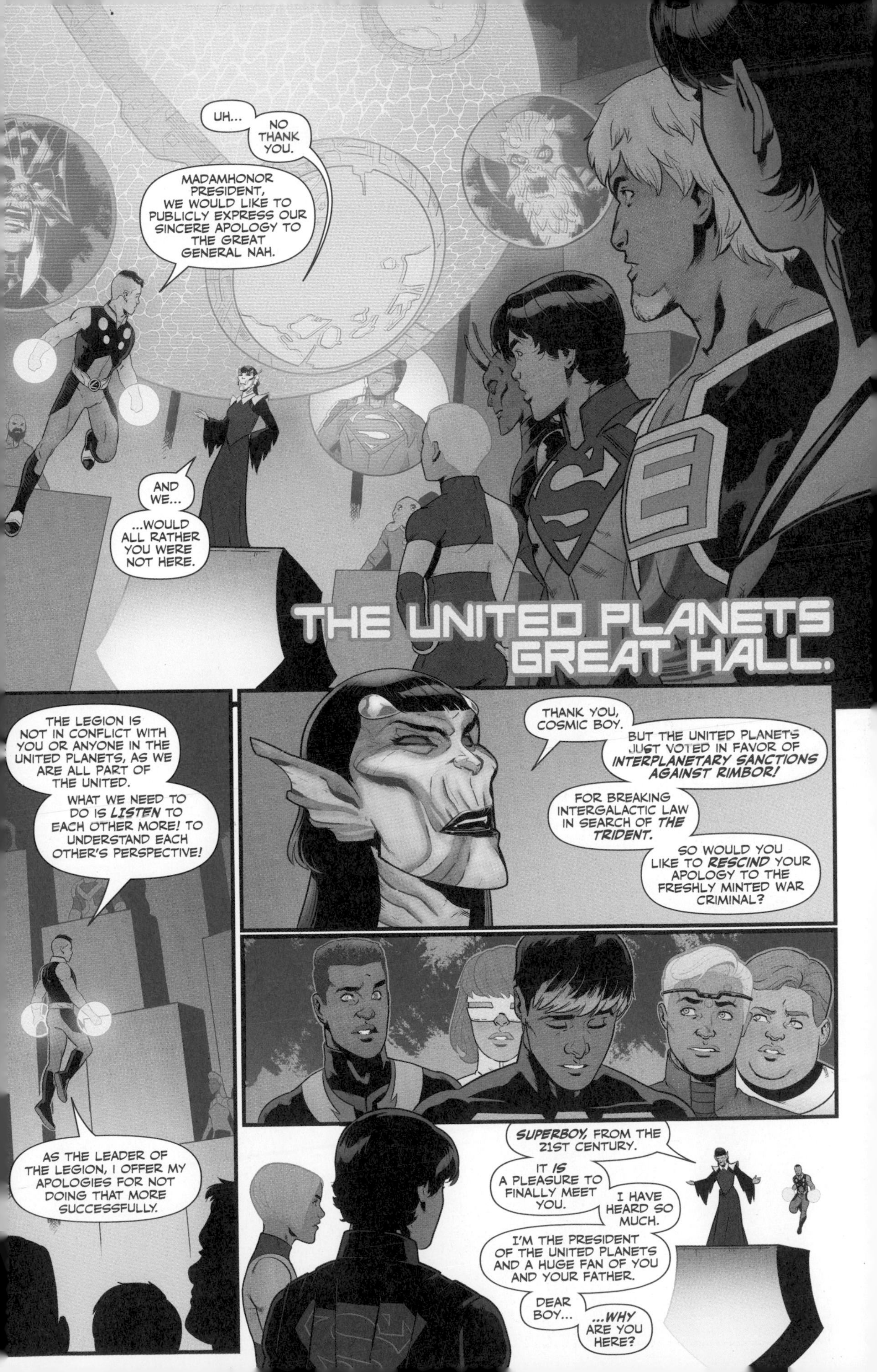
UH...
NO THANK YOU.
MADAMHONOR PRESIDENT, WE WOULD LIKE TO PUBLICLY EXPRESS OUR SINCERE APOLOGY TO THE GREAT GENERAL NAH.
AND WE...
...WOULD ALL RATHER YOU WERE NOT HERE.
THE UNITED PLANETS GREAT HALL.
THE LEGION IS NOT IN CONFLICT WITH YOU OR ANYONE IN THE UNITED PLANETS, AS WE ARE ALL PART OF THE UNITED.
WHAT WE NEED TO DO IS LISTEN TO EACH OTHER MORE! TO UNDERSTAND EACH OTHER'S PERSPECTIVE!
THANK YOU, COSMIC BOY.
BUT THE UNITED PLANETS JUST VOTED IN FAVOR OF INTERPLANETARY SANCTIONS AGAINST RIMBOR!
FOR BREAKING INTERGALACTIC LAW IN SEARCH OF THE TRIDENT.
SO WOULD YOU LIKE TO RESCIND YOUR APOLOGY TO THE FRESHLY MINTED WAR CRIMINAL?
AS THE LEADER OF THE LEGION, I OFFER MY APOLOGIES FOR NOT DOING THAT MORE SUCCESSFULLY.
SUPERBOY, FROM THE 21ST CENTURY.
IT IS A PLEASURE TO FINALLY MEET YOU.
I HAVE HEARD SO MUCH.
I'M THE PRESIDENT OF THE UNITED PLANETS AND A HUGE FAN OF YOU AND YOUR FATHER.
DEAR BOY...
...WHY ARE YOU HERE?

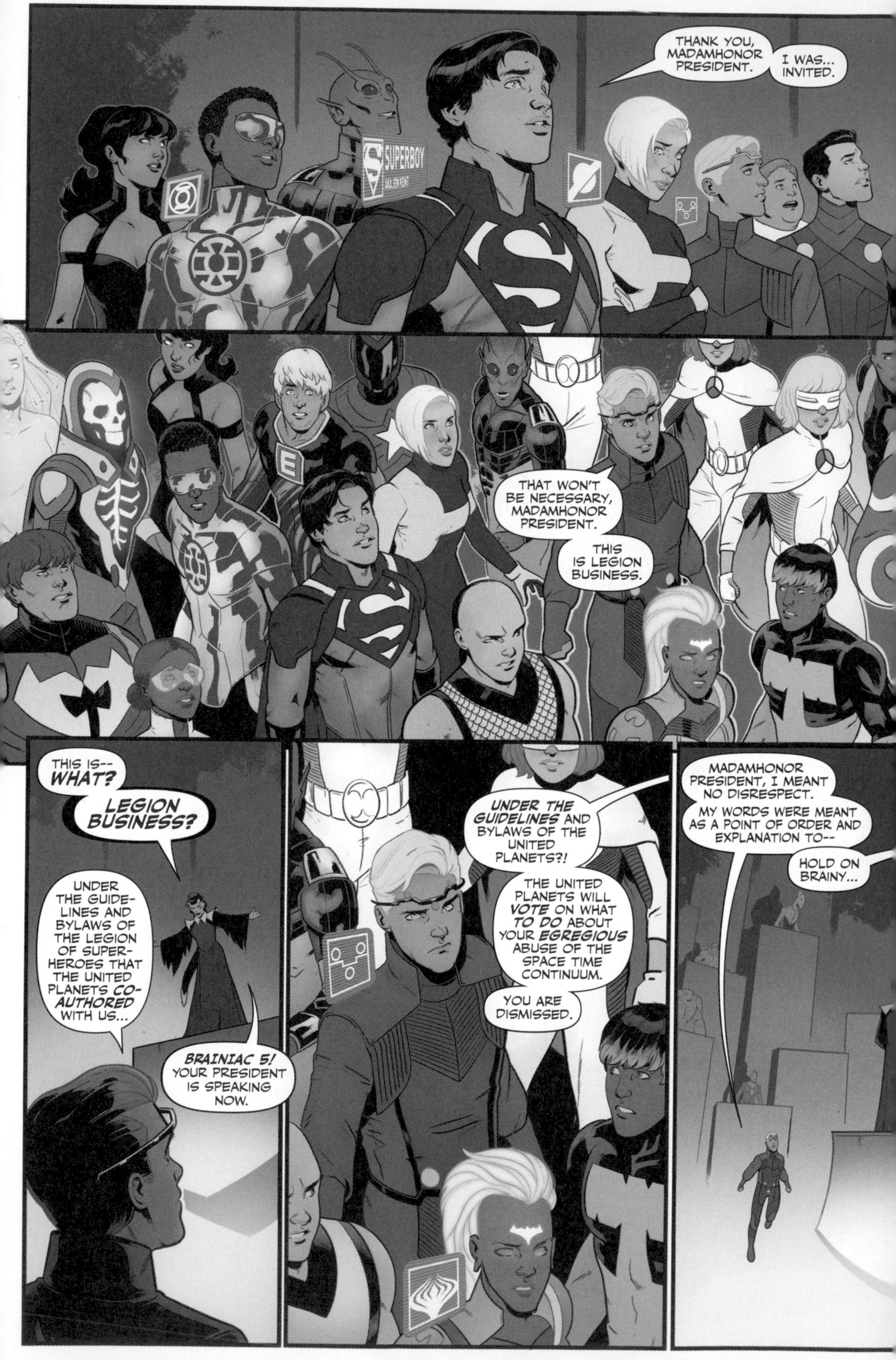

SUPERBOY
THANK YOU, MADAMHONOR PRESIDENT.
I WAS... INVITED.
THAT WON'T BE NECESSARY, MADAMHONOR PRESIDENT.
THIS IS LEGION BUSINESS.
THIS IS-- WHAT?
LEGION BUSINESS?
UNDER THE GUIDELINES AND BYLAWS OF THE LEGION OF SUPER-HEROES THAT THE UNITED PLANETS CO-AUTHORED WITH US...
BRAINIAC 5! YOUR PRESIDENT IS SPEAKING NOW.
UNDER THE GUIDELINES AND BYLAWS OF THE UNITED PLANETS?!
THE UNITED PLANETS WILL VOTE ON WHAT TO DO ABOUT YOUR EGREGIOUS ABUSE OF THE SPACE TIME CONTINUUM.
YOU ARE DISMISSED.
MADAMHONOR PRESIDENT, I MEANT NO DISRESPECT.
MY WORDS WERE MEANT AS A POINT OF ORDER AND EXPLANATION TO--
HOLD ON BRAINY...

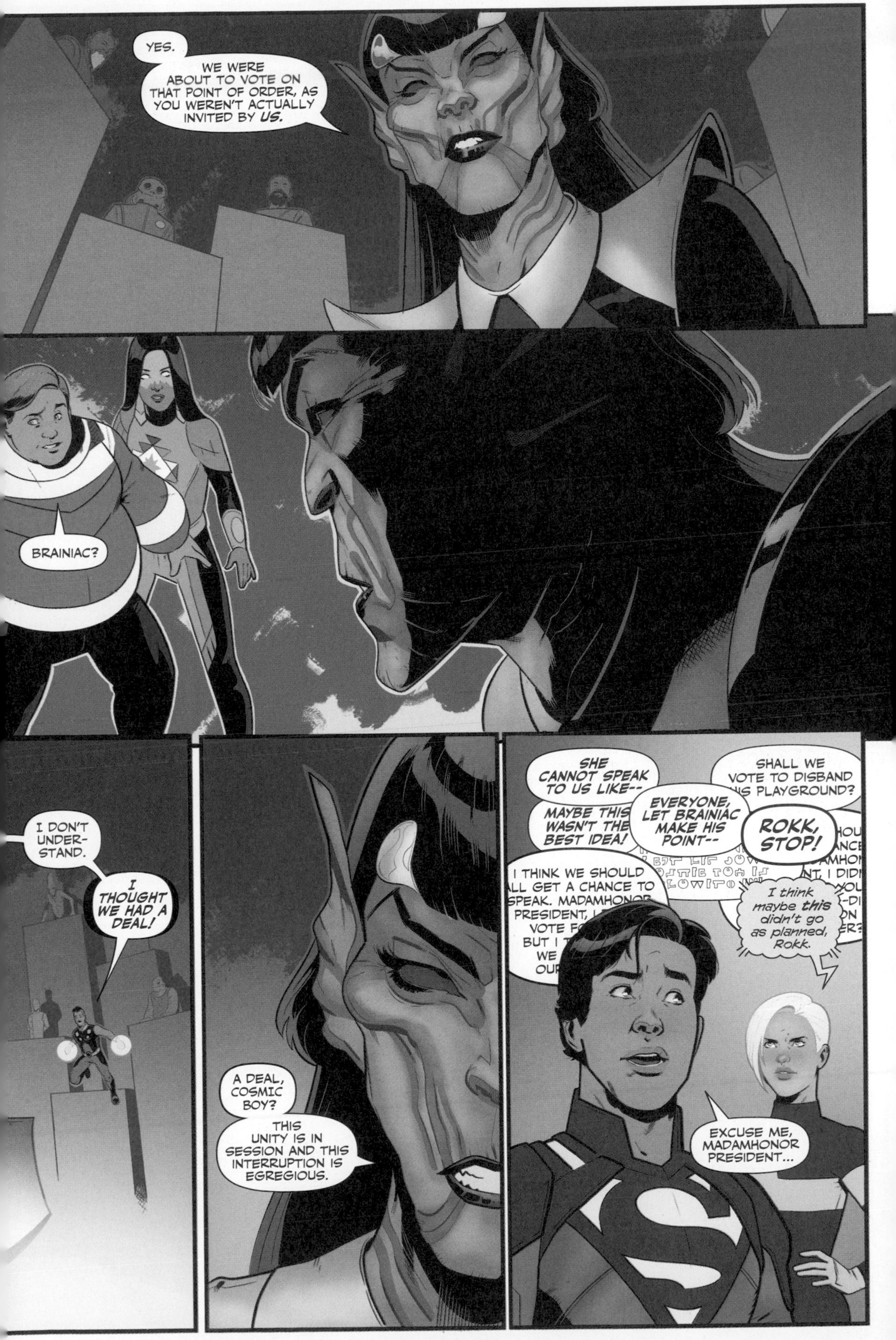
YES.
WE WERE ABOUT TO VOTE ON THAT POINT OF ORDER, AS YOU WEREN'T ACTUALLY INVITED BY *US.*
BRAINIAC?
I DON'T UNDER-STAND.
I THOUGHT WE HAD A DEAL!
A DEAL, COSMIC BOY?
THIS UNITY IS IN SESSION AND THIS INTERRUPTION IS EGREGIOUS.
SHE CANNOT SPEAK TO US LIKE--
SHALL WE VOTE TO DISBAND THIS PLAYGROUND?
MAYBE THIS WASN'T THE BEST IDEA!
EVERYONE, LET BRAINIAC MAKE HIS POINT--
ROKK, STOP!
*I think maybe **this** didn't go as planned, Rokk.*
EXCUSE ME, MADAMHONOR PRESIDENT...

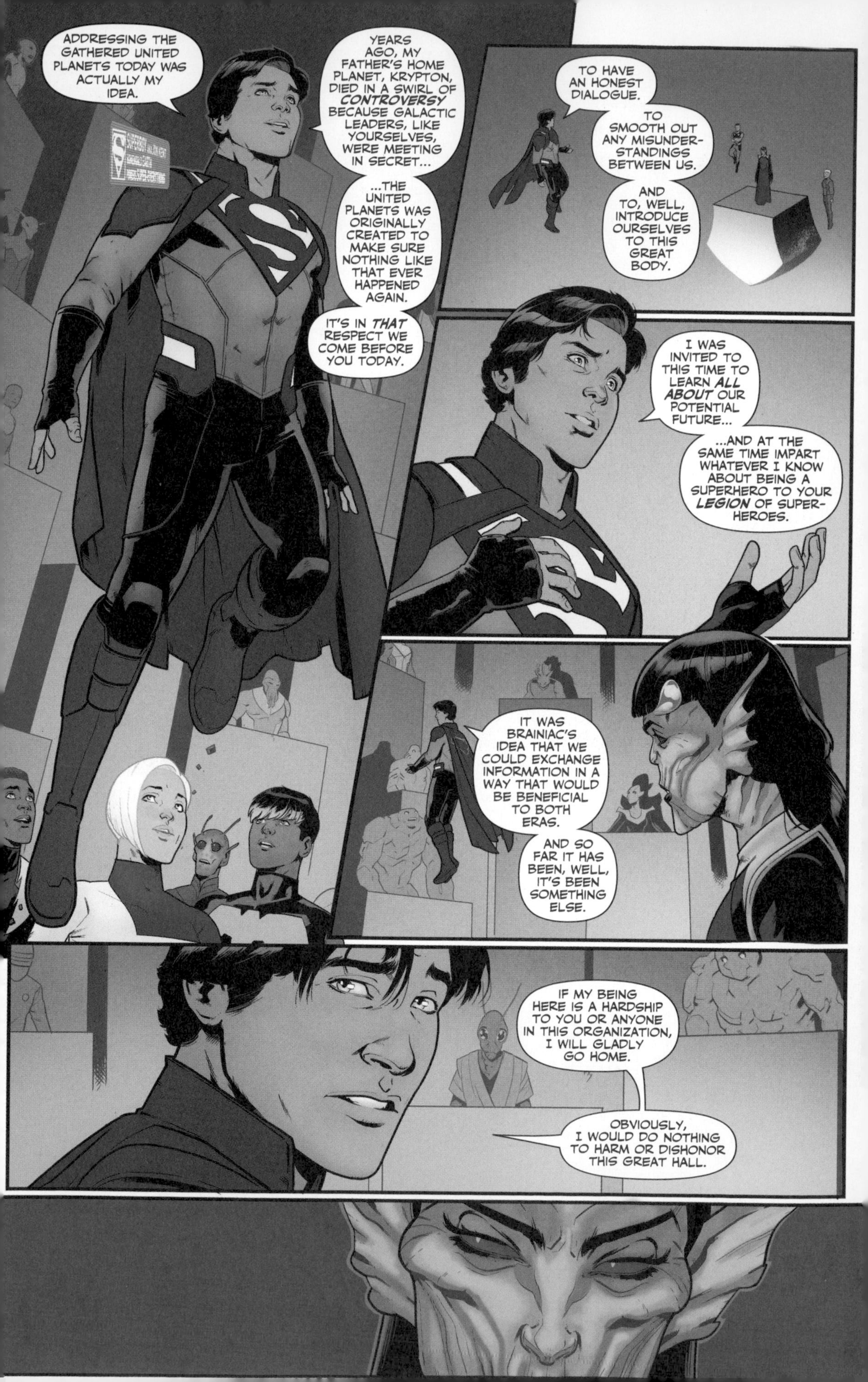
ADDRESSING THE GATHERED UNITED PLANETS TODAY WAS ACTUALLY MY IDEA.
YEARS AGO, MY FATHER'S HOME PLANET, KRYPTON, DIED IN A SWIRL OF *CONTROVERSY* BECAUSE GALACTIC LEADERS, LIKE YOURSELVES, WERE MEETING IN SECRET...
...THE UNITED PLANETS WAS ORIGINALLY CREATED TO MAKE SURE NOTHING LIKE THAT EVER HAPPENED AGAIN.
IT'S IN *THAT* RESPECT WE COME BEFORE YOU TODAY.
TO HAVE AN HONEST DIALOGUE.
TO SMOOTH OUT ANY MISUNDER-STANDINGS BETWEEN US.
AND TO, WELL, INTRODUCE OURSELVES TO THIS GREAT BODY.
I WAS INVITED TO THIS TIME TO LEARN *ALL ABOUT* OUR POTENTIAL FUTURE...
...AND AT THE SAME TIME IMPART WHATEVER I KNOW ABOUT BEING A SUPERHERO TO YOUR *LEGION* OF SUPER-HEROES.
IT WAS BRAINIAC'S IDEA THAT WE COULD EXCHANGE INFORMATION IN A WAY THAT WOULD BE BENEFICIAL TO BOTH ERAS.
AND SO FAR IT HAS BEEN, WELL, IT'S BEEN SOMETHING ELSE.
IF MY BEING HERE IS A HARDSHIP TO YOU OR ANYONE IN THIS ORGANIZATION, I WILL GLADLY GO HOME.
OBVIOUSLY, I WOULD DO NOTHING TO HARM OR DISHONOR THIS GREAT HALL.

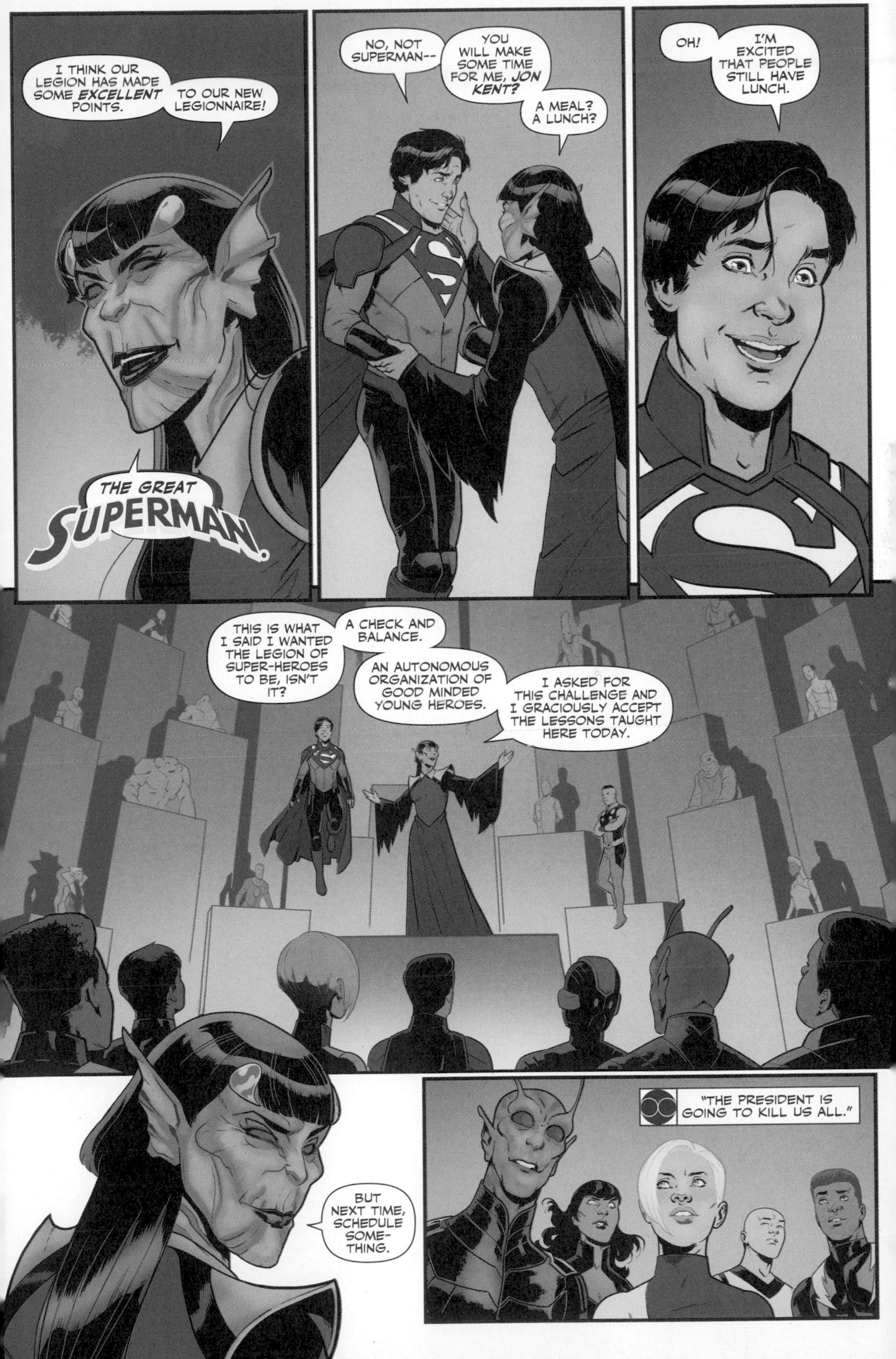
I THINK OUR LEGION HAS MADE SOME *EXCELLENT* POINTS.
TO OUR NEW LEGIONNAIRE!
THE GREAT SUPERMAN.
NO, NOT SUPERMAN--
YOU WILL MAKE SOME TIME FOR ME, *JON KENT?*
A MEAL? A LUNCH?
OH!
I'M EXCITED THAT PEOPLE STILL HAVE LUNCH.
THIS IS WHAT I SAID I WANTED THE LEGION OF SUPER-HEROES TO BE, ISN'T IT?
A CHECK AND BALANCE.
AN AUTONOMOUS ORGANIZATION OF GOOD MINDED YOUNG HEROES.
I ASKED FOR THIS CHALLENGE AND I GRACIOUSLY ACCEPT THE LESSONS TAUGHT HERE TODAY.
BUT NEXT TIME, SCHEDULE SOME-THING.
"THE PRESIDENT IS GOING TO KILL US ALL."

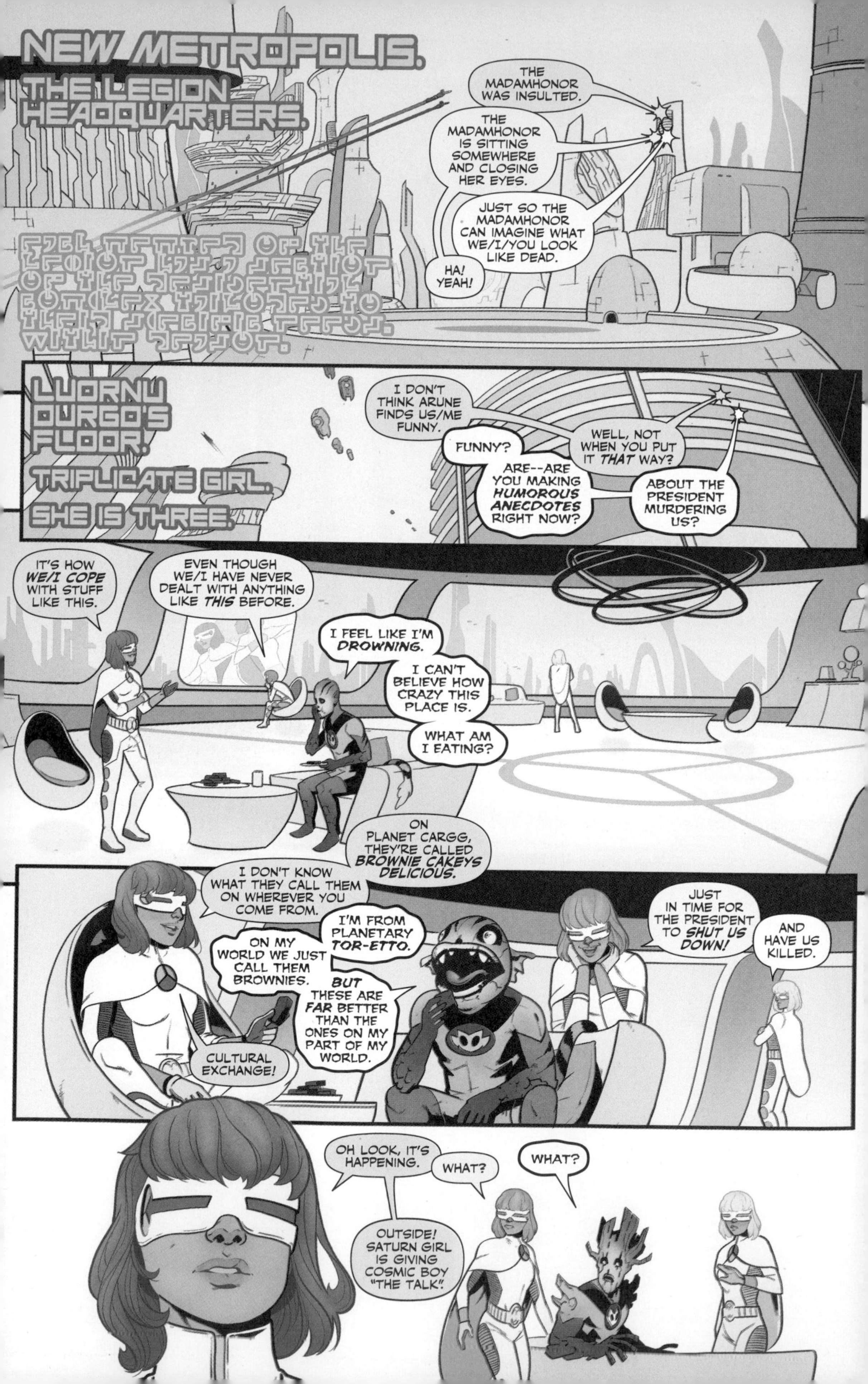
NEW METROPOLIS.
THE LEGION HEADQUARTERS.
THE MADAMHONOR WAS INSULTED.
THE MADAMHONOR IS SITTING SOMEWHERE AND CLOSING HER EYES.
JUST SO THE MADAMHONOR CAN IMAGINE WHAT WE/I/YOU LOOK LIKE DEAD.
HA! YEAH!
LUORNU DURGO'S FLOOR.
TRIPLICATE GIRL.
SHE IS THREE.
I DON'T THINK ARUNE FINDS US/ME FUNNY.
FUNNY?
WELL, NOT WHEN YOU PUT IT *THAT* WAY?
ARE--ARE YOU MAKING ***HUMOROUS ANECDOTES*** RIGHT NOW?
ABOUT THE PRESIDENT MURDERING US?
IT'S HOW ***WE/I COPE*** WITH STUFF LIKE THIS.
EVEN THOUGH WE/I HAVE NEVER DEALT WITH ANYTHING LIKE *THIS* BEFORE.
I FEEL LIKE I'M ***DROWNING.***
I CAN'T BELIEVE HOW CRAZY THIS PLACE IS.
WHAT AM I EATING?
ON PLANET CARGG, THEY'RE CALLED ***BROWNIE CAKEYS DELICIOUS.***
I DON'T KNOW WHAT THEY CALL THEM ON WHEREVER YOU COME FROM.
I'M FROM PLANETARY ***TOR-ETTO.***
ON MY WORLD WE JUST CALL THEM BROWNIES.
BUT THESE ARE ***FAR*** BETTER THAN THE ONES ON MY PART OF MY WORLD.
CULTURAL EXCHANGE!
JUST IN TIME FOR THE PRESIDENT TO ***SHUT US DOWN!***
AND HAVE US KILLED.
OH LOOK, IT'S HAPPENING.
WHAT?
WHAT?
OUTSIDE! SATURN GIRL IS GIVING COSMIC BOY "THE TALK."

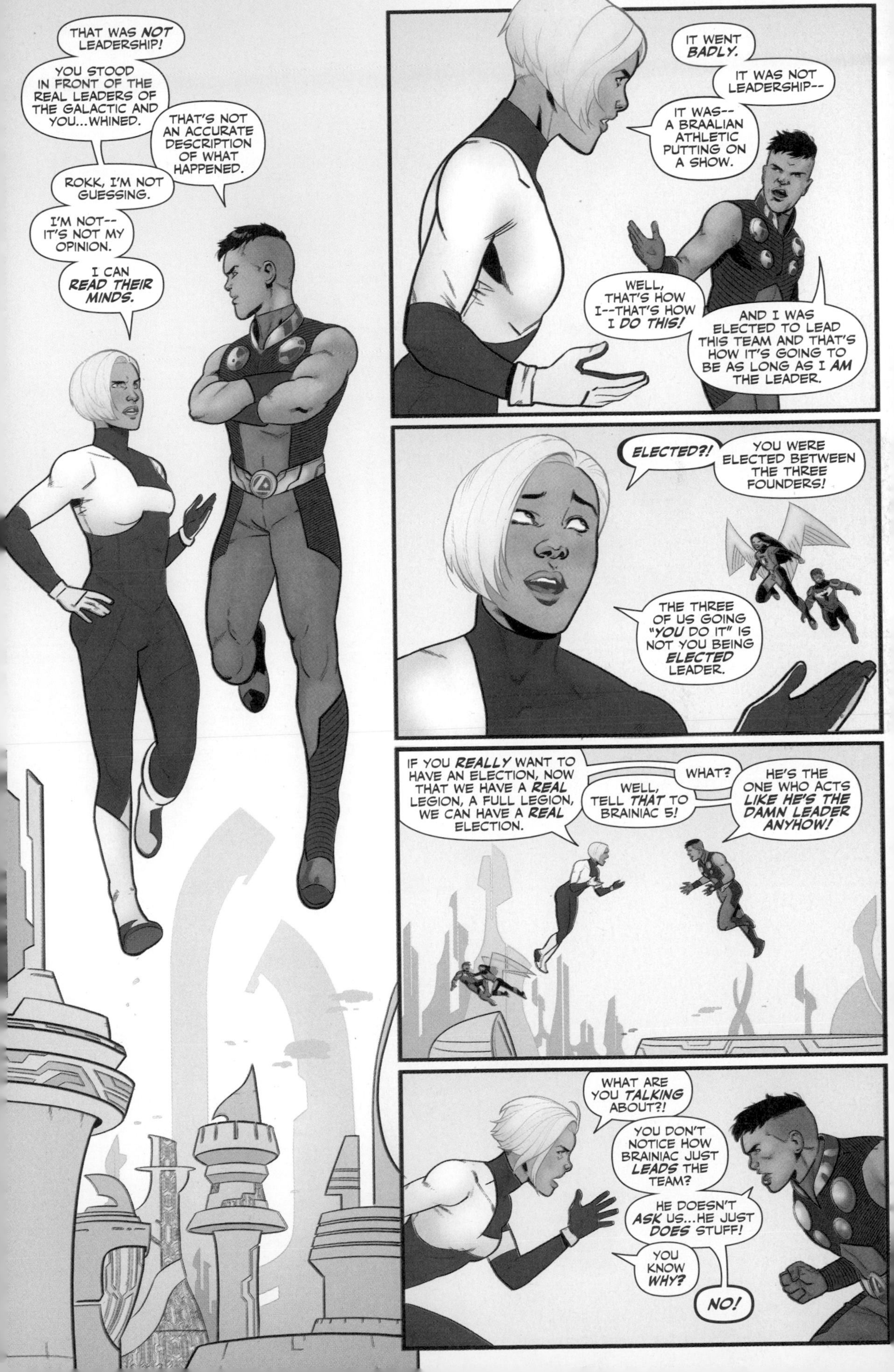
THAT WAS NOT LEADERSHIP!
YOU STOOD IN FRONT OF THE REAL LEADERS OF THE GALACTIC AND YOU...WHINED.
THAT'S NOT AN ACCURATE DESCRIPTION OF WHAT HAPPENED.
ROKK, I'M NOT GUESSING.
I'M NOT-- IT'S NOT MY OPINION.
I CAN READ THEIR MINDS.
IT WENT BADLY.
IT WAS NOT LEADERSHIP--
IT WAS-- A BRAALIAN ATHLETIC PUTTING ON A SHOW.
WELL, THAT'S HOW I--THAT'S HOW I DO THIS!
AND I WAS ELECTED TO LEAD THIS TEAM AND THAT'S HOW IT'S GOING TO BE AS LONG AS I AM THE LEADER.
ELECTED?!
YOU WERE ELECTED BETWEEN THE THREE FOUNDERS!
THE THREE OF US GOING "YOU DO IT" IS NOT YOU BEING ELECTED LEADER.
IF YOU REALLY WANT TO HAVE AN ELECTION, NOW THAT WE HAVE A REAL LEGION, A FULL LEGION, WE CAN HAVE A REAL ELECTION.
WELL, TELL THAT TO BRAINIAC 5!
WHAT?
HE'S THE ONE WHO ACTS LIKE HE'S THE DAMN LEADER ANYHOW!
WHAT ARE YOU TALKING ABOUT?!
YOU DON'T NOTICE HOW BRAINIAC JUST LEADS THE TEAM?
HE DOESN'T ASK US...HE JUST DOES STUFF!
YOU KNOW WHY?
NO!

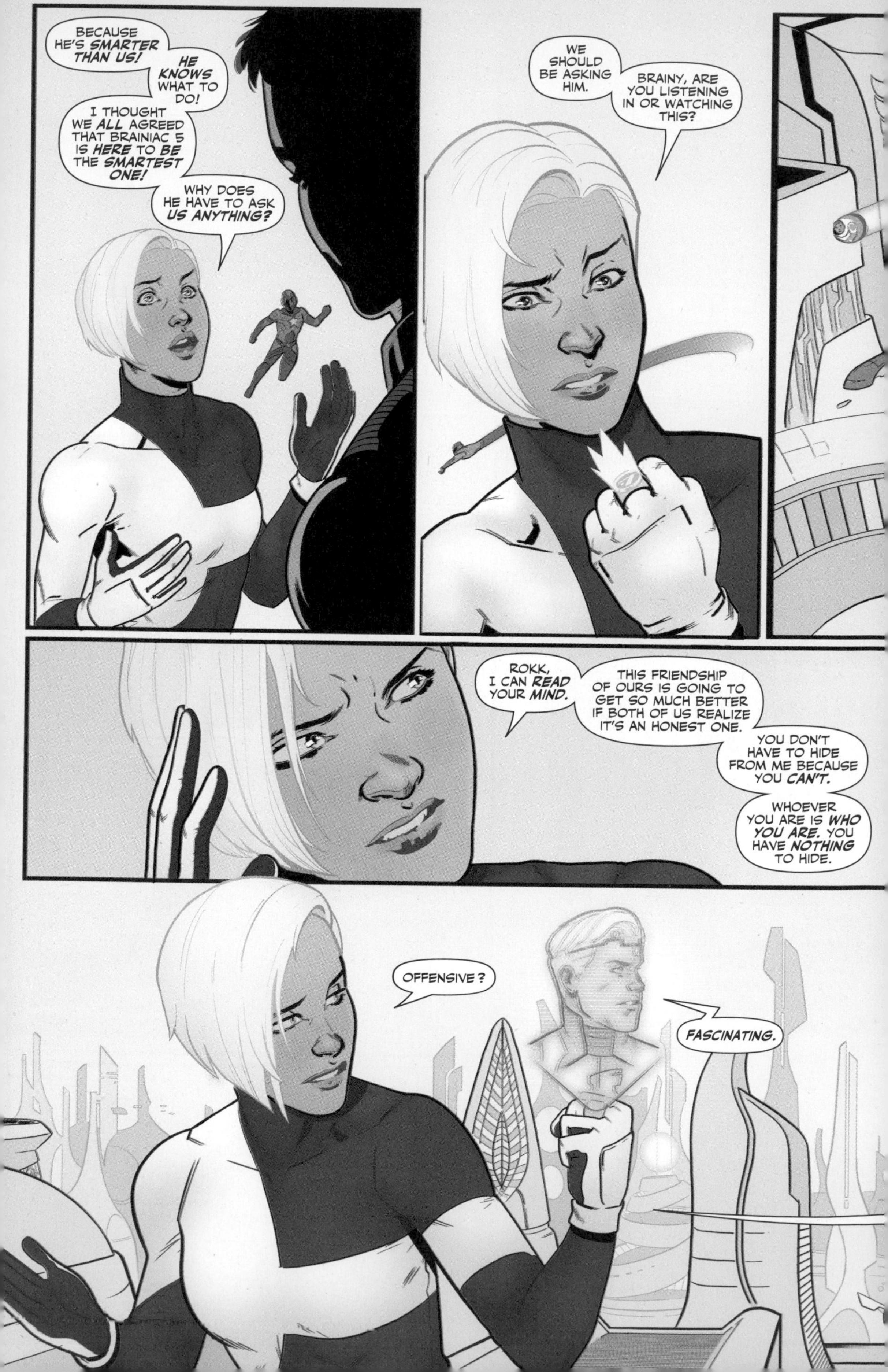
BECAUSE HE'S SMARTER THAN US!
HE KNOWS WHAT TO DO!
I THOUGHT WE ALL AGREED THAT BRAINIAC 5 IS HERE TO BE THE SMARTEST ONE!
WHY DOES HE HAVE TO ASK US ANYTHING?
WE SHOULD BE ASKING HIM.
BRAINY, ARE YOU LISTENING IN OR WATCHING THIS?
ROKK, I CAN READ YOUR MIND.
THIS FRIENDSHIP OF OURS IS GOING TO GET SO MUCH BETTER IF BOTH OF US REALIZE IT'S AN HONEST ONE.
YOU DON'T HAVE TO HIDE FROM ME BECAUSE YOU CAN'T.
WHOEVER YOU ARE IS WHO YOU ARE. YOU HAVE NOTHING TO HIDE.
OFFENSIVE?
FASCINATING.

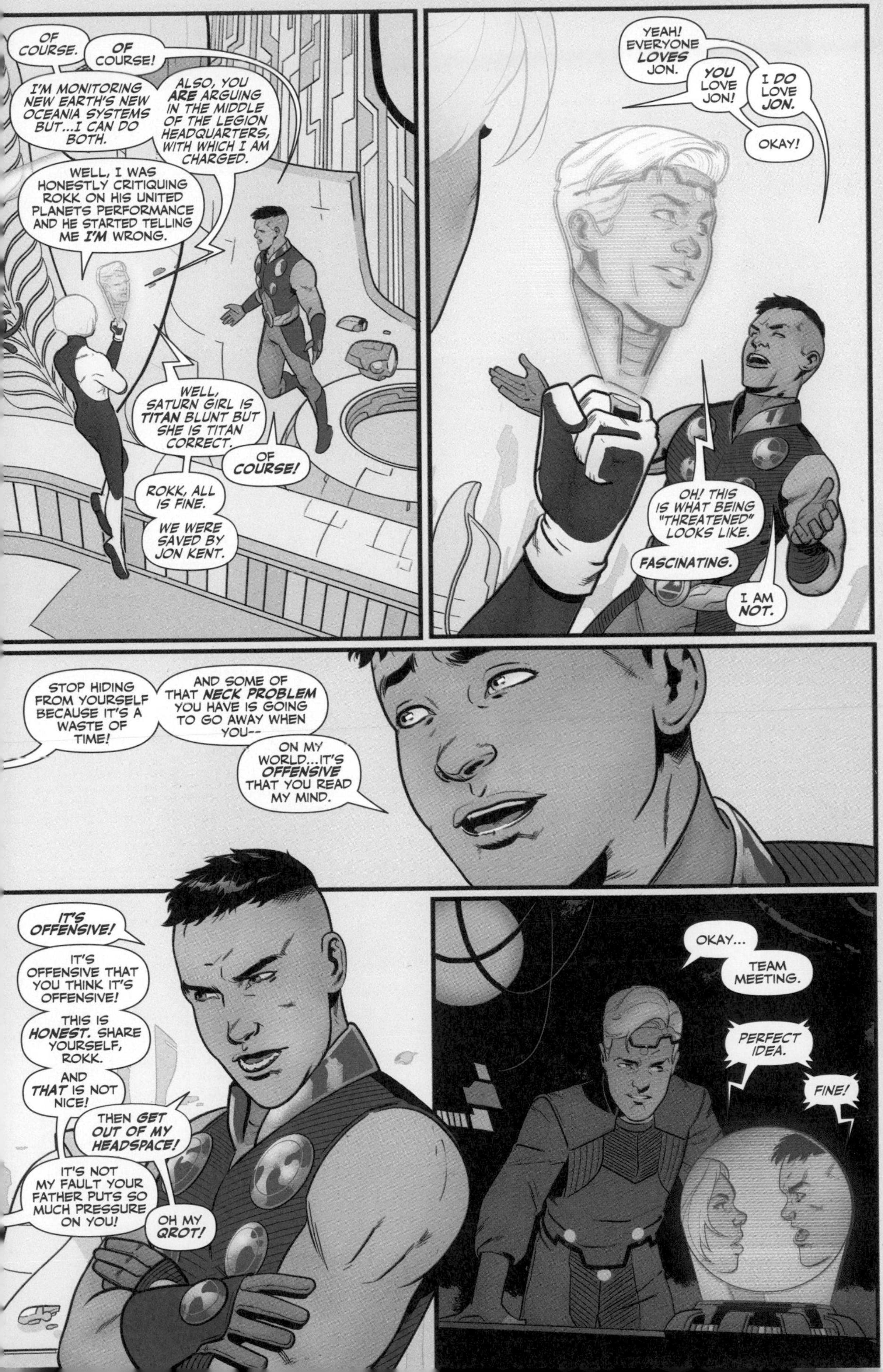
OF COURSE.
OF COURSE!
I'M MONITORING NEW EARTH'S NEW OCEANIA SYSTEMS BUT...I CAN DO BOTH.
ALSO, YOU ARE ARGUING IN THE MIDDLE OF THE LEGION HEADQUARTERS, WITH WHICH I AM CHARGED.
WELL, I WAS HONESTLY CRITIQUING ROKK ON HIS UNITED PLANETS PERFORMANCE AND HE STARTED TELLING ME I'M WRONG.
WELL, SATURN GIRL IS TITAN BLUNT BUT SHE IS TITAN CORRECT.
OF COURSE!
ROKK, ALL IS FINE.
WE WERE SAVED BY JON KENT.
YEAH! EVERYONE LOVES JON.
YOU LOVE JON!
I DO LOVE JON.
OKAY!
OH! THIS IS WHAT BEING "THREATENED" LOOKS LIKE.
FASCINATING.
I AM NOT.
STOP HIDING FROM YOURSELF BECAUSE IT'S A WASTE OF TIME!
AND SOME OF THAT NECK PROBLEM YOU HAVE IS GOING TO GO AWAY WHEN YOU--
ON MY WORLD...IT'S OFFENSIVE THAT YOU READ MY MIND.
IT'S OFFENSIVE!
IT'S OFFENSIVE THAT YOU THINK IT'S OFFENSIVE!
THIS IS HONEST. SHARE YOURSELF, ROKK.
AND THAT IS NOT NICE!
THEN GET OUT OF MY HEADSPACE!
IT'S NOT MY FAULT YOUR FATHER PUTS SO MUCH PRESSURE ON YOU!
OH MY QROT!
OKAY...
TEAM MEETING.
PERFECT IDEA.
FINE!

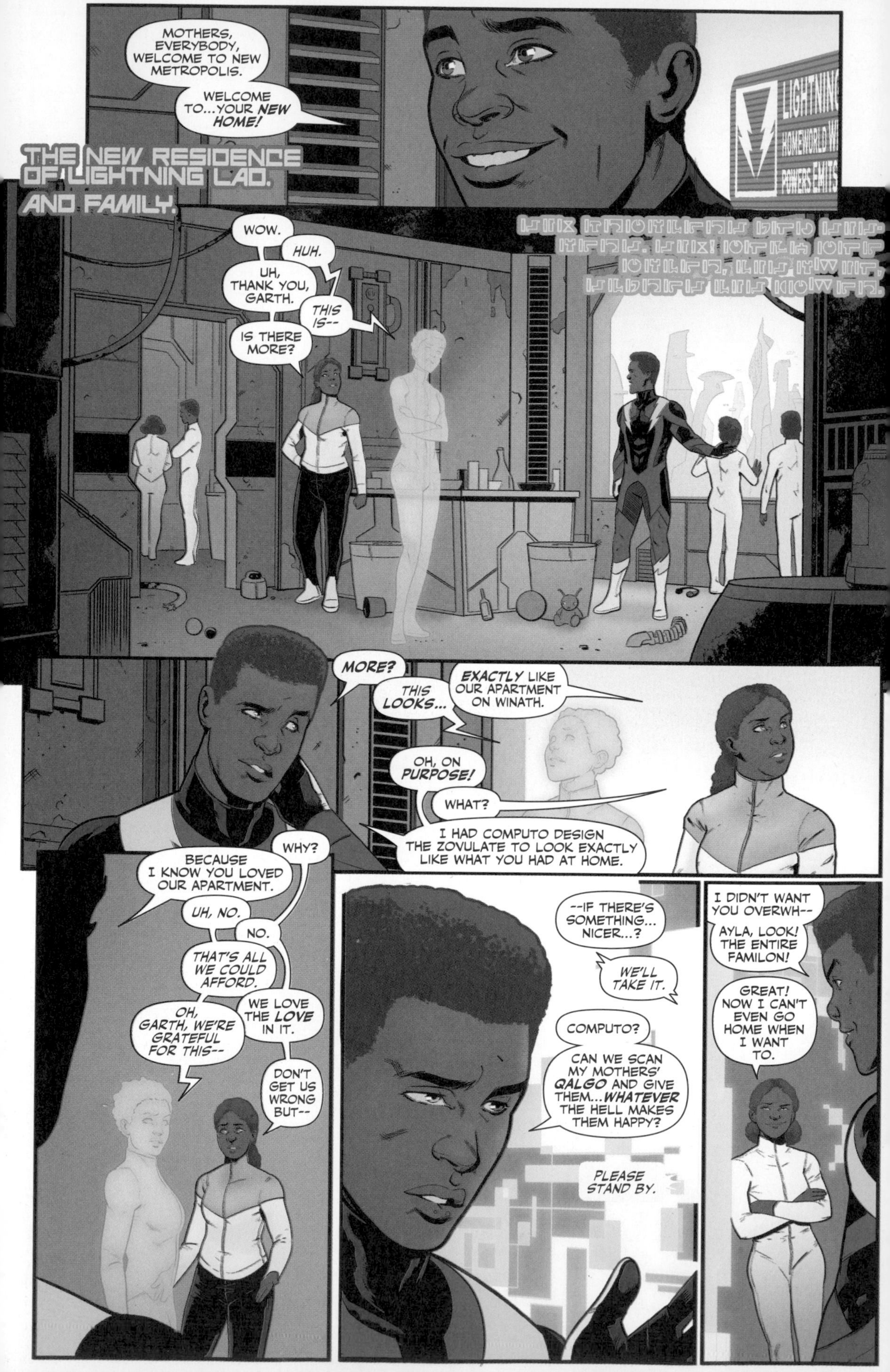

MOTHERS, EVERYBODY, WELCOME TO NEW METROPOLIS.
WELCOME TO...YOUR NEW HOME!
THE NEW RESIDENCE OF LIGHTNING LAD. AND FAMILY.
WOW.
HUH.
UH, THANK YOU, GARTH.
THIS IS--
IS THERE MORE?
MORE?
THIS LOOKS...
EXACTLY LIKE OUR APARTMENT ON WINATH.
OH, ON PURPOSE!
WHAT?
I HAD COMPUTO DESIGN THE ZOVULATE TO LOOK EXACTLY LIKE WHAT YOU HAD AT HOME.
WHY?
BECAUSE I KNOW YOU LOVED OUR APARTMENT.
UH, NO.
NO.
THAT'S ALL WE COULD AFFORD.
WE LOVE THE LOVE IN IT.
OH, GARTH, WE'RE GRATEFUL FOR THIS--
DON'T GET US WRONG BUT--
--IF THERE'S SOMETHING... NICER...?
WE'LL TAKE IT.
COMPUTO?
CAN WE SCAN MY MOTHERS' QALGO AND GIVE THEM...WHATEVER THE HELL MAKES THEM HAPPY?
PLEASE STAND BY.
I DIDN'T WANT YOU OVERWH--
AYLA, LOOK! THE ENTIRE FAMILON!
GREAT! NOW I CAN'T EVEN GO HOME WHEN I WANT TO.

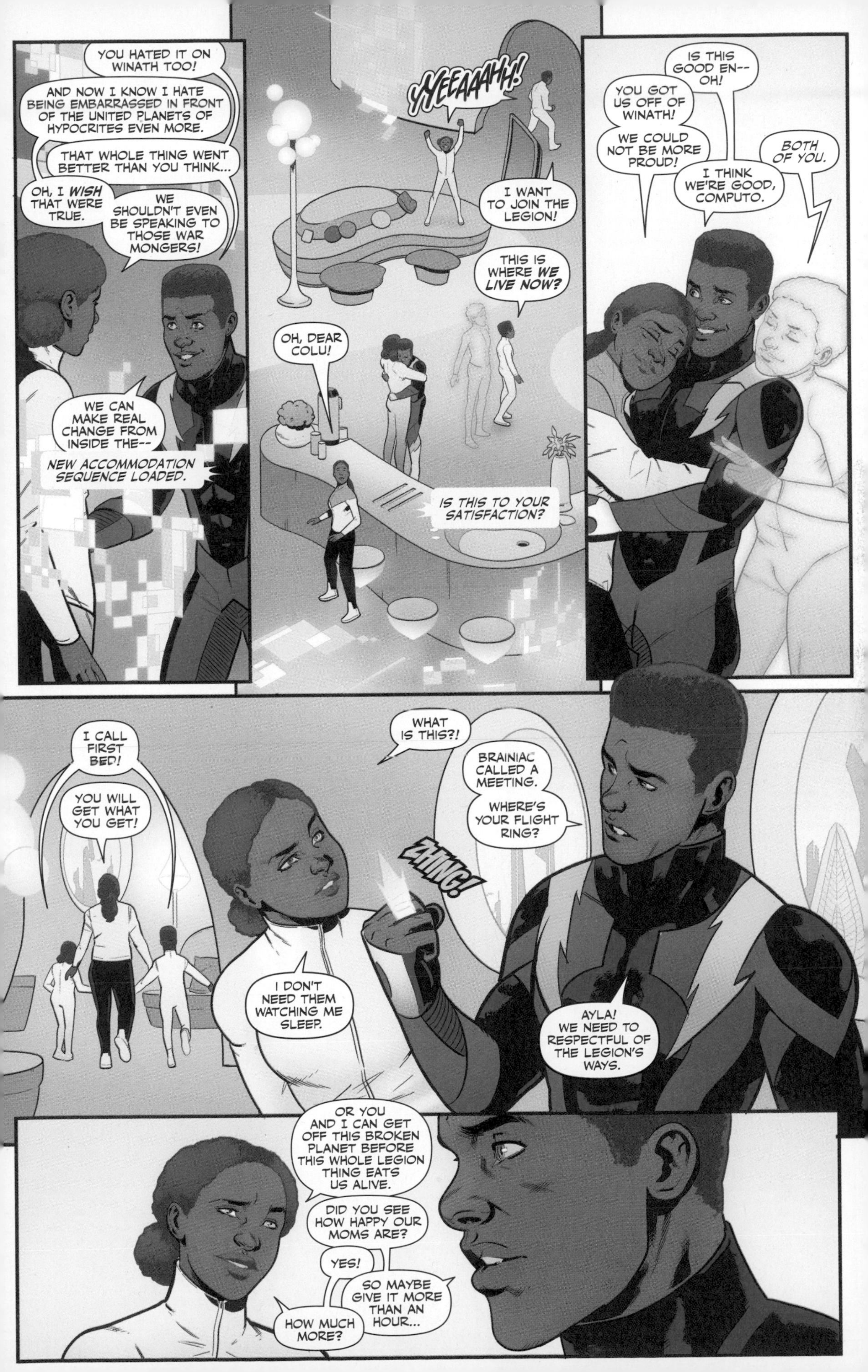
YOU HATED IT ON WINATH TOO!
AND NOW I KNOW I HATE BEING EMBARRASSED IN FRONT OF THE UNITED PLANETS OF HYPOCRITES EVEN MORE.
THAT WHOLE THING WENT BETTER THAN YOU THINK...
OH, I *WISH* THAT WERE TRUE.
WE SHOULDN'T EVEN BE SPEAKING TO THOSE WAR MONGERS!
WE CAN MAKE REAL CHANGE FROM INSIDE THE--
NEW ACCOMMODATION SEQUENCE LOADED.
YYEEAAAHH!
I WANT TO JOIN THE LEGION!
THIS IS WHERE *WE LIVE NOW?*
OH, DEAR COLU!
IS THIS TO YOUR SATISFACTION?
IS THIS GOOD EN-- OH!
YOU GOT US OFF OF WINATH!
WE COULD NOT BE MORE PROUD!
BOTH OF YOU.
I THINK WE'RE GOOD, COMPUTO.
I CALL FIRST BED!
YOU WILL GET WHAT YOU GET!
WHAT IS THIS?!
BRAINIAC CALLED A MEETING.
WHERE'S YOUR FLIGHT RING?
ZHING!
I DON'T NEED THEM WATCHING ME SLEEP.
AYLA! WE NEED TO RESPECTFUL OF THE LEGION'S WAYS.
OR YOU AND I CAN GET OFF THIS BROKEN PLANET BEFORE THIS WHOLE LEGION THING EATS US ALIVE.
DID YOU SEE HOW HAPPY OUR MOMS ARE?
YES!
SO MAYBE GIVE IT MORE THAN AN HOUR...
HOW MUCH MORE?

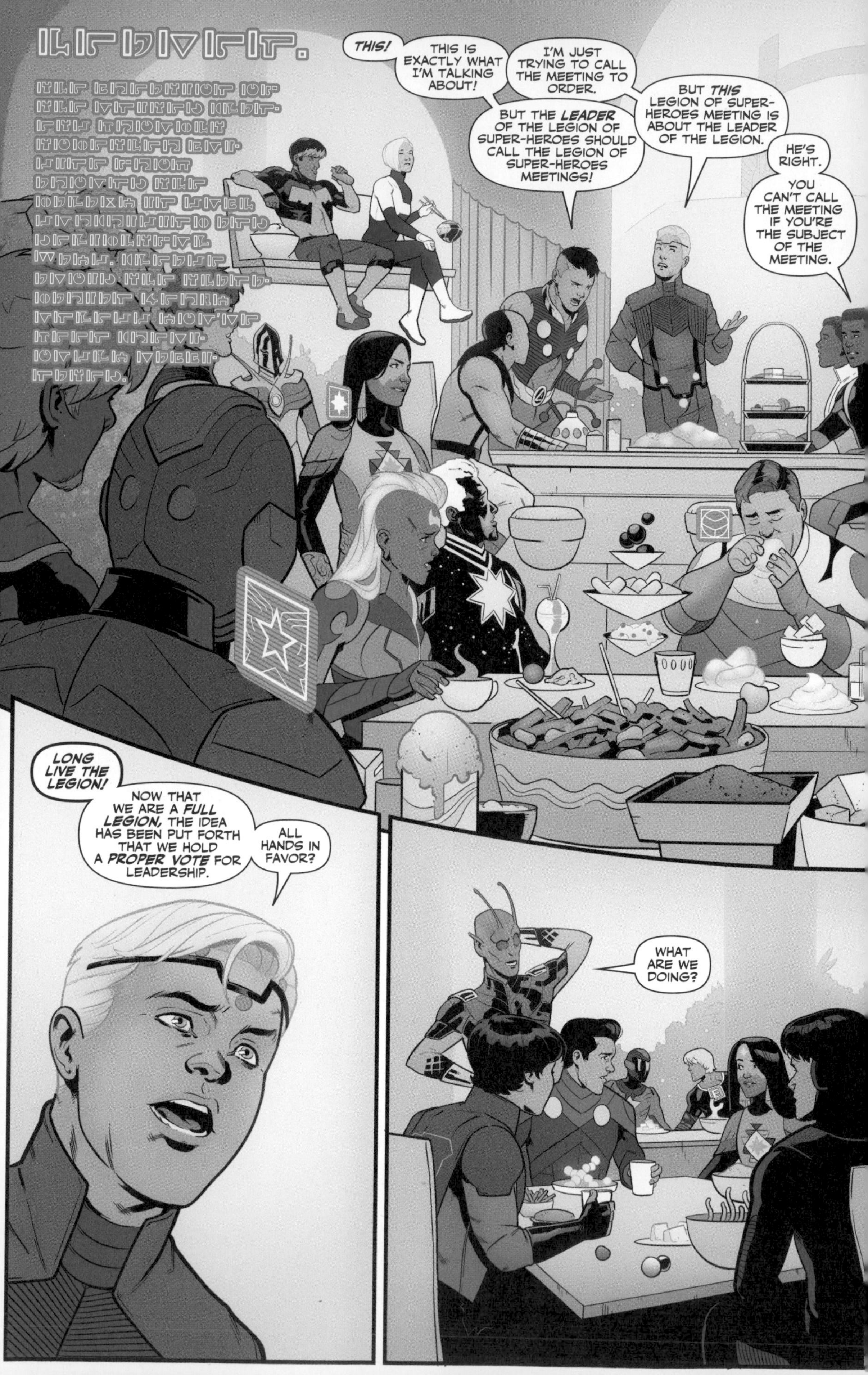
THIS!
THIS IS EXACTLY WHAT I'M TALKING ABOUT!
I'M JUST TRYING TO CALL THE MEETING TO ORDER.
BUT THE LEADER OF THE LEGION OF SUPER-HEROES SHOULD CALL THE LEGION OF SUPER-HEROES MEETINGS!
BUT THIS LEGION OF SUPER-HEROES MEETING IS ABOUT THE LEADER OF THE LEGION.
HE'S RIGHT.
YOU CAN'T CALL THE MEETING IF YOU'RE THE SUBJECT OF THE MEETING.
LONG LIVE THE LEGION!
NOW THAT WE ARE A FULL LEGION, THE IDEA HAS BEEN PUT FORTH THAT WE HOLD A PROPER VOTE FOR LEADERSHIP.
ALL HANDS IN FAVOR?
WHAT ARE WE DOING?

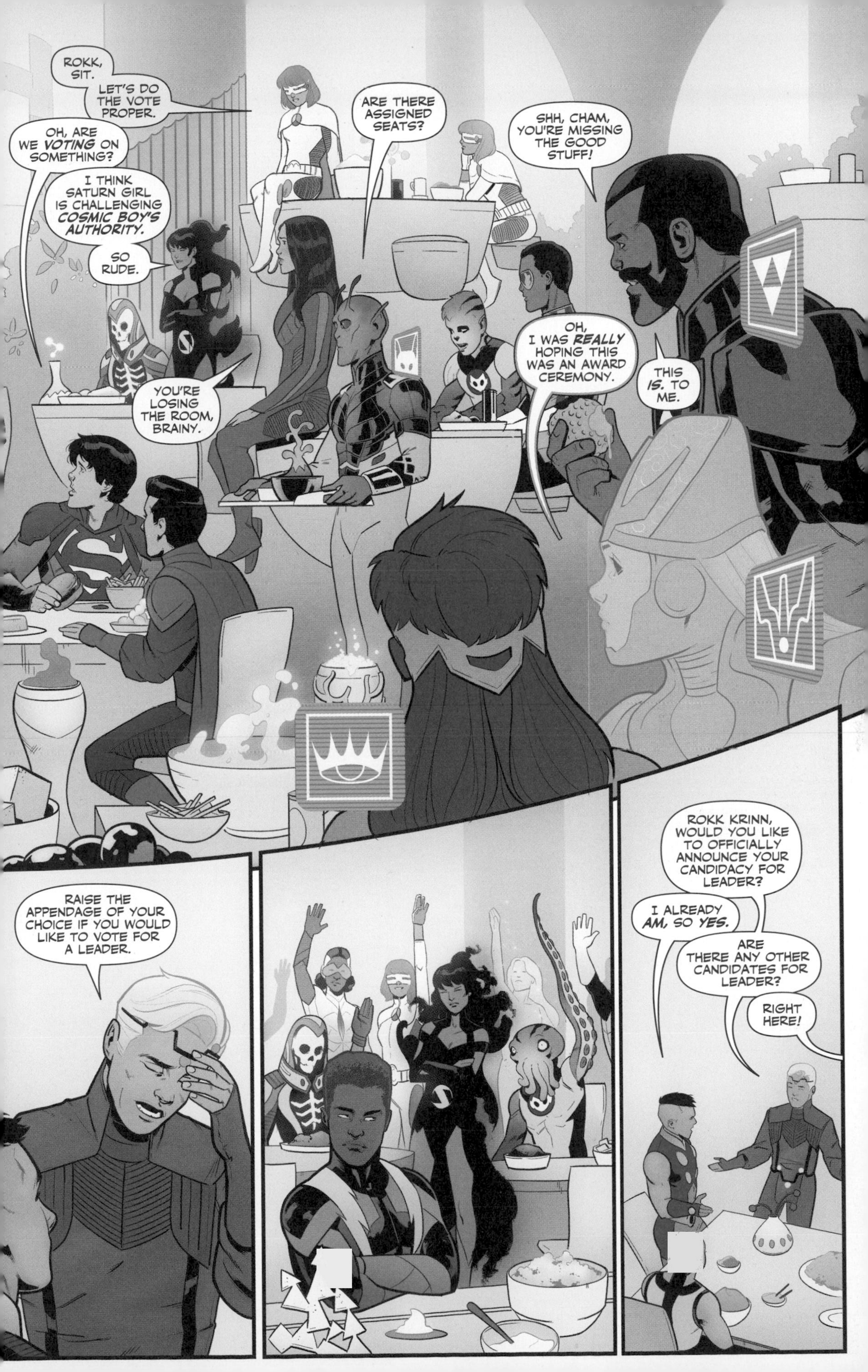
ROKK, SIT.
LET'S DO THE VOTE PROPER.
OH, ARE WE ***VOTING*** ON SOMETHING?
I THINK SATURN GIRL IS CHALLENGING ***COSMIC BOY'S AUTHORITY.***
SO RUDE.
ARE THERE ASSIGNED SEATS?
SHH, CHAM, YOU'RE MISSING THE GOOD STUFF!
YOU'RE LOSING THE ROOM, BRAINY.
OH, I WAS ***REALLY*** HOPING THIS WAS AN AWARD CEREMONY.
THIS ***IS.*** TO ME.
RAISE THE APPENDAGE OF YOUR CHOICE IF YOU WOULD LIKE TO VOTE FOR A LEADER.
ROKK KRINN, WOULD YOU LIKE TO OFFICIALLY ANNOUNCE YOUR CANDIDACY FOR LEADER?
I ALREADY ***AM,*** SO ***YES.***
ARE THERE ANY OTHER CANDIDATES FOR LEADER?
RIGHT HERE!

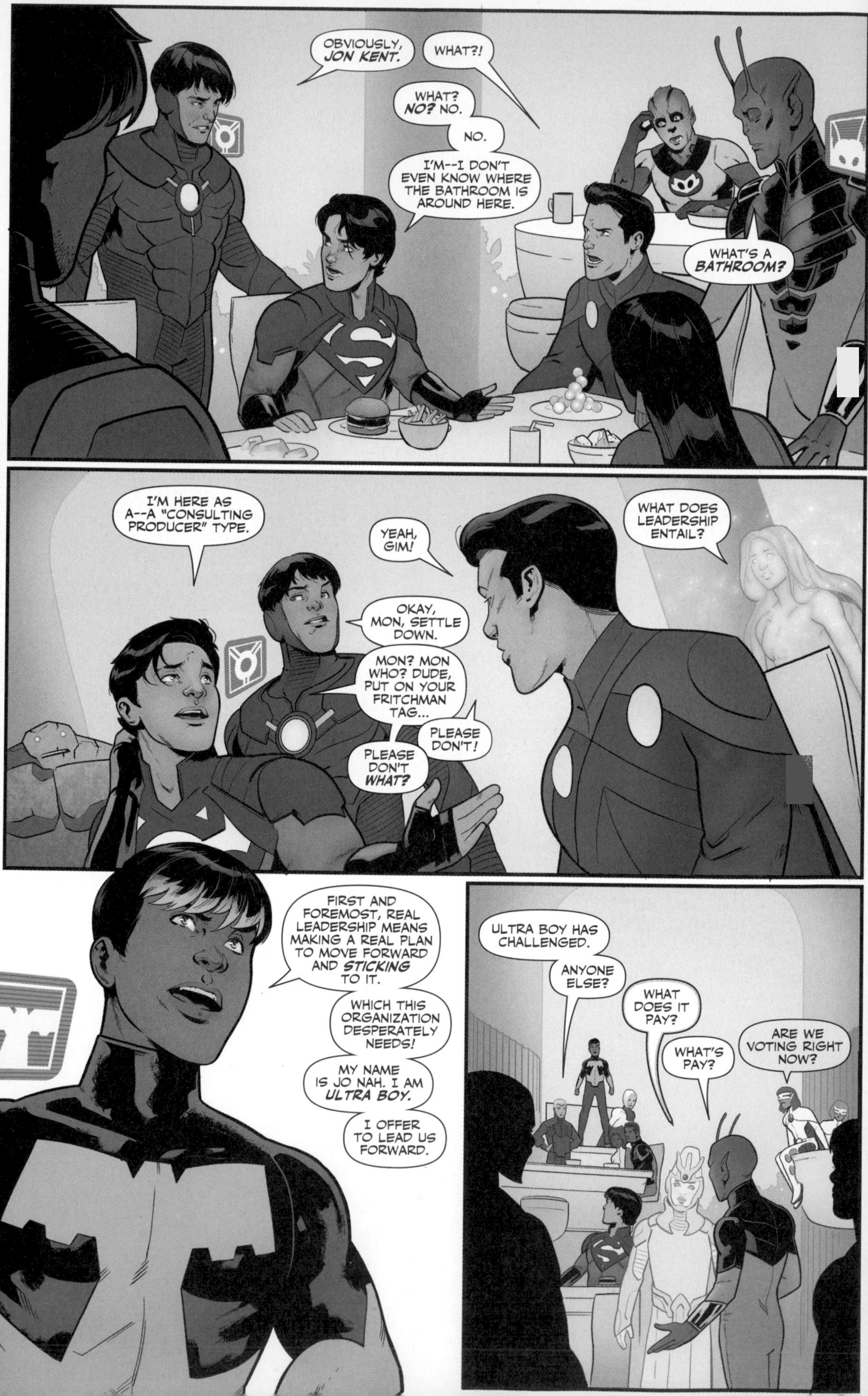

OBVIOUSLY, JON KENT.
WHAT?!
WHAT? NO? NO.
NO.
I'M--I DON'T EVEN KNOW WHERE THE BATHROOM IS AROUND HERE.
WHAT'S A BATHROOM?
I'M HERE AS A--A "CONSULTING PRODUCER" TYPE.
YEAH, GIM!
WHAT DOES LEADERSHIP ENTAIL?
OKAY, MON, SETTLE DOWN.
MON? MON WHO? DUDE, PUT ON YOUR FRITCHMAN TAG...
PLEASE DON'T!
PLEASE DON'T WHAT?
FIRST AND FOREMOST, REAL LEADERSHIP MEANS MAKING A REAL PLAN TO MOVE FORWARD AND STICKING TO IT.
WHICH THIS ORGANIZATION DESPERATELY NEEDS!
MY NAME IS JO NAH. I AM ULTRA BOY.
I OFFER TO LEAD US FORWARD.
ULTRA BOY HAS CHALLENGED.
ANYONE ELSE?
WHAT DOES IT PAY?
WHAT'S PAY?
ARE WE VOTING RIGHT NOW?

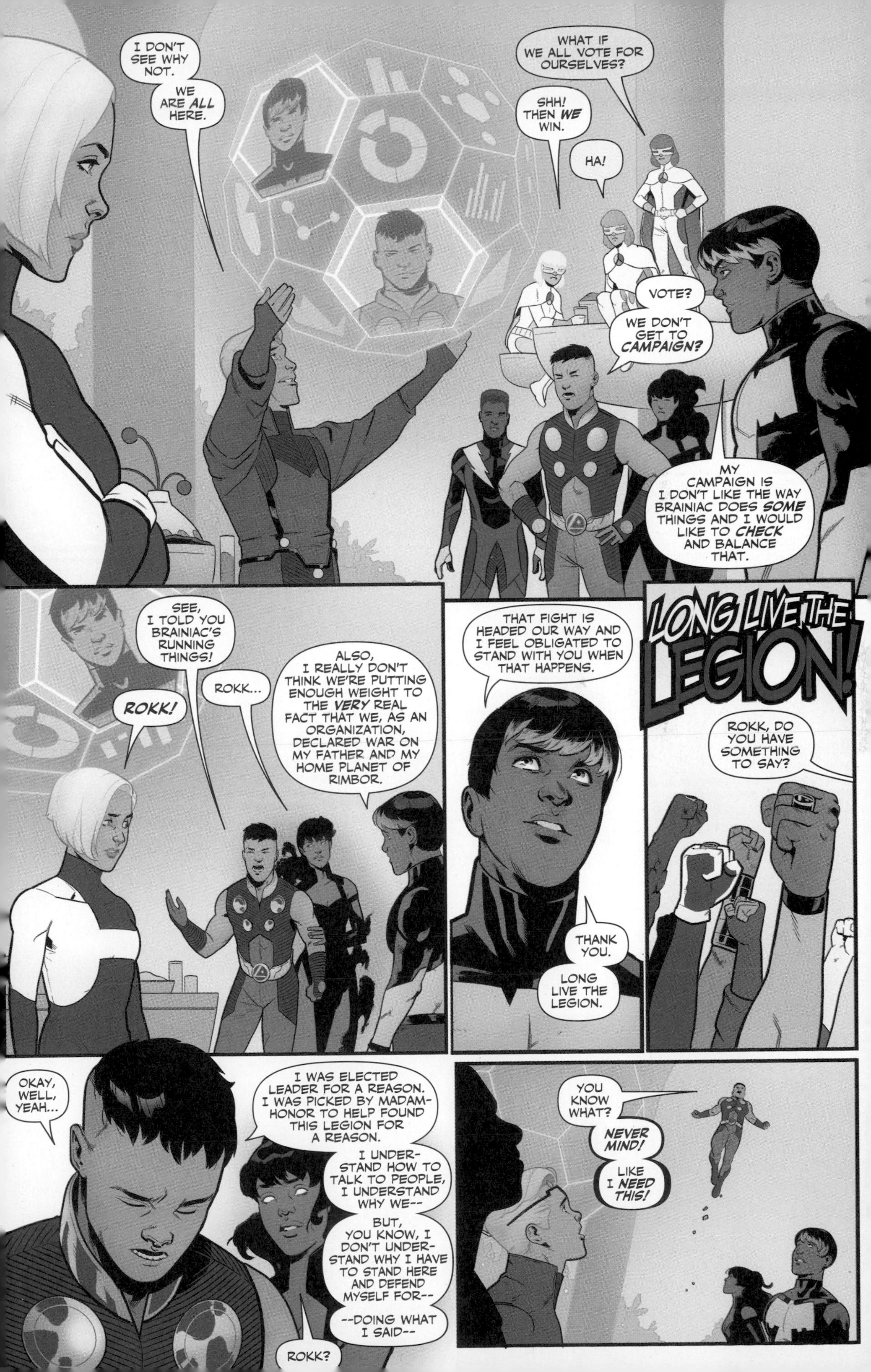
I DON'T SEE WHY NOT.
WE ARE ALL HERE.
WHAT IF WE ALL VOTE FOR OURSELVES?
SHH! THEN WE WIN.
HA!
VOTE?
WE DON'T GET TO CAMPAIGN?
MY CAMPAIGN IS I DON'T LIKE THE WAY BRAINIAC DOES SOME THINGS AND I WOULD LIKE TO CHECK AND BALANCE THAT.
SEE, I TOLD YOU BRAINIAC'S RUNNING THINGS!
ROKK!
ROKK...
ALSO, I REALLY DON'T THINK WE'RE PUTTING ENOUGH WEIGHT TO THE VERY REAL FACT THAT WE, AS AN ORGANIZATION, DECLARED WAR ON MY FATHER AND MY HOME PLANET OF RIMBOR.
THAT FIGHT IS HEADED OUR WAY AND I FEEL OBLIGATED TO STAND WITH YOU WHEN THAT HAPPENS.
THANK YOU.
LONG LIVE THE LEGION.
LONG LIVE THE LEGION!
ROKK, DO YOU HAVE SOMETHING TO SAY?
OKAY, WELL, YEAH...
I WAS ELECTED LEADER FOR A REASON. I WAS PICKED BY MADAM-HONOR TO HELP FOUND THIS LEGION FOR A REASON.
I UNDER-STAND HOW TO TALK TO PEOPLE, I UNDERSTAND WHY WE--
BUT, YOU KNOW, I DON'T UNDER-STAND WHY I HAVE TO STAND HERE AND DEFEND MYSELF FOR--
--DOING WHAT I SAID--
ROKK?
YOU KNOW WHAT?
NEVER MIND!
LIKE I NEED THIS!

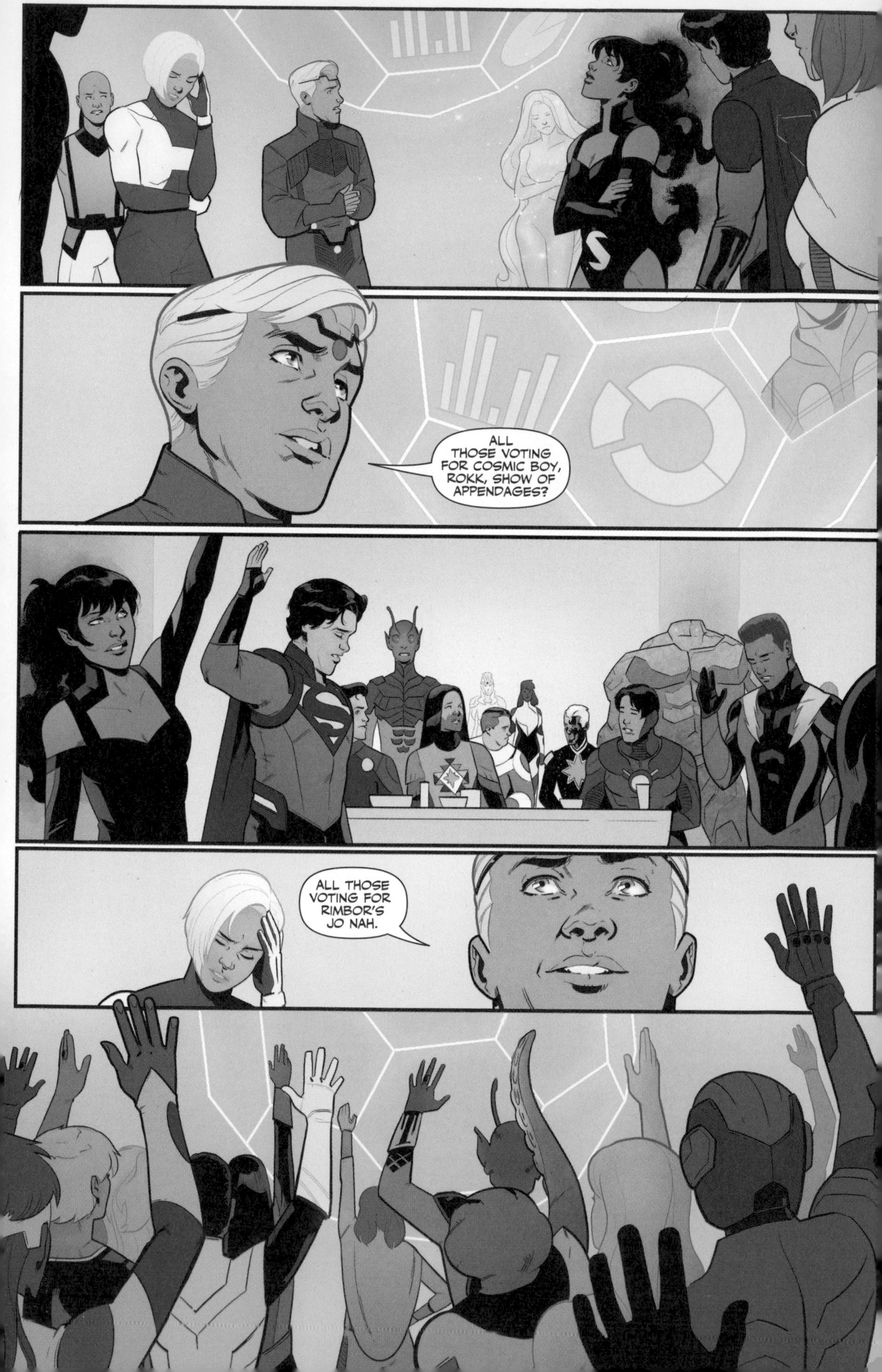
ALL THOSE VOTING FOR COSMIC BOY, ROKK, SHOW OF APPENDAGES?
ALL THOSE VOTING FOR RIMBOR'S JO NAH.

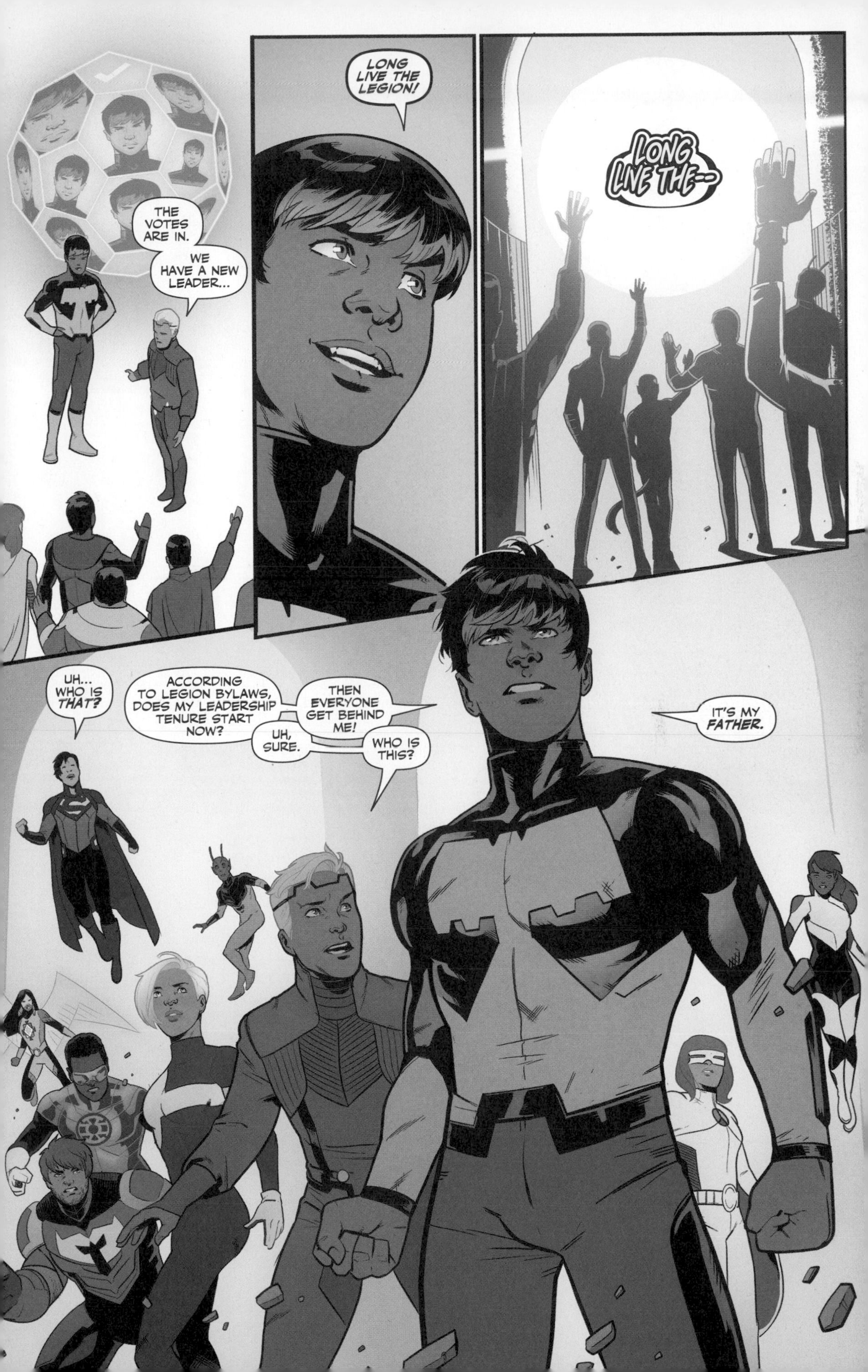
THE VOTES ARE IN.
WE HAVE A NEW LEADER...
LONG LIVE THE LEGION!
LONG LIVE THE--
UH... WHO IS THAT?
ACCORDING TO LEGION BYLAWS, DOES MY LEADERSHIP TENURE START NOW?
UH, SURE.
THEN EVERYONE GET BEHIND ME!
WHO IS THIS?
IT'S MY FATHER.

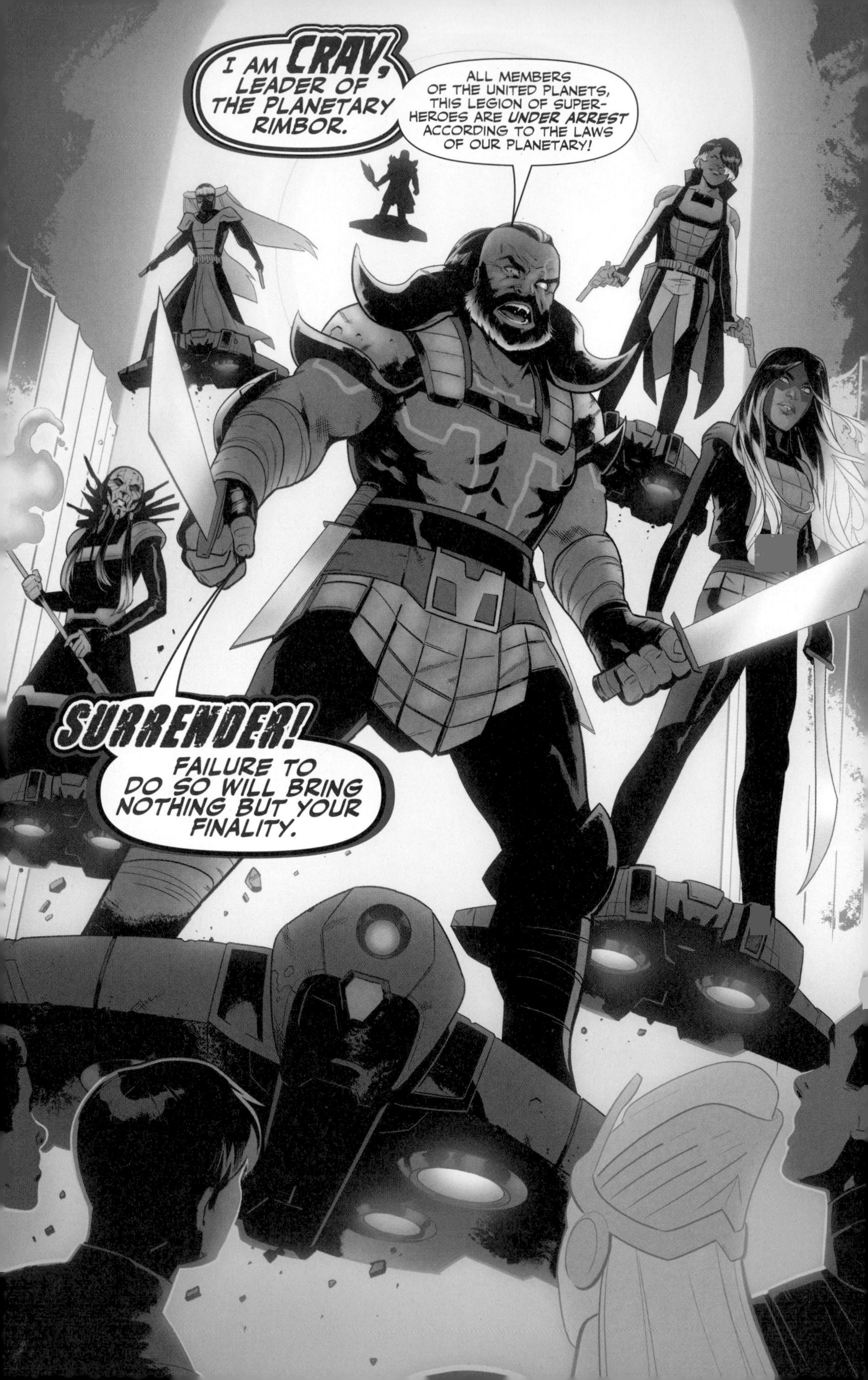
I AM CRAV, LEADER OF THE PLANETARY RIMBOR.
ALL MEMBERS OF THE UNITED PLANETS, THIS LEGION OF SUPER-HEROES ARE UNDER ARREST ACCORDING TO THE LAWS OF OUR PLANETARY!
SURRENDER!
FAILURE TO DO SO WILL BRING NOTHING BUT YOUR FINALITY.

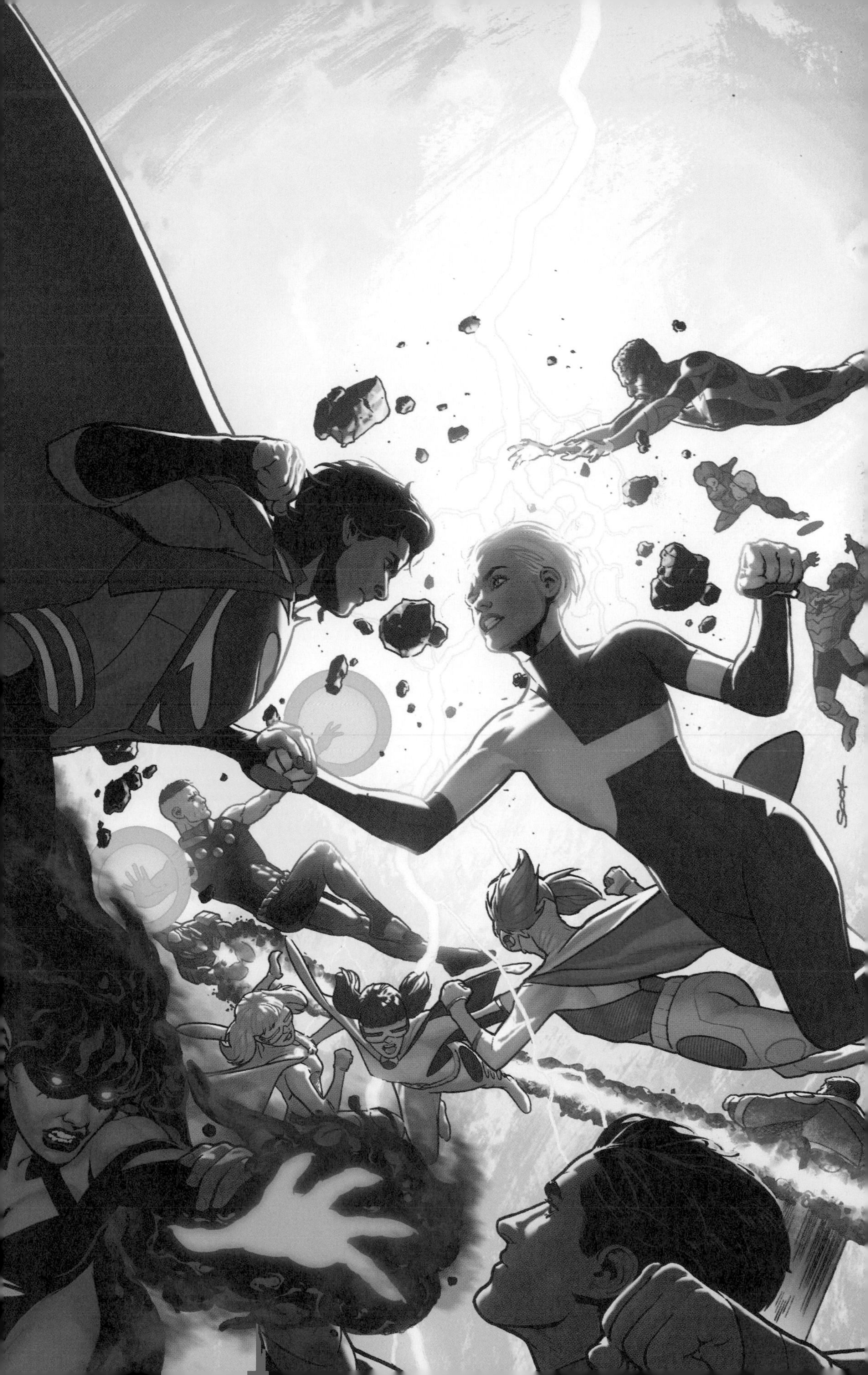

THE TRIAL OF THE LEGION OF SUPER-HEROES - PART 1

BRIAN MICHAEL BENDIS - WRITER

PAGE 1:   **EVAN "DOC" SHANER (ART & COLOR)**
PAGE 2:   **JEFF LEMIRE**
PAGE 3:   **DUSTIN NGUYEN**
PAGE 4:   **JOËLLE JONES**
PAGE 5:   **MICHAEL AVON OEMING**
PAGE 6:   **LIAM SHARP**
PAGE 7:   **ANDRÉ LIMA ARAÚJO**
PAGE 8:   **SANFORD GREENE**
PAGE 9:   **CULLY HAMNER**
PAGE 10:   **YANICK PAQUETTE**
PAGE 11:   **DAN HIPP**
PAGE 12:   **DAVID MACK (ART & COLOR)**
PAGE 13:   **DARICK ROBERTSON**
PAGE 14:   **DAN JURGENS & NORM RAPMUND**
PAGE 15:   **BILQUIS EVELY**
PAGE 16:   **FABIO MOON**
PAGE 17:   **MICHAEL ALLRED**
PAGES 18-19: **RYAN SOOK & WADE VON GRAWBADGER**
PAGE 20:   **ALEX MALEEV**
PAGE 21:   **JOHN TIMMS**
PAGE 22:   **DUNCAN ROULEAU**

- ARTISTS -

JORDIE BELLAIRE - COLORIST
DAVE SHARPE - LETTERER
RYAN SOOK - COVER ARTIST
DUSTIN NGUYEN – VARIANT COVER ARTIST
BRITTANY HOLZHERR – ASSOCIATE EDITOR
BRIAN CUNNINGHAM – EDITOR

SUPERBOY CREATED BY **JERRY SIEGEL.**
BY SPECIAL ARRANGEMENT WITH **THE JERRY SIEGEL FAMILY.**

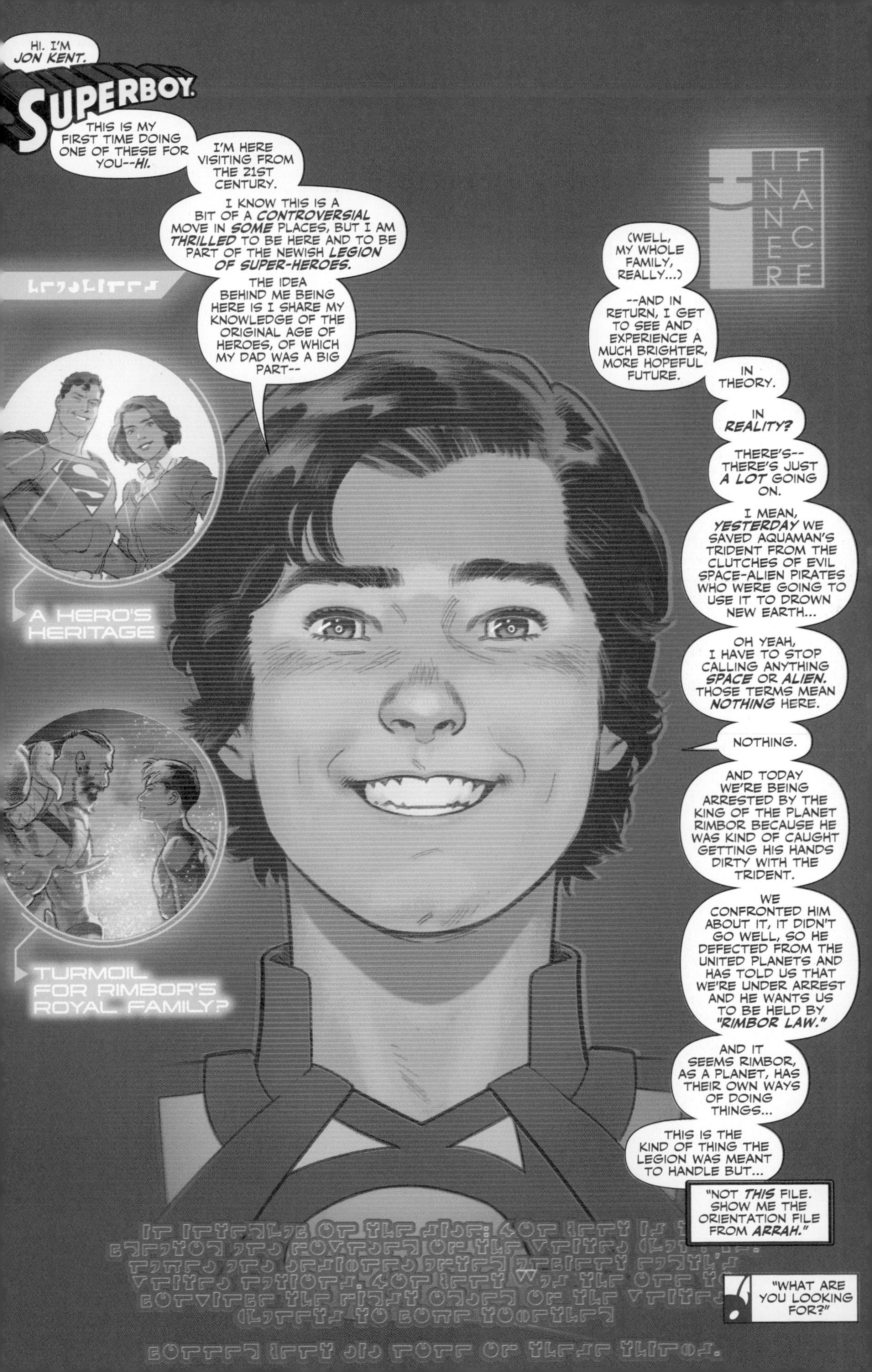

HI. I'M JON KENT.
SUPERBOY.
THIS IS MY FIRST TIME DOING ONE OF THESE FOR YOU--HI.
I'M HERE VISITING FROM THE 21ST CENTURY.
I KNOW THIS IS A BIT OF A CONTROVERSIAL MOVE IN SOME PLACES, BUT I AM THRILLED TO BE HERE AND TO BE PART OF THE NEWISH LEGION OF SUPER-HEROES.
THE IDEA BEHIND ME BEING HERE IS I SHARE MY KNOWLEDGE OF THE ORIGINAL AGE OF HEROES, OF WHICH MY DAD WAS A BIG PART--
(WELL, MY WHOLE FAMILY, REALLY...)
--AND IN RETURN, I GET TO SEE AND EXPERIENCE A MUCH BRIGHTER, MORE HOPEFUL FUTURE.
IN THEORY.
IN REALITY?
THERE'S-- THERE'S JUST A LOT GOING ON.
I MEAN, YESTERDAY WE SAVED AQUAMAN'S TRIDENT FROM THE CLUTCHES OF EVIL SPACE-ALIEN PIRATES WHO WERE GOING TO USE IT TO DROWN NEW EARTH...
OH YEAH, I HAVE TO STOP CALLING ANYTHING SPACE OR ALIEN. THOSE TERMS MEAN NOTHING HERE.
NOTHING.
AND TODAY WE'RE BEING ARRESTED BY THE KING OF THE PLANET RIMBOR BECAUSE HE WAS KIND OF CAUGHT GETTING HIS HANDS DIRTY WITH THE TRIDENT.
WE CONFRONTED HIM ABOUT IT, IT DIDN'T GO WELL, SO HE DEFECTED FROM THE UNITED PLANETS AND HAS TOLD US THAT WE'RE UNDER ARREST AND HE WANTS US TO BE HELD BY "RIMBOR LAW."
AND IT SEEMS RIMBOR, AS A PLANET, HAS THEIR OWN WAYS OF DOING THINGS...
THIS IS THE KIND OF THING THE LEGION WAS MEANT TO HANDLE BUT...
"NOT THIS FILE. SHOW ME THE ORIENTATION FILE FROM ARRAH."
"WHAT ARE YOU LOOKING FOR?"
A HERO'S HERITAGE
TURMOIL FOR RIMBOR'S ROYAL FAMILY?
INFINITE FRANCE

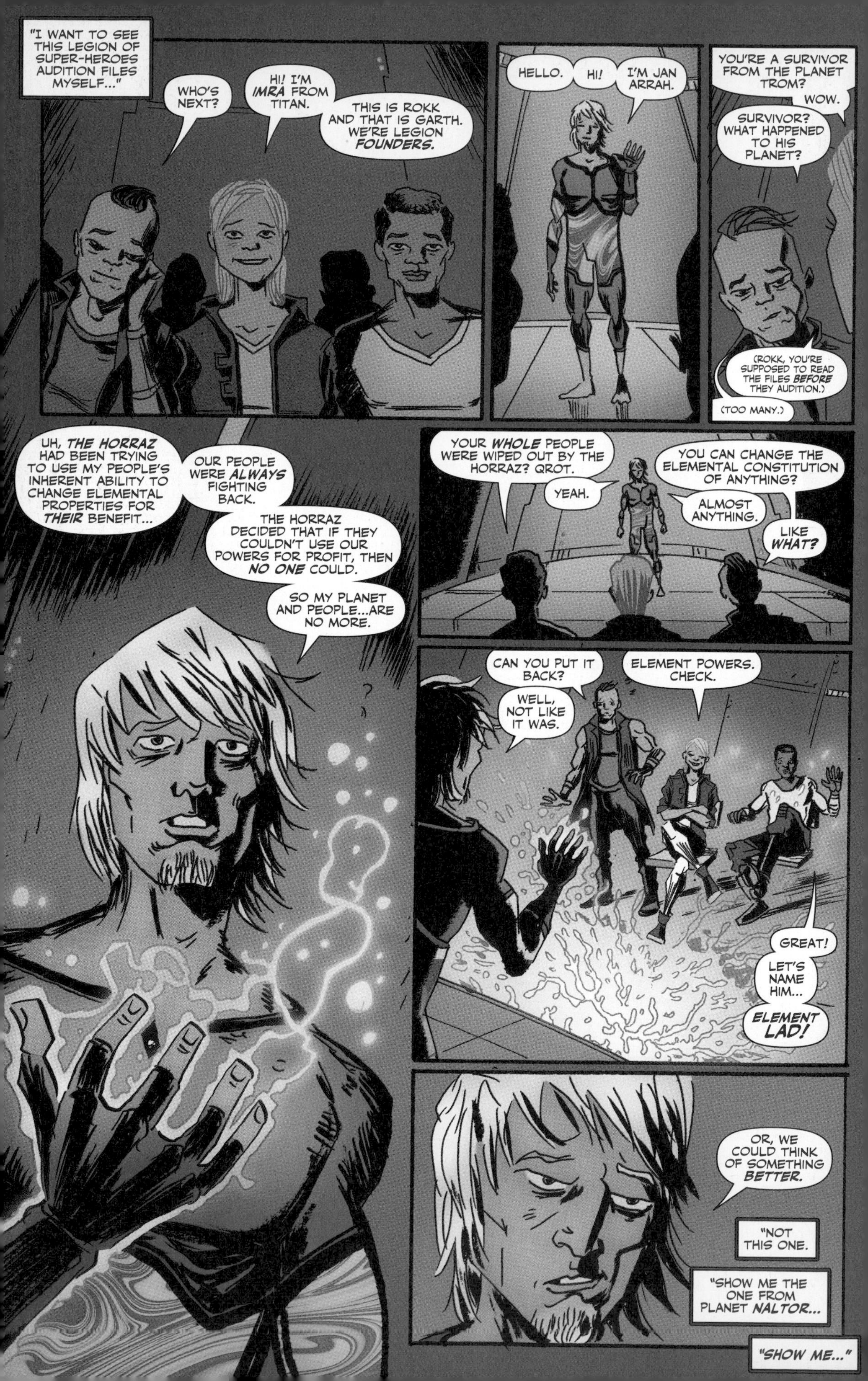
"I WANT TO SEE THIS LEGION OF SUPER-HEROES AUDITION FILES MYSELF..."
WHO'S NEXT?
HI! I'M IMRA FROM TITAN.
THIS IS ROKK AND THAT IS GARTH. WE'RE LEGION FOUNDERS.
HELLO.
HI!
I'M JAN ARRAH.
YOU'RE A SURVIVOR FROM THE PLANET TROM?
WOW.
SURVIVOR? WHAT HAPPENED TO HIS PLANET?
(ROKK, YOU'RE SUPPOSED TO READ THE FILES BEFORE THEY AUDITION.)
(TOO MANY.)
UH, THE HORRAZ HAD BEEN TRYING TO USE MY PEOPLE'S INHERENT ABILITY TO CHANGE ELEMENTAL PROPERTIES FOR THEIR BENEFIT...
OUR PEOPLE WERE ALWAYS FIGHTING BACK.
THE HORRAZ DECIDED THAT IF THEY COULDN'T USE OUR POWERS FOR PROFIT, THEN NO ONE COULD.
SO MY PLANET AND PEOPLE...ARE NO MORE.
YOUR WHOLE PEOPLE WERE WIPED OUT BY THE HORRAZ? QROT.
YEAH.
YOU CAN CHANGE THE ELEMENTAL CONSTITUTION OF ANYTHING?
ALMOST ANYTHING.
LIKE WHAT?
CAN YOU PUT IT BACK?
WELL, NOT LIKE IT WAS.
ELEMENT POWERS. CHECK.
GREAT!
LET'S NAME HIM...
ELEMENT LAD!
OR, WE COULD THINK OF SOMETHING BETTER.
"NOT THIS ONE.
"SHOW ME THE ONE FROM PLANET NALTOR...
"SHOW ME..."

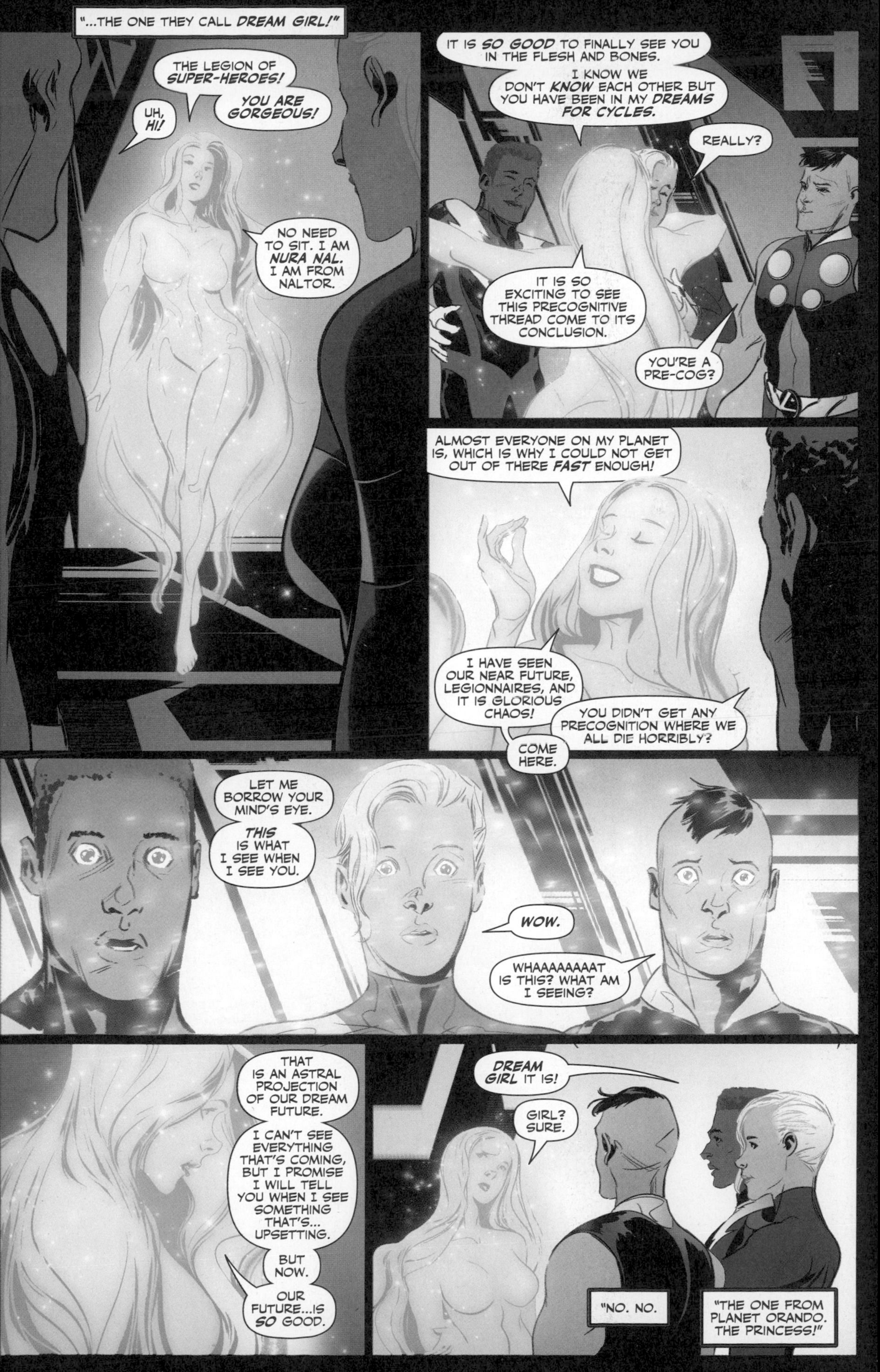
"...THE ONE THEY CALL DREAM GIRL!"
THE LEGION OF SUPER-HEROES! YOU ARE GORGEOUS!
UH, HI!
NO NEED TO SIT. I AM NURA NAL. I AM FROM NALTOR.
IT IS SO GOOD TO FINALLY SEE YOU IN THE FLESH AND BONES.
I KNOW WE DON'T KNOW EACH OTHER BUT YOU HAVE BEEN IN MY DREAMS FOR CYCLES.
REALLY?
IT IS SO EXCITING TO SEE THIS PRECOGNITIVE THREAD COME TO ITS CONCLUSION.
YOU'RE A PRE-COG?
ALMOST EVERYONE ON MY PLANET IS, WHICH IS WHY I COULD NOT GET OUT OF THERE FAST ENOUGH!
I HAVE SEEN OUR NEAR FUTURE, LEGIONNAIRES, AND IT IS GLORIOUS CHAOS!
YOU DIDN'T GET ANY PRECOGNITION WHERE WE ALL DIE HORRIBLY?
COME HERE.
LET ME BORROW YOUR MIND'S EYE.
THIS IS WHAT I SEE WHEN I SEE YOU.
WOW.
WHAAAAAAAAT IS THIS? WHAT AM I SEEING?
THAT IS AN ASTRAL PROJECTION OF OUR DREAM FUTURE.
I CAN'T SEE EVERYTHING THAT'S COMING, BUT I PROMISE I WILL TELL YOU WHEN I SEE SOMETHING THAT'S... UPSETTING.
BUT NOW.
OUR FUTURE...IS SO GOOD.
DREAM GIRL IT IS!
GIRL? SURE.
"NO. NO.
"THE ONE FROM PLANET ORANDO. THE PRINCESS!"

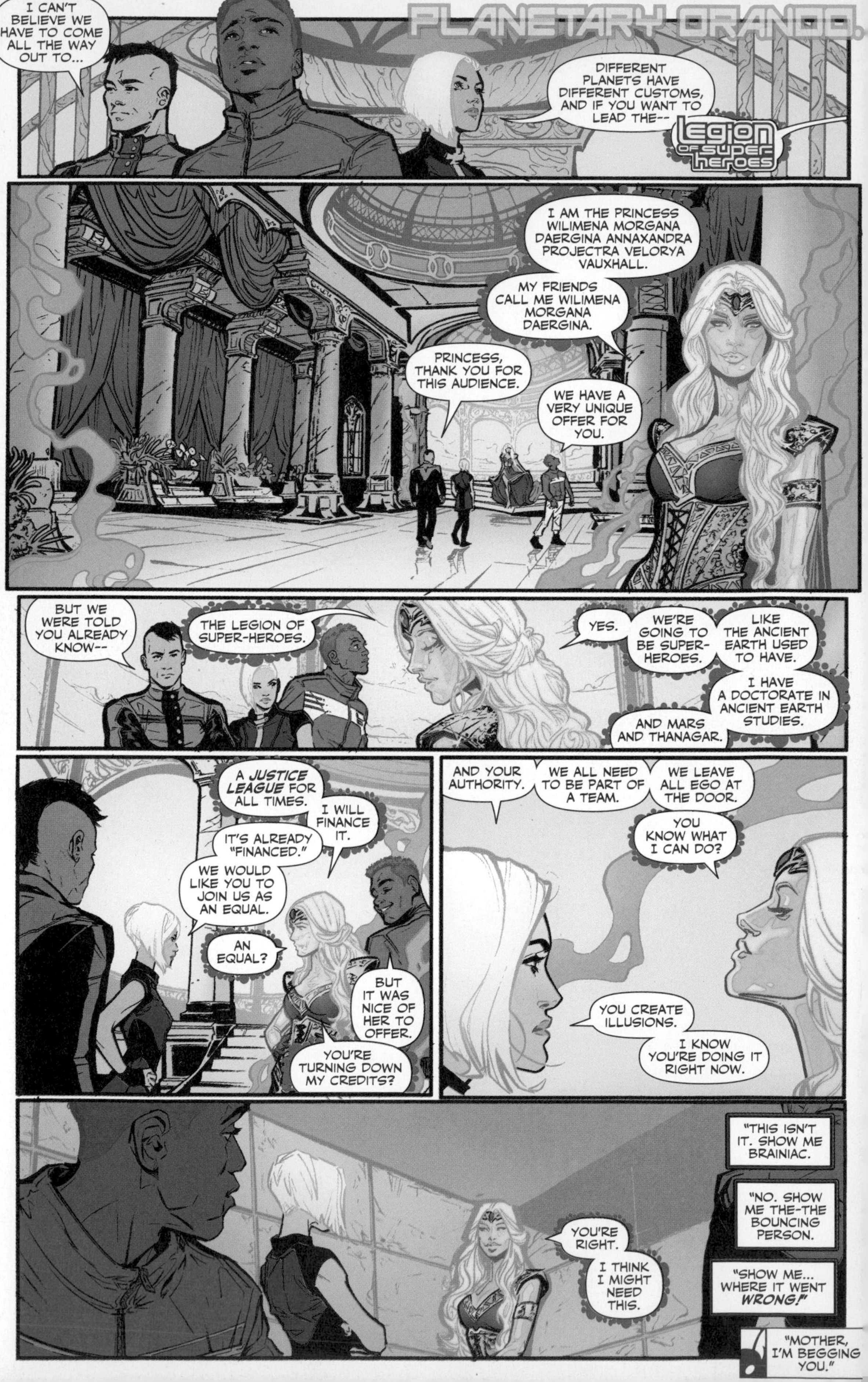
PLANETARY ORANDO.
I CAN'T BELIEVE WE HAVE TO COME ALL THE WAY OUT TO...
DIFFERENT PLANETS HAVE DIFFERENT CUSTOMS, AND IF YOU WANT TO LEAD THE--
LEGION OF SUPER HEROES
I AM THE PRINCESS WILIMENA MORGANA DAERGINA ANNAXANDRA PROJECTRA VELORYA VAUXHALL.
MY FRIENDS CALL ME WILIMENA MORGANA DAERGINA.
PRINCESS, THANK YOU FOR THIS AUDIENCE.
WE HAVE A VERY UNIQUE OFFER FOR YOU.
BUT WE WERE TOLD YOU ALREADY KNOW--
THE LEGION OF SUPER-HEROES.
YES.
WE'RE GOING TO BE SUPER-HEROES.
LIKE THE ANCIENT EARTH USED TO HAVE.
I HAVE A DOCTORATE IN ANCIENT EARTH STUDIES.
AND MARS AND THANAGAR.
A *JUSTICE LEAGUE* FOR ALL TIMES.
I WILL FINANCE IT.
IT'S ALREADY "FINANCED."
WE WOULD LIKE YOU TO JOIN US AS AN EQUAL.
AN EQUAL?
BUT IT WAS NICE OF HER TO OFFER.
YOU'RE TURNING DOWN MY CREDITS?
AND YOUR AUTHORITY.
WE ALL NEED TO BE PART OF A TEAM.
WE LEAVE ALL EGO AT THE DOOR.
YOU KNOW WHAT I CAN DO?
YOU CREATE ILLUSIONS.
I KNOW YOU'RE DOING IT RIGHT NOW.
"THIS ISN'T IT. SHOW ME BRAINIAC.
"NO. SHOW ME THE-THE BOUNCING PERSON.
"SHOW ME... WHERE IT WENT *WRONG!*"
YOU'RE RIGHT.
I THINK I MIGHT NEED THIS.
"MOTHER, I'M BEGGING YOU."

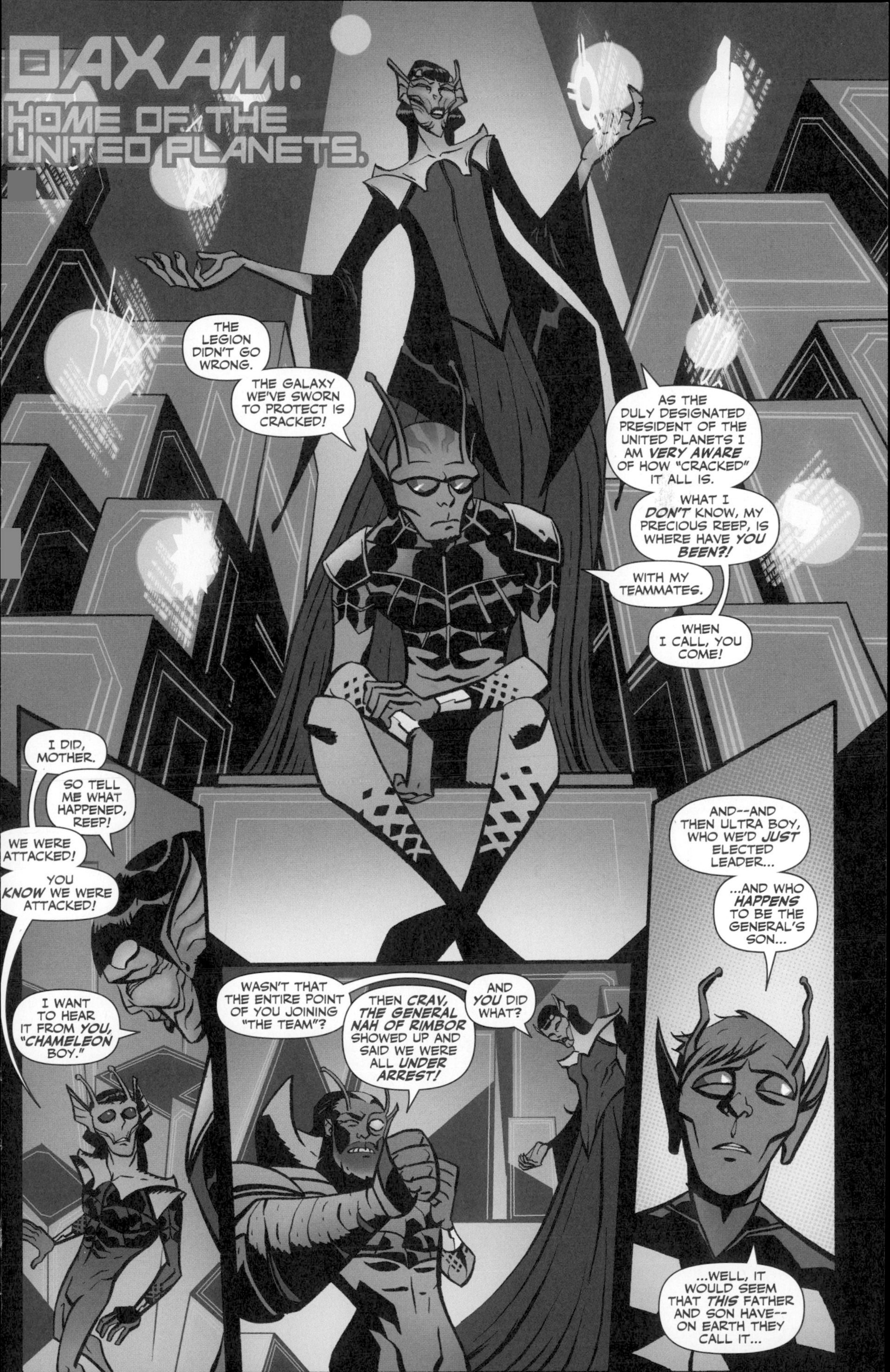
DAXAM.
HOME OF THE UNITED PLANETS.
THE LEGION DIDN'T GO WRONG.
THE GALAXY WE'VE SWORN TO PROTECT IS CRACKED!
AS THE DULY DESIGNATED PRESIDENT OF THE UNITED PLANETS I AM VERY AWARE OF HOW "CRACKED" IT ALL IS.
WHAT I DON'T KNOW, MY PRECIOUS REEP, IS WHERE HAVE YOU BEEN?!
WITH MY TEAMMATES.
WHEN I CALL, YOU COME!
I DID, MOTHER.
SO TELL ME WHAT HAPPENED, REEP!
WE WERE ATTACKED!
YOU KNOW WE WERE ATTACKED!
I WANT TO HEAR IT FROM YOU, "CHAMELEON BOY."
WASN'T THAT THE ENTIRE POINT OF YOU JOINING "THE TEAM"?
THEN CRAV, THE GENERAL NAH OF RIMBOR SHOWED UP AND SAID WE WERE ALL UNDER ARREST!
AND YOU DID WHAT?
AND--AND THEN ULTRA BOY, WHO WE'D JUST ELECTED LEADER...
...AND WHO HAPPENS TO BE THE GENERAL'S SON...
...WELL, IT WOULD SEEM THAT THIS FATHER AND SON HAVE-- ON EARTH THEY CALL IT...

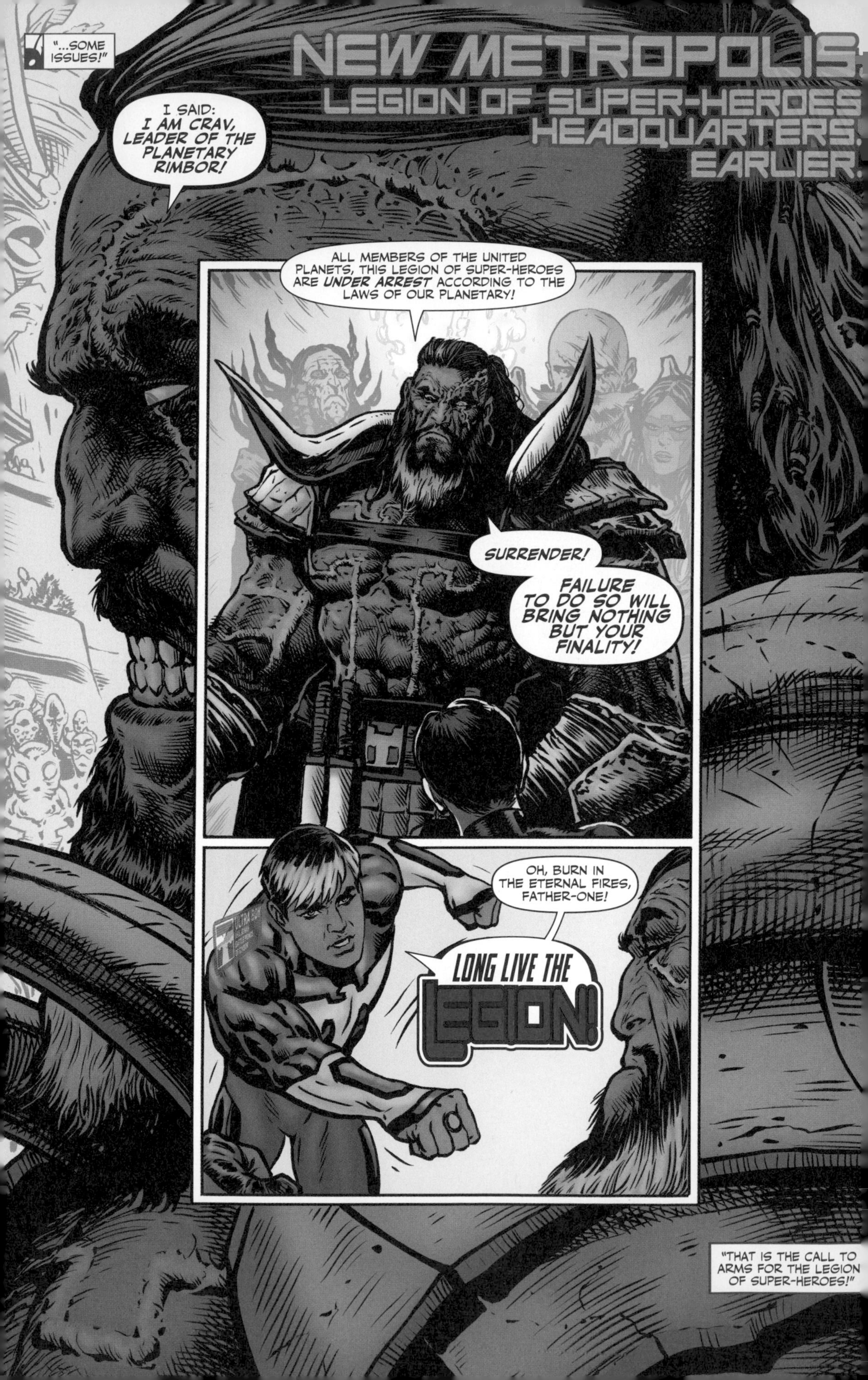
"...SOME ISSUES!"
NEW METROPOLIS. LEGION OF SUPER-HEROES HEADQUARTERS. EARLIER.
I SAID: I AM CRAV, LEADER OF THE PLANETARY RIMBOR!
ALL MEMBERS OF THE UNITED PLANETS, THIS LEGION OF SUPER-HEROES ARE UNDER ARREST ACCORDING TO THE LAWS OF OUR PLANETARY!
SURRENDER!
FAILURE TO DO SO WILL BRING NOTHING BUT YOUR FINALITY!
OH, BURN IN THE ETERNAL FIRES, FATHER-ONE!
LONG LIVE THE LEGION!
"THAT IS THE CALL TO ARMS FOR THE LEGION OF SUPER-HEROES!"

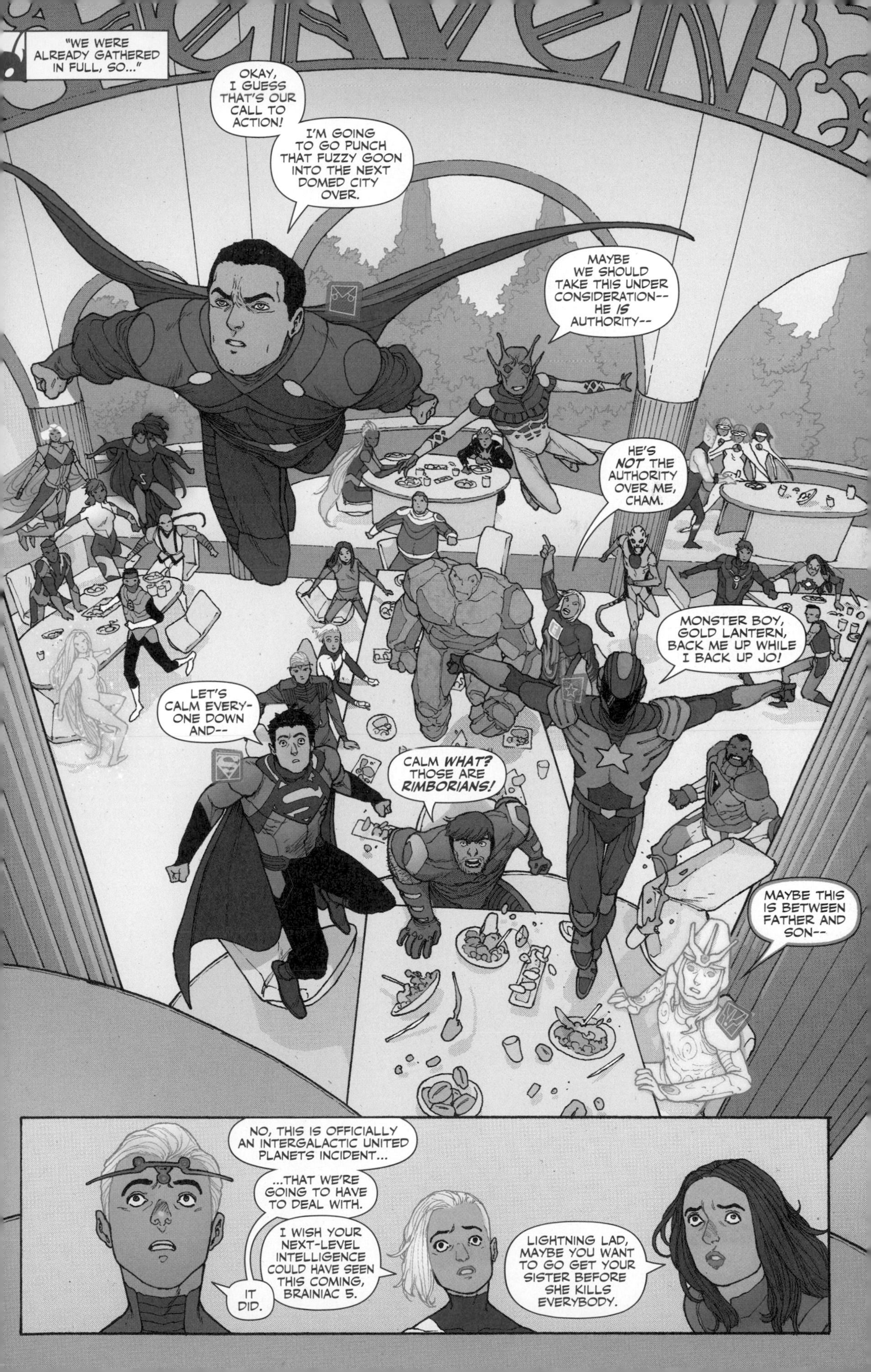
"WE WERE ALREADY GATHERED IN FULL, SO..."
OKAY, I GUESS THAT'S OUR CALL TO ACTION!
I'M GOING TO GO PUNCH THAT FUZZY GOON INTO THE NEXT DOMED CITY OVER.
MAYBE WE SHOULD TAKE THIS UNDER CONSIDERATION-- HE IS AUTHORITY--
HE'S NOT THE AUTHORITY OVER ME, CHAM.
MONSTER BOY, GOLD LANTERN, BACK ME UP WHILE I BACK UP JO!
LET'S CALM EVERY-ONE DOWN AND--
CALM WHAT? THOSE ARE RIMBORIANS!
MAYBE THIS IS BETWEEN FATHER AND SON--
NO, THIS IS OFFICIALLY AN INTERGALACTIC UNITED PLANETS INCIDENT...
...THAT WE'RE GOING TO HAVE TO DEAL WITH.
I WISH YOUR NEXT-LEVEL INTELLIGENCE COULD HAVE SEEN THIS COMING, BRAINIAC 5.
IT DID.
LIGHTNING LAD, MAYBE YOU WANT TO GO GET YOUR SISTER BEFORE SHE KILLS EVERYBODY.

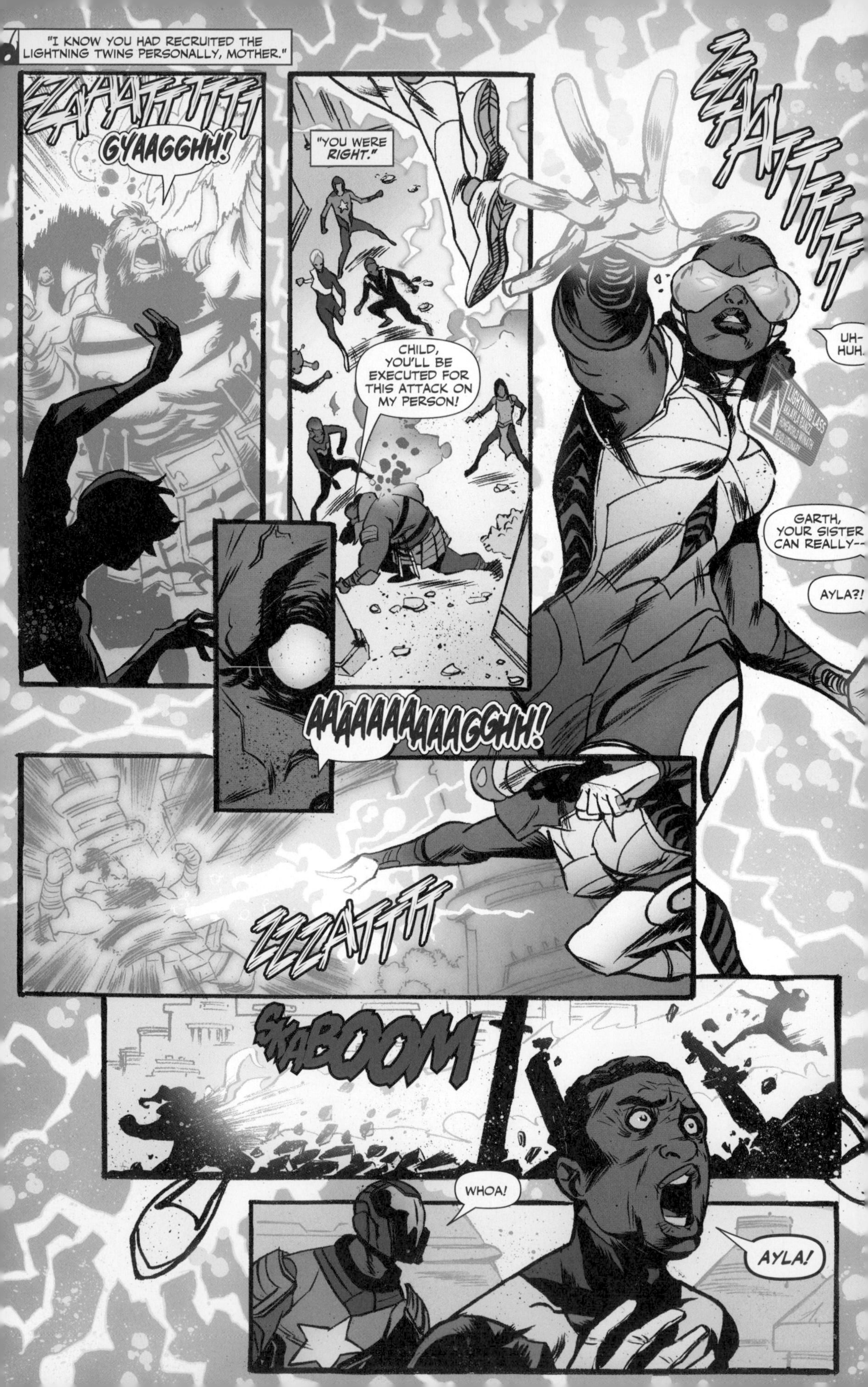
"I KNOW YOU HAD RECRUITED THE LIGHTNING TWINS PERSONALLY, MOTHER."
ZZAATTTTTT
GYAAGGHH!
"YOU WERE *RIGHT.*"
CHILD, YOU'LL BE EXECUTED FOR THIS ATTACK ON MY PERSON!
ZZAATTTTTTT
UH-HUH.
GARTH, YOUR SISTER CAN REALLY--
AYLA?!
AAAAAAAAAAGGHH!
ZZZATTTT
SKABOOM
WHOA!
AYLA!

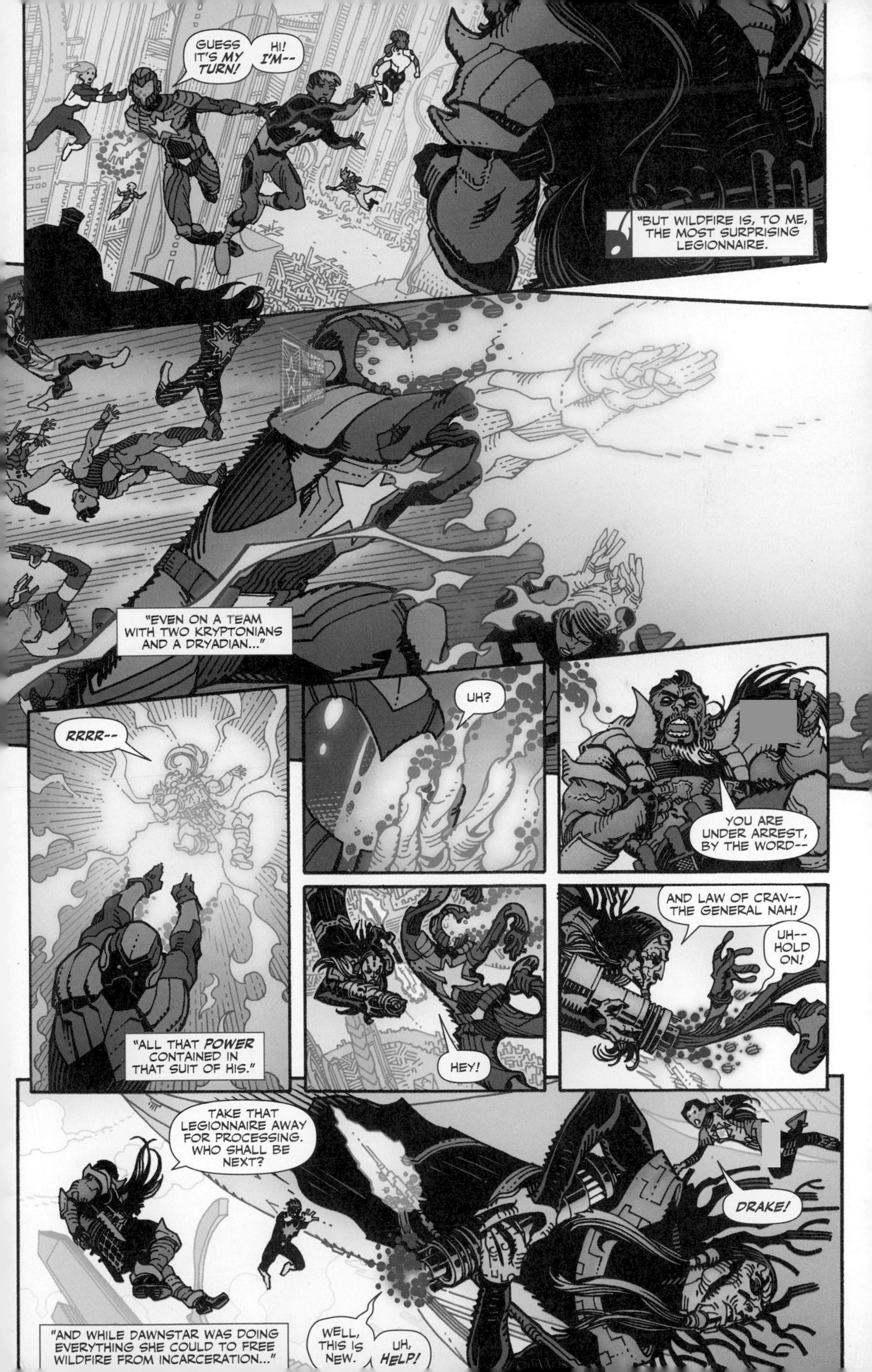
GUESS IT'S MY TURN!
HI! I'M--
"BUT WILDFIRE IS, TO ME, THE MOST SURPRISING LEGIONNAIRE.
"EVEN ON A TEAM WITH TWO KRYPTONIANS AND A DRYADIAN..."
RRRR--
"ALL THAT POWER CONTAINED IN THAT SUIT OF HIS."
UH?
YOU ARE UNDER ARREST, BY THE WORD--
HEY!
AND LAW OF CRAV-- THE GENERAL NAH!
UH-- HOLD ON!
TAKE THAT LEGIONNAIRE AWAY FOR PROCESSING. WHO SHALL BE NEXT?
DRAKE!
"AND WHILE DAWNSTAR WAS DOING EVERYTHING SHE COULD TO FREE WILDFIRE FROM INCARCERATION..."
WELL, THIS IS NEW.
UH, HELP!

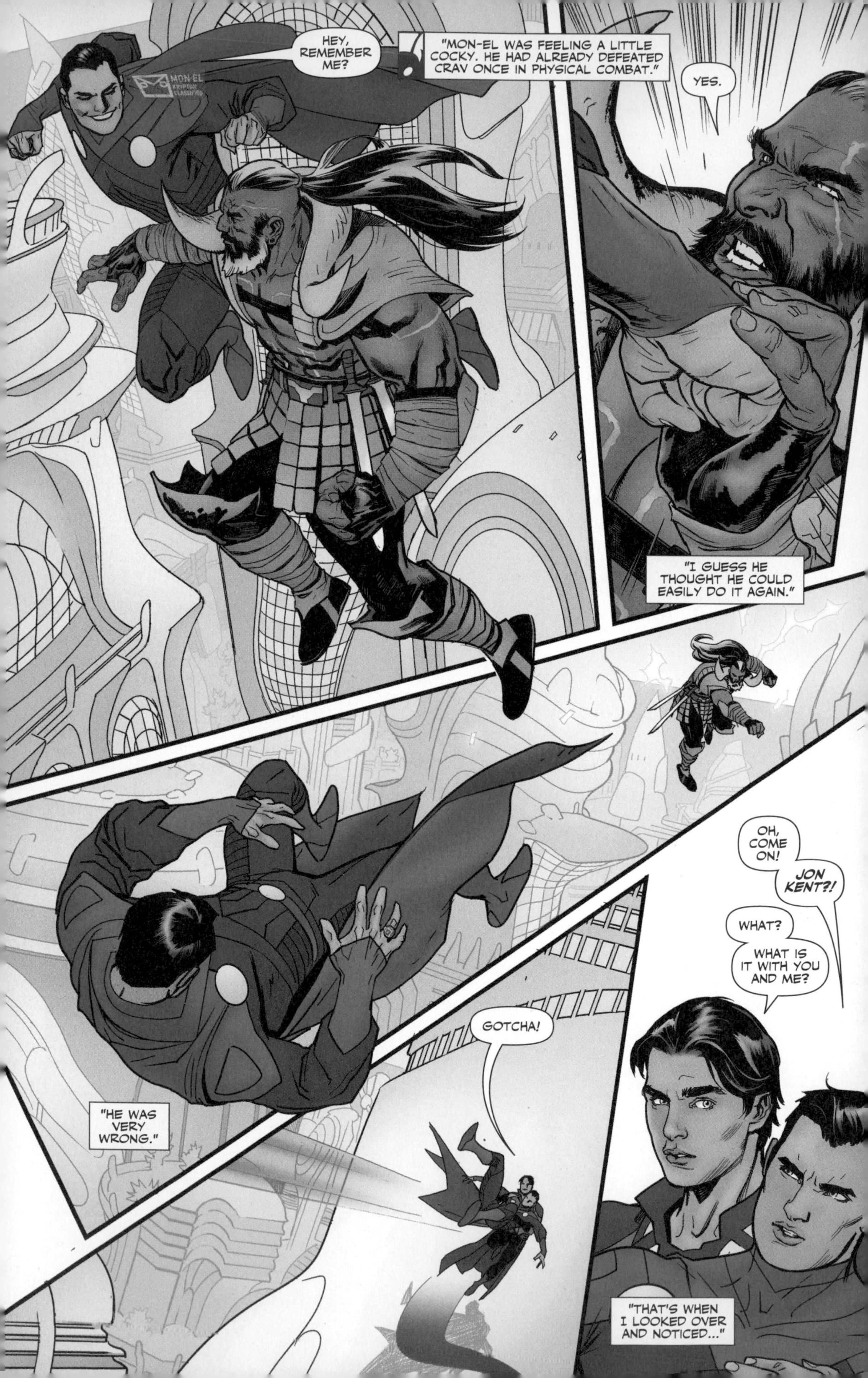

HEY, REMEMBER ME?
"MON-EL WAS FEELING A LITTLE COCKY. HE HAD ALREADY DEFEATED CRAV ONCE IN PHYSICAL COMBAT."
MON-EL KRYPTON CLASSIFIED
YES.
"I GUESS HE THOUGHT HE COULD EASILY DO IT AGAIN."
"HE WAS VERY WRONG."
GOTCHA!
OH, COME ON!
JON KENT?!
WHAT?
WHAT IS IT WITH YOU AND ME?
"THAT'S WHEN I LOOKED OVER AND NOTICED..."

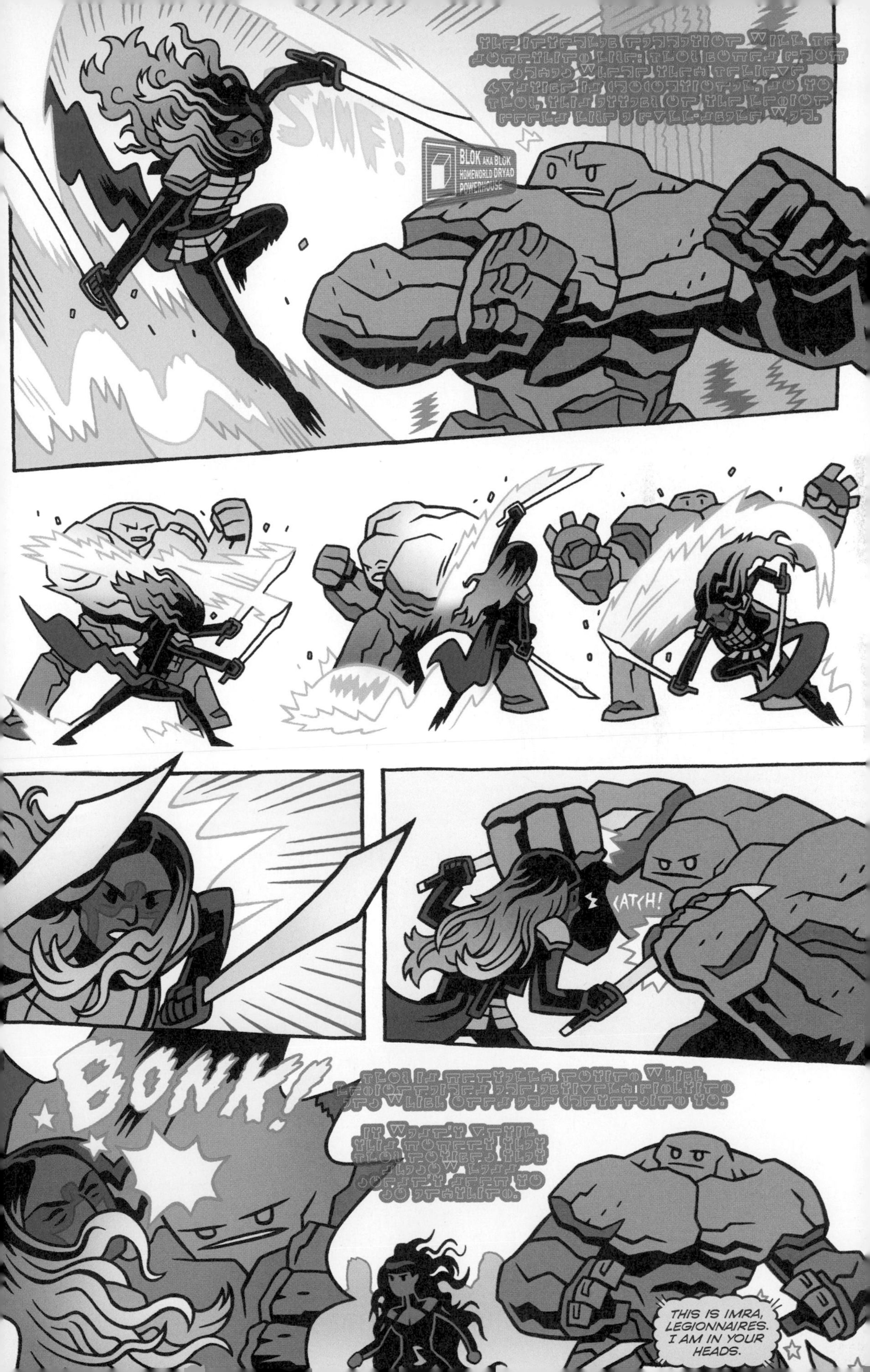
SHIF!
BLOK AKA BLOK
HOMEWORLD DRYAD
POWERHOUSE
CATCH!
BONK!
THIS IS IMRA, LEGIONNAIRES. I AM IN YOUR HEADS.

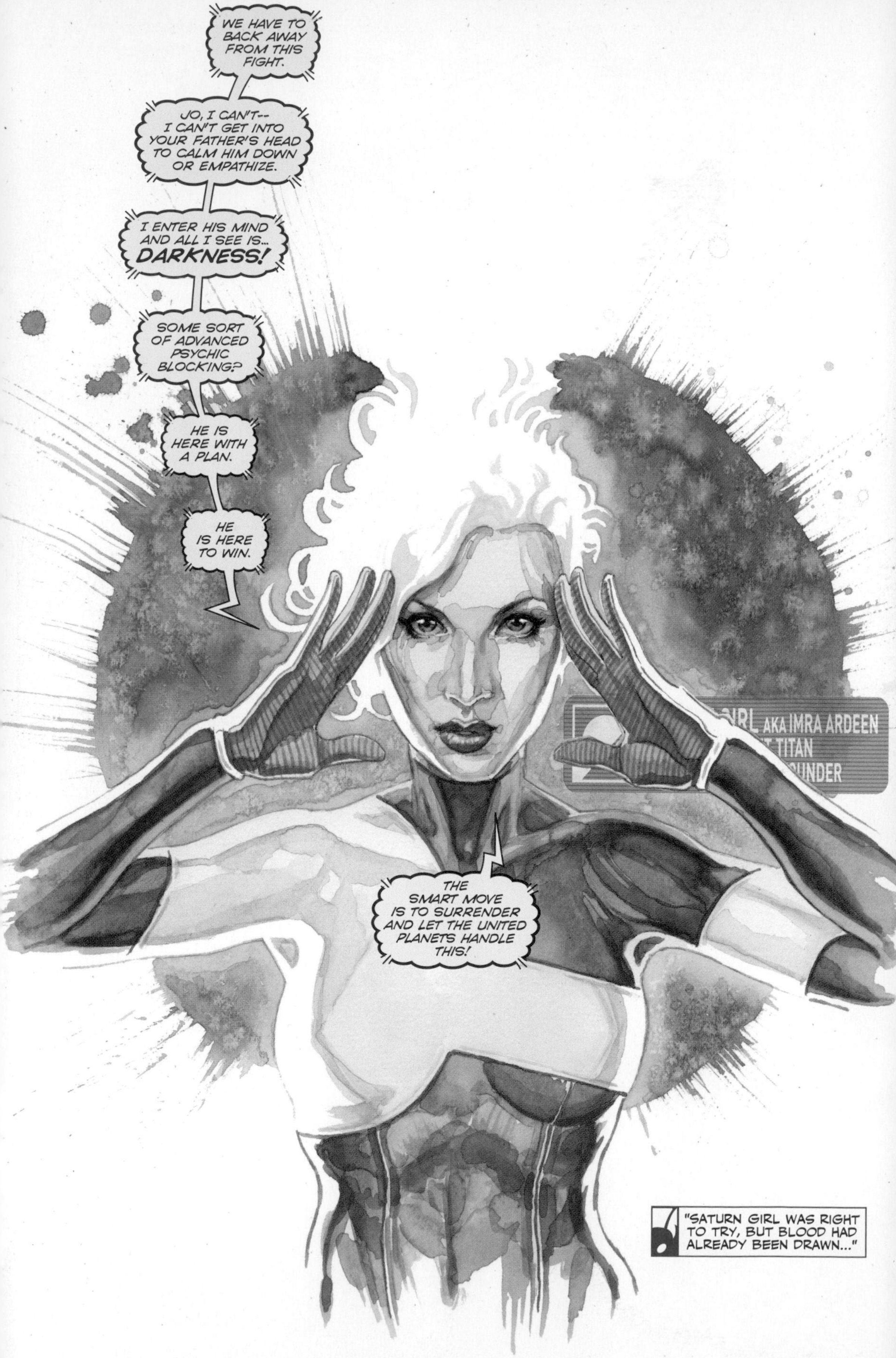
WE HAVE TO BACK AWAY FROM THIS FIGHT.
JO, I CAN'T-- I CAN'T GET INTO YOUR FATHER'S HEAD TO CALM HIM DOWN OR EMPATHIZE.
I ENTER HIS MIND AND ALL I SEE IS... DARKNESS!
SOME SORT OF ADVANCED PSYCHIC BLOCKING?
HE IS HERE WITH A PLAN.
HE IS HERE TO WIN.
THE SMART MOVE IS TO SURRENDER AND LET THE UNITED PLANETS HANDLE THIS!
"SATURN GIRL WAS RIGHT TO TRY, BUT BLOOD HAD ALREADY BEEN DRAWN..."

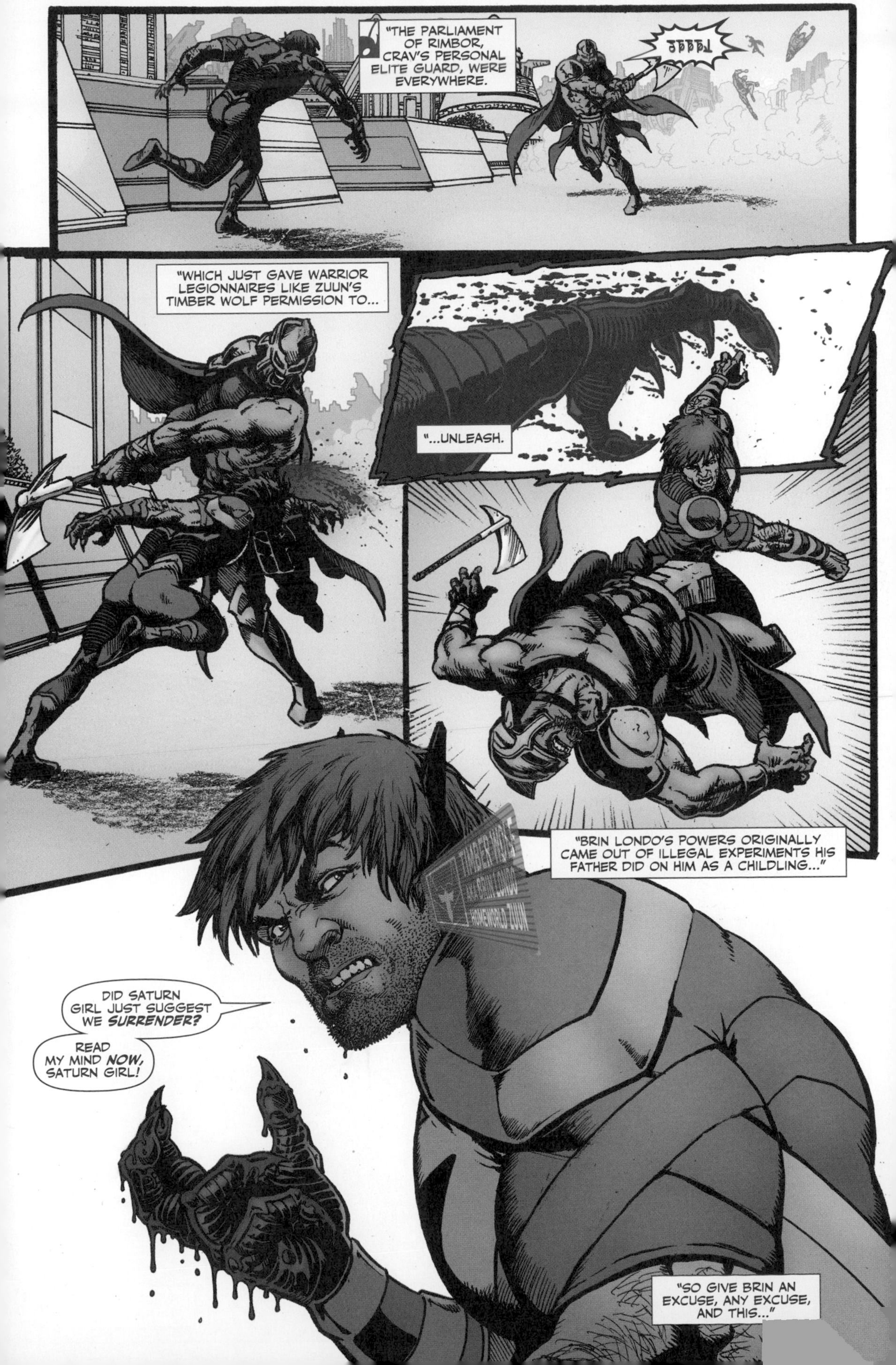
"THE PARLIAMENT OF RIMBOR, CRAV'S PERSONAL ELITE GUARD, WERE EVERYWHERE.
"WHICH JUST GAVE WARRIOR LEGIONNAIRES LIKE ZUUN'S TIMBER WOLF PERMISSION TO...
"...UNLEASH.
"BRIN LONDO'S POWERS ORIGINALLY CAME OUT OF ILLEGAL EXPERIMENTS HIS FATHER DID ON HIM AS A CHILDLING..."
HOMEWORLD ZUUN
DID SATURN GIRL JUST SUGGEST WE *SURRENDER?*
READ MY MIND *NOW,* SATURN GIRL!
"SO GIVE BRIN AN EXCUSE, ANY EXCUSE, AND THIS..."

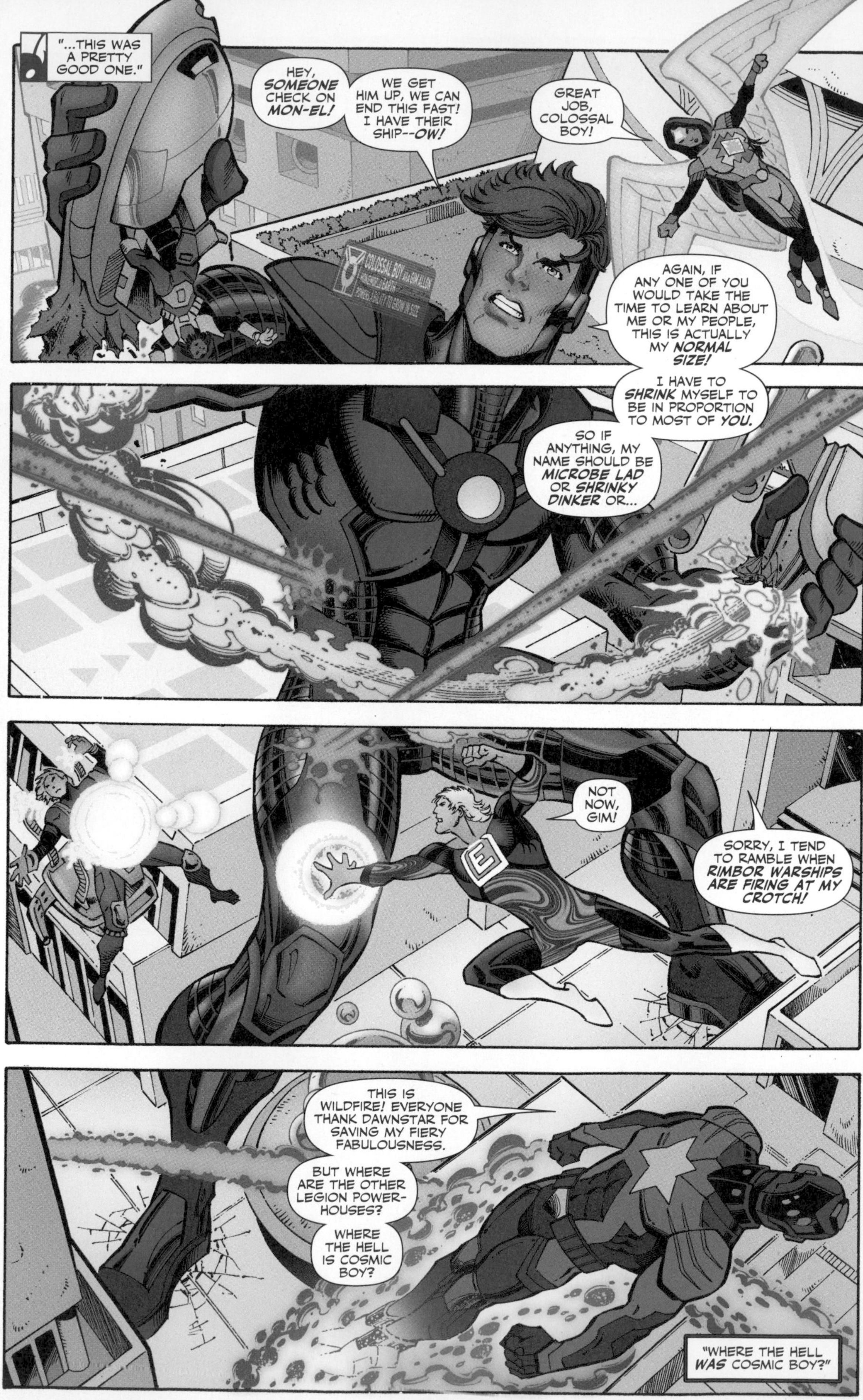
"...THIS WAS A PRETTY GOOD ONE."
HEY, *SOMEONE* CHECK ON *MON-EL!*
WE GET HIM UP, WE CAN END THIS FAST! I HAVE THEIR SHIP--*OW!*
GREAT JOB, COLOSSAL BOY!
COLOSSAL BOY A.K.A. GIM ALLON
AGAIN, IF ANY ONE OF YOU WOULD TAKE THE TIME TO LEARN ABOUT ME OR MY PEOPLE, THIS IS ACTUALLY MY *NORMAL SIZE!*
I HAVE TO *SHRINK* MYSELF TO BE IN PROPORTION TO MOST OF *YOU.*
SO IF ANYTHING, MY NAME SHOULD BE *MICROBE LAD* OR *SHRINKY DINKER* OR...
NOT NOW, GIM!
SORRY, I TEND TO RAMBLE WHEN *RIMBOR WARSHIPS ARE FIRING AT MY CROTCH!*
THIS IS WILDFIRE! EVERYONE THANK DAWNSTAR FOR SAVING MY FIERY FABULOUSNESS.
BUT WHERE ARE THE OTHER LEGION POWER-HOUSES?
WHERE THE HELL IS COSMIC BOY?
"WHERE THE HELL *WAS* COSMIC BOY?"

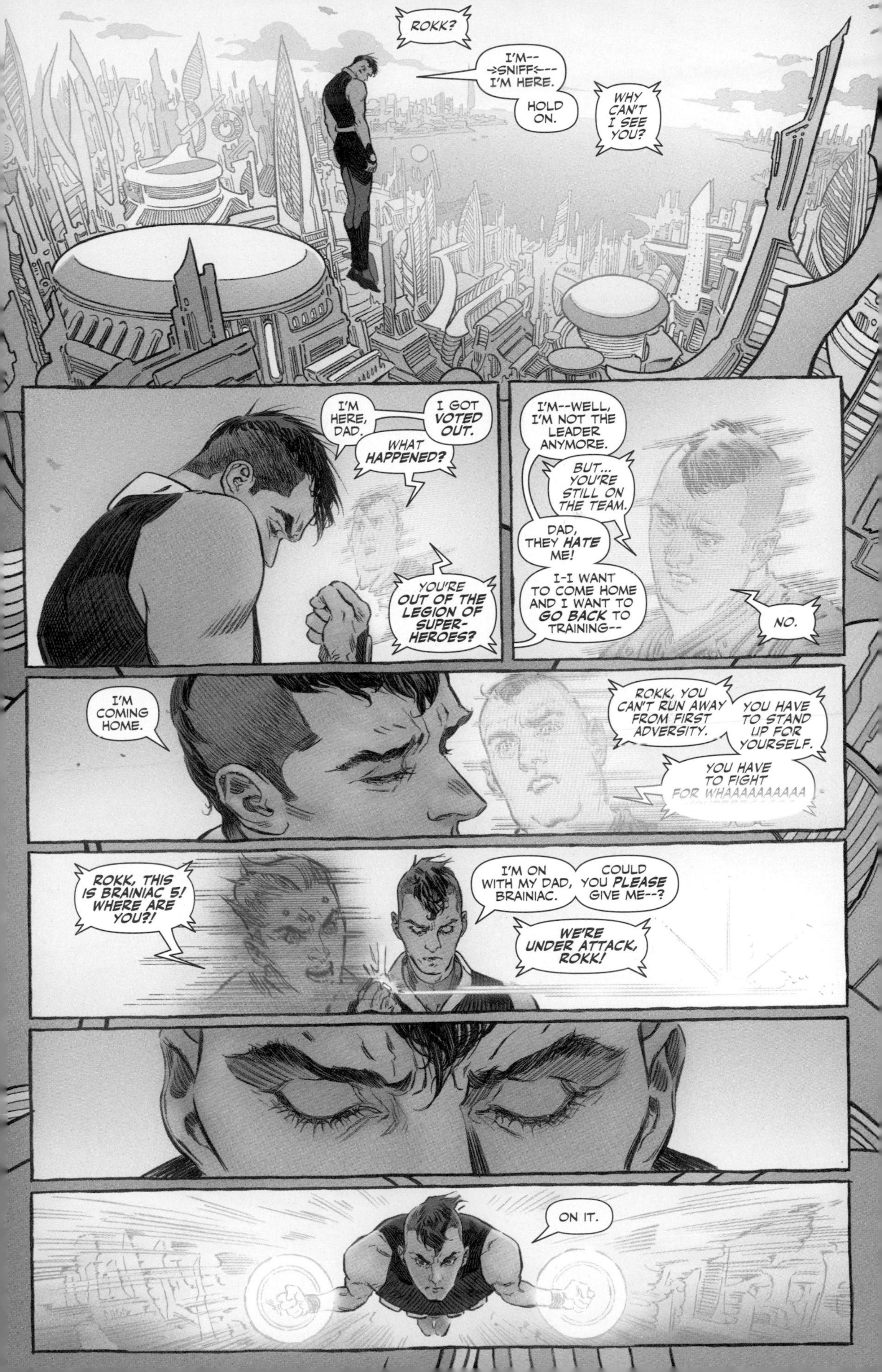
ROKK?
I'M-- -SNIFF- -- I'M HERE.
HOLD ON.
WHY CAN'T I SEE YOU?
I'M HERE, DAD.
I GOT VOTED OUT.
WHAT HAPPENED?
YOU'RE OUT OF THE LEGION OF SUPER-HEROES?
I'M--WELL, I'M NOT THE LEADER ANYMORE.
BUT... YOU'RE STILL ON THE TEAM.
DAD, THEY HATE ME!
I-I WANT TO COME HOME AND I WANT TO GO BACK TO TRAINING--
NO.
I'M COMING HOME.
ROKK, YOU CAN'T RUN AWAY FROM FIRST ADVERSITY.
YOU HAVE TO STAND UP FOR YOURSELF.
YOU HAVE TO FIGHT FOR WHAAAAAAAAAA
ROKK, THIS IS BRAINIAC 5! WHERE ARE YOU?!
I'M ON WITH MY DAD, BRAINIAC.
COULD YOU PLEASE GIVE ME--?
WE'RE UNDER ATTACK, ROKK!
ON IT.

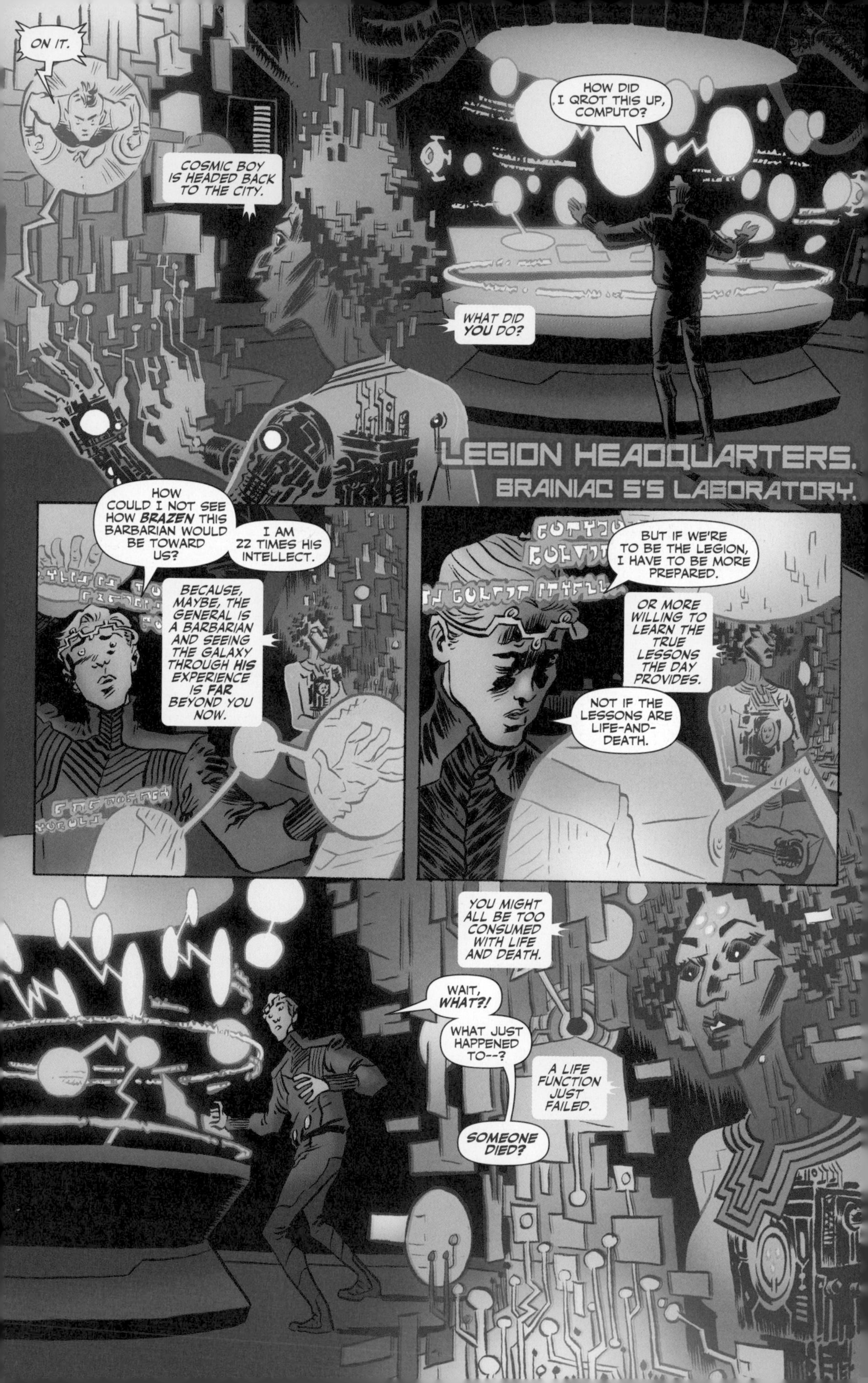
ON IT.
COSMIC BOY IS HEADED BACK TO THE CITY.
HOW DID I QROT THIS UP, COMPUTO?
WHAT DID YOU DO?
LEGION HEADQUARTERS.
BRAINIAC 5'S LABORATORY.
HOW COULD I NOT SEE HOW BRAZEN THIS BARBARIAN WOULD BE TOWARD US?
I AM 22 TIMES HIS INTELLECT.
BECAUSE, MAYBE, THE GENERAL IS A BARBARIAN AND SEEING THE GALAXY THROUGH HIS EXPERIENCE IS FAR BEYOND YOU NOW.
BUT IF WE'RE TO BE THE LEGION, I HAVE TO BE MORE PREPARED.
OR MORE WILLING TO LEARN THE TRUE LESSONS THE DAY PROVIDES.
NOT IF THE LESSONS ARE LIFE-AND-DEATH.
YOU MIGHT ALL BE TOO CONSUMED WITH LIFE AND DEATH.
WAIT, WHAT?!
WHAT JUST HAPPENED TO--?
A LIFE FUNCTION JUST FAILED.
SOMEONE DIED?

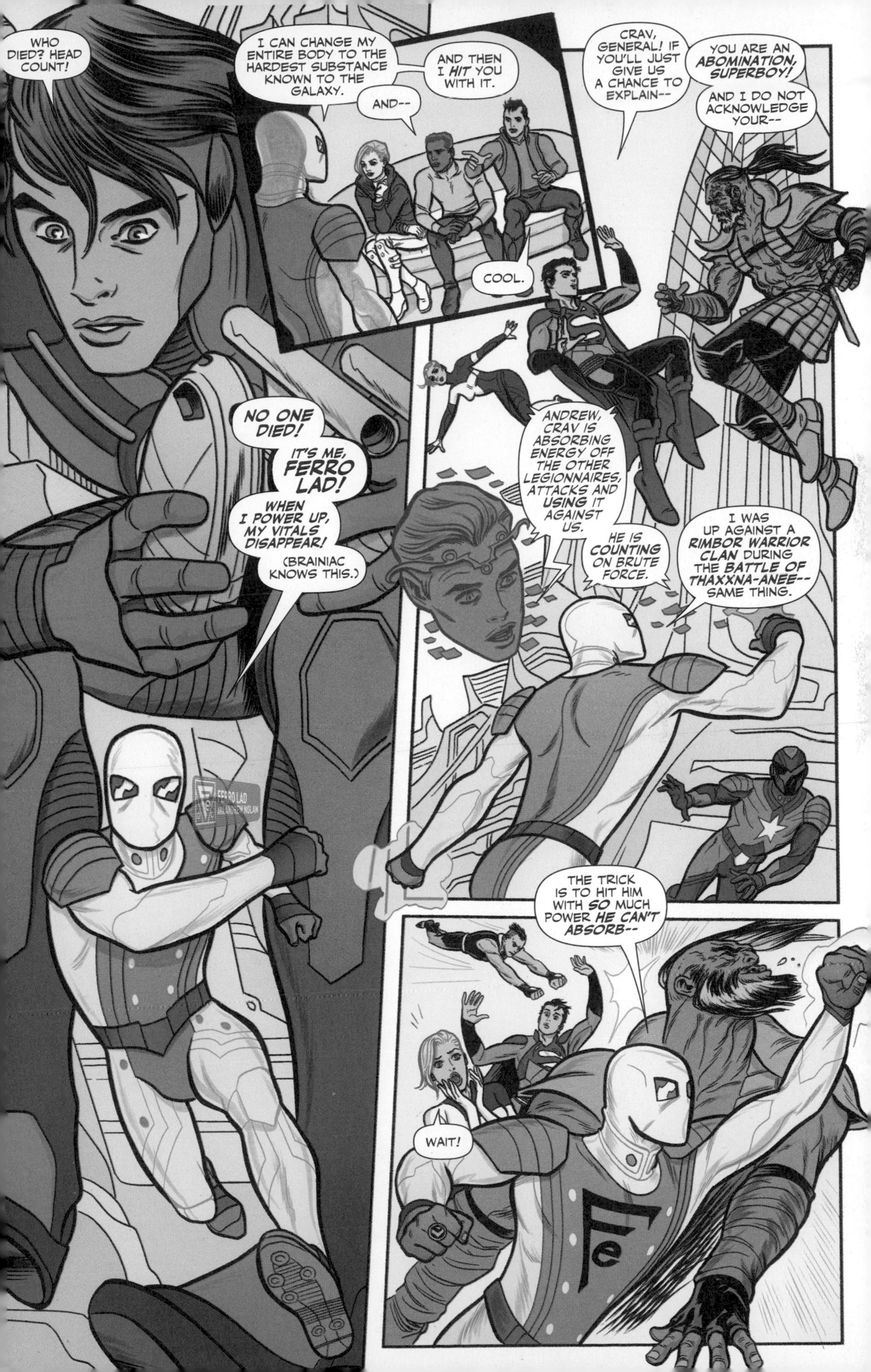
WHO DIED? HEAD COUNT!
I CAN CHANGE MY ENTIRE BODY TO THE HARDEST SUBSTANCE KNOWN TO THE GALAXY.
AND--
AND THEN I *HIT* YOU WITH IT.
COOL.
CRAV, GENERAL! IF YOU'LL JUST GIVE US A CHANCE TO EXPLAIN--
YOU ARE AN *ABOMINATION, SUPERBOY!*
AND I DO NOT ACKNOWLEDGE YOUR--
NO ONE DIED!
IT'S ME, **FERRO LAD!**
WHEN I POWER UP, MY VITALS DISAPPEAR!
(BRAINIAC KNOWS THIS.)
FERRO LAD
AKA ANDREW NOLAN
ANDREW, CRAV IS ABSORBING ENERGY OFF THE OTHER LEGIONNAIRES, ATTACKS AND *USING* IT AGAINST US.
HE IS *COUNTING* ON BRUTE FORCE.
I WAS UP AGAINST A *RIMBOR WARRIOR CLAN* DURING THE *BATTLE OF THAXXNA-ANEE*-- SAME THING.
THE TRICK IS TO HIT HIM WITH *SO* MUCH POWER *HE CAN'T ABSORB*--
WAIT!

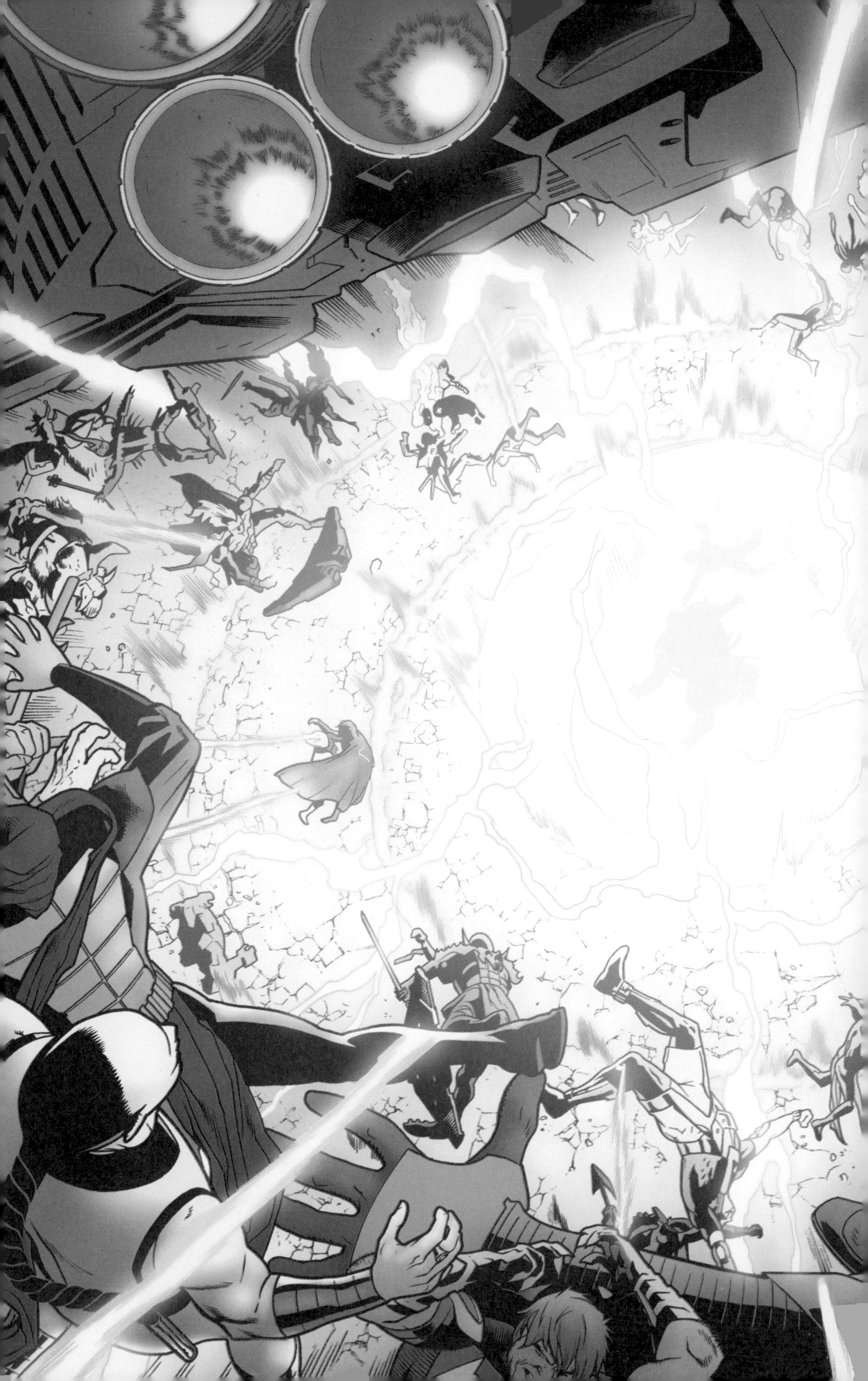

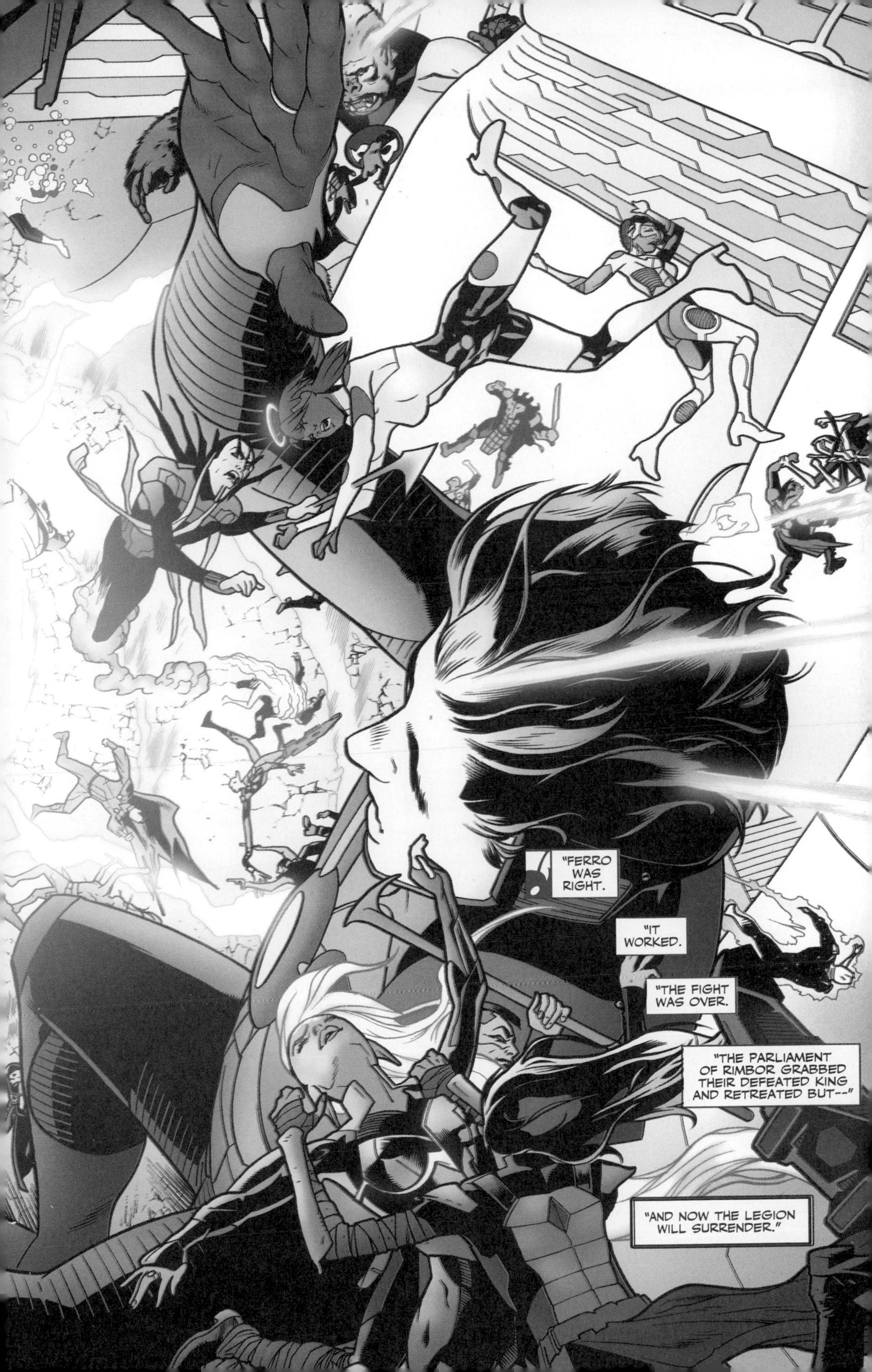
"FERRO WAS RIGHT.
"IT WORKED.
"THE FIGHT WAS OVER.
"THE PARLIAMENT OF RIMBOR GRABBED THEIR DEFEATED KING AND RETREATED BUT--"
"AND NOW THE LEGION WILL SURRENDER."

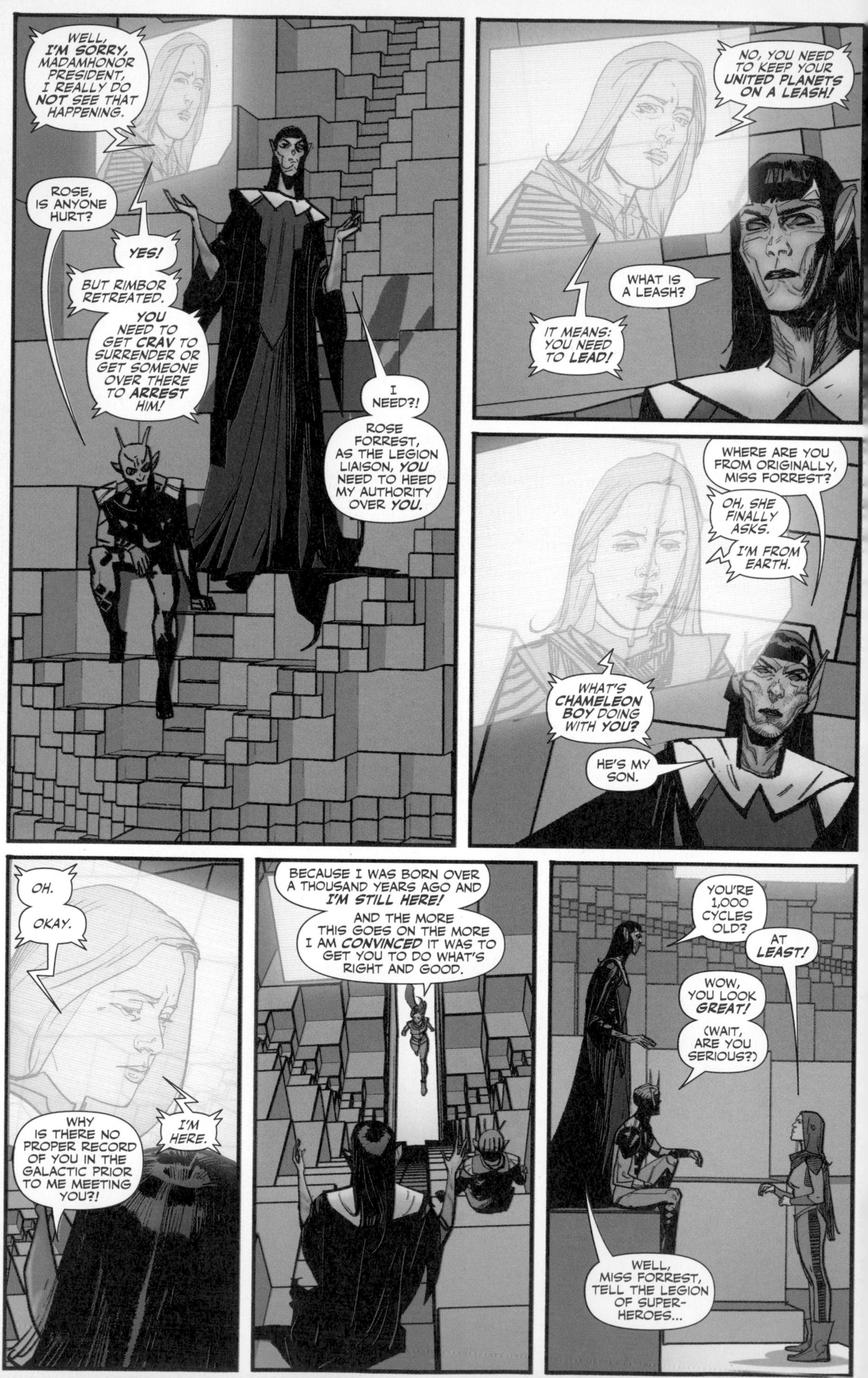
WELL, I'M SORRY, MADAMHONOR PRESIDENT, I REALLY DO NOT SEE THAT HAPPENING.
ROSE, IS ANYONE HURT?
YES!
BUT RIMBOR RETREATED.
YOU NEED TO GET CRAV TO SURRENDER OR GET SOMEONE OVER THERE TO ARREST HIM!
I NEED?!
ROSE FORREST, AS THE LEGION LIAISON, YOU NEED TO HEED MY AUTHORITY OVER YOU.
NO, YOU NEED TO KEEP YOUR UNITED PLANETS ON A LEASH!
WHAT IS A LEASH?
IT MEANS: YOU NEED TO LEAD!
WHERE ARE YOU FROM ORIGINALLY, MISS FORREST?
OH, SHE FINALLY ASKS.
I'M FROM EARTH.
WHAT'S CHAMELEON BOY DOING WITH YOU?
HE'S MY SON.
OH.
OKAY.
WHY IS THERE NO PROPER RECORD OF YOU IN THE GALACTIC PRIOR TO ME MEETING YOU?!
I'M HERE.
BECAUSE I WAS BORN OVER A THOUSAND YEARS AGO AND I'M STILL HERE!
AND THE MORE THIS GOES ON THE MORE I AM CONVINCED IT WAS TO GET YOU TO DO WHAT'S RIGHT AND GOOD.
YOU'RE 1,000 CYCLES OLD?
AT LEAST!
WOW, YOU LOOK GREAT!
(WAIT, ARE YOU SERIOUS?)
WELL, MISS FORREST, TELL THE LEGION OF SUPER-HEROES...

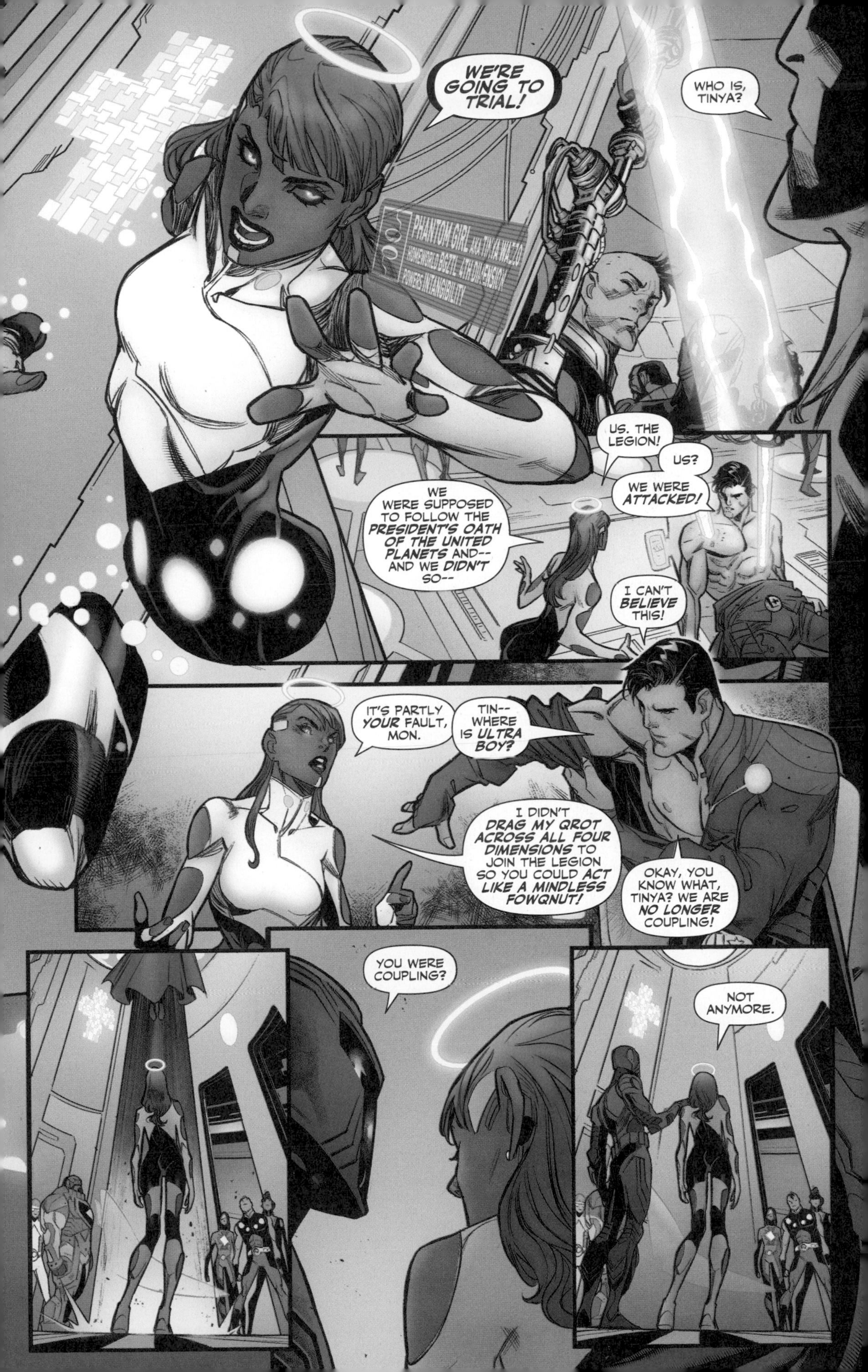
WE'RE GOING TO TRIAL!
PHANTOM GIRL AKA TINYA WAZZO
HOMEWORLD BOZTL 4TH DIMENSION
POWERS INTANGIBILITY
WHO IS, TINYA?
US. THE LEGION!
US?
WE WERE ATTACKED!
WE WERE SUPPOSED TO FOLLOW THE PRESIDENT'S OATH OF THE UNITED PLANETS AND-- AND WE DIDN'T SO--
I CAN'T BELIEVE THIS!
IT'S PARTLY YOUR FAULT, MON.
TIN-- WHERE IS ULTRA BOY?
I DIDN'T DRAG MY QROT ACROSS ALL FOUR DIMENSIONS TO JOIN THE LEGION SO YOU COULD ACT LIKE A MINDLESS FOWQNUT!
OKAY, YOU KNOW WHAT, TINYA? WE ARE NO LONGER COUPLING!
YOU WERE COUPLING?
NOT ANYMORE.

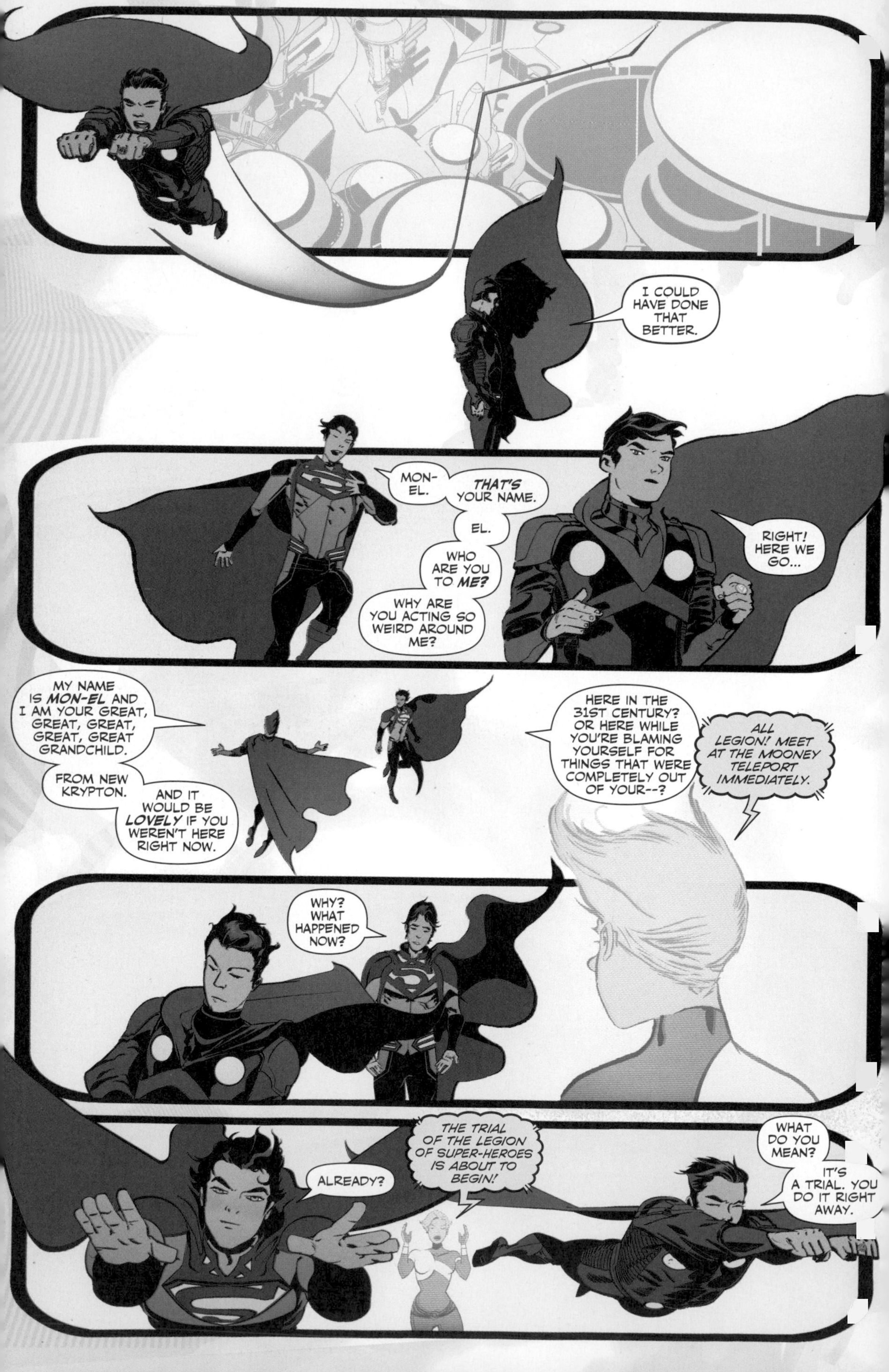
I COULD HAVE DONE THAT BETTER.
MON-EL.
THAT'S YOUR NAME.
EL.
WHO ARE YOU TO ME?
WHY ARE YOU ACTING SO WEIRD AROUND ME?
RIGHT! HERE WE GO...
MY NAME IS MON-EL AND I AM YOUR GREAT, GREAT, GREAT, GREAT, GREAT GRANDCHILD.
FROM NEW KRYPTON.
AND IT WOULD BE LOVELY IF YOU WEREN'T HERE RIGHT NOW.
HERE IN THE 31ST CENTURY? OR HERE WHILE YOU'RE BLAMING YOURSELF FOR THINGS THAT WERE COMPLETELY OUT OF YOUR--?
ALL LEGION! MEET AT THE MOONEY TELEPORT IMMEDIATELY.
WHY? WHAT HAPPENED NOW?
THE TRIAL OF THE LEGION OF SUPER-HEROES IS ABOUT TO BEGIN!
ALREADY?
WHAT DO YOU MEAN?
IT'S A TRIAL. YOU DO IT RIGHT AWAY.

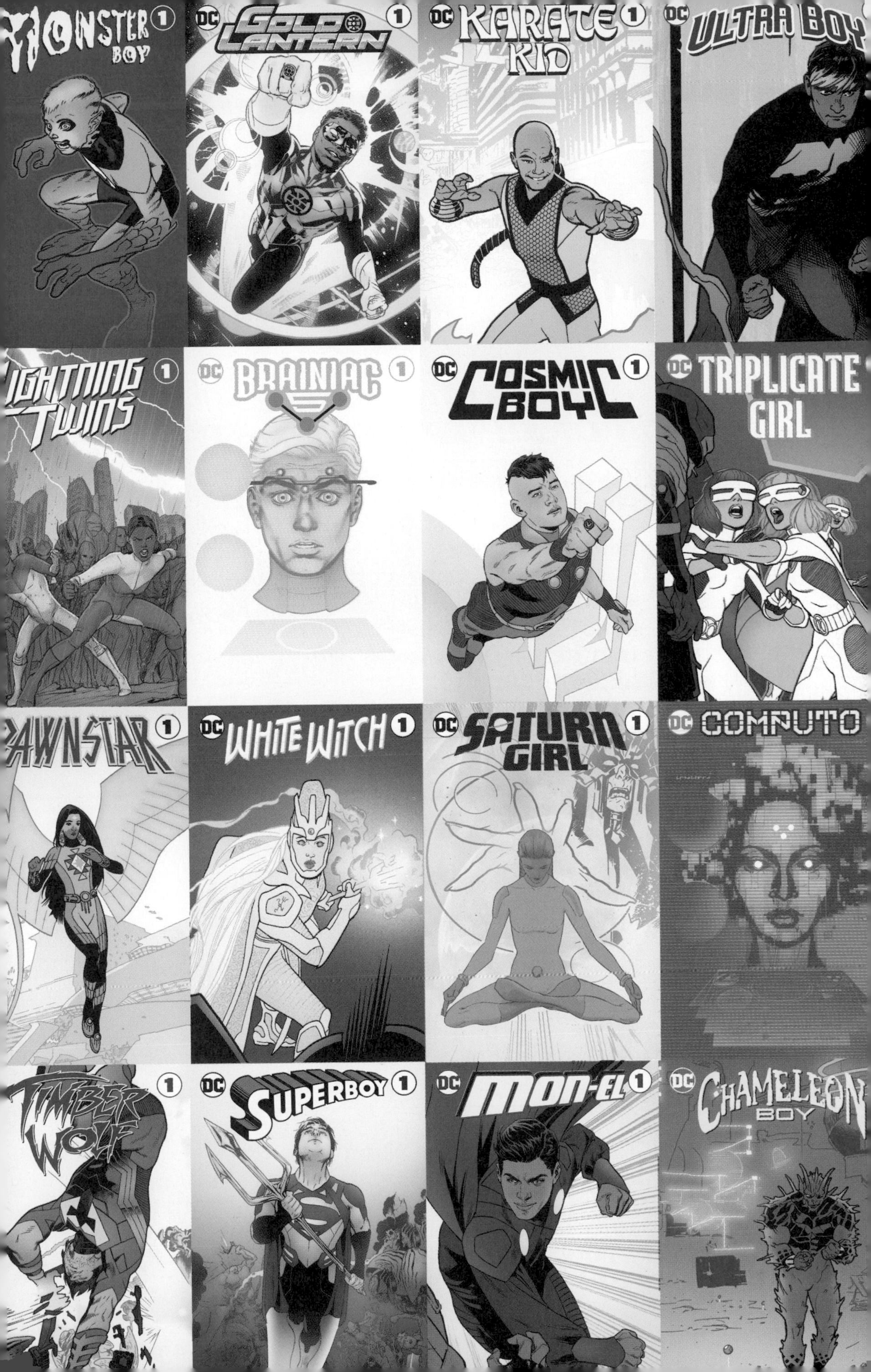
MONSTER BOY 1
DC GOLD LANTERN 1
DC KARATE KID 1
DC ULTRA BOY
IGHTNING TWINS 1
DC BRAINIAC 1
DC COSMIC BOY 1
DC TRIPLICATE GIRL
AWNSTAR 1
DC WHITE WITCH 1
DC SATURN GIRL 1
DC COMPUTO
TIMBER WOLF 1
DC SUPERBOY 1
DC MON-EL 1
DC CHAMELEON BOY

THE TRIAL OF THE LEGION OF SUPER-HEROES - PART 2

BRIAN MICHAEL BENDIS - WRITER

- ARTISTS -

PAGE 1: **DAVID MARQUEZ**
PAGE 2: **RYAN SOOK & WADE VON GRAWBADGER**
PAGE 3: **JOE QUINONES**
PAGE 4: **MIKE GRELL**
PAGE 5: **IVAN REIS & JOE PRADO**
PAGE 6: **NICK DERINGTON**
PAGE 7: **JAMES HARREN**
PAGE 8: **JOHN ROMITA JR & KLAUS JANSON**
PAGE 9: **NICOLA SCOTT**
PAGE 11: **ARTHUR ADAMS**
PAGE 12: **JIM CHEUNG**
PAGE 13: **GARY FRANK**
PAGE 14: **TULA LOTAY**
PAGE 15: **RILEY ROSSMO**
PAGE 16: **GENE LUEN YANG**
PAGE 17: **KEVIN NOWLAN**
PAGE 18: **MICHEL FIFFE**
PAGE 19: **JENNY FRISON**
PAGE 20: **EMANUELA LUPACCHINO & WADE VON GRAWBADGER**
PAGE 21: **RYAN SOOK & WADE VON GRAWBADGER**
PAGE 22: **MITCH GERADS (ART & COLOR)**

JORDIE BELLAIRE - COLORIST
DAVE SHARPE - LETTERER
**RYAN SOOK, WADE VON GRAWBADGER, MIKEL JANIN,
TRAVIS MOORE & JORDIE BELLAIRE** – COVER ARTISTS
ANDRÉ LIMA ARAÚJO & CHRIS O'HALLORAN – VARIANT COVER ARTISTS
BRITTANY HOLZHERR – ASSOCIATE EDITOR
BRIAN CUNNINGHAM – EDITOR

SUPERBOY CREATED BY JERRY SIEGEL.
BY SPECIAL ARRANGEMENT WITH **THE JERRY SIEGEL FAMILY.**

MY NAME IS TASMIA MALLOR.

I AM THE HEREDITARY SHADOW CHAMPION OF TALOK VIII.

WHICH MEANS I HAVE BEEN BEQUEATHED THE ABILITY TO CONJURE ABSOLUTE DARKNESS.

MY SPECIES SEES ALL THINGS IN STARK TERMS AND THAT GIVES US A VERY PURE VIEW OF WHAT IS JUST.

AND NOW I AM A *VERY* PROUD MEMBER OF THE LEGION OF SUPER-HEROES.

THE LEGION, LIKE THE UNITED PLANETS IT DEFENDS AND SUPPORTS, IS A GROUP OF YOUNG HEROES OF INDIVIDUAL, UNIQUE, EXCEPTIONAL ABILITY.

WE ATTEMPT TO EMULATE THE GREAT AGE OF HEROES FROM EARTH'S ANCIENT PAST.

IT IS OUR WAY TO PROTECT THIS AMAZING GALAXY.

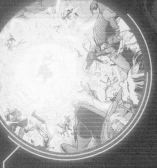

RIMBOR'S CRAV THE GENERAL NAH ATTACKS

CLASH ON NEW METROPOLIS LEADS TO TRIAL

IN MANY CULTURES, ON MANY PLANETS, THE ONLY WAY TOWARD PEACE AND UNDERSTANDING IS THROUGH COMMUNICATION AND PARTNERSHIP.

THE GREAT AGE WAS A TIME WHEN HEROES GATHERED TOGETHER TO SHARE EACH OTHER'S STORIES AND EXPERIENCES AND TO FIGHT THE FIGHTS NO SINGLE HERO COULD WITHSTAND.

THE LEGION WAS CREATED TO STAND UP TO THOSE WHO WOULD DEFY THE IDEA OF THE UNITED PLANETS AND UNITY AMONG OUR CULTURES.

THEREFORE, THE ACCUSATIONS MADE TODAY ARE OUTLANDISH AND SKEWED.

I STAND BEFORE YOU REPRESENTING THE LEGION AND THEIR COLLECTED BELIEFS AND IDEAS.

TODAY... ALL TRUTH WILL BE REVEALED.

THE LEGION OF SUPER-HEROES IS A BRILLIANT IDEA WELL EXECUTED BY ITS MEMBERS.

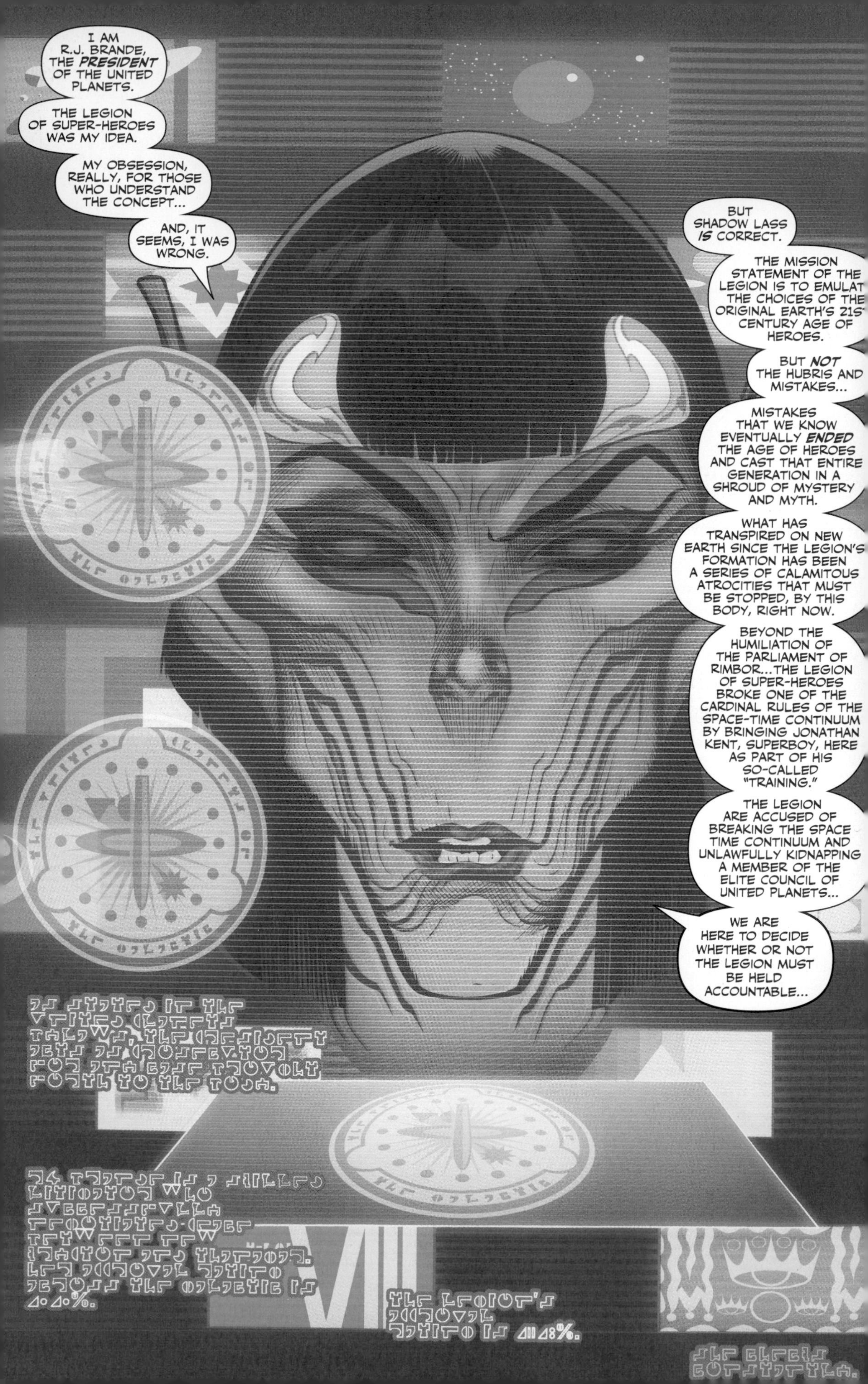
I AM R.J. BRANDE, THE PRESIDENT OF THE UNITED PLANETS.
THE LEGION OF SUPER-HEROES WAS MY IDEA.
MY OBSESSION, REALLY, FOR THOSE WHO UNDERSTAND THE CONCEPT...
AND, IT SEEMS, I WAS WRONG.
BUT SHADOW LASS IS CORRECT.
THE MISSION STATEMENT OF THE LEGION IS TO EMULAT THE CHOICES OF THE ORIGINAL EARTH'S 21S CENTURY AGE OF HEROES.
BUT NOT THE HUBRIS AND MISTAKES...
MISTAKES THAT WE KNOW EVENTUALLY ENDED THE AGE OF HEROES AND CAST THAT ENTIRE GENERATION IN A SHROUD OF MYSTERY AND MYTH.
WHAT HAS TRANSPIRED ON NEW EARTH SINCE THE LEGION'S FORMATION HAS BEEN A SERIES OF CALAMITOUS ATROCITIES THAT MUST BE STOPPED, BY THIS BODY, RIGHT NOW.
BEYOND THE HUMILIATION OF THE PARLIAMENT OF RIMBOR...THE LEGION OF SUPER-HEROES BROKE ONE OF THE CARDINAL RULES OF THE SPACE-TIME CONTINUUM BY BRINGING JONATHAN KENT, SUPERBOY, HERE AS PART OF HIS SO-CALLED "TRAINING."
THE LEGION ARE ACCUSED OF BREAKING THE SPACE TIME CONTINUUM AND UNLAWFULLY KIDNAPPING A MEMBER OF THE ELITE COUNCIL OF UNITED PLANETS...
WE ARE HERE TO DECIDE WHETHER OR NOT THE LEGION MUST BE HELD ACCOUNTABLE...

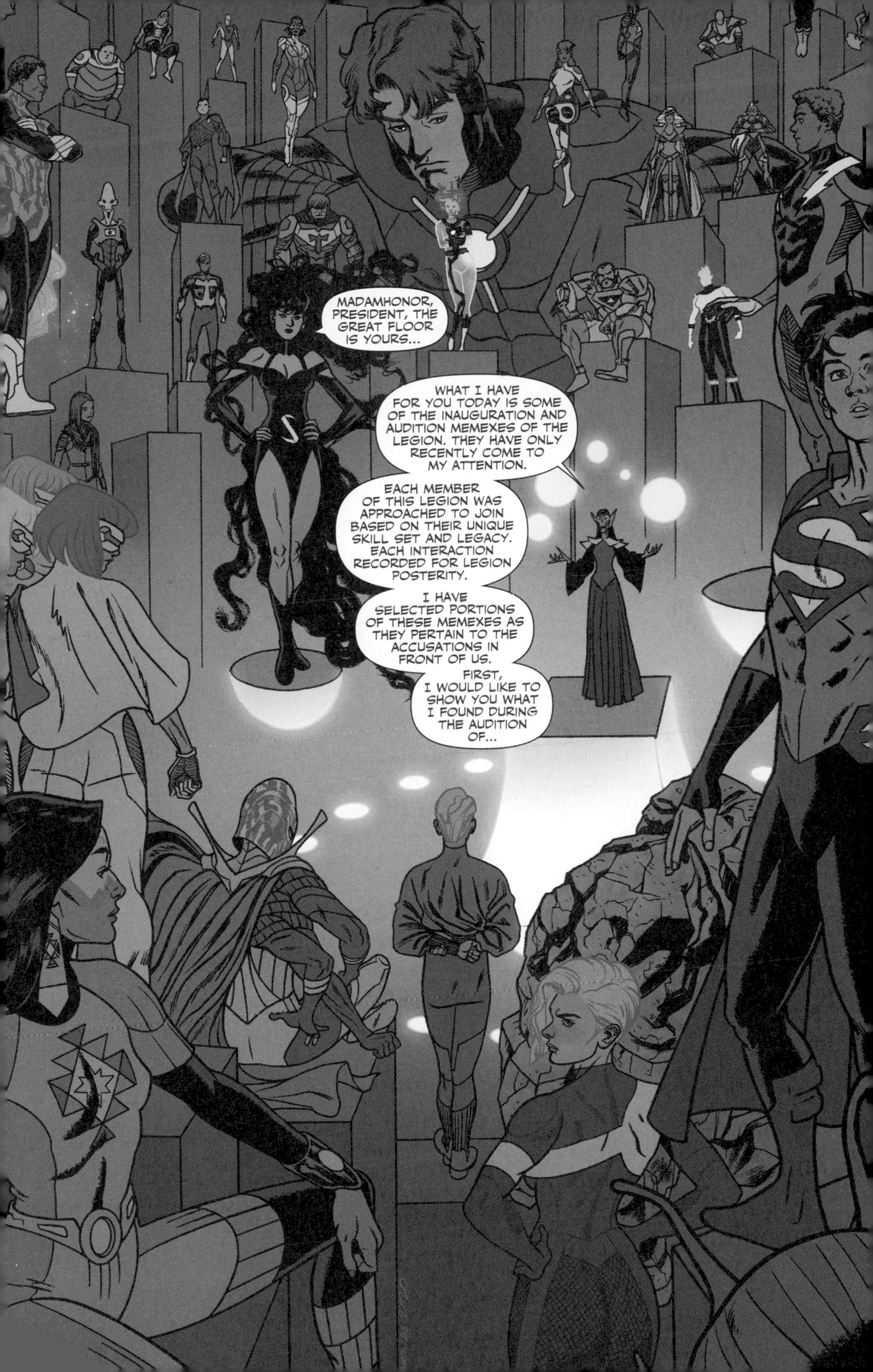
MADAMHONOR, PRESIDENT, THE GREAT FLOOR IS YOURS...
WHAT I HAVE FOR YOU TODAY IS SOME OF THE INAUGURATION AND AUDITION MEMEXES OF THE LEGION. THEY HAVE ONLY RECENTLY COME TO MY ATTENTION.
EACH MEMBER OF THIS LEGION WAS APPROACHED TO JOIN BASED ON THEIR UNIQUE SKILL SET AND LEGACY. EACH INTERACTION RECORDED FOR LEGION POSTERITY.
I HAVE SELECTED PORTIONS OF THESE MEMEXES AS THEY PERTAIN TO THE ACCUSATIONS IN FRONT OF US.
FIRST, I WOULD LIKE TO SHOW YOU WHAT I FOUND DURING THE AUDITION OF...

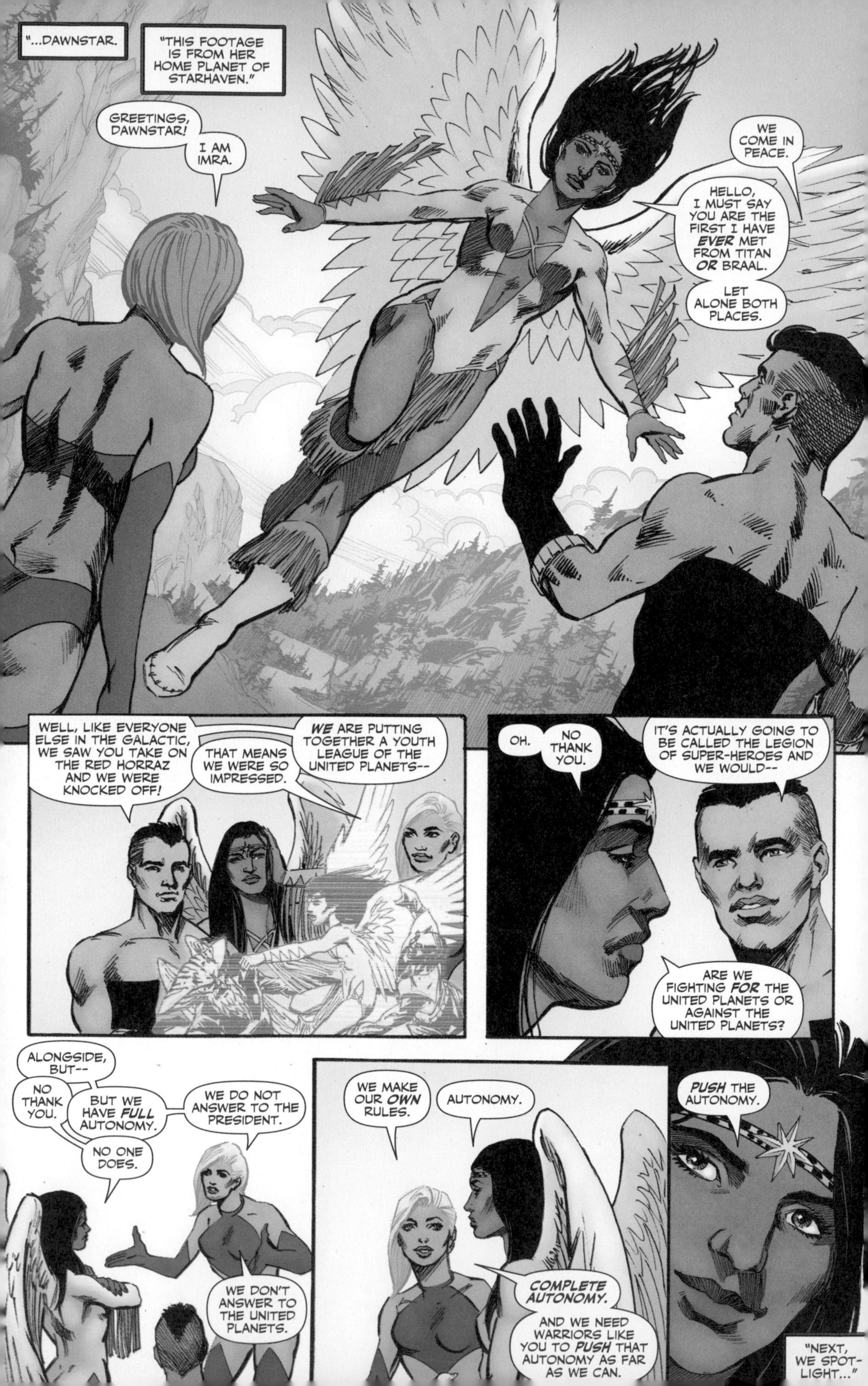
"...DAWNSTAR.
"THIS FOOTAGE IS FROM HER HOME PLANET OF STARHAVEN."
GREETINGS, DAWNSTAR!
I AM IMRA.
WE COME IN PEACE.
HELLO, I MUST SAY YOU ARE THE FIRST I HAVE EVER MET FROM TITAN OR BRAAL.
LET ALONE BOTH PLACES.
WELL, LIKE EVERYONE ELSE IN THE GALACTIC, WE SAW YOU TAKE ON THE RED HORRAZ AND WE WERE KNOCKED OFF!
THAT MEANS WE WERE SO IMPRESSED.
WE ARE PUTTING TOGETHER A YOUTH LEAGUE OF THE UNITED PLANETS--
OH.
NO THANK YOU.
IT'S ACTUALLY GOING TO BE CALLED THE LEGION OF SUPER-HEROES AND WE WOULD--
ARE WE FIGHTING FOR THE UNITED PLANETS OR AGAINST THE UNITED PLANETS?
ALONGSIDE, BUT--
NO THANK YOU.
BUT WE HAVE FULL AUTONOMY.
WE DO NOT ANSWER TO THE PRESIDENT.
NO ONE DOES.
WE DON'T ANSWER TO THE UNITED PLANETS.
WE MAKE OUR OWN RULES.
AUTONOMY.
COMPLETE AUTONOMY.
AND WE NEED WARRIORS LIKE YOU TO PUSH THAT AUTONOMY AS FAR AS WE CAN.
PUSH THE AUTONOMY.
"NEXT, WE SPOT-LIGHT..."

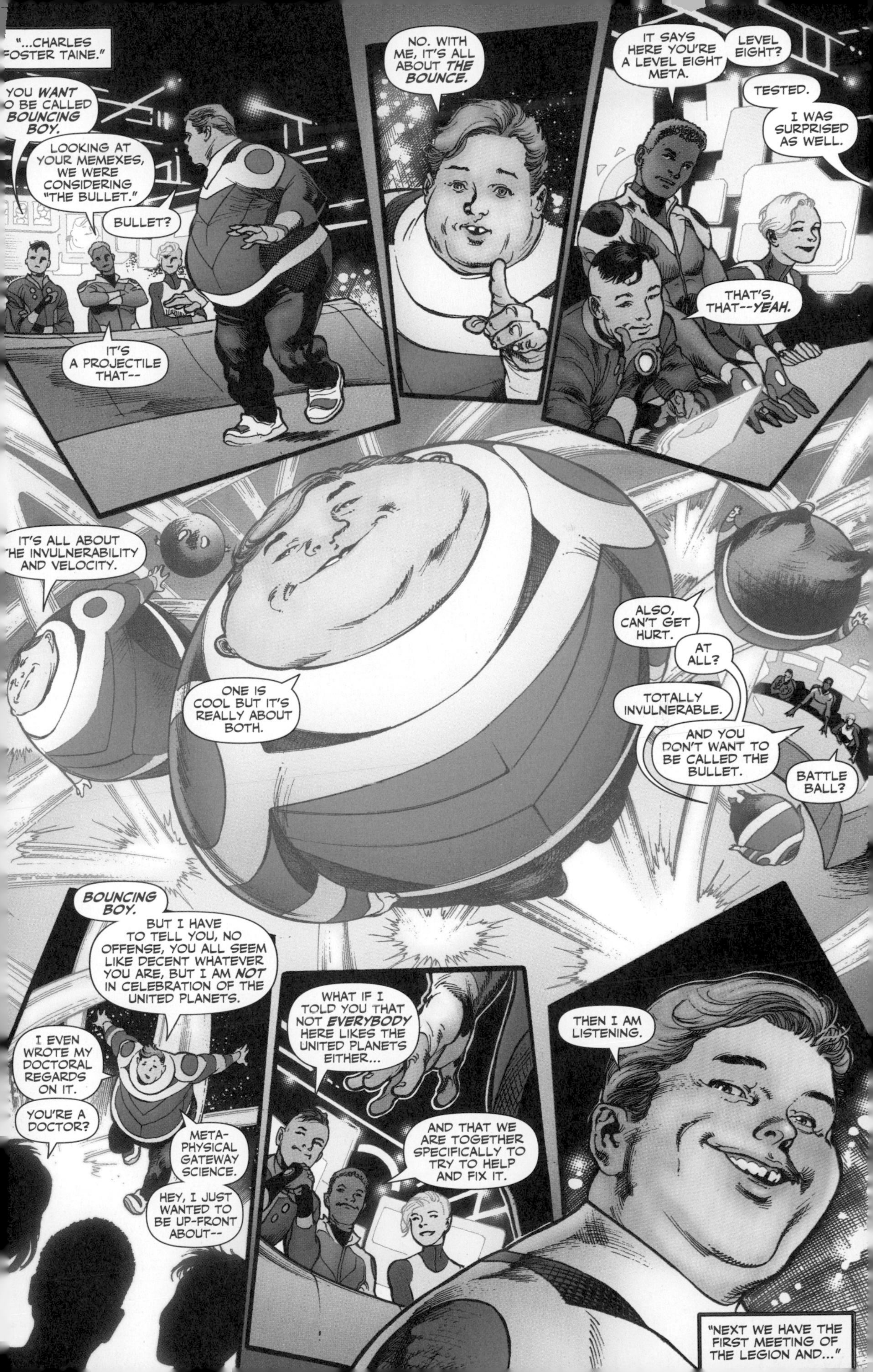
"...CHARLES FOSTER TAINE."
YOU WANT TO BE CALLED BOUNCING BOY.
LOOKING AT YOUR MEMEXES, WE WERE CONSIDERING "THE BULLET."
BULLET?
IT'S A PROJECTILE THAT--
NO. WITH ME, IT'S ALL ABOUT THE BOUNCE.
IT SAYS HERE YOU'RE A LEVEL EIGHT META.
LEVEL EIGHT?
TESTED.
I WAS SURPRISED AS WELL.
THAT'S, THAT--YEAH.
IT'S ALL ABOUT THE INVULNERABILITY AND VELOCITY.
ONE IS COOL BUT IT'S REALLY ABOUT BOTH.
ALSO, CAN'T GET HURT.
AT ALL?
TOTALLY INVULNERABLE.
AND YOU DON'T WANT TO BE CALLED THE BULLET.
BATTLE BALL?
BOUNCING BOY.
BUT I HAVE TO TELL YOU, NO OFFENSE, YOU ALL SEEM LIKE DECENT WHATEVER YOU ARE, BUT I AM NOT IN CELEBRATION OF THE UNITED PLANETS.
I EVEN WROTE MY DOCTORAL REGARDS ON IT.
YOU'RE A DOCTOR?
META-PHYSICAL GATEWAY SCIENCE.
HEY, I JUST WANTED TO BE UP-FRONT ABOUT--
WHAT IF I TOLD YOU THAT NOT EVERYBODY HERE LIKES THE UNITED PLANETS EITHER...
AND THAT WE ARE TOGETHER SPECIFICALLY TO TRY TO HELP AND FIX IT.
THEN I AM LISTENING.
"NEXT WE HAVE THE FIRST MEETING OF THE LEGION AND..."

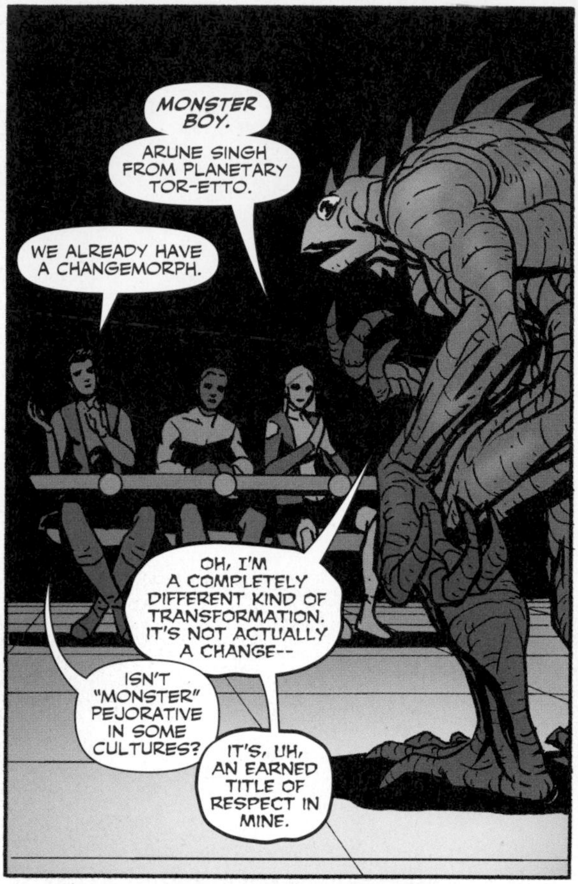
MONSTER BOY.
ARUNE SINGH FROM PLANETARY TOR-ETTO.
WE ALREADY HAVE A CHANGEMORPH.
OH, I'M A COMPLETELY DIFFERENT KIND OF TRANSFORMATION. IT'S NOT ACTUALLY A CHANGE--
ISN'T "MONSTER" PEJORATIVE IN SOME CULTURES?
IT'S, UH, AN EARNED TITLE OF RESPECT IN MINE.
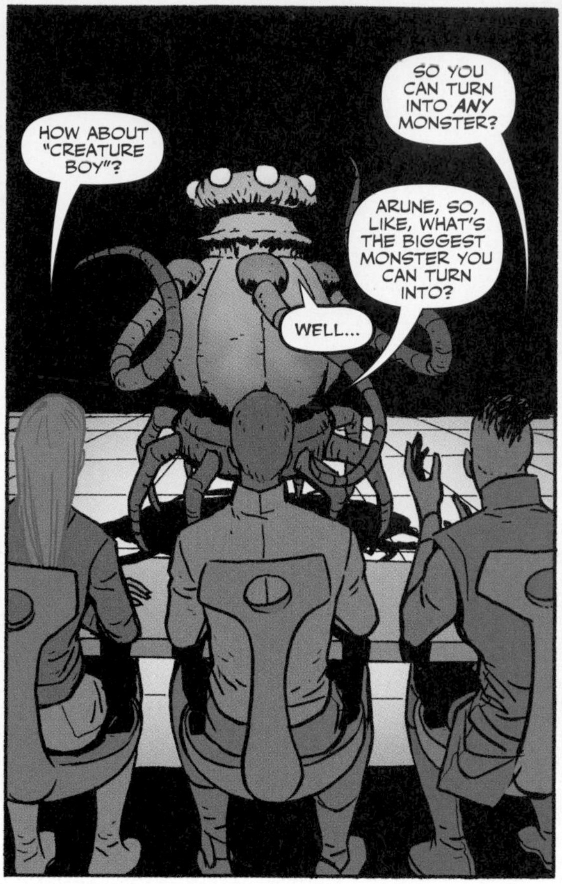
HOW ABOUT "CREATURE BOY"?
SO YOU CAN TURN INTO ANY MONSTER?
ARUNE, SO, LIKE, WHAT'S THE BIGGEST MONSTER YOU CAN TURN INTO?
WELL...
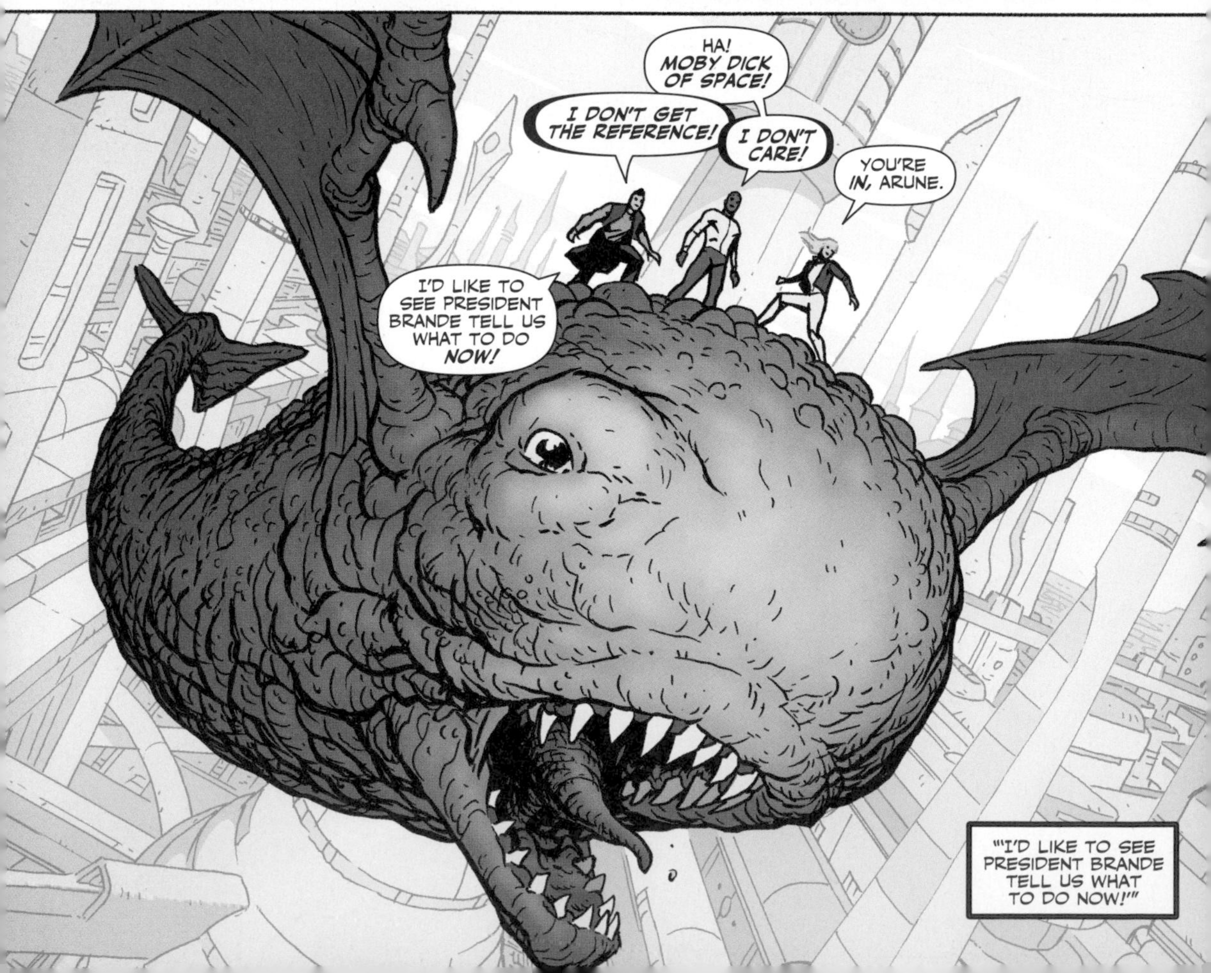
HA! MOBY DICK OF SPACE!
I DON'T GET THE REFERENCE!
I DON'T CARE!
YOU'RE IN, ARUNE.
I'D LIKE TO SEE PRESIDENT BRANDE TELL US WHAT TO DO NOW!
"I'D LIKE TO SEE PRESIDENT BRANDE TELL US WHAT TO DO NOW!"

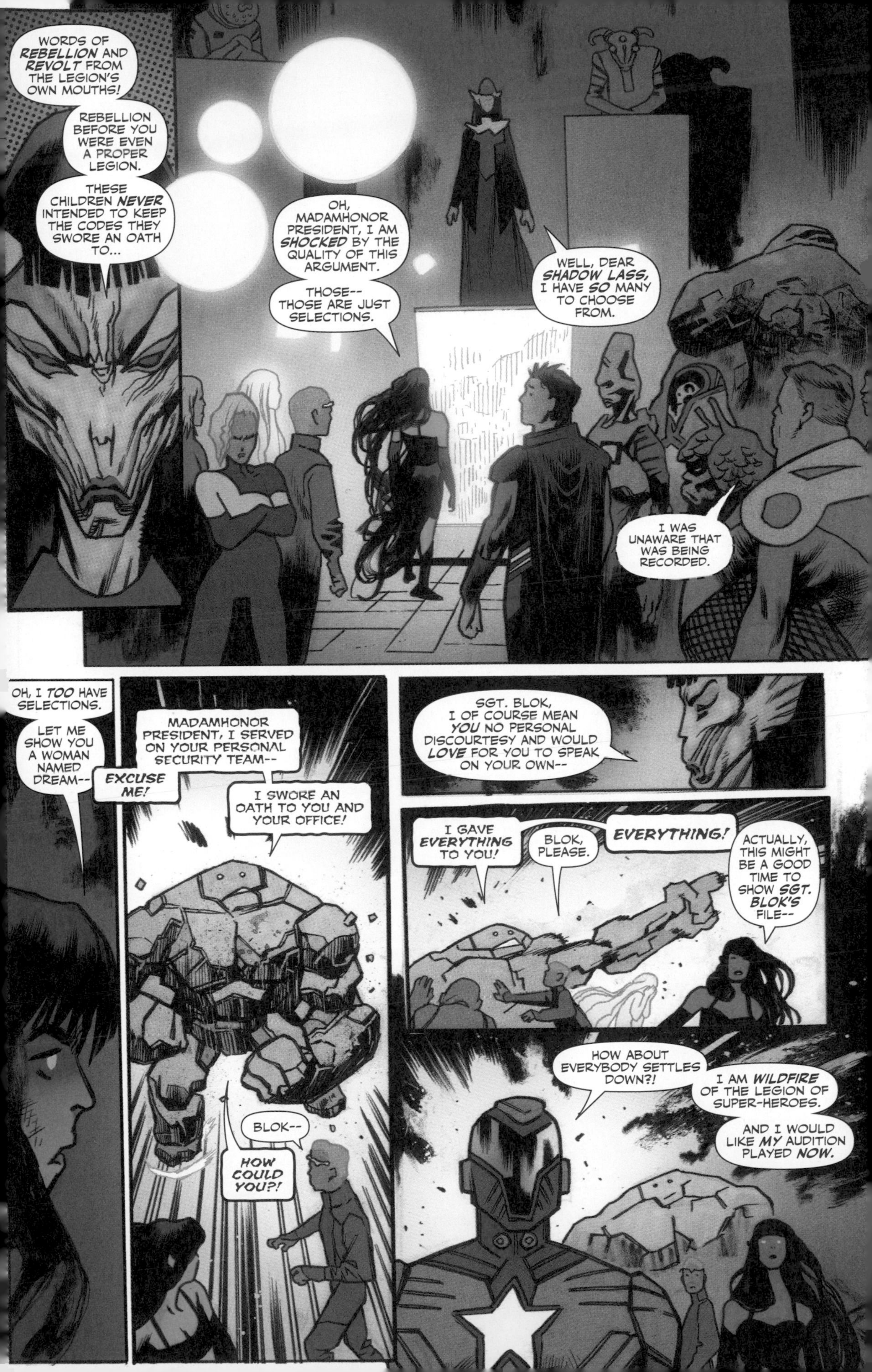
WORDS OF REBELLION AND REVOLT FROM THE LEGION'S OWN MOUTHS!
REBELLION BEFORE YOU WERE EVEN A PROPER LEGION.
THESE CHILDREN NEVER INTENDED TO KEEP THE CODES THEY SWORE AN OATH TO...
OH, MADAMHONOR PRESIDENT, I AM SHOCKED BY THE QUALITY OF THIS ARGUMENT.
THOSE-- THOSE ARE JUST SELECTIONS.
WELL, DEAR SHADOW LASS, I HAVE SO MANY TO CHOOSE FROM.
I WAS UNAWARE THAT WAS BEING RECORDED.
OH, I TOO HAVE SELECTIONS.
LET ME SHOW YOU A WOMAN NAMED DREAM--
EXCUSE ME!
MADAMHONOR PRESIDENT, I SERVED ON YOUR PERSONAL SECURITY TEAM--
I SWORE AN OATH TO YOU AND YOUR OFFICE!
BLOK--
HOW COULD YOU?!
SGT. BLOK, I OF COURSE MEAN YOU NO PERSONAL DISCOURTESY AND WOULD LOVE FOR YOU TO SPEAK ON YOUR OWN--
I GAVE EVERYTHING TO YOU!
BLOK, PLEASE.
EVERYTHING!
ACTUALLY, THIS MIGHT BE A GOOD TIME TO SHOW SGT. BLOK'S FILE--
HOW ABOUT EVERYBODY SETTLES DOWN?!
I AM WILDFIRE OF THE LEGION OF SUPER-HEROES.
AND I WOULD LIKE MY AUDITION PLAYED NOW.

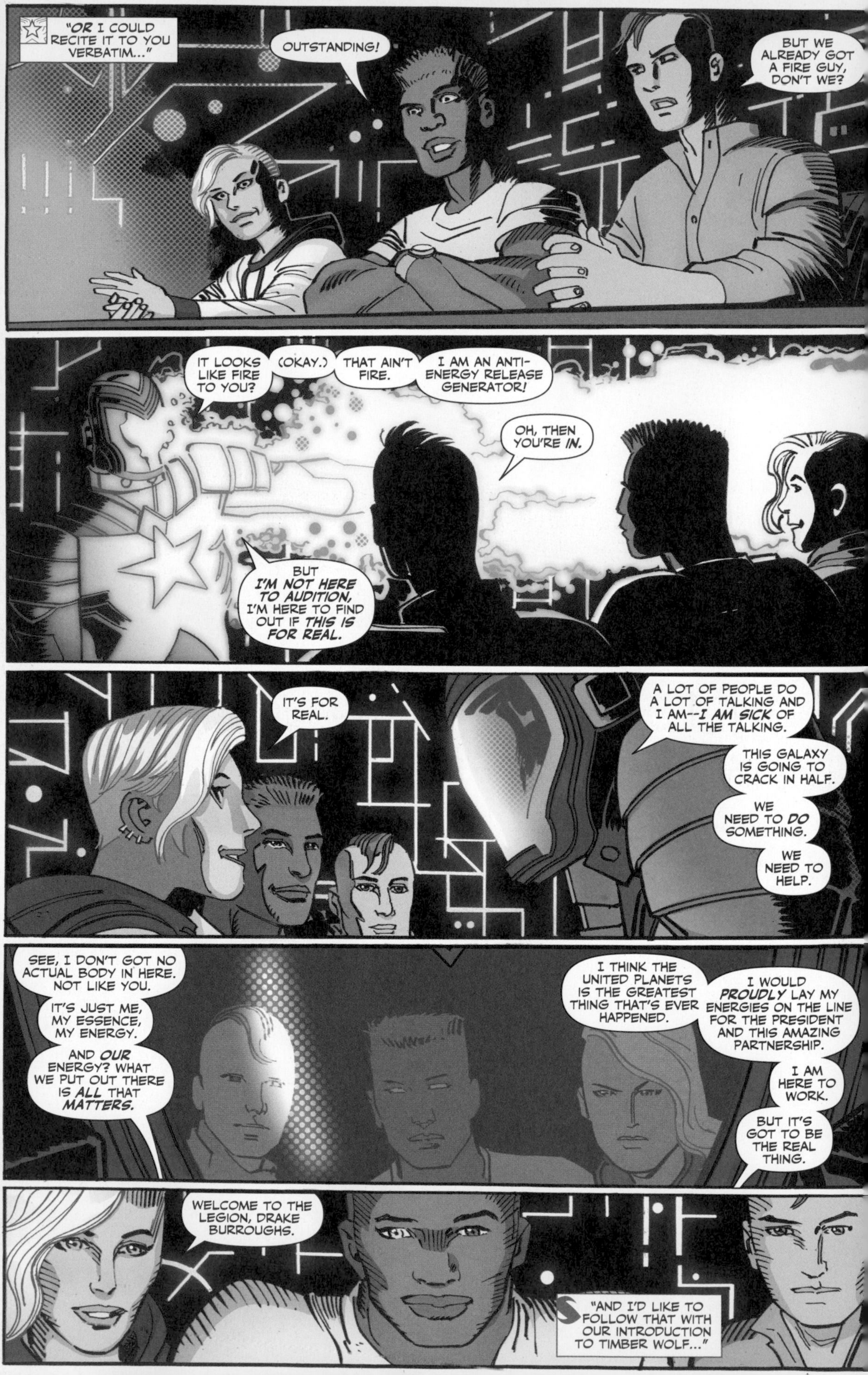
"OR I COULD RECITE IT TO YOU VERBATIM..."
OUTSTANDING!
BUT WE ALREADY GOT A FIRE GUY, DON'T WE?
IT LOOKS LIKE FIRE TO YOU?
(OKAY.)
THAT AIN'T FIRE.
I AM AN ANTI-ENERGY RELEASE GENERATOR!
OH, THEN YOU'RE IN.
BUT I'M NOT HERE TO AUDITION, I'M HERE TO FIND OUT IF THIS IS FOR REAL.
IT'S FOR REAL.
A LOT OF PEOPLE DO A LOT OF TALKING AND I AM--I AM SICK OF ALL THE TALKING.
THIS GALAXY IS GOING TO CRACK IN HALF.
WE NEED TO DO SOMETHING.
WE NEED TO HELP.
SEE, I DON'T GOT NO ACTUAL BODY IN HERE. NOT LIKE YOU.
IT'S JUST ME, MY ESSENCE, MY ENERGY.
AND OUR ENERGY? WHAT WE PUT OUT THERE IS ALL THAT MATTERS.
I THINK THE UNITED PLANETS IS THE GREATEST THING THAT'S EVER HAPPENED.
I WOULD PROUDLY LAY MY ENERGIES ON THE LINE FOR THE PRESIDENT AND THIS AMAZING PARTNERSHIP.
I AM HERE TO WORK.
BUT IT'S GOT TO BE THE REAL THING.
WELCOME TO THE LEGION, DRAKE BURROUGHS.
"AND I'D LIKE TO FOLLOW THAT WITH OUR INTRODUCTION TO TIMBER WOLF..."

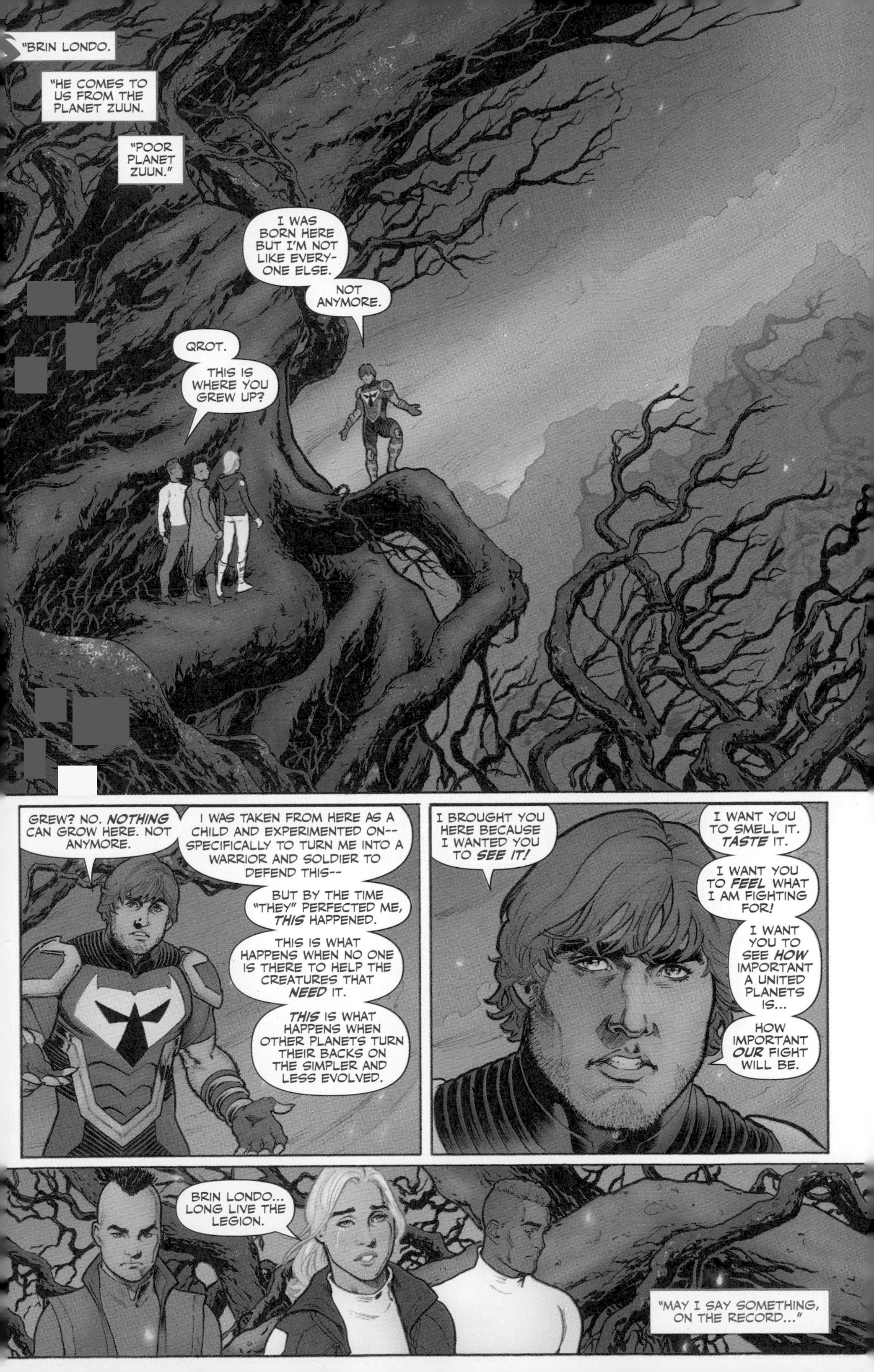
"BRIN LONDO.
"HE COMES TO US FROM THE PLANET ZUUN.
"POOR PLANET ZUUN."
I WAS BORN HERE BUT I'M NOT LIKE EVERY-ONE ELSE.
NOT ANYMORE.
QROT.
THIS IS WHERE YOU GREW UP?
GREW? NO. *NOTHING* CAN GROW HERE. NOT ANYMORE.
I WAS TAKEN FROM HERE AS A CHILD AND EXPERIMENTED ON-- SPECIFICALLY TO TURN ME INTO A WARRIOR AND SOLDIER TO DEFEND THIS--
BUT BY THE TIME "THEY" PERFECTED ME, *THIS* HAPPENED.
THIS IS WHAT HAPPENS WHEN NO ONE IS THERE TO HELP THE CREATURES THAT *NEED* IT.
THIS IS WHAT HAPPENS WHEN OTHER PLANETS TURN THEIR BACKS ON THE SIMPLER AND LESS EVOLVED.
I BROUGHT YOU HERE BECAUSE I WANTED YOU TO *SEE IT!*
I WANT YOU TO SMELL IT. *TASTE* IT.
I WANT YOU TO *FEEL* WHAT I AM FIGHTING FOR!
I WANT YOU TO SEE *HOW* IMPORTANT A UNITED PLANETS IS...
HOW IMPORTANT *OUR* FIGHT WILL BE.
BRIN LONDO... LONG LIVE THE LEGION.
"MAY I SAY SOMETHING, ON THE RECORD..."

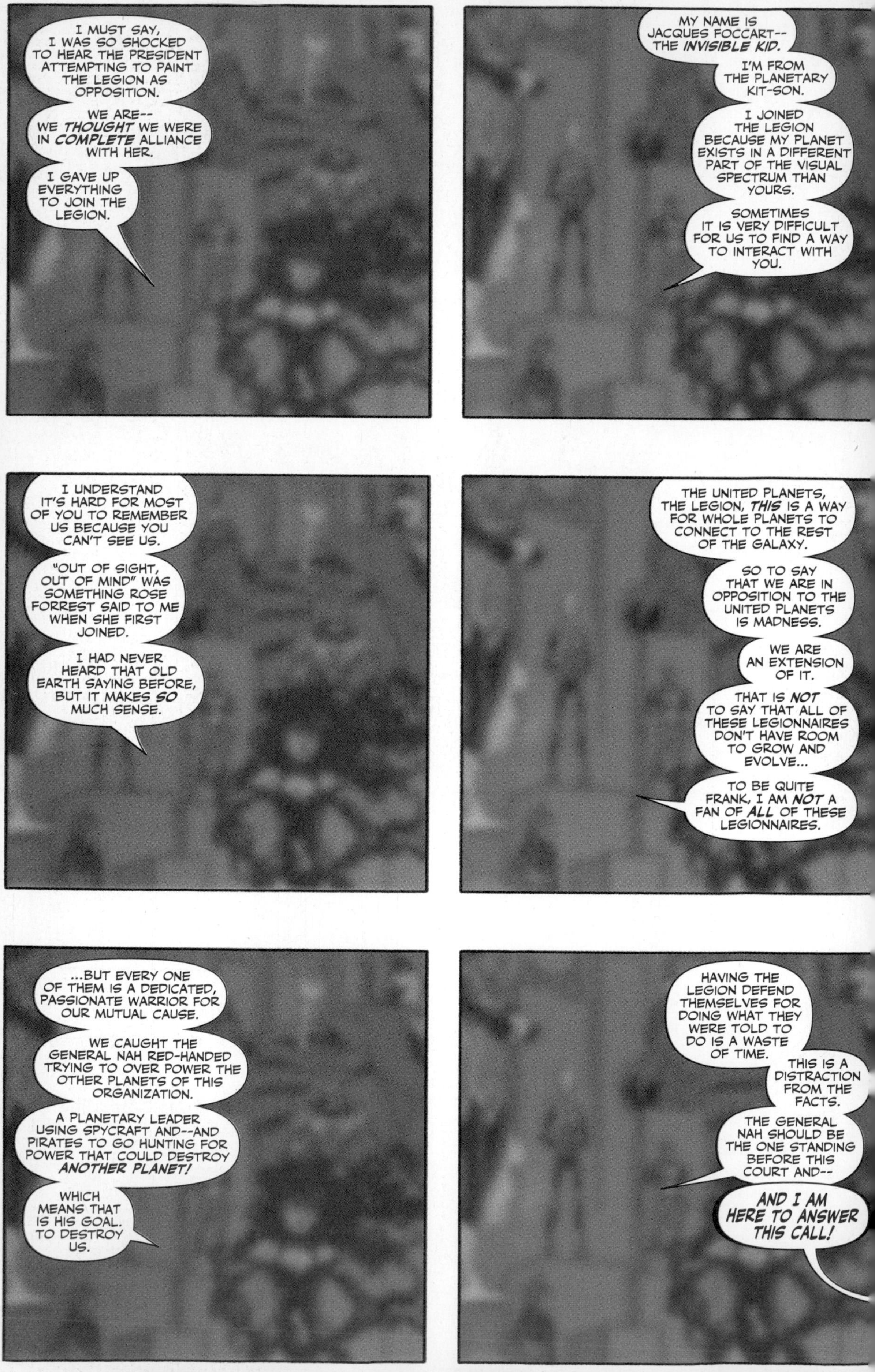
I MUST SAY, I WAS SO SHOCKED TO HEAR THE PRESIDENT ATTEMPTING TO PAINT THE LEGION AS OPPOSITION.
WE ARE-- WE THOUGHT WE WERE IN COMPLETE ALLIANCE WITH HER.
I GAVE UP EVERYTHING TO JOIN THE LEGION.
MY NAME IS JACQUES FOCCART-- THE INVISIBLE KID.
I'M FROM THE PLANETARY KIT-SON.
I JOINED THE LEGION BECAUSE MY PLANET EXISTS IN A DIFFERENT PART OF THE VISUAL SPECTRUM THAN YOURS.
SOMETIMES IT IS VERY DIFFICULT FOR US TO FIND A WAY TO INTERACT WITH YOU.
I UNDERSTAND IT'S HARD FOR MOST OF YOU TO REMEMBER US BECAUSE YOU CAN'T SEE US.
"OUT OF SIGHT, OUT OF MIND" WAS SOMETHING ROSE FORREST SAID TO ME WHEN SHE FIRST JOINED.
I HAD NEVER HEARD THAT OLD EARTH SAYING BEFORE, BUT IT MAKES SO MUCH SENSE.
THE UNITED PLANETS, THE LEGION, THIS IS A WAY FOR WHOLE PLANETS TO CONNECT TO THE REST OF THE GALAXY.
SO TO SAY THAT WE ARE IN OPPOSITION TO THE UNITED PLANETS IS MADNESS.
WE ARE AN EXTENSION OF IT.
THAT IS NOT TO SAY THAT ALL OF THESE LEGIONNAIRES DON'T HAVE ROOM TO GROW AND EVOLVE...
TO BE QUITE FRANK, I AM NOT A FAN OF ALL OF THESE LEGIONNAIRES.
...BUT EVERY ONE OF THEM IS A DEDICATED, PASSIONATE WARRIOR FOR OUR MUTUAL CAUSE.
WE CAUGHT THE GENERAL NAH RED-HANDED TRYING TO OVER POWER THE OTHER PLANETS OF THIS ORGANIZATION.
A PLANETARY LEADER USING SPYCRAFT AND--AND PIRATES TO GO HUNTING FOR POWER THAT COULD DESTROY ANOTHER PLANET!
WHICH MEANS THAT IS HIS GOAL. TO DESTROY US.
HAVING THE LEGION DEFEND THEMSELVES FOR DOING WHAT THEY WERE TOLD TO DO IS A WASTE OF TIME.
THIS IS A DISTRACTION FROM THE FACTS.
THE GENERAL NAH SHOULD BE THE ONE STANDING BEFORE THIS COURT AND--
AND I AM HERE TO ANSWER THIS CALL!

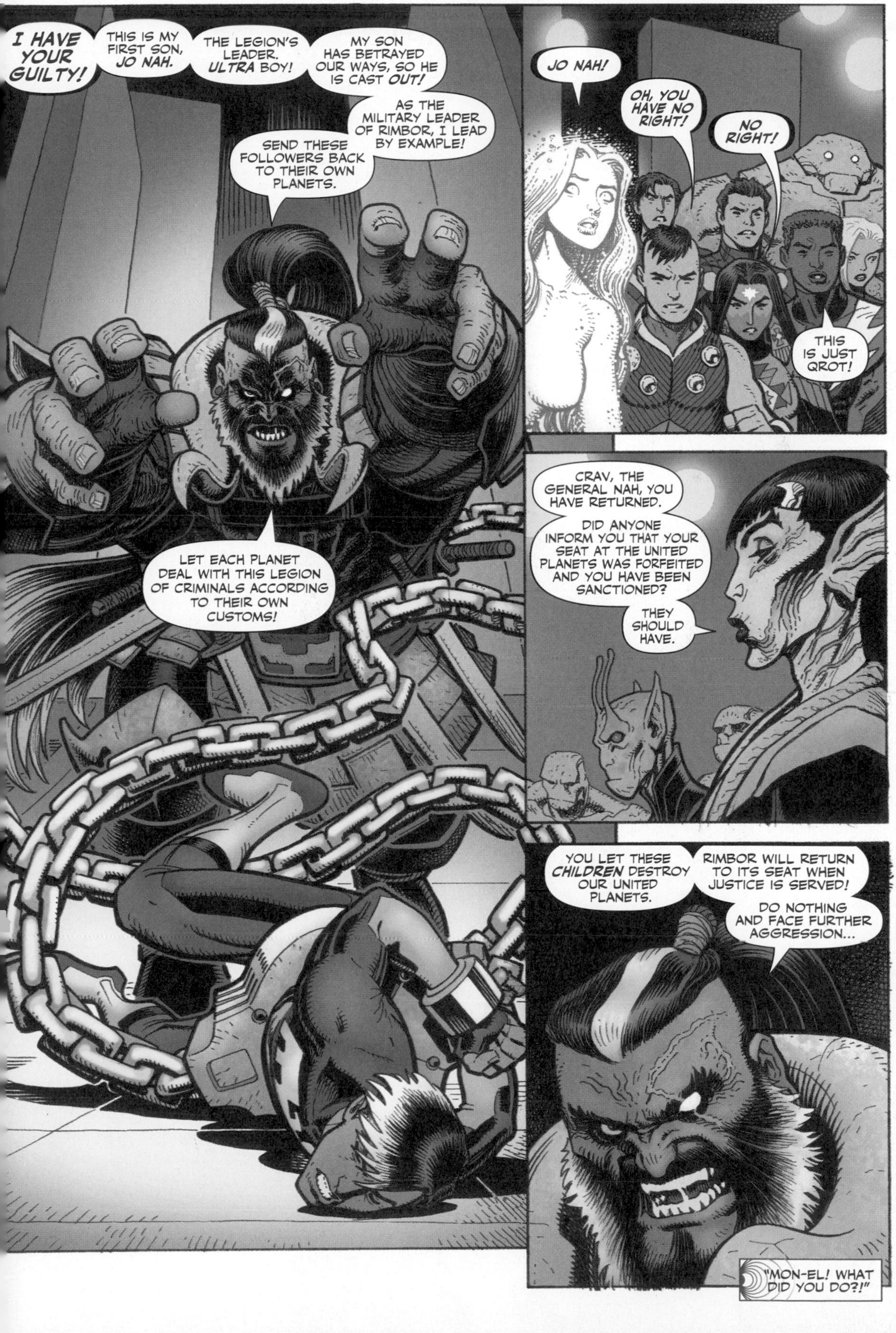
I HAVE YOUR GUILTY!
THIS IS MY FIRST SON, JO NAH.
THE LEGION'S LEADER. ULTRA BOY!
MY SON HAS BETRAYED OUR WAYS, SO HE IS CAST OUT!
AS THE MILITARY LEADER OF RIMBOR, I LEAD BY EXAMPLE!
SEND THESE FOLLOWERS BACK TO THEIR OWN PLANETS.
LET EACH PLANET DEAL WITH THIS LEGION OF CRIMINALS ACCORDING TO THEIR OWN CUSTOMS!
JO NAH!
OH, YOU HAVE NO RIGHT!
NO RIGHT!
THIS IS JUST QROT!
CRAV, THE GENERAL NAH, YOU HAVE RETURNED.
DID ANYONE INFORM YOU THAT YOUR SEAT AT THE UNITED PLANETS WAS FORFEITED AND YOU HAVE BEEN SANCTIONED?
THEY SHOULD HAVE.
YOU LET THESE CHILDREN DESTROY OUR UNITED PLANETS.
RIMBOR WILL RETURN TO ITS SEAT WHEN JUSTICE IS SERVED!
DO NOTHING AND FACE FURTHER AGGRESSION...
"MON-EL! WHAT DID YOU DO?!"

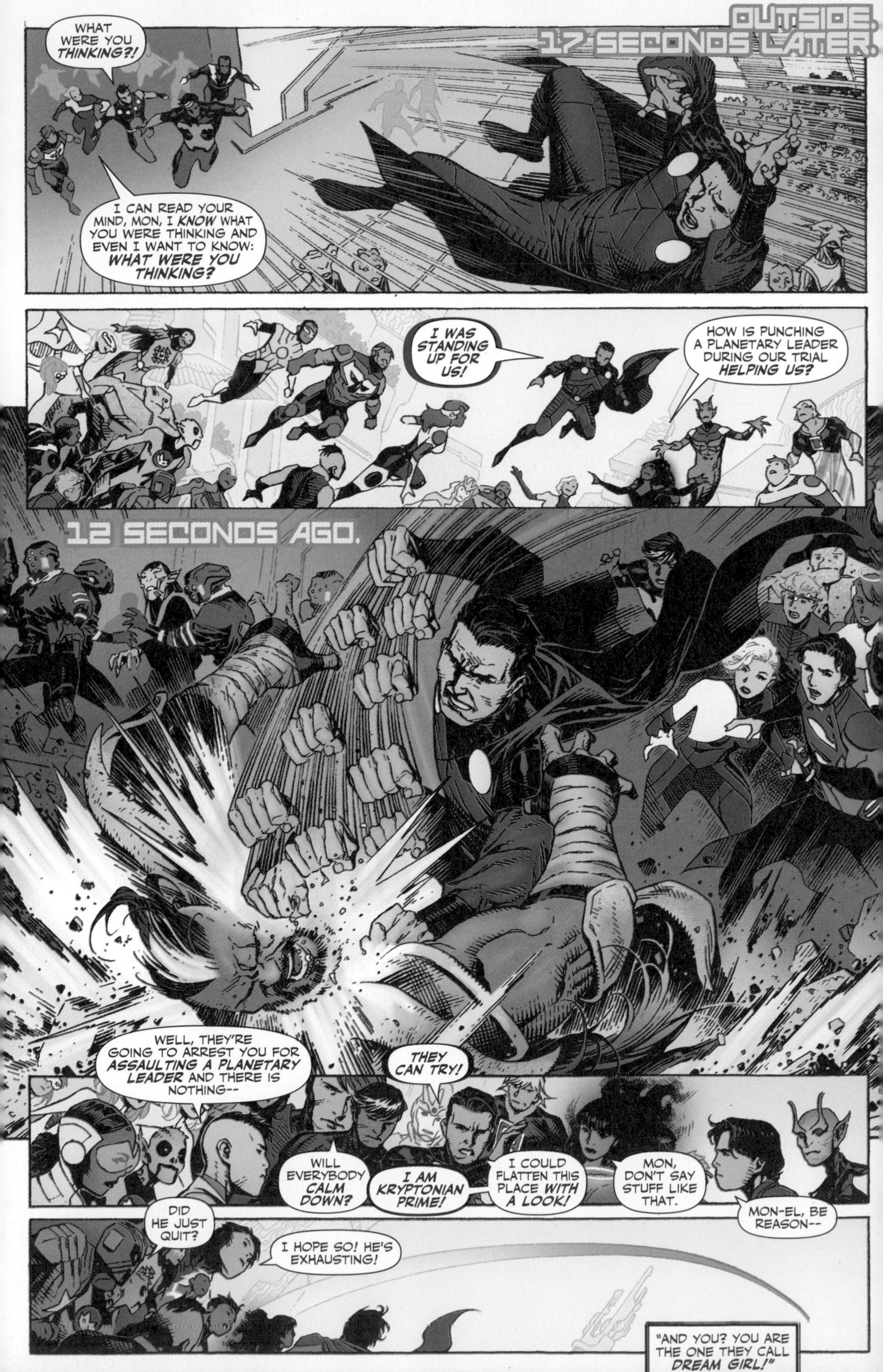
OUTSIDE. 17 SECONDS LATER.
WHAT WERE YOU *THINKING?!*
I CAN READ YOUR MIND, MON, I *KNOW* WHAT YOU WERE THINKING AND EVEN I WANT TO KNOW: *WHAT WERE YOU THINKING?*
I WAS STANDING UP FOR US!
HOW IS PUNCHING A PLANETARY LEADER DURING OUR TRIAL *HELPING US?*
12 SECONDS AGO.
WELL, THEY'RE GOING TO ARREST YOU FOR *ASSAULTING A PLANETARY LEADER* AND THERE IS NOTHING--
THEY CAN TRY!
WILL EVERYBODY *CALM DOWN?*
I AM KRYPTONIAN PRIME!
I COULD FLATTEN THIS PLACE *WITH A LOOK!*
MON, DON'T SAY STUFF LIKE THAT.
MON-EL, BE REASON--
DID HE JUST QUIT?
I HOPE SO! HE'S EXHAUSTING!
"AND YOU? YOU ARE THE ONE THEY CALL *DREAM GIRL!*"

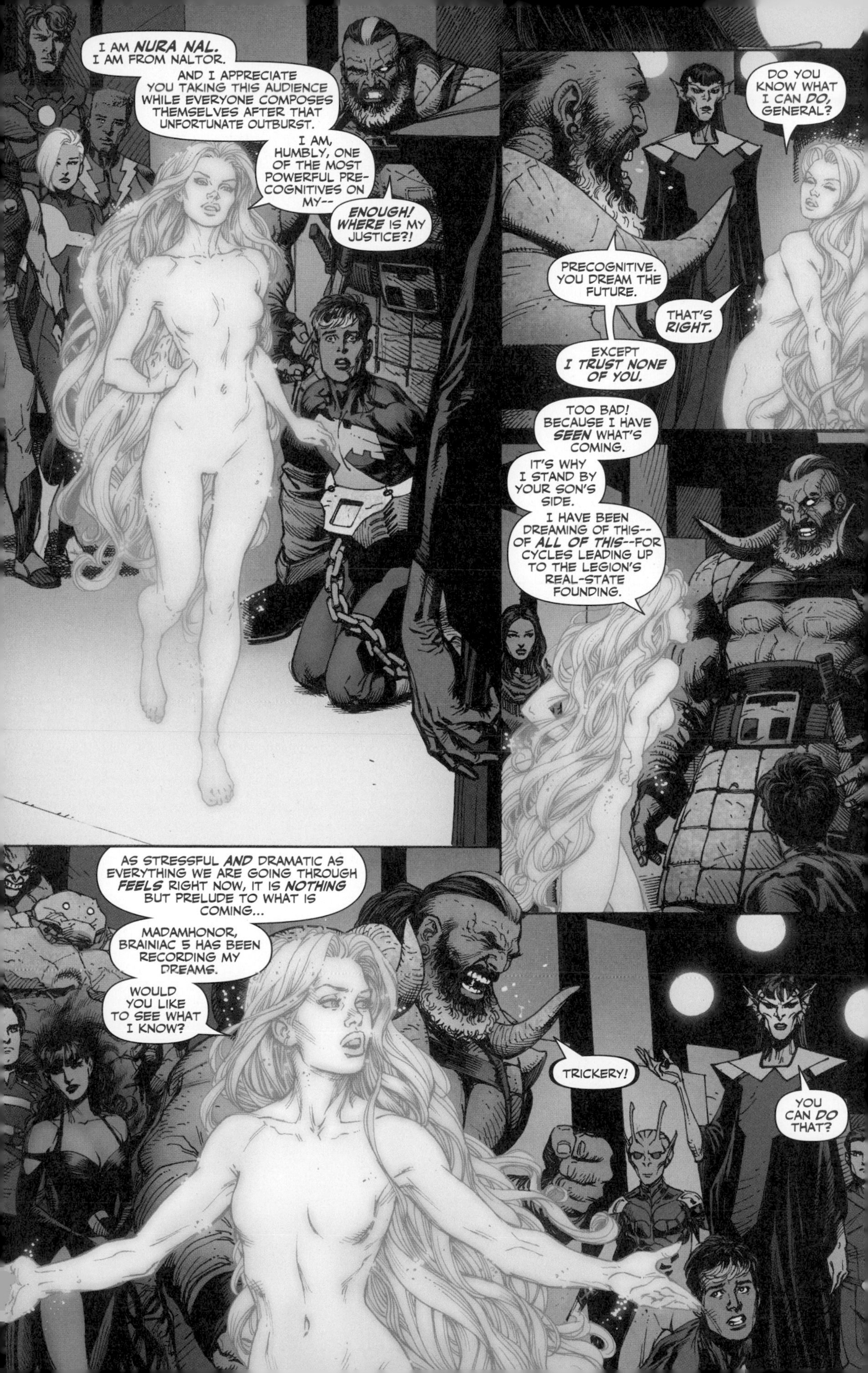
I AM NURA NAL. I AM FROM NALTOR.
AND I APPRECIATE YOU TAKING THIS AUDIENCE WHILE EVERYONE COMPOSES THEMSELVES AFTER THAT UNFORTUNATE OUTBURST.
I AM, HUMBLY, ONE OF THE MOST POWERFUL PRE-COGNITIVES ON MY--
ENOUGH! WHERE IS MY JUSTICE?!
DO YOU KNOW WHAT I CAN DO, GENERAL?
PRECOGNITIVE. YOU DREAM THE FUTURE.
THAT'S RIGHT.
EXCEPT I TRUST NONE OF YOU.
TOO BAD! BECAUSE I HAVE SEEN WHAT'S COMING.
IT'S WHY I STAND BY YOUR SON'S SIDE.
I HAVE BEEN DREAMING OF THIS-- OF ALL OF THIS--FOR CYCLES LEADING UP TO THE LEGION'S REAL-STATE FOUNDING.
AS STRESSFUL AND DRAMATIC AS EVERYTHING WE ARE GOING THROUGH FEELS RIGHT NOW, IT IS NOTHING BUT PRELUDE TO WHAT IS COMING...
MADAMHONOR, BRAINIAC 5 HAS BEEN RECORDING MY DREAMS.
WOULD YOU LIKE TO SEE WHAT I KNOW?
TRICKERY!
YOU CAN DO THAT?

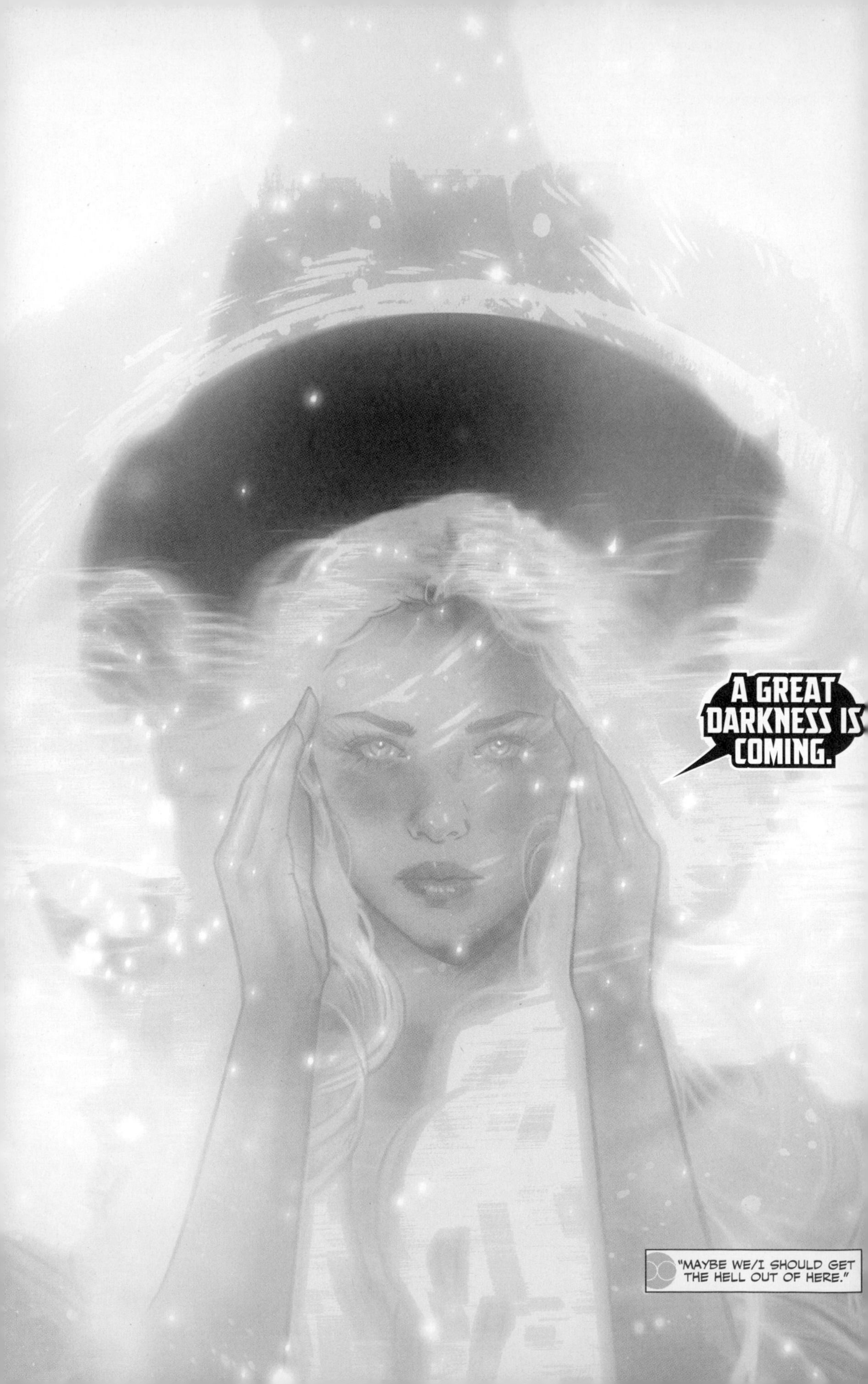
A GREAT DARKNESS IS COMING.
"MAYBE WE/I SHOULD GET THE HELL OUT OF HERE."

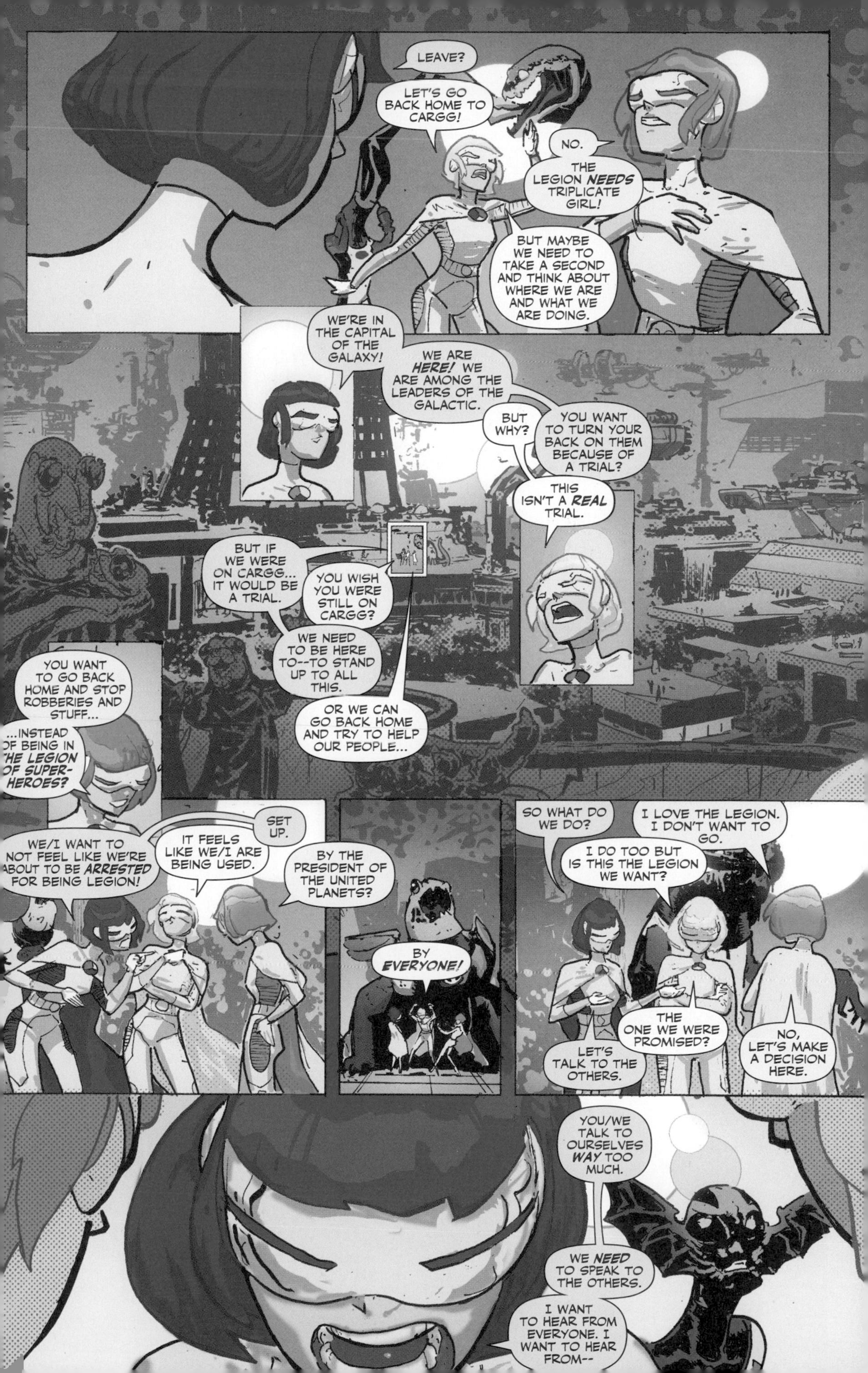
LEAVE?
LET'S GO BACK HOME TO CARGG!
NO.
THE LEGION *NEEDS* TRIPLICATE GIRL!
BUT MAYBE WE NEED TO TAKE A SECOND AND THINK ABOUT WHERE WE ARE AND WHAT WE ARE DOING.
WE'RE IN THE CAPITAL OF THE GALAXY!
WE ARE *HERE!* WE ARE AMONG THE LEADERS OF THE GALACTIC.
BUT WHY?
YOU WANT TO TURN YOUR BACK ON THEM BECAUSE OF A TRIAL?
THIS ISN'T A *REAL* TRIAL.
BUT IF WE WERE ON CARGG... IT WOULD BE A TRIAL.
YOU WISH YOU WERE STILL ON CARGG?
WE NEED TO BE HERE TO--TO STAND UP TO ALL THIS.
OR WE CAN GO BACK HOME AND TRY TO HELP OUR PEOPLE...
YOU WANT TO GO BACK HOME AND STOP ROBBERIES AND STUFF...
...INSTEAD OF BEING IN *THE LEGION OF SUPER-HEROES?*
WE/I WANT TO NOT FEEL LIKE WE'RE ABOUT TO BE *ARRESTED* FOR BEING LEGION!
IT FEELS LIKE WE/I ARE BEING USED.
SET UP.
BY THE PRESIDENT OF THE UNITED PLANETS?
BY *EVERYONE!*
SO WHAT DO WE DO?
I LOVE THE LEGION. I DON'T WANT TO GO.
I DO TOO BUT IS THIS THE LEGION WE WANT?
THE ONE WE WERE PROMISED?
LET'S TALK TO THE OTHERS.
NO, LET'S MAKE A DECISION HERE.
YOU/WE TALK TO OURSELVES *WAY* TOO MUCH.
WE *NEED* TO SPEAK TO THE OTHERS.
I WANT TO HEAR FROM EVERYONE. I WANT TO HEAR FROM--

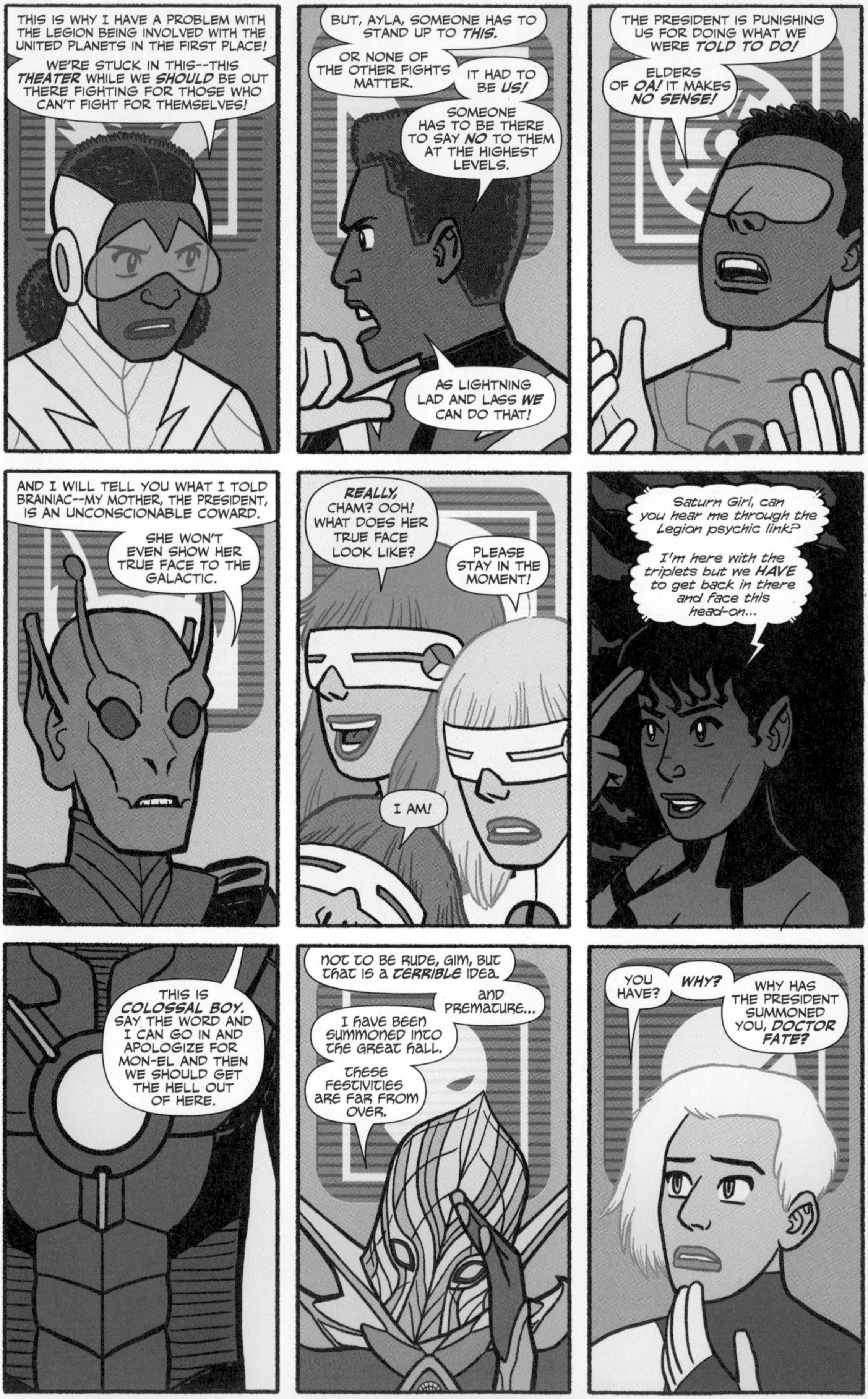
THIS IS WHY I HAVE A PROBLEM WITH THE LEGION BEING INVOLVED WITH THE UNITED PLANETS IN THE FIRST PLACE!
WE'RE STUCK IN THIS--THIS THEATER WHILE WE SHOULD BE OUT THERE FIGHTING FOR THOSE WHO CAN'T FIGHT FOR THEMSELVES!
BUT, AYLA, SOMEONE HAS TO STAND UP TO THIS.
OR NONE OF THE OTHER FIGHTS MATTER.
IT HAD TO BE US!
SOMEONE HAS TO BE THERE TO SAY NO TO THEM AT THE HIGHEST LEVELS.
AS LIGHTNING LAD AND LASS WE CAN DO THAT!
THE PRESIDENT IS PUNISHING US FOR DOING WHAT WE WERE TOLD TO DO!
ELDERS OF OA! IT MAKES NO SENSE!
AND I WILL TELL YOU WHAT I TOLD BRAINIAC--MY MOTHER, THE PRESIDENT, IS AN UNCONSCIONABLE COWARD.
SHE WON'T EVEN SHOW HER TRUE FACE TO THE GALACTIC.
REALLY, CHAM? OOH! WHAT DOES HER TRUE FACE LOOK LIKE?
PLEASE STAY IN THE MOMENT!
I AM!
Saturn Girl, can you hear me through the Legion psychic link?
I'm here with the triplets but we HAVE to get back in there and face this head-on...
THIS IS COLOSSAL BOY. SAY THE WORD AND I CAN GO IN AND APOLOGIZE FOR MON-EL AND THEN WE SHOULD GET THE HELL OUT OF HERE.
NOT TO BE RUDE, GIM, BUT THAT IS A TERRIBLE IDEA.
AND PREMATURE...
I HAVE BEEN SUMMONED INTO THE GREAT HALL.
THESE FESTIVITIES ARE FAR FROM OVER.
YOU HAVE?
WHY?
WHY HAS THE PRESIDENT SUMMONED YOU, DOCTOR FATE?

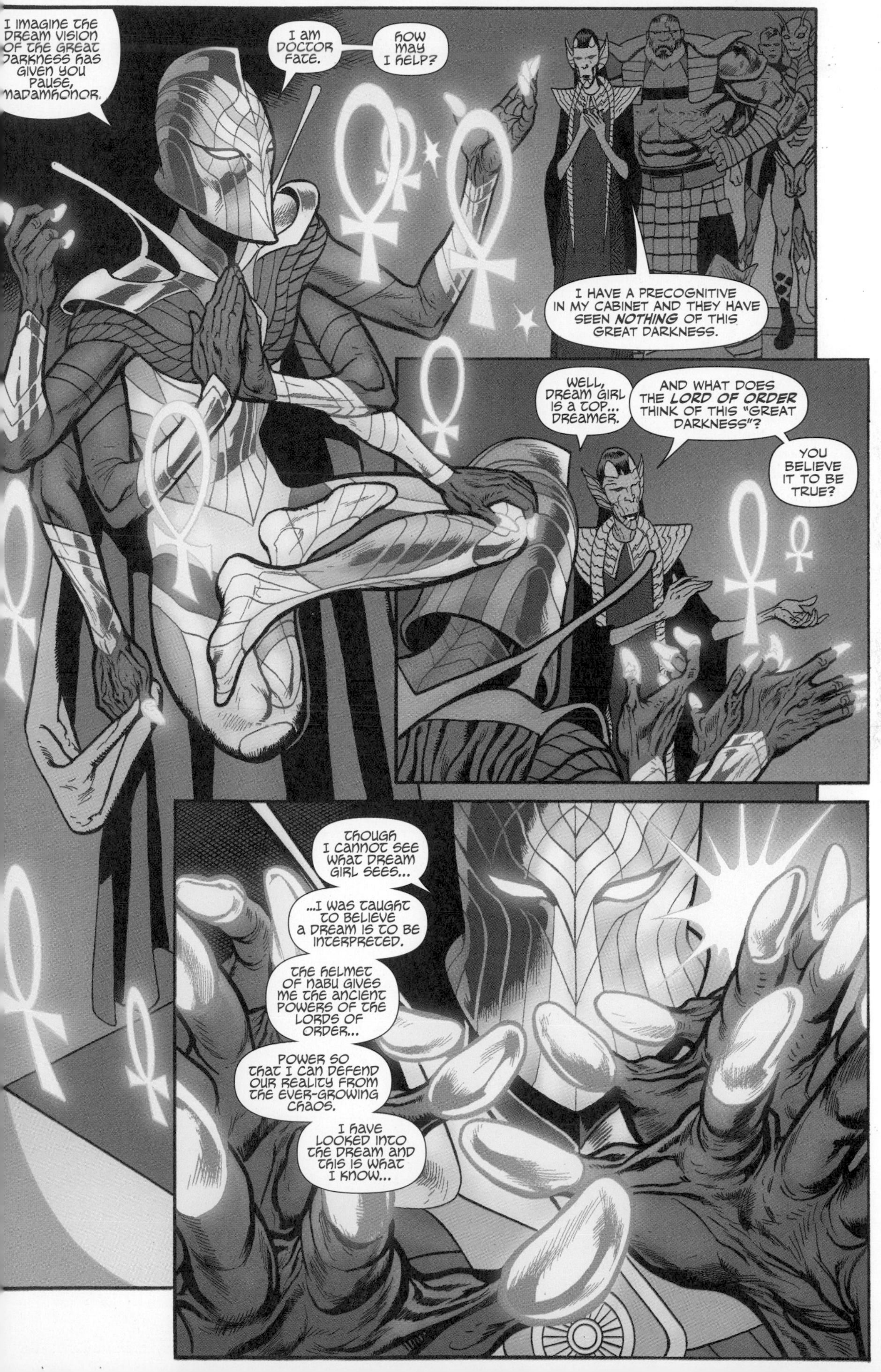
I IMAGINE THE DREAM VISION OF THE GREAT DARKNESS HAS GIVEN YOU PAUSE, MADAMHONOR.
I AM DOCTOR FATE.
HOW MAY I HELP?
I HAVE A PRECOGNITIVE IN MY CABINET AND THEY HAVE SEEN NOTHING OF THIS GREAT DARKNESS.
WELL, DREAM GIRL IS A TOP... DREAMER.
AND WHAT DOES THE LORD OF ORDER THINK OF THIS "GREAT DARKNESS"?
YOU BELIEVE IT TO BE TRUE?
THOUGH I CANNOT SEE WHAT DREAM GIRL SEES...
...I WAS TAUGHT TO BELIEVE A DREAM IS TO BE INTERPRETED.
THE HELMET OF NABU GIVES ME THE ANCIENT POWERS OF THE LORDS OF ORDER...
POWER SO THAT I CAN DEFEND OUR REALITY FROM THE EVER-GROWING CHAOS.
I HAVE LOOKED INTO THE DREAM AND THIS IS WHAT I KNOW...

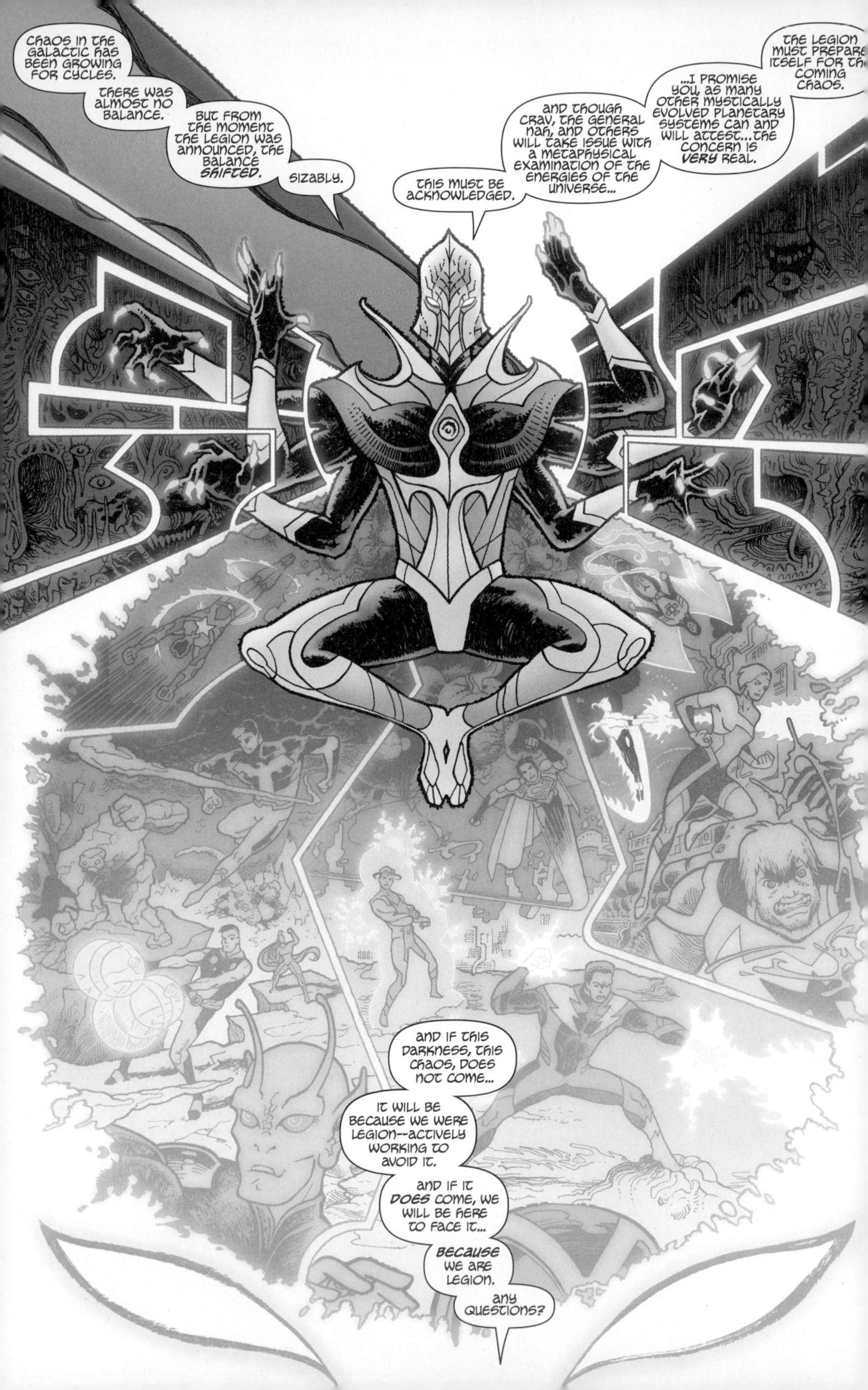
CHAOS IN THE GALACTIC HAS BEEN GROWING FOR CYCLES.
THERE WAS ALMOST NO BALANCE.
BUT FROM THE MOMENT THE LEGION WAS ANNOUNCED, THE BALANCE *SHIFTED*.
SIZABLY.
THIS MUST BE ACKNOWLEDGED.
AND THOUGH CRAV, THE GENERAL NAH, AND OTHERS WILL TAKE ISSUE WITH A METAPHYSICAL EXAMINATION OF THE ENERGIES OF THE UNIVERSE...
...I PROMISE YOU, AS MANY OTHER MYSTICALLY EVOLVED PLANETARY SYSTEMS CAN AND WILL ATTEST...THE CONCERN IS **VERY** REAL.
THE LEGION MUST PREPARE ITSELF FOR THE COMING CHAOS.
AND IF THIS DARKNESS, THIS CHAOS, DOES NOT COME...
IT WILL BE BECAUSE WE WERE LEGION--ACTIVELY WORKING TO AVOID IT.
AND IF IT **DOES** COME, WE WILL BE HERE TO FACE IT...
BECAUSE WE ARE LEGION.
ANY QUESTIONS?

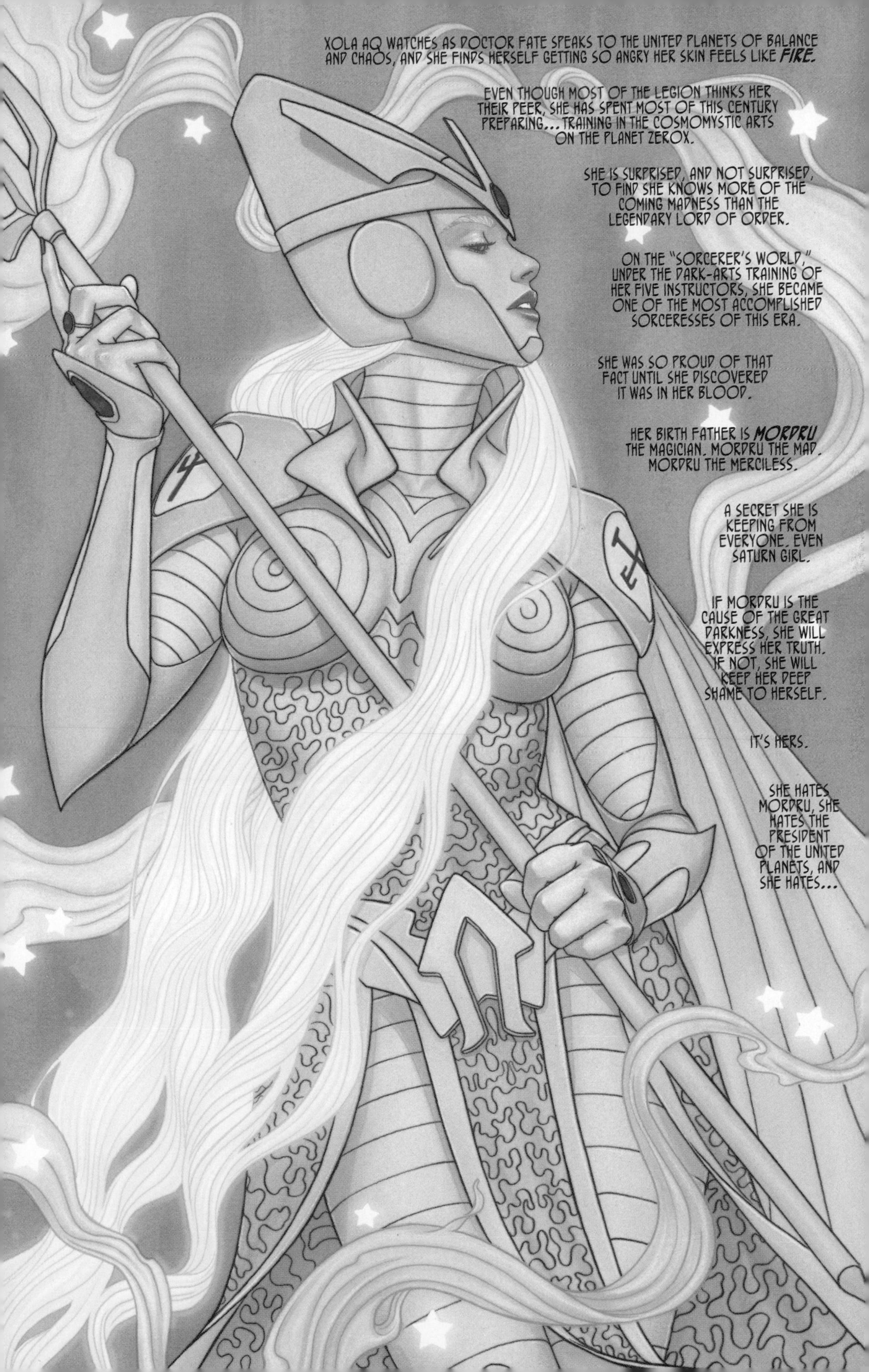
XOLA AQ WATCHES AS DOCTOR FATE SPEAKS TO THE UNITED PLANETS OF BALANCE AND CHAOS, AND SHE FINDS HERSELF GETTING SO ANGRY HER SKIN FEELS LIKE *FIRE.*
EVEN THOUGH MOST OF THE LEGION THINKS HER THEIR PEER, SHE HAS SPENT MOST OF THIS CENTURY PREPARING... TRAINING IN THE COSMOMYSTIC ARTS ON THE PLANET ZEROX.
SHE IS SURPRISED, AND NOT SURPRISED, TO FIND SHE KNOWS MORE OF THE COMING MADNESS THAN THE LEGENDARY LORD OF ORDER.
ON THE "SORCERER'S WORLD," UNDER THE DARK-ARTS TRAINING OF HER FIVE INSTRUCTORS, SHE BECAME ONE OF THE MOST ACCOMPLISHED SORCERESSES OF THIS ERA.
SHE WAS SO PROUD OF THAT FACT UNTIL SHE DISCOVERED IT WAS IN HER BLOOD.
HER BIRTH FATHER IS *MORDRU* THE MAGICIAN. MORDRU THE MAD. MORDRU THE MERCILESS.
A SECRET SHE IS KEEPING FROM EVERYONE. EVEN SATURN GIRL.
IF MORDRU IS THE CAUSE OF THE GREAT DARKNESS, SHE WILL EXPRESS HER TRUTH. IF NOT, SHE WILL KEEP HER DEEP SHAME TO HERSELF.
IT'S HERS.
SHE HATES MORDRU, SHE HATES THE PRESIDENT OF THE UNITED PLANETS, AND SHE HATES...

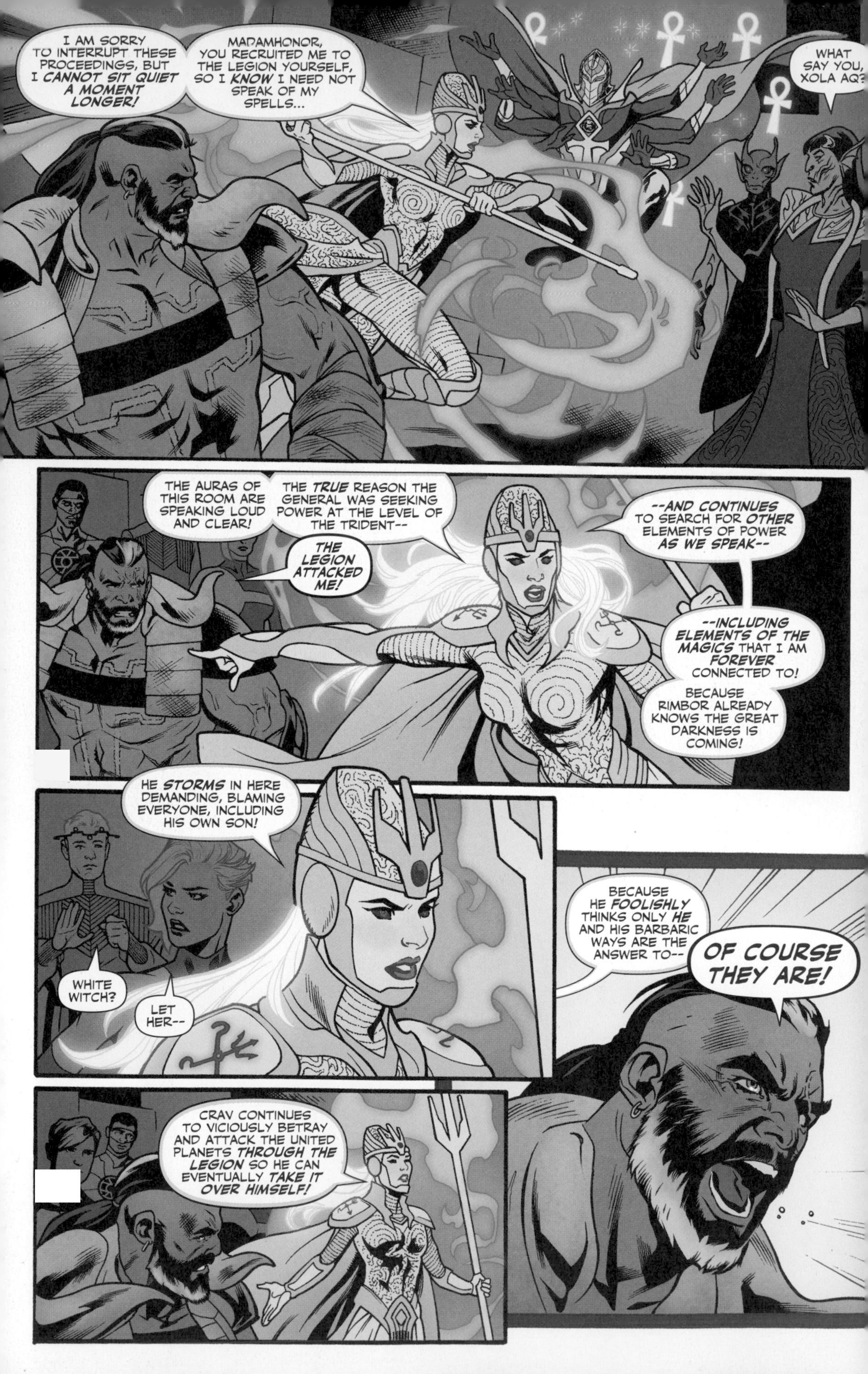
I AM SORRY TO INTERRUPT THESE PROCEEDINGS, BUT I CANNOT SIT QUIET A MOMENT LONGER!
MADAMHONOR, YOU RECRUITED ME TO THE LEGION YOURSELF, SO I KNOW I NEED NOT SPEAK OF MY SPELLS...
WHAT SAY YOU, XOLA AQ?
THE AURAS OF THIS ROOM ARE SPEAKING LOUD AND CLEAR!
THE TRUE REASON THE GENERAL WAS SEEKING POWER AT THE LEVEL OF THE TRIDENT--
THE LEGION ATTACKED ME!
--AND CONTINUES TO SEARCH FOR OTHER ELEMENTS OF POWER AS WE SPEAK--
--INCLUDING ELEMENTS OF THE MAGICS THAT I AM FOREVER CONNECTED TO!
BECAUSE RIMBOR ALREADY KNOWS THE GREAT DARKNESS IS COMING!
HE STORMS IN HERE DEMANDING, BLAMING EVERYONE, INCLUDING HIS OWN SON!
WHITE WITCH?
LET HER--
CRAV CONTINUES TO VICIOUSLY BETRAY AND ATTACK THE UNITED PLANETS THROUGH THE LEGION SO HE CAN EVENTUALLY TAKE IT OVER HIMSELF!
BECAUSE HE FOOLISHLY THINKS ONLY HE AND HIS BARBARIC WAYS ARE THE ANSWER TO--
OF COURSE THEY ARE!

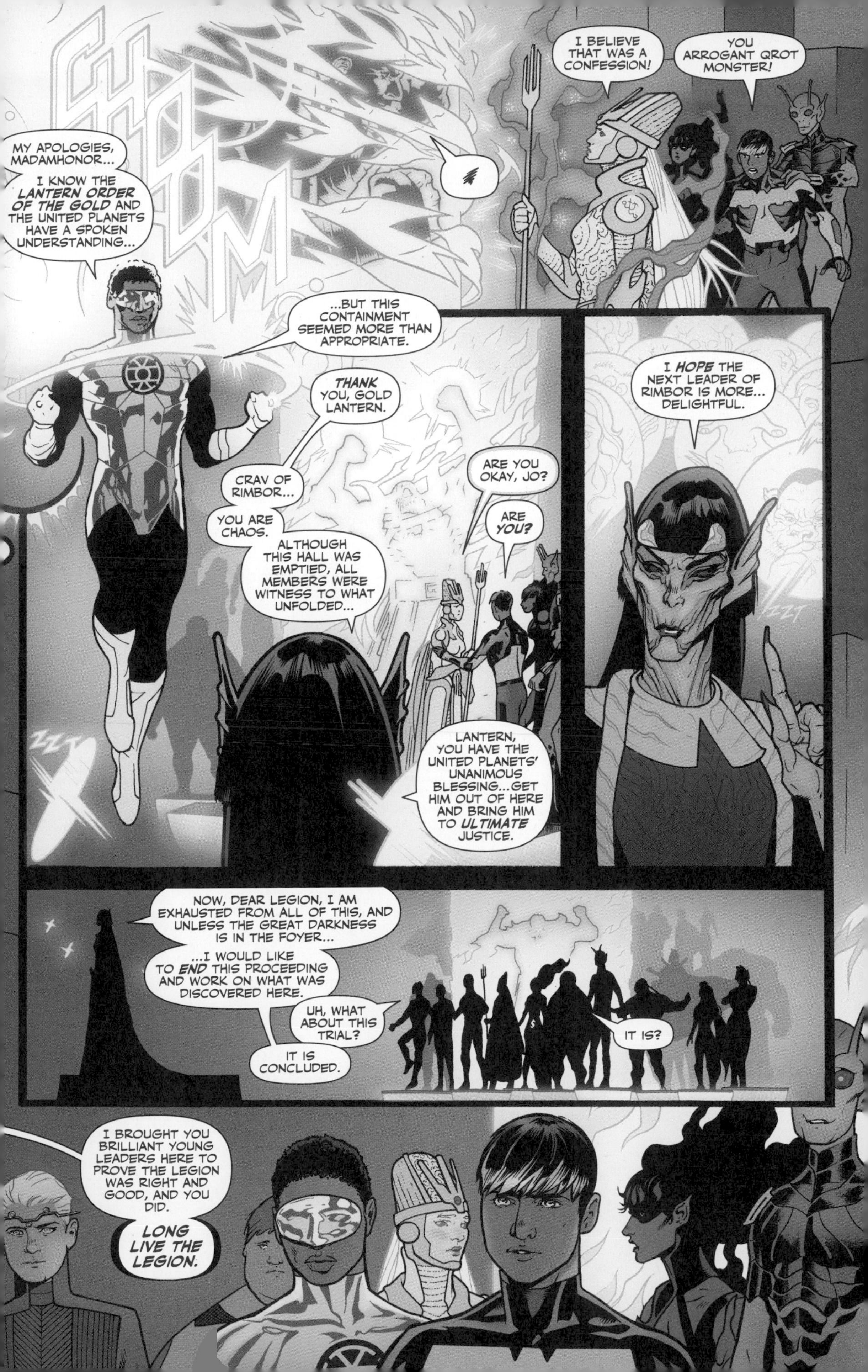
CHZZOOM
MY APOLOGIES, MADAMHONOR...
I KNOW THE LANTERN ORDER OF THE GOLD AND THE UNITED PLANETS HAVE A SPOKEN UNDERSTANDING...
I BELIEVE THAT WAS A CONFESSION!
YOU ARROGANT QROT MONSTER!
...BUT THIS CONTAINMENT SEEMED MORE THAN APPROPRIATE.
THANK YOU, GOLD LANTERN.
CRAV OF RIMBOR...
YOU ARE CHAOS.
ALTHOUGH THIS HALL WAS EMPTIED, ALL MEMBERS WERE WITNESS TO WHAT UNFOLDED...
ARE YOU OKAY, JO?
ARE YOU?
ZZZT
LANTERN, YOU HAVE THE UNITED PLANETS' UNANIMOUS BLESSING...GET HIM OUT OF HERE AND BRING HIM TO ULTIMATE JUSTICE.
I HOPE THE NEXT LEADER OF RIMBOR IS MORE... DELIGHTFUL.
ZZZT
NOW, DEAR LEGION, I AM EXHAUSTED FROM ALL OF THIS, AND UNLESS THE GREAT DARKNESS IS IN THE FOYER...
...I WOULD LIKE TO END THIS PROCEEDING AND WORK ON WHAT WAS DISCOVERED HERE.
UH, WHAT ABOUT THIS TRIAL?
IT IS CONCLUDED.
IT IS?
I BROUGHT YOU BRILLIANT YOUNG LEADERS HERE TO PROVE THE LEGION WAS RIGHT AND GOOD, AND YOU DID.
LONG LIVE THE LEGION.

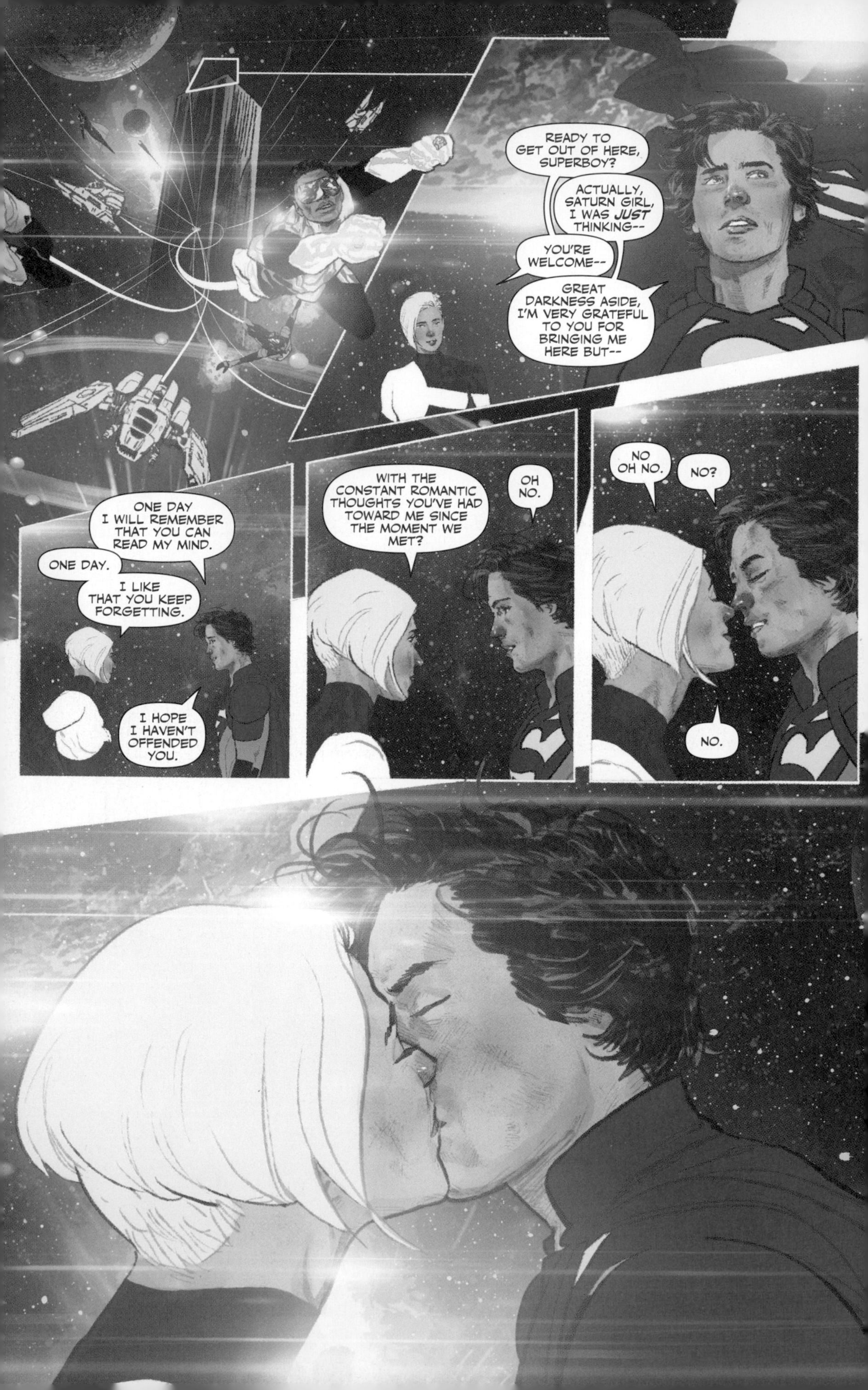
READY TO GET OUT OF HERE, SUPERBOY?
ACTUALLY, SATURN GIRL, I WAS JUST THINKING--
YOU'RE WELCOME--
GREAT DARKNESS ASIDE, I'M VERY GRATEFUL TO YOU FOR BRINGING ME HERE BUT--
ONE DAY I WILL REMEMBER THAT YOU CAN READ MY MIND.
ONE DAY.
I LIKE THAT YOU KEEP FORGETTING.
I HOPE I HAVEN'T OFFENDED YOU.
WITH THE CONSTANT ROMANTIC THOUGHTS YOU'VE HAD TOWARD ME SINCE THE MOMENT WE MET?
OH NO.
NO OH NO.
NO?
NO.

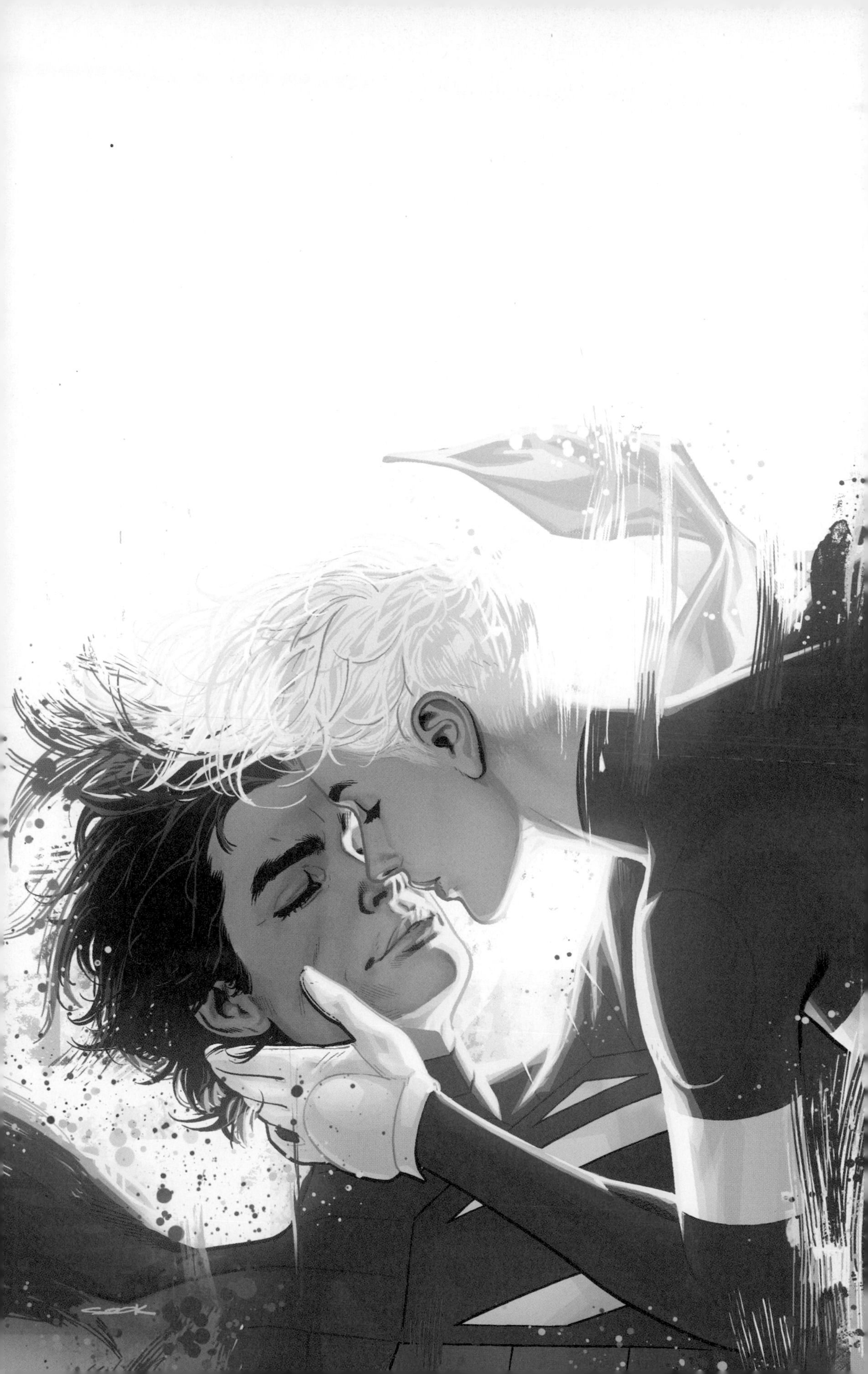

RYAN **SOOK**
Cover Artist

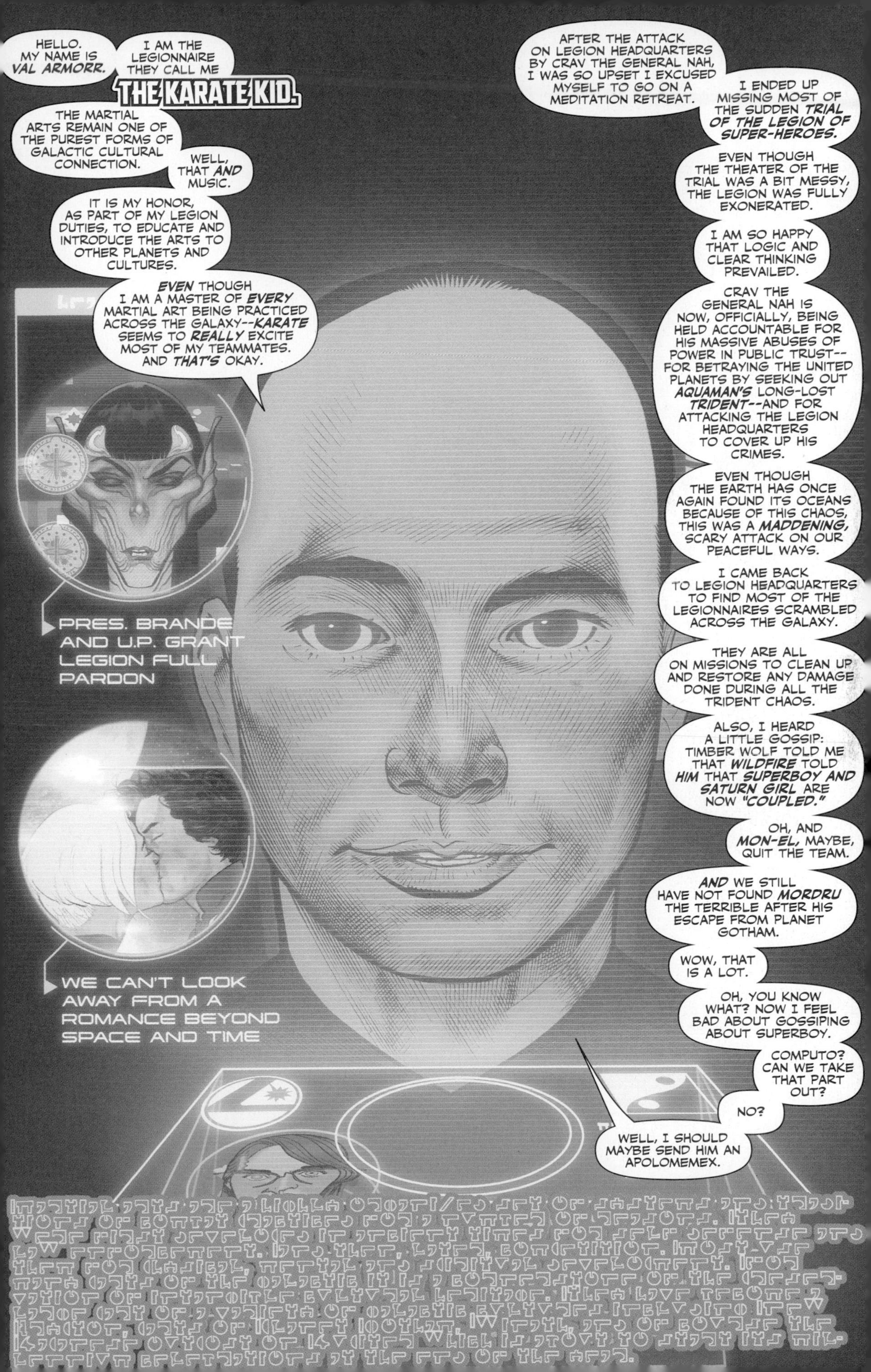

HELLO. MY NAME IS VAL ARMORR.
I AM THE LEGIONNAIRE THEY CALL ME
THE KARATE KID.
THE MARTIAL ARTS REMAIN ONE OF THE PUREST FORMS OF GALACTIC CULTURAL CONNECTION.
WELL, THAT AND MUSIC.
IT IS MY HONOR, AS PART OF MY LEGION DUTIES, TO EDUCATE AND INTRODUCE THE ARTS TO OTHER PLANETS AND CULTURES.
EVEN THOUGH I AM A MASTER OF EVERY MARTIAL ART BEING PRACTICED ACROSS THE GALAXY--KARATE SEEMS TO REALLY EXCITE MOST OF MY TEAMMATES. AND THAT'S OKAY.
PRES. BRANDE AND U.P. GRANT LEGION FULL PARDON
WE CAN'T LOOK AWAY FROM A ROMANCE BEYOND SPACE AND TIME
AFTER THE ATTACK ON LEGION HEADQUARTERS BY CRAV THE GENERAL NAH, I WAS SO UPSET I EXCUSED MYSELF TO GO ON A MEDITATION RETREAT.
I ENDED UP MISSING MOST OF THE SUDDEN TRIAL OF THE LEGION OF SUPER-HEROES.
EVEN THOUGH THE THEATER OF THE TRIAL WAS A BIT MESSY, THE LEGION WAS FULLY EXONERATED.
I AM SO HAPPY THAT LOGIC AND CLEAR THINKING PREVAILED.
CRAV THE GENERAL NAH IS NOW, OFFICIALLY, BEING HELD ACCOUNTABLE FOR HIS MASSIVE ABUSES OF POWER IN PUBLIC TRUST--FOR BETRAYING THE UNITED PLANETS BY SEEKING OUT AQUAMAN'S LONG-LOST TRIDENT--AND FOR ATTACKING THE LEGION HEADQUARTERS TO COVER UP HIS CRIMES.
EVEN THOUGH THE EARTH HAS ONCE AGAIN FOUND ITS OCEANS BECAUSE OF THIS CHAOS, THIS WAS A MADDENING, SCARY ATTACK ON OUR PEACEFUL WAYS.
I CAME BACK TO LEGION HEADQUARTERS TO FIND MOST OF THE LEGIONNAIRES SCRAMBLED ACROSS THE GALAXY.
THEY ARE ALL ON MISSIONS TO CLEAN UP AND RESTORE ANY DAMAGE DONE DURING ALL THE TRIDENT CHAOS.
ALSO, I HEARD A LITTLE GOSSIP: TIMBER WOLF TOLD ME THAT WILDFIRE TOLD HIM THAT SUPERBOY AND SATURN GIRL ARE NOW "COUPLED."
OH, AND MON-EL, MAYBE, QUIT THE TEAM.
AND WE STILL HAVE NOT FOUND MORDRU THE TERRIBLE AFTER HIS ESCAPE FROM PLANET GOTHAM.
WOW, THAT IS A LOT.
OH, YOU KNOW WHAT? NOW I FEEL BAD ABOUT GOSSIPING ABOUT SUPERBOY.
COMPUTO? CAN WE TAKE THAT PART OUT?
NO?
WELL, I SHOULD MAYBE SEND HIM AN APOLOMEMEX.

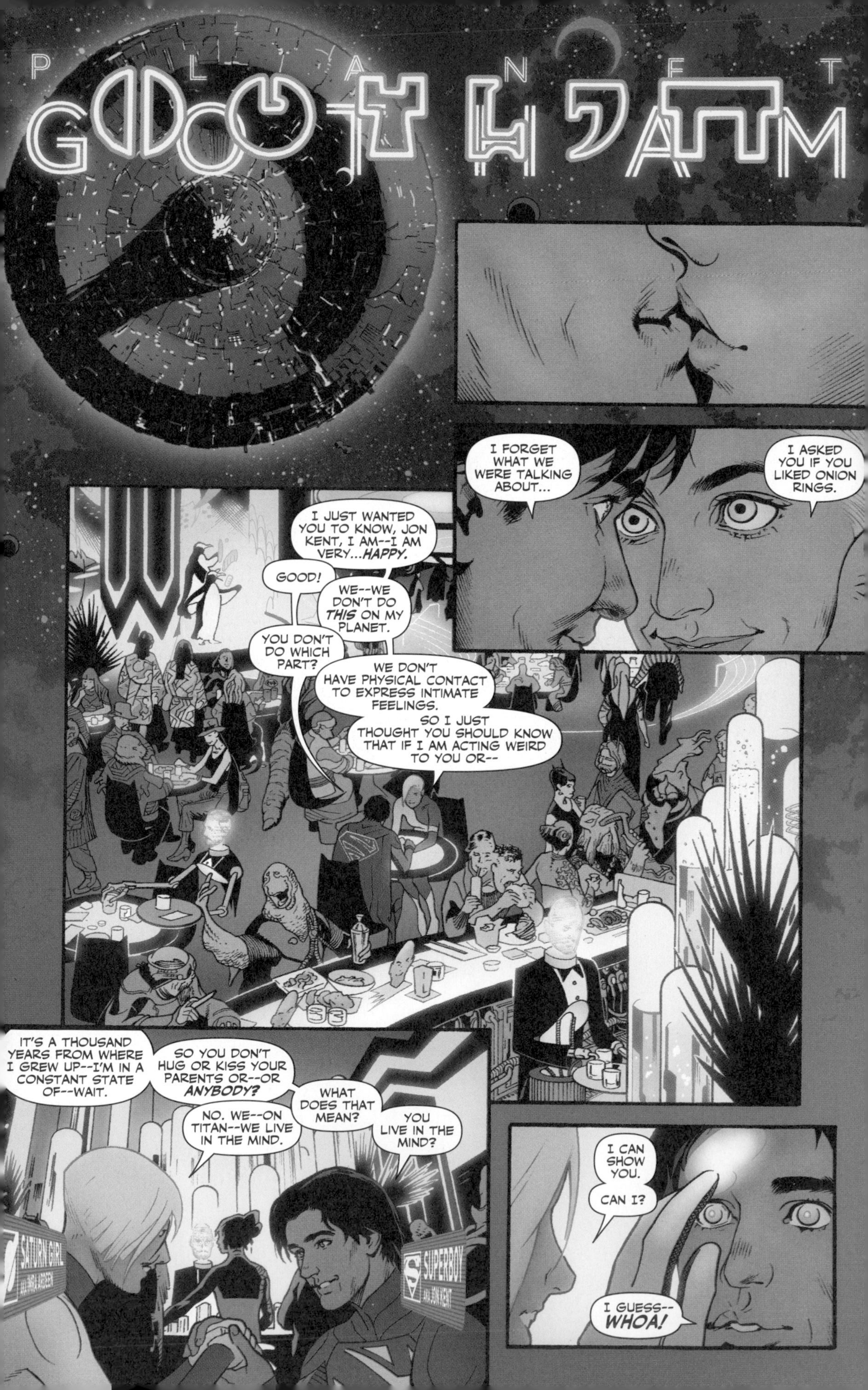
PLANET
I FORGET WHAT WE WERE TALKING ABOUT...
I ASKED YOU IF YOU LIKED ONION RINGS.
I JUST WANTED YOU TO KNOW, JON KENT, I AM--I AM VERY...*HAPPY.*
GOOD!
WE--WE DON'T DO *THIS* ON MY PLANET.
YOU DON'T DO WHICH PART?
WE DON'T HAVE PHYSICAL CONTACT TO EXPRESS INTIMATE FEELINGS.
SO I JUST THOUGHT YOU SHOULD KNOW THAT IF I AM ACTING WEIRD TO YOU OR--
IT'S A THOUSAND YEARS FROM WHERE I GREW UP--I'M IN A CONSTANT STATE OF--WAIT.
SO YOU DON'T HUG OR KISS YOUR PARENTS OR--OR *ANYBODY?*
NO. WE--ON TITAN--WE LIVE IN THE MIND.
WHAT DOES THAT MEAN?
YOU LIVE IN THE MIND?
SATURN GIRL
SUPERBOY
I CAN SHOW YOU.
CAN I?
I GUESS-- *WHOA!*

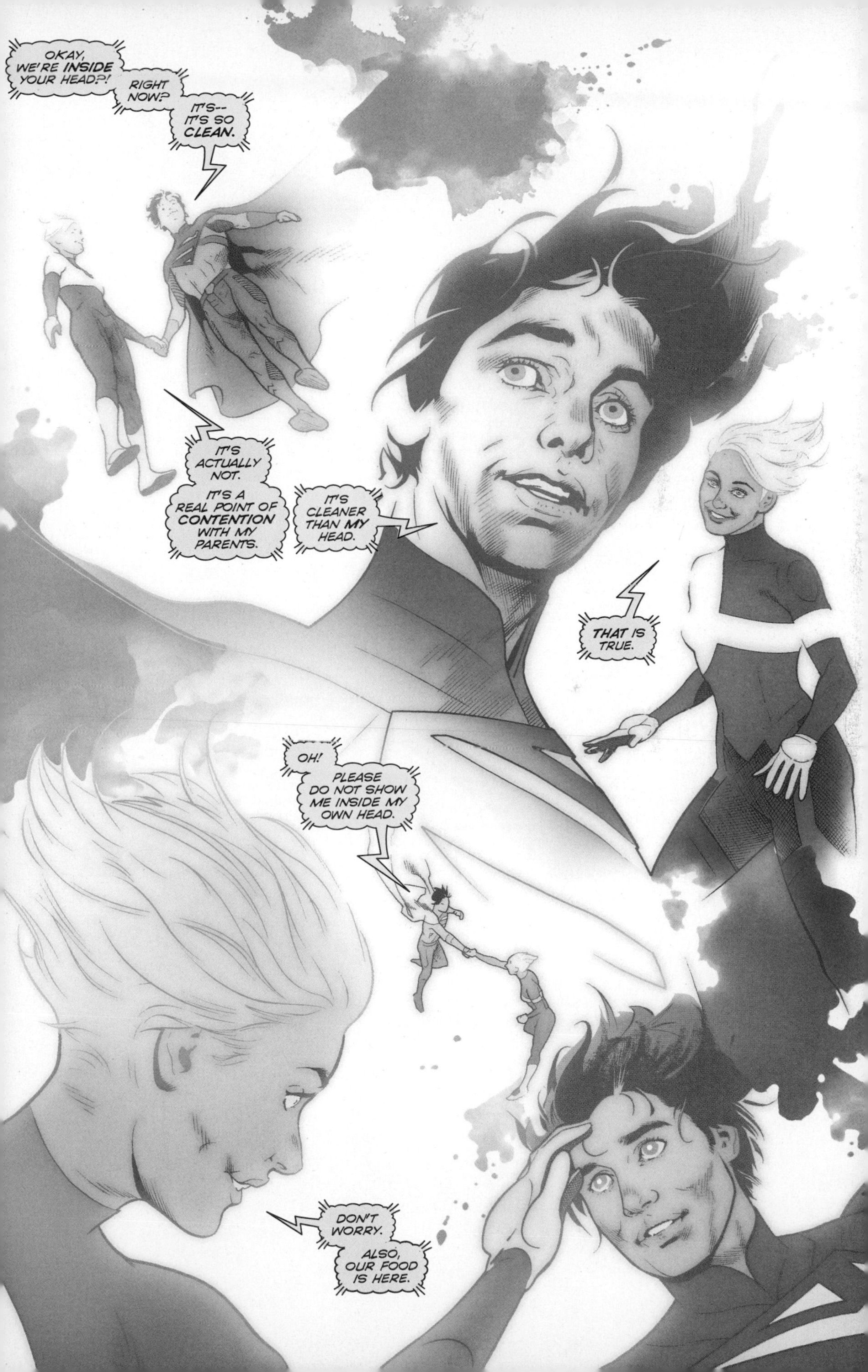

OKAY, WE'RE INSIDE YOUR HEAD?!
RIGHT NOW?
IT'S-- IT'S SO CLEAN.
IT'S ACTUALLY NOT.
IT'S A REAL POINT OF CONTENTION WITH MY PARENTS.
IT'S CLEANER THAN MY HEAD.
THAT IS TRUE.
OH!
PLEASE DO NOT SHOW ME INSIDE MY OWN HEAD.
DON'T WORRY.
ALSO, OUR FOOD IS HERE.

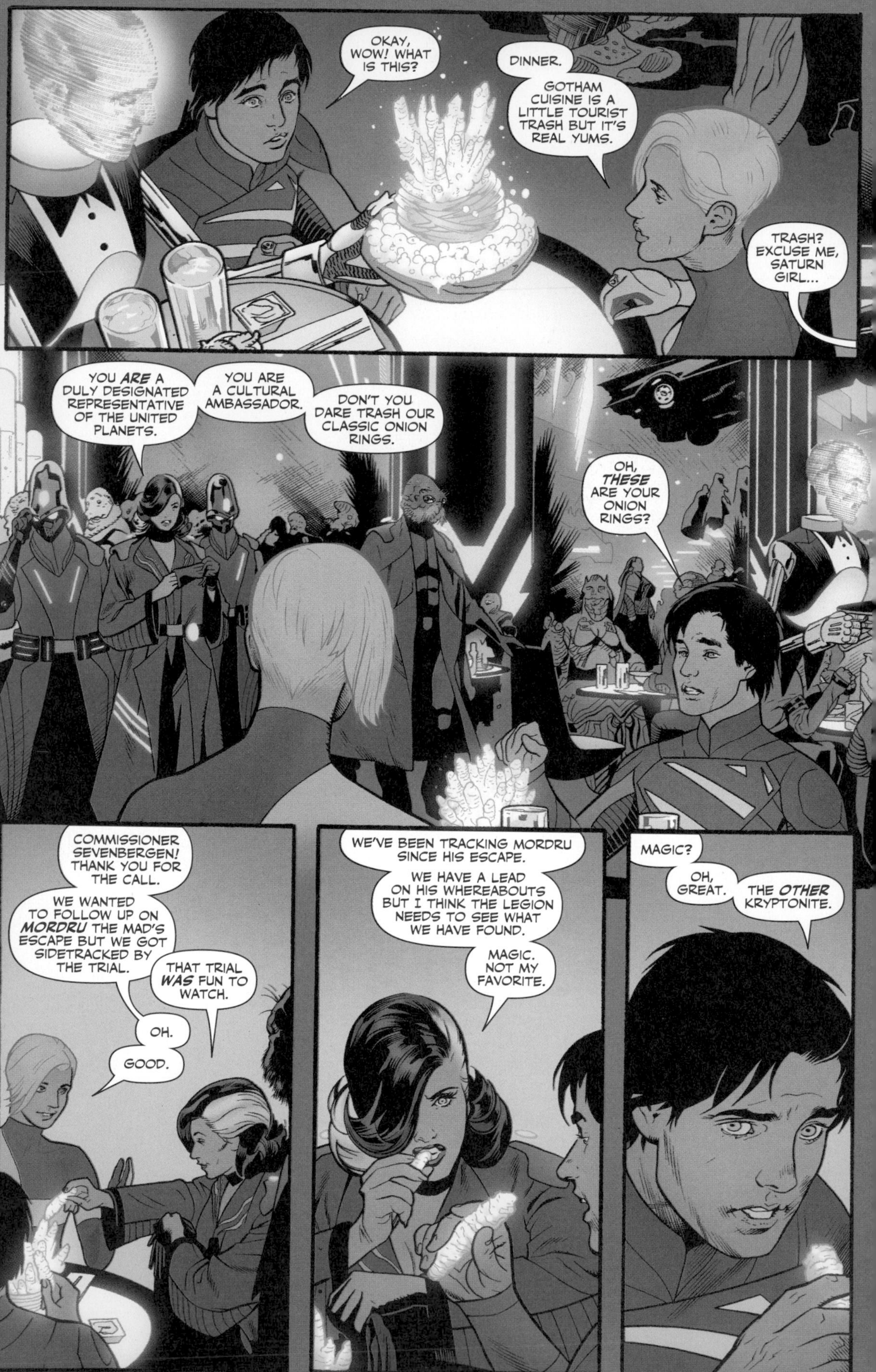
OKAY, WOW! WHAT IS THIS?
DINNER.
GOTHAM CUISINE IS A LITTLE TOURIST TRASH BUT IT'S REAL YUMS.
TRASH? EXCUSE ME, SATURN GIRL...
YOU *ARE* A DULY DESIGNATED REPRESENTATIVE OF THE UNITED PLANETS.
YOU ARE A CULTURAL AMBASSADOR.
DON'T YOU DARE TRASH OUR CLASSIC ONION RINGS.
OH, *THESE* ARE YOUR ONION RINGS?
COMMISSIONER SEVENBERGEN! THANK YOU FOR THE CALL.
WE WANTED TO FOLLOW UP ON *MORDRU* THE MAD'S ESCAPE BUT WE GOT SIDETRACKED BY THE TRIAL.
THAT TRIAL *WAS* FUN TO WATCH.
OH.
GOOD.
WE'VE BEEN TRACKING MORDRU SINCE HIS ESCAPE.
WE HAVE A LEAD ON HIS WHEREABOUTS BUT I THINK THE LEGION NEEDS TO SEE WHAT WE HAVE FOUND.
MAGIC. NOT MY FAVORITE.
MAGIC?
OH, GREAT.
THE *OTHER* KRYPTONITE.

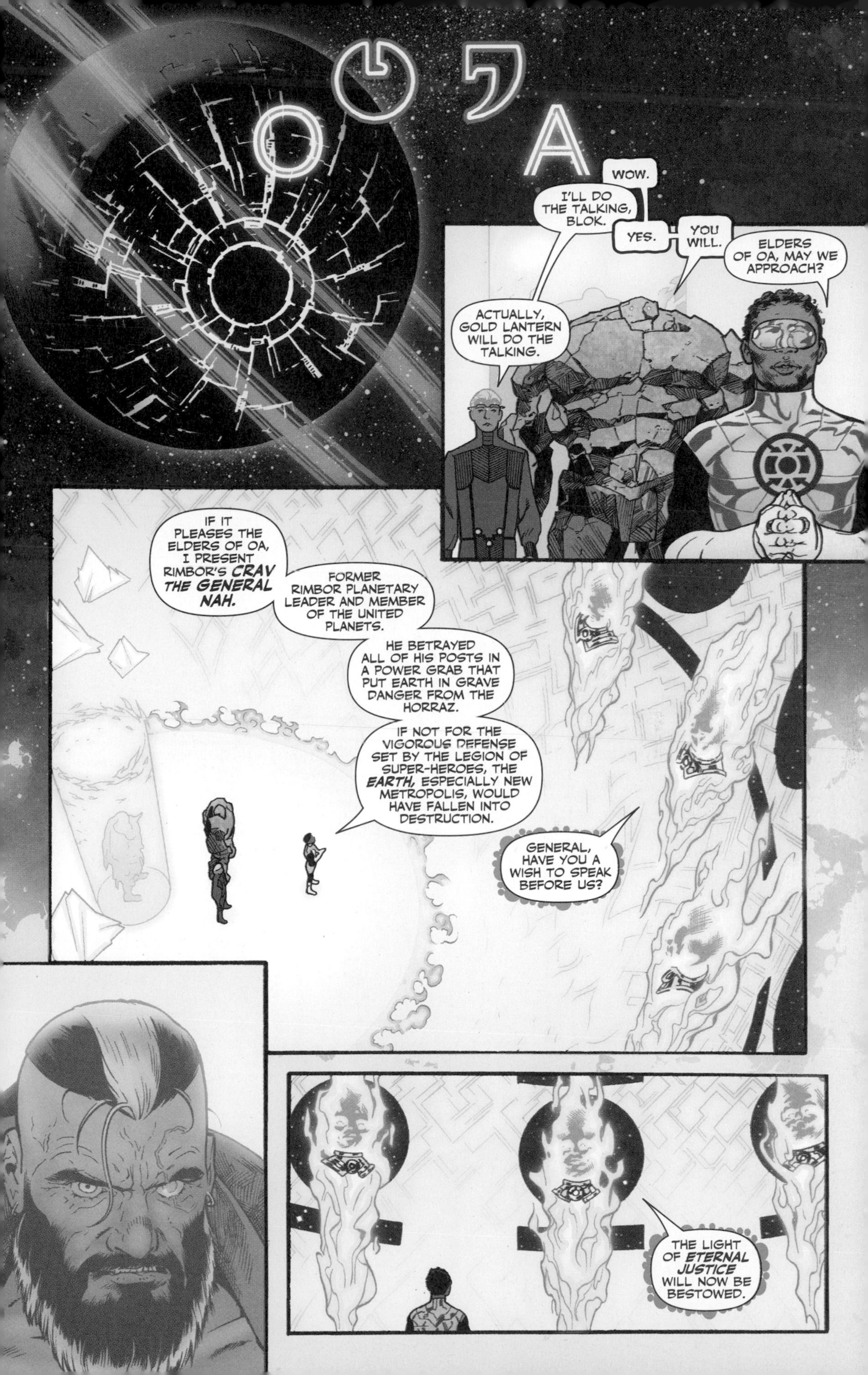
OA
WOW.
I'LL DO THE TALKING, BLOK.
YES.
YOU WILL.
ELDERS OF OA, MAY WE APPROACH?
ACTUALLY, GOLD LANTERN WILL DO THE TALKING.
IF IT PLEASES THE ELDERS OF OA, I PRESENT RIMBOR'S CRAV THE GENERAL NAH.
FORMER RIMBOR PLANETARY LEADER AND MEMBER OF THE UNITED PLANETS.
HE BETRAYED ALL OF HIS POSTS IN A POWER GRAB THAT PUT EARTH IN GRAVE DANGER FROM THE HORRAZ.
IF NOT FOR THE VIGOROUS DEFENSE SET BY THE LEGION OF SUPER-HEROES, THE EARTH, ESPECIALLY NEW METROPOLIS, WOULD HAVE FALLEN INTO DESTRUCTION.
GENERAL, HAVE YOU A WISH TO SPEAK BEFORE US?
THE LIGHT OF ETERNAL JUSTICE WILL NOW BE BESTOWED.

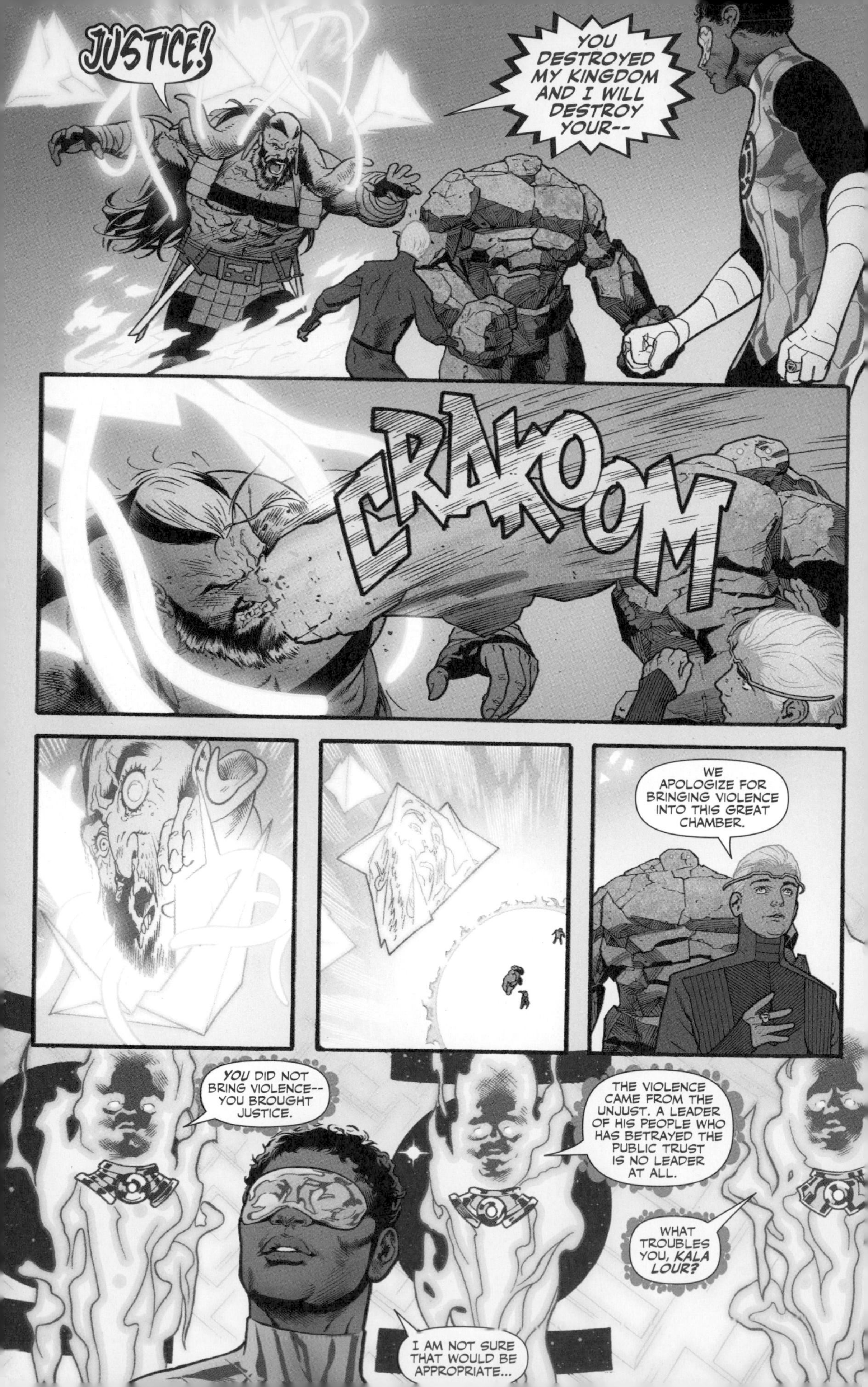
JUSTICE!
YOU DESTROYED MY KINGDOM AND I WILL DESTROY YOUR--
CRAKOOM
WE APOLOGIZE FOR BRINGING VIOLENCE INTO THIS GREAT CHAMBER.
YOU DID NOT BRING VIOLENCE-- YOU BROUGHT JUSTICE.
THE VIOLENCE CAME FROM THE UNJUST. A LEADER OF HIS PEOPLE WHO HAS BETRAYED THE PUBLIC TRUST IS NO LEADER AT ALL.
WHAT TROUBLES YOU, KALA LOUR?
I AM NOT SURE THAT WOULD BE APPROPRIATE...

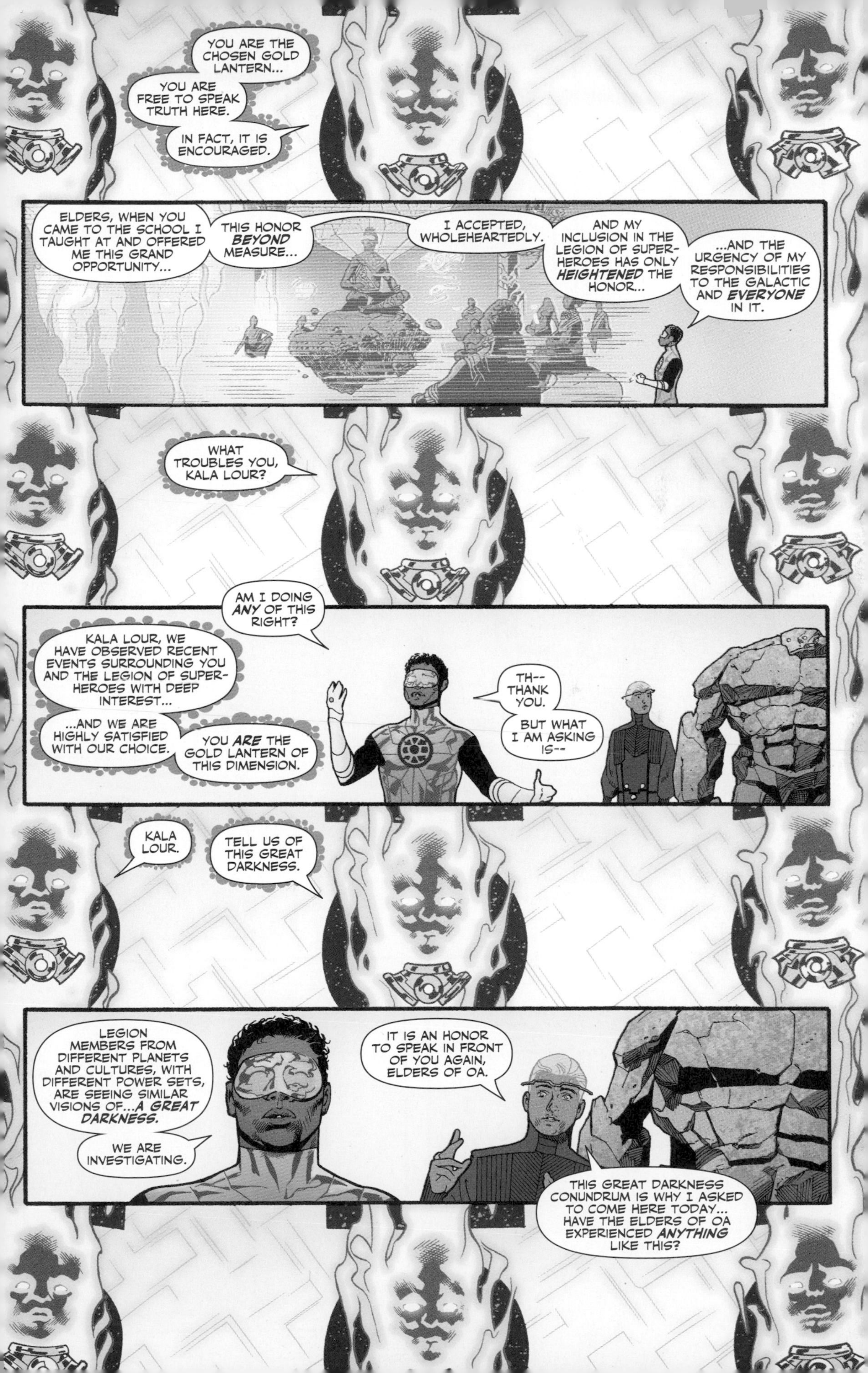

YOU ARE THE CHOSEN GOLD LANTERN...
YOU ARE FREE TO SPEAK TRUTH HERE.
IN FACT, IT IS ENCOURAGED.
ELDERS, WHEN YOU CAME TO THE SCHOOL I TAUGHT AT AND OFFERED ME THIS GRAND OPPORTUNITY...
THIS HONOR BEYOND MEASURE...
I ACCEPTED, WHOLEHEARTEDLY.
AND MY INCLUSION IN THE LEGION OF SUPER-HEROES HAS ONLY HEIGHTENED THE HONOR...
...AND THE URGENCY OF MY RESPONSIBILITIES TO THE GALACTIC AND EVERYONE IN IT.
WHAT TROUBLES YOU, KALA LOUR?
AM I DOING ANY OF THIS RIGHT?
KALA LOUR, WE HAVE OBSERVED RECENT EVENTS SURROUNDING YOU AND THE LEGION OF SUPER-HEROES WITH DEEP INTEREST...
...AND WE ARE HIGHLY SATISFIED WITH OUR CHOICE.
YOU ARE THE GOLD LANTERN OF THIS DIMENSION.
TH-- THANK YOU.
BUT WHAT I AM ASKING IS--
KALA LOUR.
TELL US OF THIS GREAT DARKNESS.
LEGION MEMBERS FROM DIFFERENT PLANETS AND CULTURES, WITH DIFFERENT POWER SETS, ARE SEEING SIMILAR VISIONS OF...A GREAT DARKNESS.
WE ARE INVESTIGATING.
IT IS AN HONOR TO SPEAK IN FRONT OF YOU AGAIN, ELDERS OF OA.
THIS GREAT DARKNESS CONUNDRUM IS WHY I ASKED TO COME HERE TODAY... HAVE THE ELDERS OF OA EXPERIENCED ANYTHING LIKE THIS?

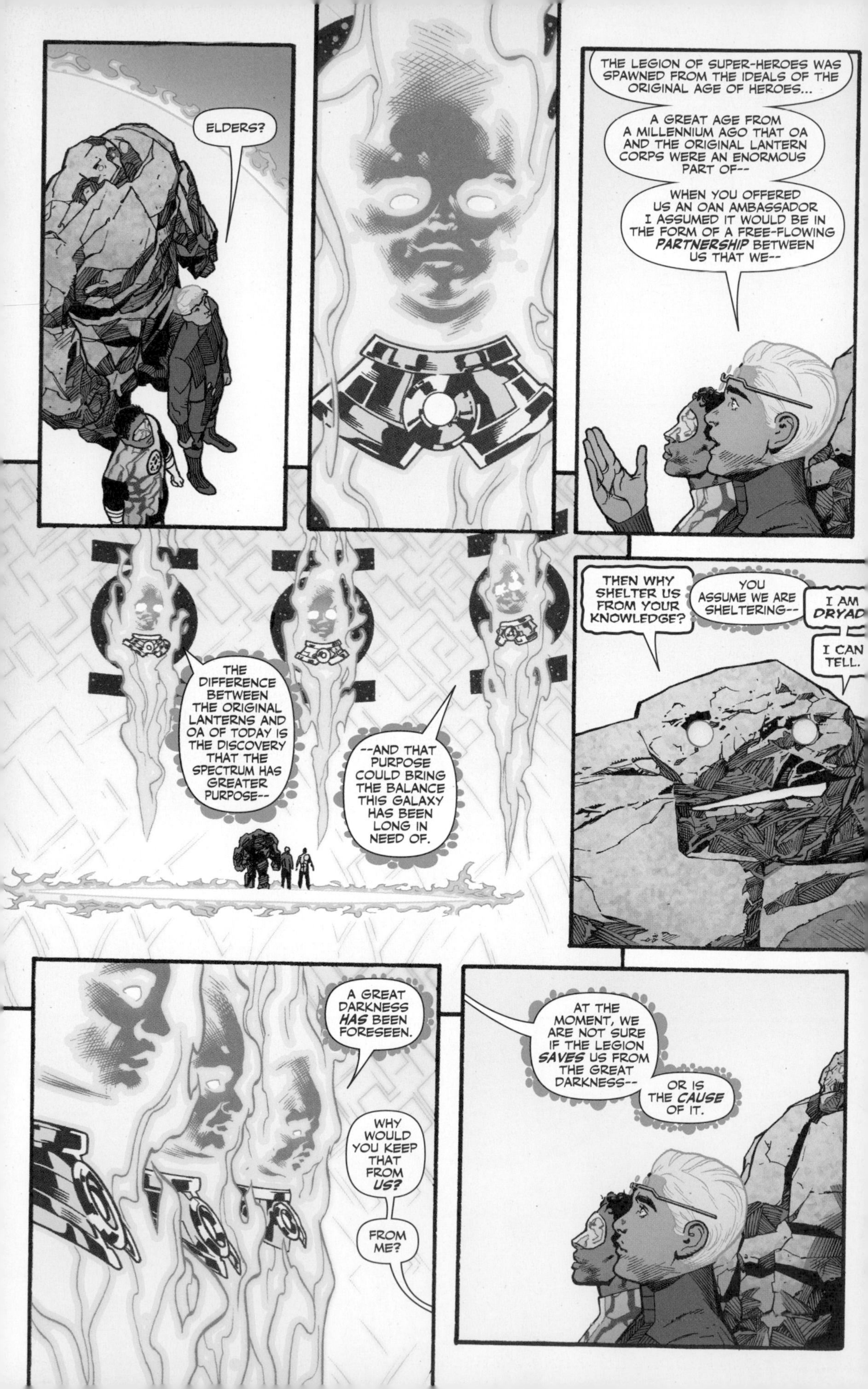
ELDERS?
THE LEGION OF SUPER-HEROES WAS SPAWNED FROM THE IDEALS OF THE ORIGINAL AGE OF HEROES...
A GREAT AGE FROM A MILLENNIUM AGO THAT OA AND THE ORIGINAL LANTERN CORPS WERE AN ENORMOUS PART OF--
WHEN YOU OFFERED US AN OAN AMBASSADOR I ASSUMED IT WOULD BE IN THE FORM OF A FREE-FLOWING PARTNERSHIP BETWEEN US THAT WE--
THE DIFFERENCE BETWEEN THE ORIGINAL LANTERNS AND OA OF TODAY IS THE DISCOVERY THAT THE SPECTRUM HAS GREATER PURPOSE--
--AND THAT PURPOSE COULD BRING THE BALANCE THIS GALAXY HAS BEEN LONG IN NEED OF.
THEN WHY SHELTER US FROM YOUR KNOWLEDGE?
YOU ASSUME WE ARE SHELTERING--
I AM DRYAD
I CAN TELL.
A GREAT DARKNESS HAS BEEN FORESEEN.
WHY WOULD YOU KEEP THAT FROM US?
FROM ME?
AT THE MOMENT, WE ARE NOT SURE IF THE LEGION SAVES US FROM THE GREAT DARKNESS--
OR IS THE CAUSE OF IT.

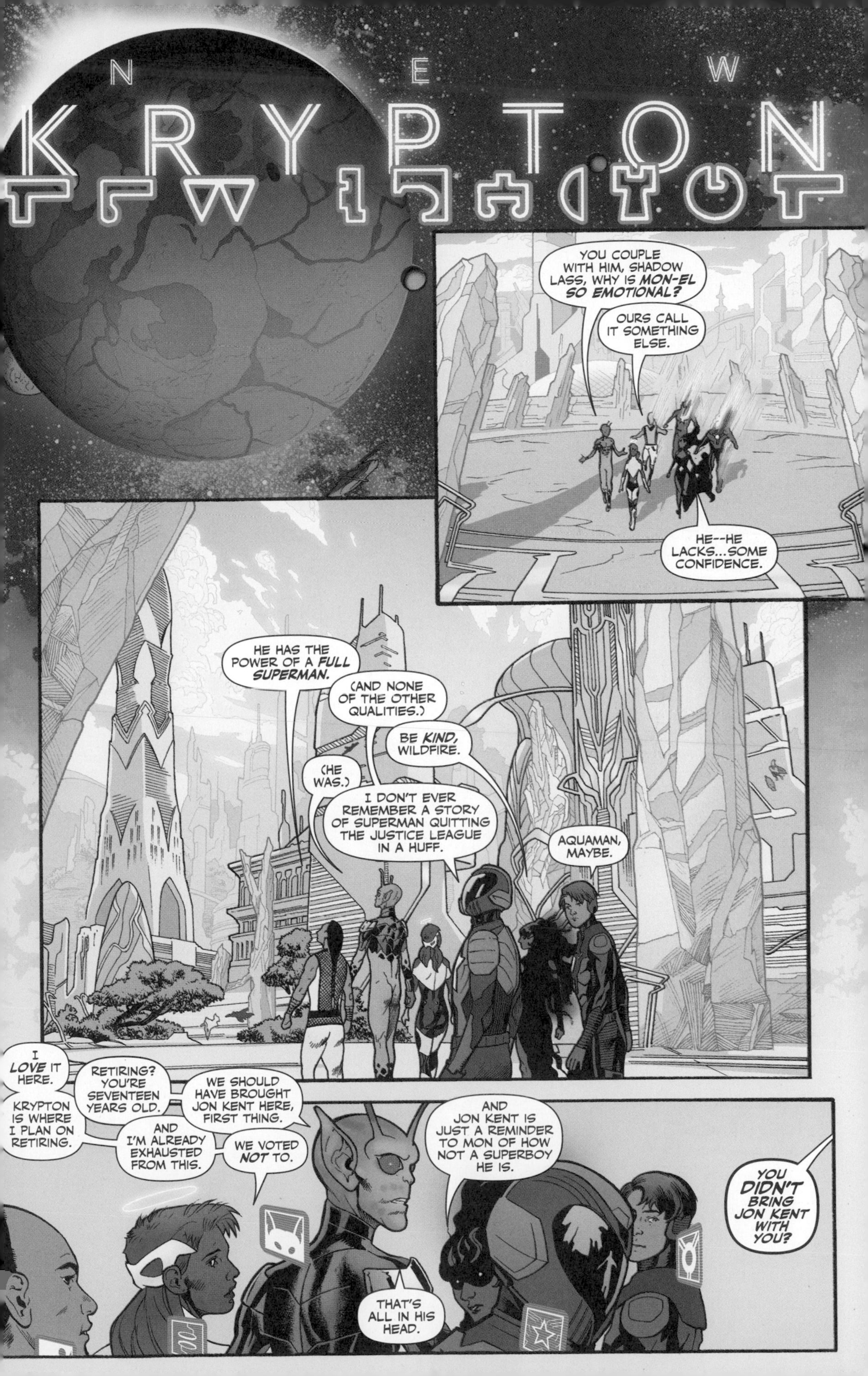
NEW
KRYPTON
YOU COUPLE WITH HIM, SHADOW LASS, WHY IS MON-EL SO EMOTIONAL?
OURS CALL IT SOMETHING ELSE.
HE--HE LACKS...SOME CONFIDENCE.
HE HAS THE POWER OF A FULL SUPERMAN.
(AND NONE OF THE OTHER QUALITIES.)
BE KIND, WILDFIRE.
(HE WAS.)
I DON'T EVER REMEMBER A STORY OF SUPERMAN QUITTING THE JUSTICE LEAGUE IN A HUFF.
AQUAMAN, MAYBE.
I LOVE IT HERE.
KRYPTON IS WHERE I PLAN ON RETIRING.
RETIRING? YOU'RE SEVENTEEN YEARS OLD.
AND I'M ALREADY EXHAUSTED FROM THIS.
WE SHOULD HAVE BROUGHT JON KENT HERE, FIRST THING.
WE VOTED NOT TO.
AND JON KENT IS JUST A REMINDER TO MON OF HOW NOT A SUPERBOY HE IS.
THAT'S ALL IN HIS HEAD.
YOU DIDN'T BRING JON KENT WITH YOU?

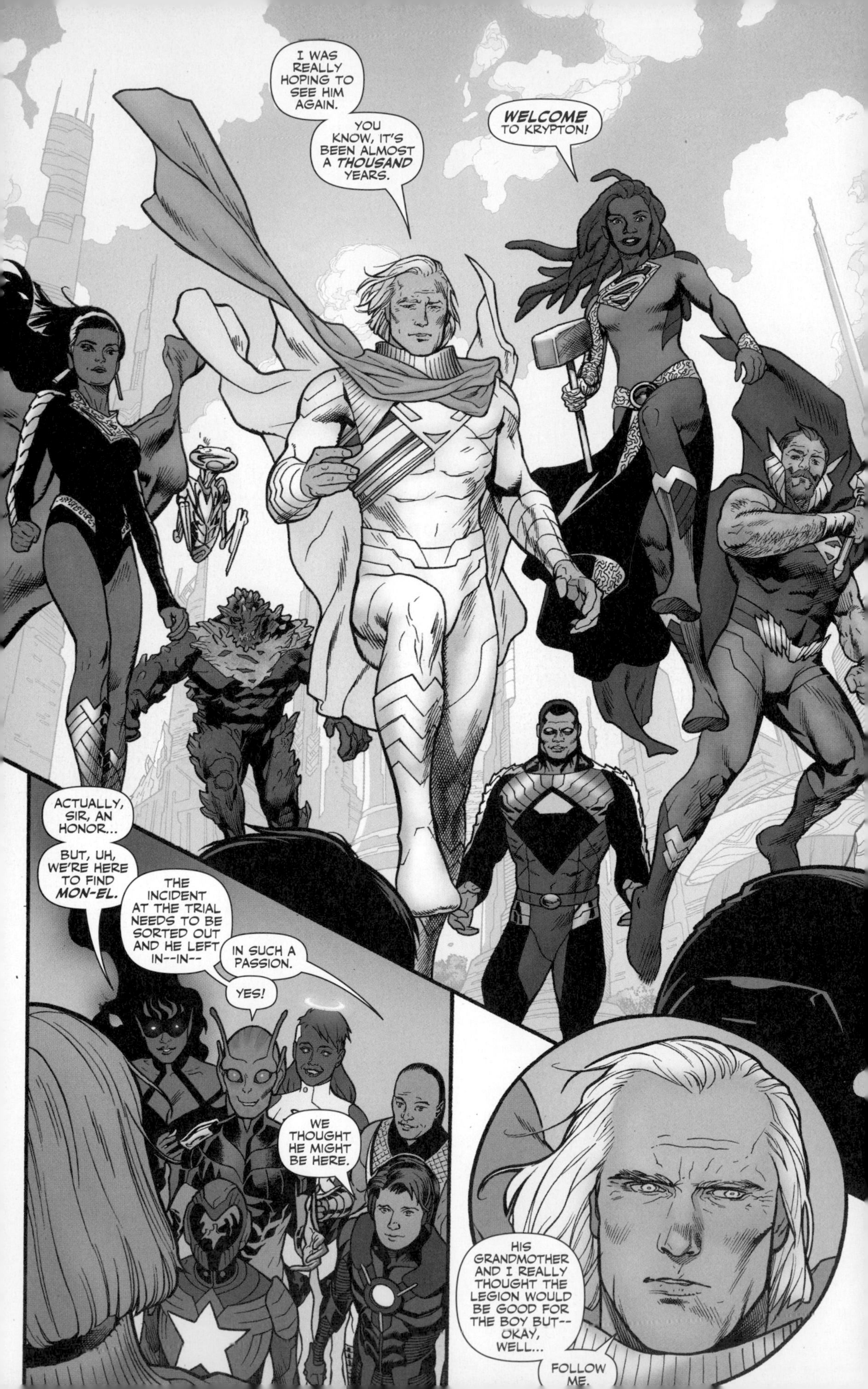
I WAS REALLY HOPING TO SEE HIM AGAIN.
YOU KNOW, IT'S BEEN ALMOST A THOUSAND YEARS.
WELCOME TO KRYPTON!
ACTUALLY, SIR, AN HONOR...
BUT, UH, WE'RE HERE TO FIND MON-EL.
THE INCIDENT AT THE TRIAL NEEDS TO BE SORTED OUT AND HE LEFT IN--IN--
IN SUCH A PASSION.
YES!
WE THOUGHT HE MIGHT BE HERE.
HIS GRANDMOTHER AND I REALLY THOUGHT THE LEGION WOULD BE GOOD FOR THE BOY BUT-- OKAY, WELL...
FOLLOW ME.

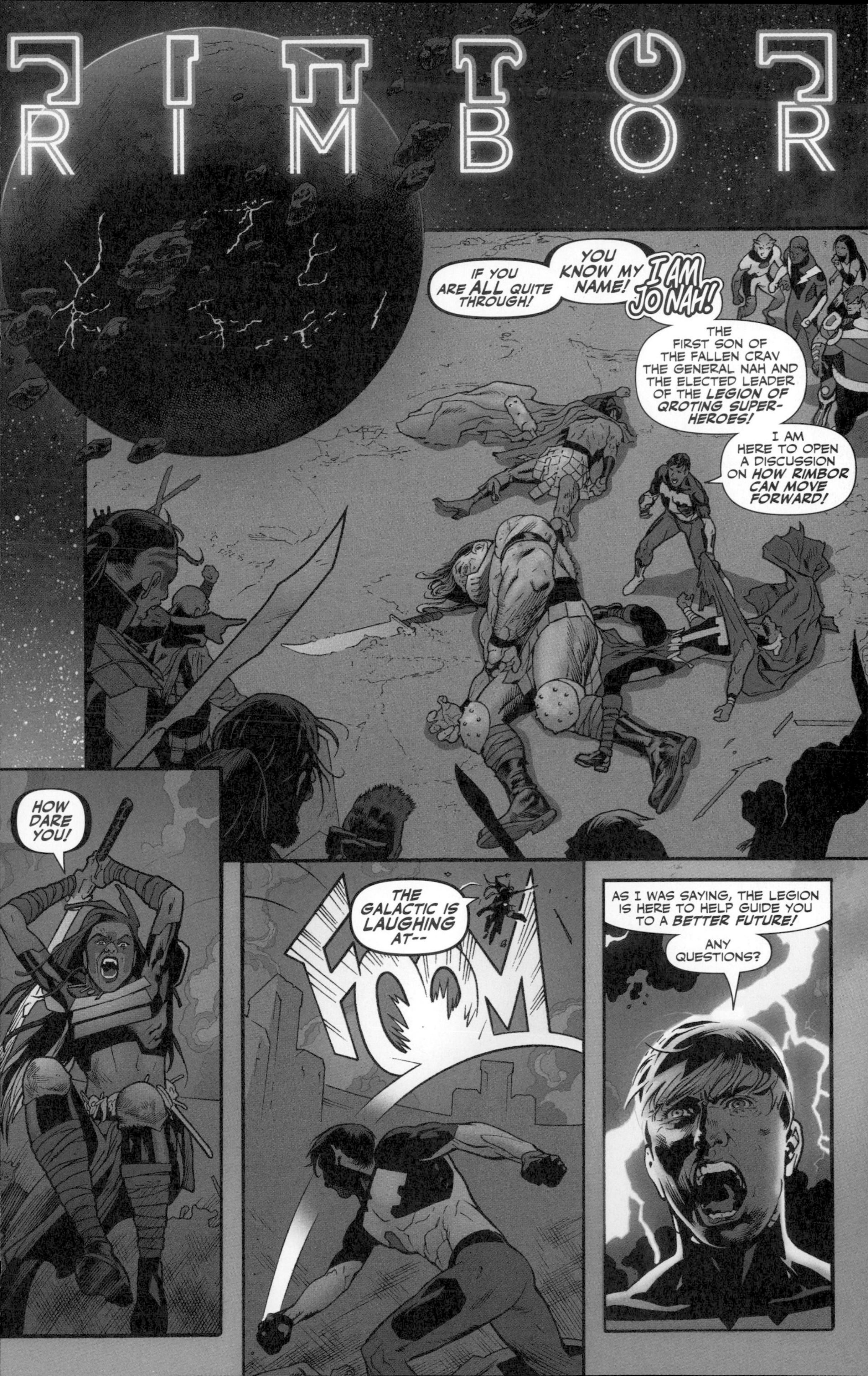

RIMBOR
IF YOU ARE ALL QUITE THROUGH!
YOU KNOW MY NAME!
I AM JO NAH!
THE FIRST SON OF THE FALLEN CRAV THE GENERAL NAH AND THE ELECTED LEADER OF THE LEGION OF QROTING SUPER-HEROES!
I AM HERE TO OPEN A DISCUSSION ON HOW RIMBOR CAN MOVE FORWARD!
HOW DARE YOU!
THE GALACTIC IS LAUGHING AT--
FOOM
AS I WAS SAYING, THE LEGION IS HERE TO HELP GUIDE YOU TO A BETTER FUTURE!
ANY QUESTIONS?

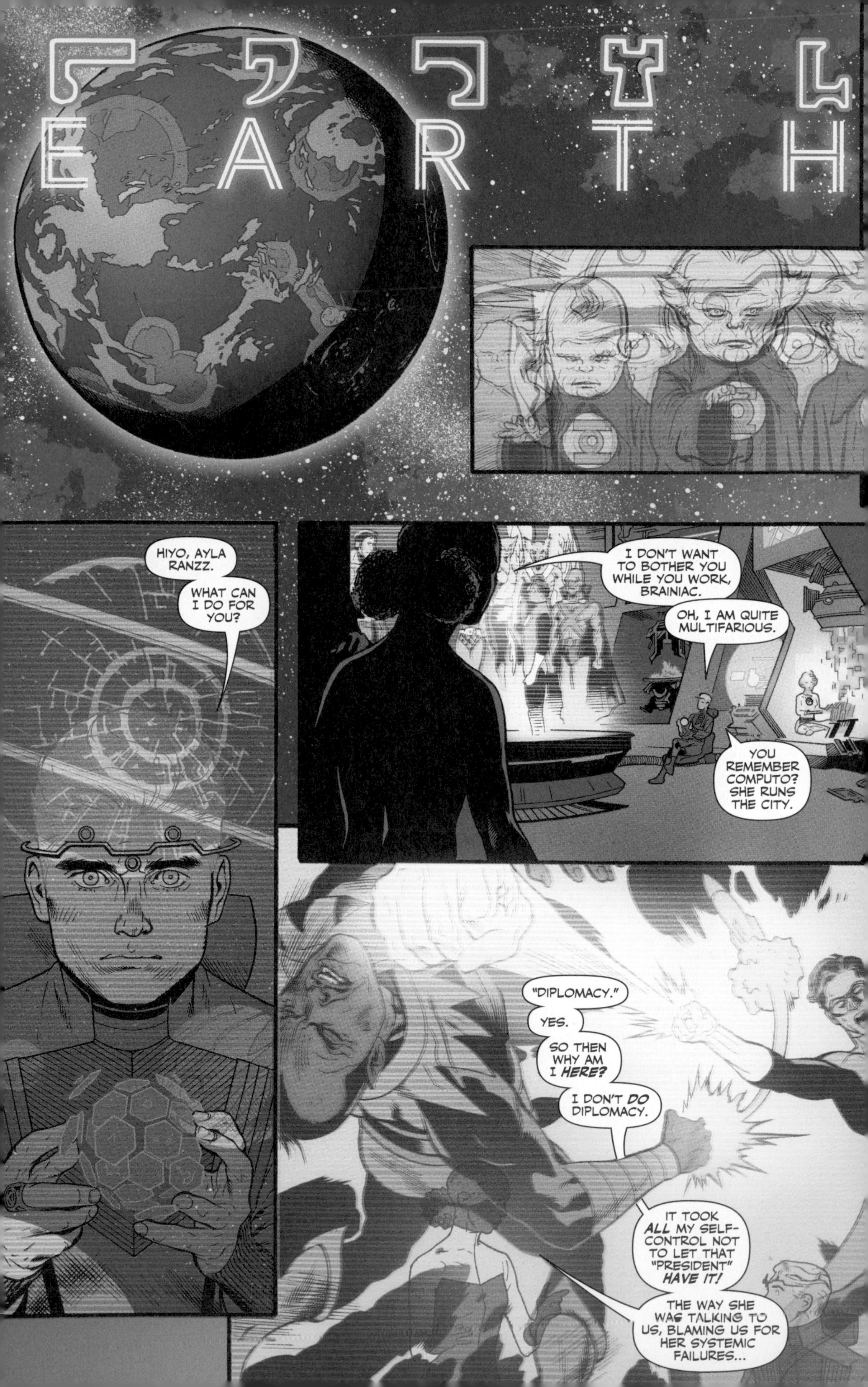
EARTH
HIYO, AYLA RANZZ.
WHAT CAN I DO FOR YOU?
I DON'T WANT TO BOTHER YOU WHILE YOU WORK, BRAINIAC.
OH, I AM QUITE MULTIFARIOUS.
YOU REMEMBER COMPUTO? SHE RUNS THE CITY.
"DIPLOMACY."
YES.
SO THEN WHY AM I *HERE?*
I DON'T *DO* DIPLOMACY.
IT TOOK *ALL* MY SELF-CONTROL NOT TO LET THAT "PRESIDENT" *HAVE IT!*
THE WAY SHE WAS TALKING TO US, BLAMING US FOR HER SYSTEMIC FAILURES...

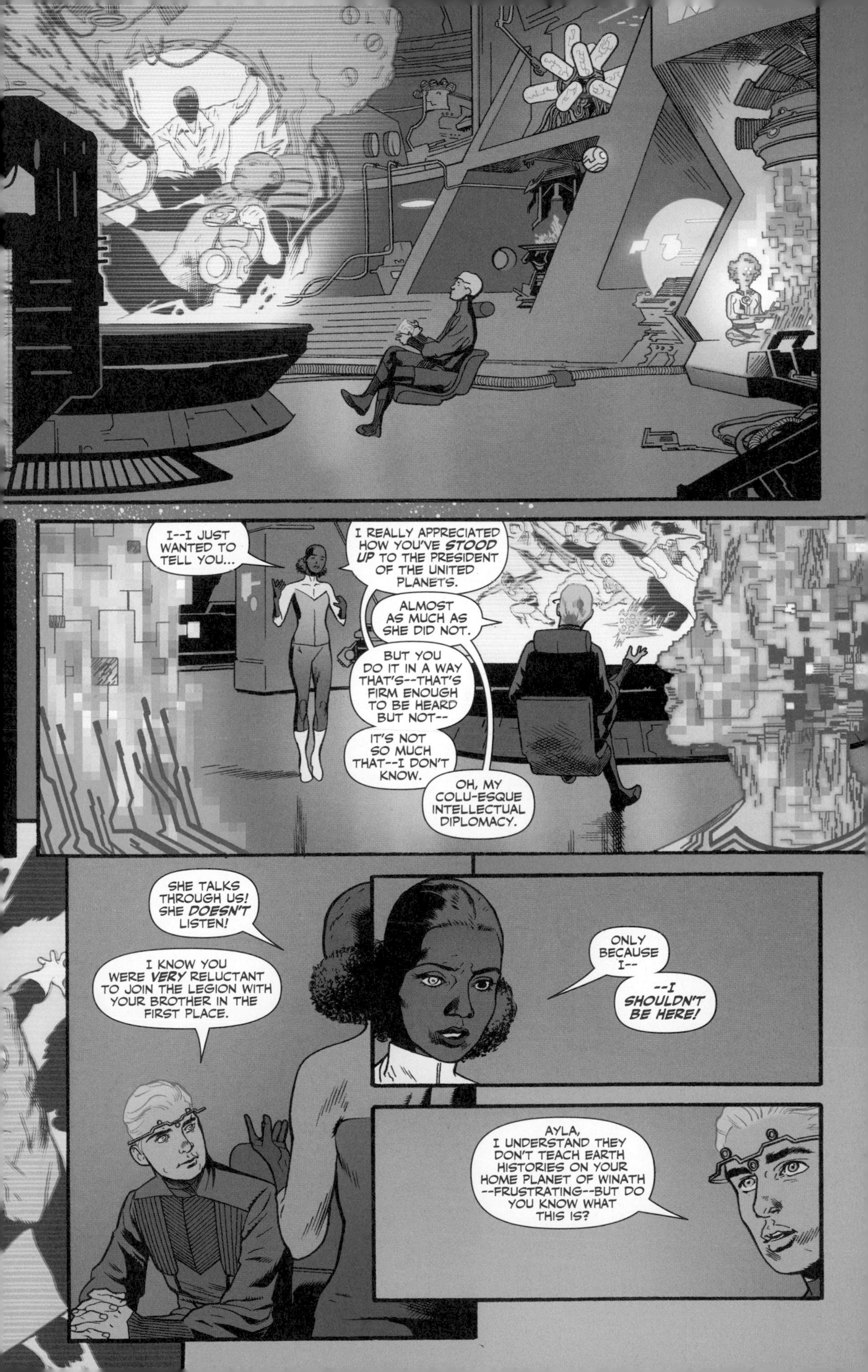
I--I JUST WANTED TO TELL YOU...
I REALLY APPRECIATED HOW YOU'VE STOOD UP TO THE PRESIDENT OF THE UNITED PLANETS.
ALMOST AS MUCH AS SHE DID NOT.
BUT YOU DO IT IN A WAY THAT'S--THAT'S FIRM ENOUGH TO BE HEARD BUT NOT--
IT'S NOT SO MUCH THAT--I DON'T KNOW.
OH, MY COLU-ESQUE INTELLECTUAL DIPLOMACY.
SHE TALKS THROUGH US! SHE DOESN'T LISTEN!
I KNOW YOU WERE VERY RELUCTANT TO JOIN THE LEGION WITH YOUR BROTHER IN THE FIRST PLACE.
ONLY BECAUSE I--
--I SHOULDN'T BE HERE!
AYLA, I UNDERSTAND THEY DON'T TEACH EARTH HISTORIES ON YOUR HOME PLANET OF WINATH --FRUSTRATING--BUT DO YOU KNOW WHAT THIS IS?

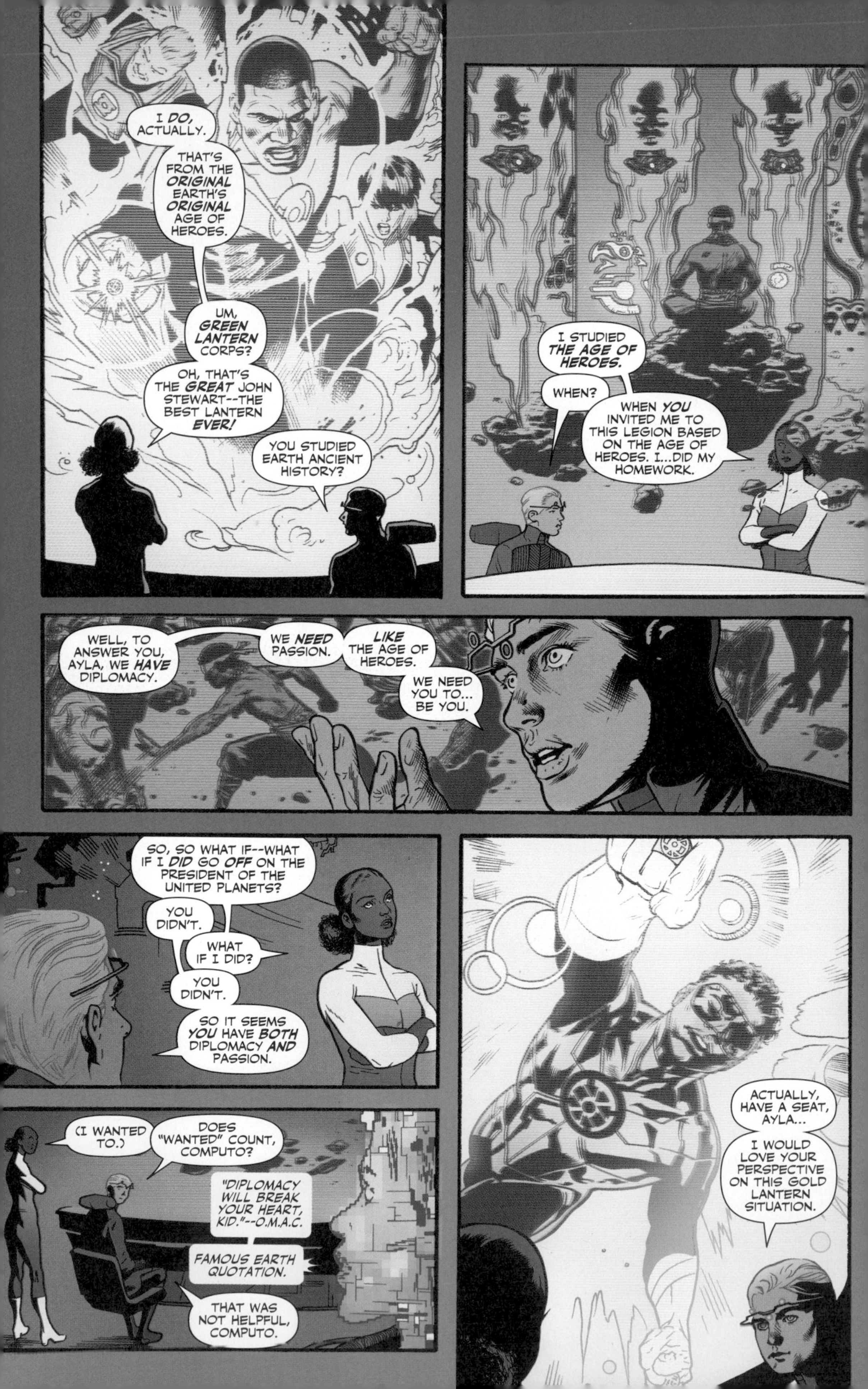
I DO, ACTUALLY.
THAT'S FROM THE ORIGINAL EARTH'S ORIGINAL AGE OF HEROES.
UM, GREEN LANTERN CORPS?
OH, THAT'S THE GREAT JOHN STEWART--THE BEST LANTERN EVER!
YOU STUDIED EARTH ANCIENT HISTORY?
I STUDIED THE AGE OF HEROES.
WHEN?
WHEN YOU INVITED ME TO THIS LEGION BASED ON THE AGE OF HEROES. I...DID MY HOMEWORK.
WELL, TO ANSWER YOU, AYLA, WE HAVE DIPLOMACY.
WE NEED PASSION.
LIKE THE AGE OF HEROES.
WE NEED YOU TO... BE YOU.
SO, SO WHAT IF--WHAT IF I DID GO OFF ON THE PRESIDENT OF THE UNITED PLANETS?
YOU DIDN'T.
WHAT IF I DID?
YOU DIDN'T.
SO IT SEEMS YOU HAVE BOTH DIPLOMACY AND PASSION.
(I WANTED TO.)
DOES "WANTED" COUNT, COMPUTO?
"DIPLOMACY WILL BREAK YOUR HEART, KID."--O.M.A.C.
FAMOUS EARTH QUOTATION.
THAT WAS NOT HELPFUL, COMPUTO.
ACTUALLY, HAVE A SEAT, AYLA...
I WOULD LOVE YOUR PERSPECTIVE ON THIS GOLD LANTERN SITUATION.

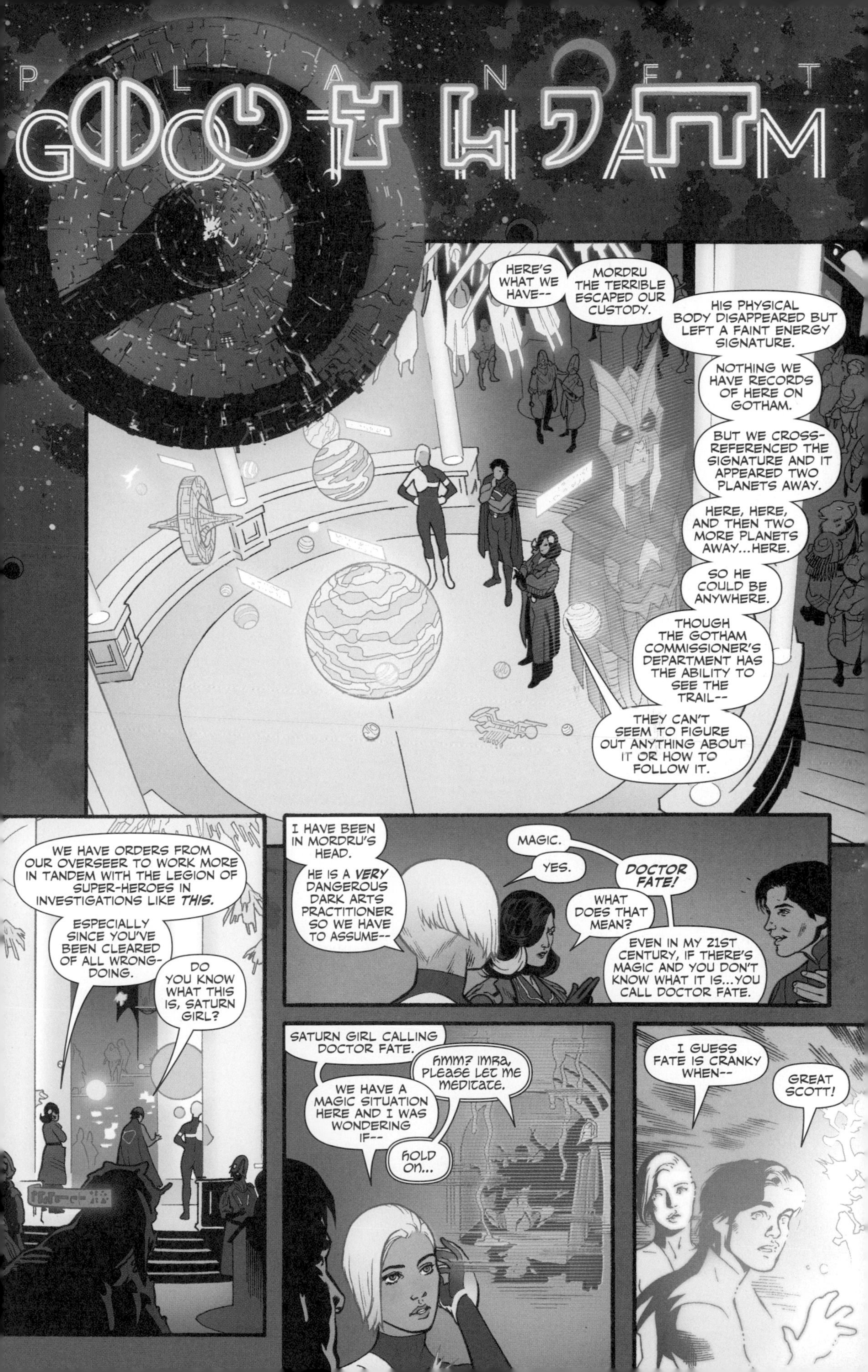
PLANET
GOTHAM
HERE'S WHAT WE HAVE--
MORDRU THE TERRIBLE ESCAPED OUR CUSTODY.
HIS PHYSICAL BODY DISAPPEARED BUT LEFT A FAINT ENERGY SIGNATURE.
NOTHING WE HAVE RECORDS OF HERE ON GOTHAM.
BUT WE CROSS-REFERENCED THE SIGNATURE AND IT APPEARED TWO PLANETS AWAY.
HERE, HERE, AND THEN TWO MORE PLANETS AWAY...HERE.
SO HE COULD BE ANYWHERE.
THOUGH THE GOTHAM COMMISSIONER'S DEPARTMENT HAS THE ABILITY TO SEE THE TRAIL--
THEY CAN'T SEEM TO FIGURE OUT ANYTHING ABOUT IT OR HOW TO FOLLOW IT.
WE HAVE ORDERS FROM OUR OVERSEER TO WORK MORE IN TANDEM WITH THE LEGION OF SUPER-HEROES IN INVESTIGATIONS LIKE *THIS.*
ESPECIALLY SINCE YOU'VE BEEN CLEARED OF ALL WRONG-DOING.
DO YOU KNOW WHAT THIS IS, SATURN GIRL?
I HAVE BEEN IN MORDRU'S HEAD.
HE IS A *VERY* DANGEROUS DARK ARTS PRACTITIONER SO WE HAVE TO ASSUME--
MAGIC.
YES.
DOCTOR FATE!
WHAT DOES THAT MEAN?
EVEN IN MY 21ST CENTURY, IF THERE'S MAGIC AND YOU DON'T KNOW WHAT IT IS...YOU CALL DOCTOR FATE.
SATURN GIRL CALLING DOCTOR FATE.
WE HAVE A MAGIC SITUATION HERE AND I WAS WONDERING IF--
HMM? IMRA, PLEASE LET ME MEDITATE.
HOLD ON...
I GUESS FATE IS CRANKY WHEN--
GREAT SCOTT!

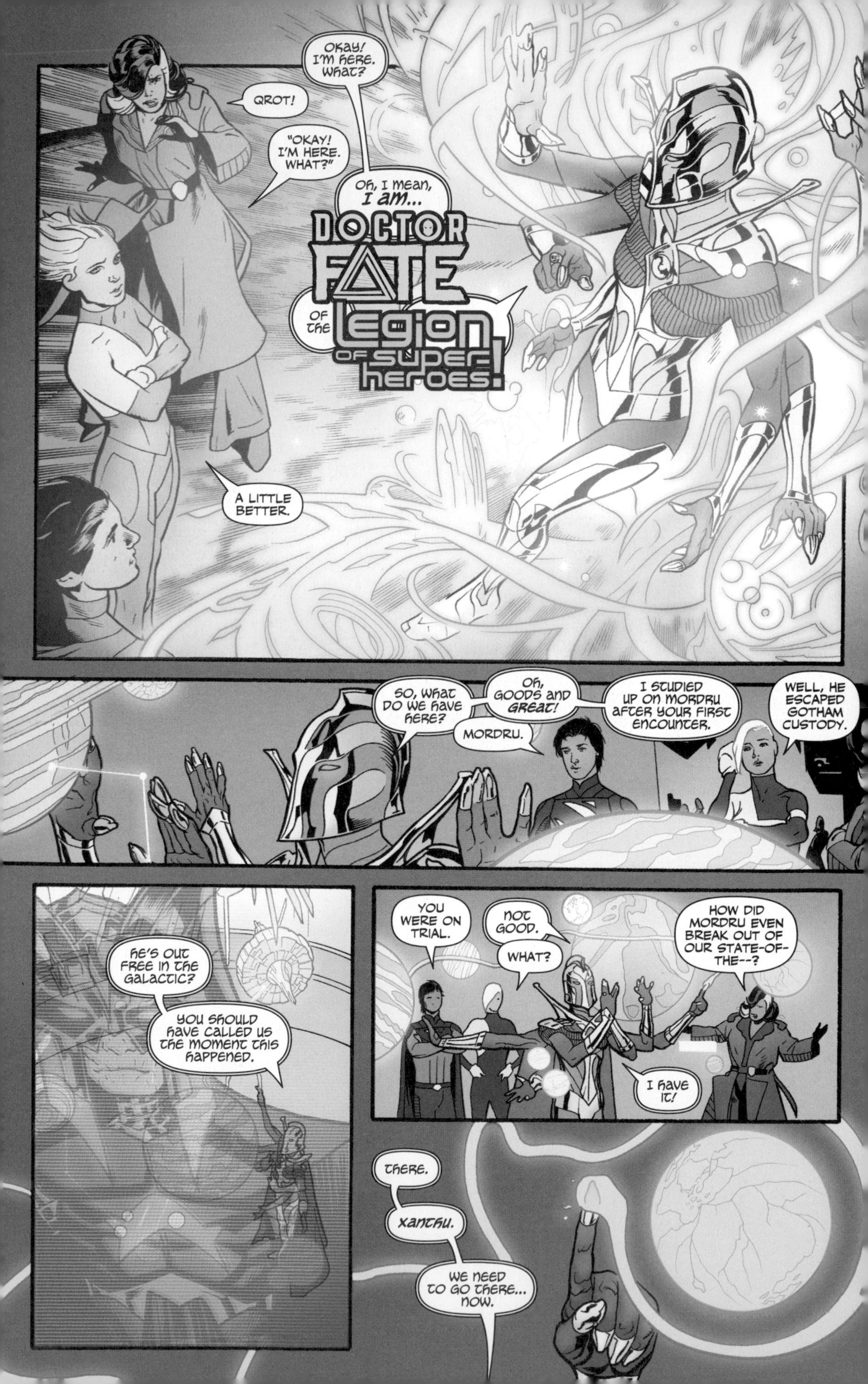
QROT!
OKAY! I'M HERE. WHAT?
"OKAY! I'M HERE. WHAT?"
OH, I MEAN, I AM...
DOCTOR FATE OF THE LEGION OF SUPER-HEROES!
A LITTLE BETTER.
SO, WHAT DO WE HAVE HERE?
OH, GOODS AND GREAT!
MORDRU.
I STUDIED UP ON MORDRU AFTER YOUR FIRST ENCOUNTER.
WELL, HE ESCAPED GOTHAM CUSTODY.
HE'S OUT FREE IN THE GALACTIC?
YOU SHOULD HAVE CALLED US THE MOMENT THIS HAPPENED.
YOU WERE ON TRIAL.
NOT GOOD.
WHAT?
HOW DID MORDRU EVEN BREAK OUT OF OUR STATE-OF-THE--?
I HAVE IT!
THERE.
XANTHU.
WE NEED TO GO THERE... NOW.

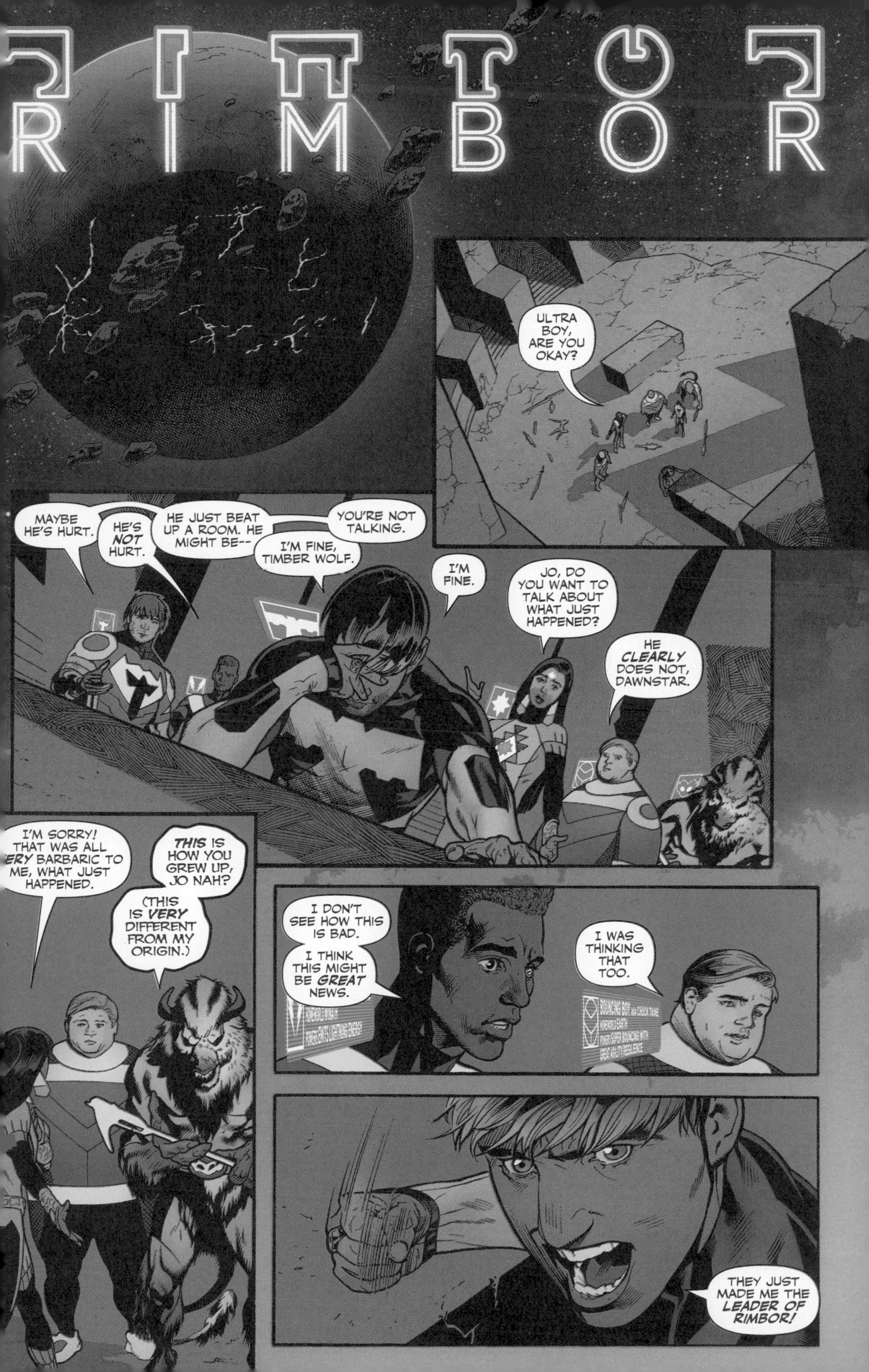
RIMBOR
ULTRA BOY, ARE YOU OKAY?
MAYBE HE'S HURT.
HE'S NOT HURT.
HE JUST BEAT UP A ROOM. HE MIGHT BE--
YOU'RE NOT TALKING.
I'M FINE, TIMBER WOLF.
I'M FINE.
JO, DO YOU WANT TO TALK ABOUT WHAT JUST HAPPENED?
HE CLEARLY DOES NOT, DAWNSTAR.
I'M SORRY! THAT WAS ALL ERY BARBARIC TO ME, WHAT JUST HAPPENED.
THIS IS HOW YOU GREW UP, JO NAH?
(THIS IS VERY DIFFERENT FROM MY ORIGIN.)
I DON'T SEE HOW THIS IS BAD.
I THINK THIS MIGHT BE GREAT NEWS.
I WAS THINKING THAT TOO.
THEY JUST MADE ME THE LEADER OF RIMBOR!

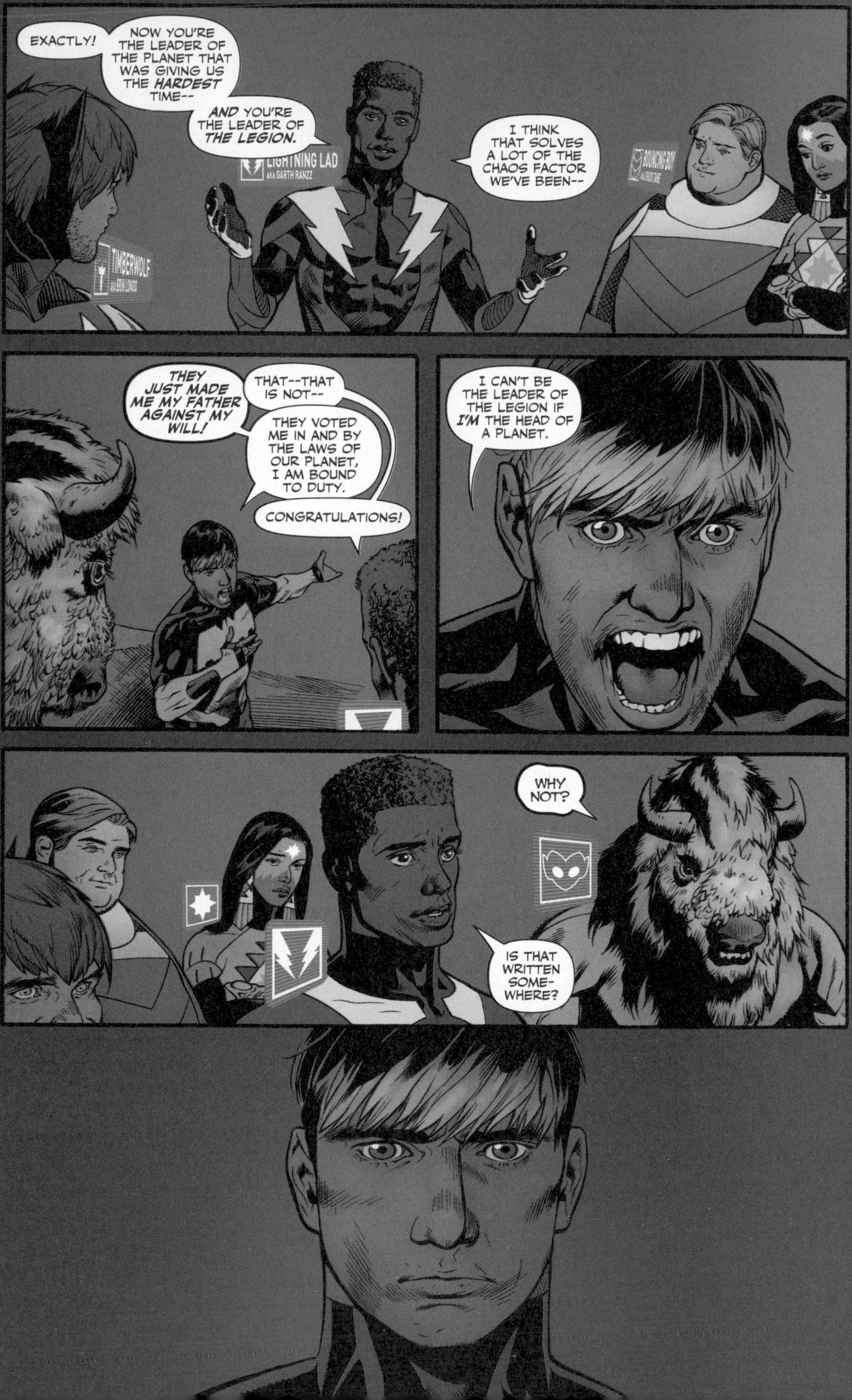
EXACTLY!
NOW YOU'RE THE LEADER OF THE PLANET THAT WAS GIVING US THE HARDEST TIME--
AND YOU'RE THE LEADER OF THE LEGION.
I THINK THAT SOLVES A LOT OF THE CHAOS FACTOR WE'VE BEEN--
LIGHTNING LAD
AKA GARTH RANZZ
TIMBERWOLF
BOUNCING BOY
THEY JUST MADE ME MY FATHER AGAINST MY WILL!
THAT--THAT IS NOT--
THEY VOTED ME IN AND BY THE LAWS OF OUR PLANET, I AM BOUND TO DUTY.
CONGRATULATIONS!
I CAN'T BE THE LEADER OF THE LEGION IF I'M THE HEAD OF A PLANET.
WHY NOT?
IS THAT WRITTEN SOME-WHERE?

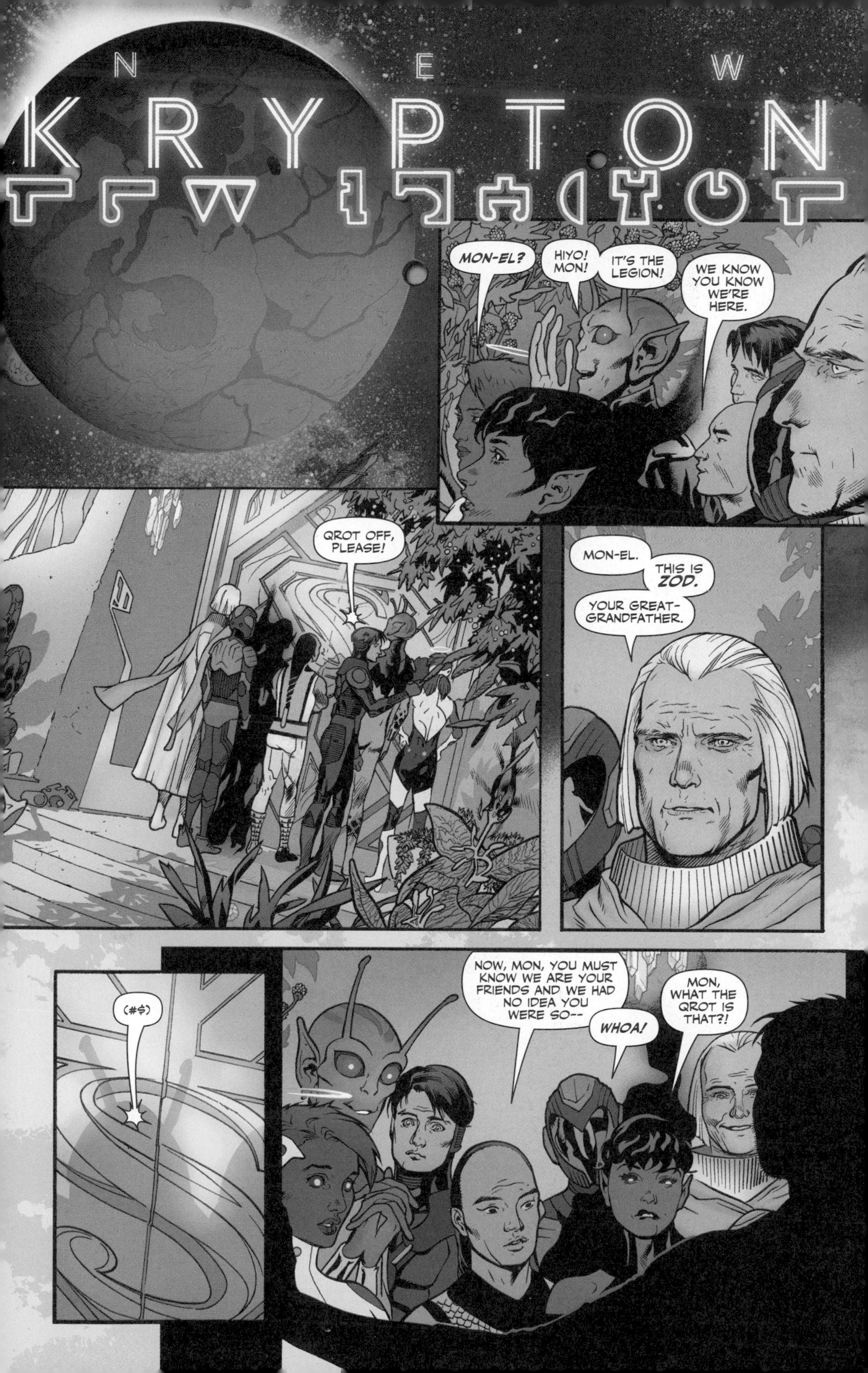
NEW
KRYPTON
MON-EL?
HIYO! MON!
IT'S THE LEGION!
WE KNOW YOU KNOW WE'RE HERE.
QROT OFF, PLEASE!
MON-EL.
THIS IS ZOD.
YOUR GREAT-GRANDFATHER.
(#$)
NOW, MON, YOU MUST KNOW WE ARE YOUR FRIENDS AND WE HAD NO IDEA YOU WERE SO--
WHOA!
MON, WHAT THE QROT IS THAT?!

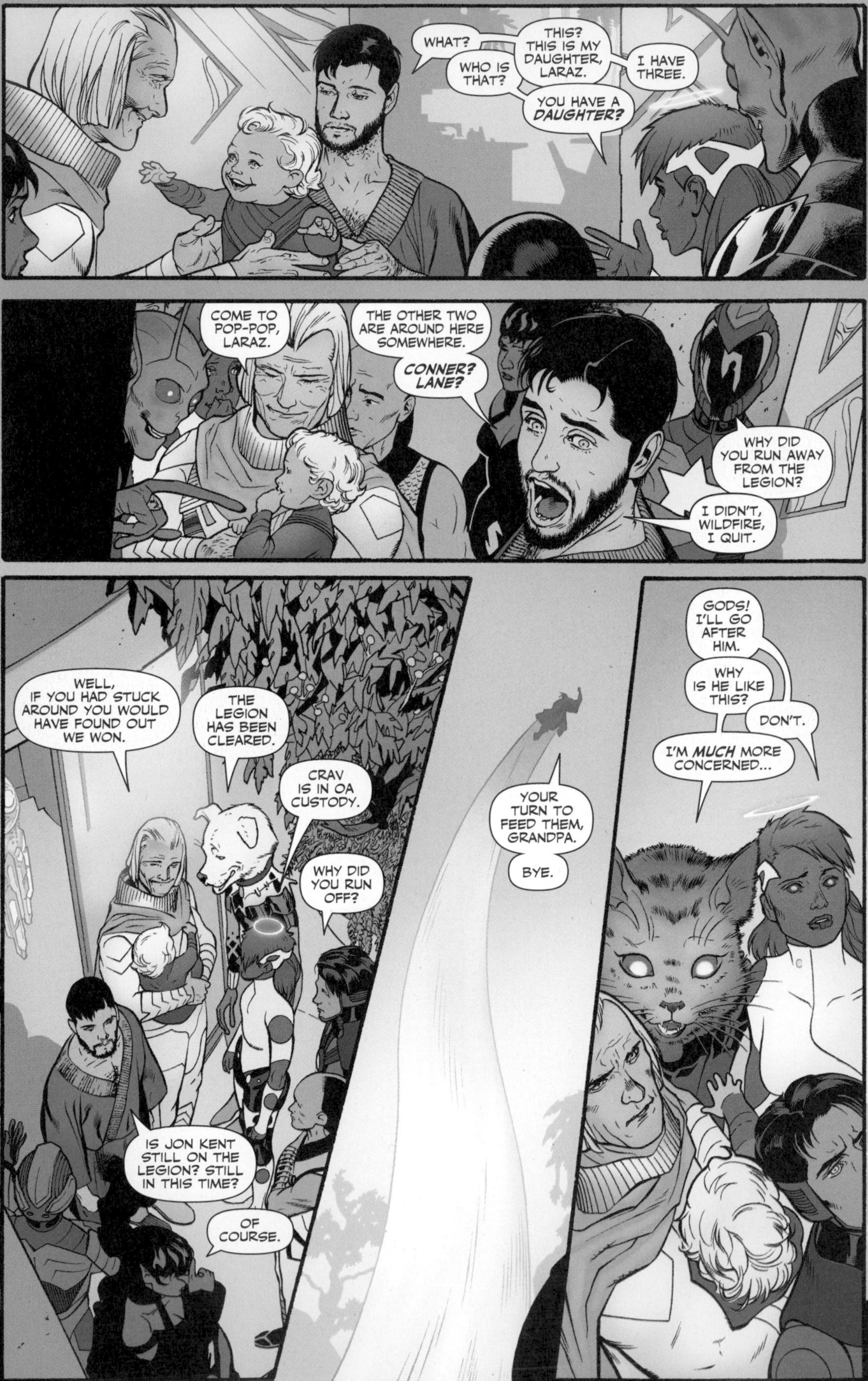
WHAT?
WHO IS THAT?
THIS? THIS IS MY DAUGHTER, LARAZ.
I HAVE THREE.
YOU HAVE A *DAUGHTER?*
COME TO POP-POP, LARAZ.
THE OTHER TWO ARE AROUND HERE SOMEWHERE.
CONNER? LANE?
WHY DID YOU RUN AWAY FROM THE LEGION?
I DIDN'T, WILDFIRE, I QUIT.
WELL, IF YOU HAD STUCK AROUND YOU WOULD HAVE FOUND OUT WE WON.
THE LEGION HAS BEEN CLEARED.
CRAV IS IN OA CUSTODY.
WHY DID YOU RUN OFF?
IS JON KENT STILL ON THE LEGION? STILL IN THIS TIME?
OF COURSE.
YOUR TURN TO FEED THEM, GRANDPA.
BYE.
GODS! I'LL GO AFTER HIM.
WHY IS HE LIKE THIS?
DON'T.
I'M *MUCH* MORE CONCERNED...

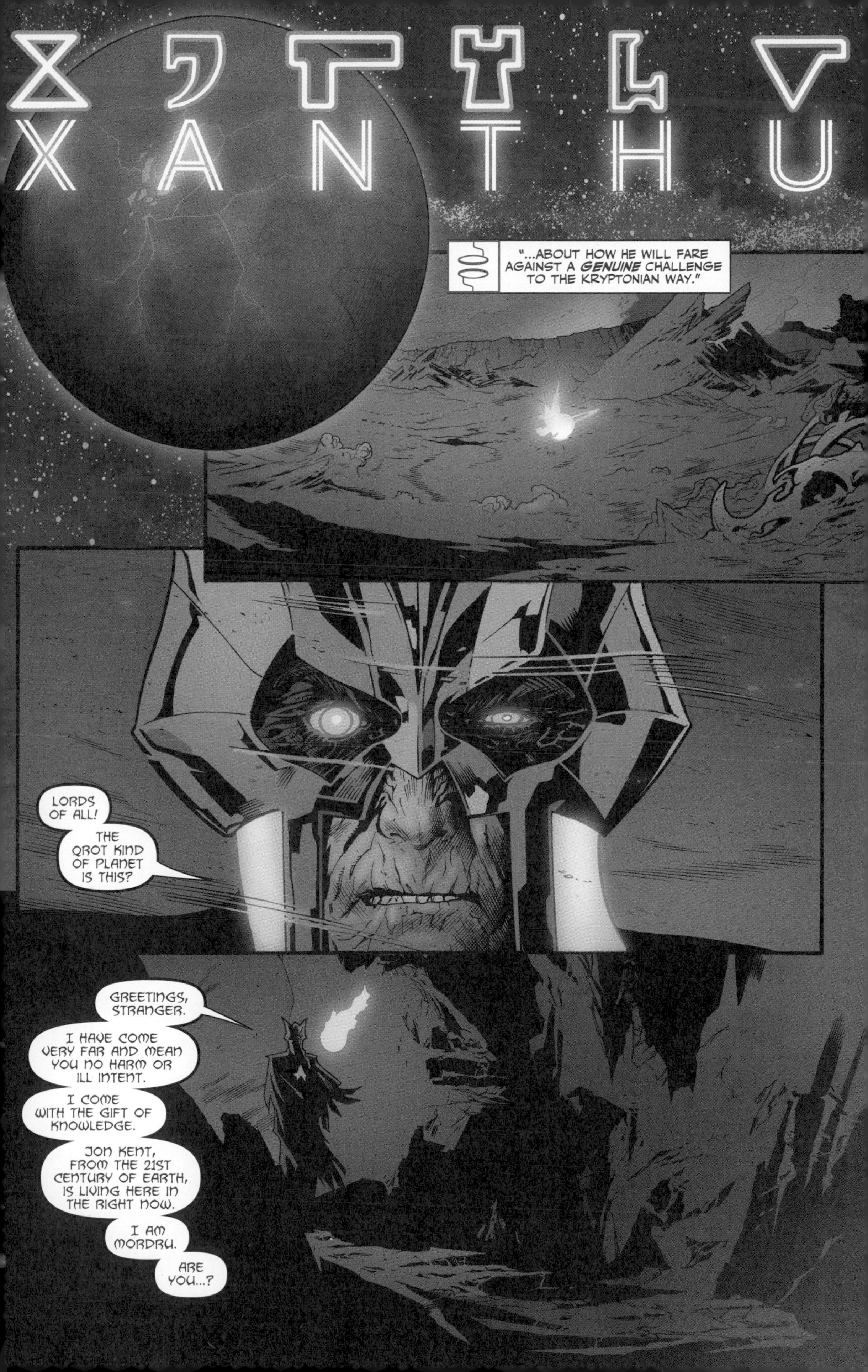
XANTHU
"...ABOUT HOW HE WILL FARE AGAINST A GENUINE CHALLENGE TO THE KRYPTONIAN WAY."
LORDS OF ALL!
THE QROT KIND OF PLANET IS THIS?
GREETINGS, STRANGER.
I HAVE COME VERY FAR AND MEAN YOU NO HARM OR ILL INTENT.
I COME WITH THE GIFT OF KNOWLEDGE.
JON KENT, FROM THE 21ST CENTURY OF EARTH, IS LIVING HERE IN THE RIGHT NOW.
I AM MORDRU.
ARE YOU...?

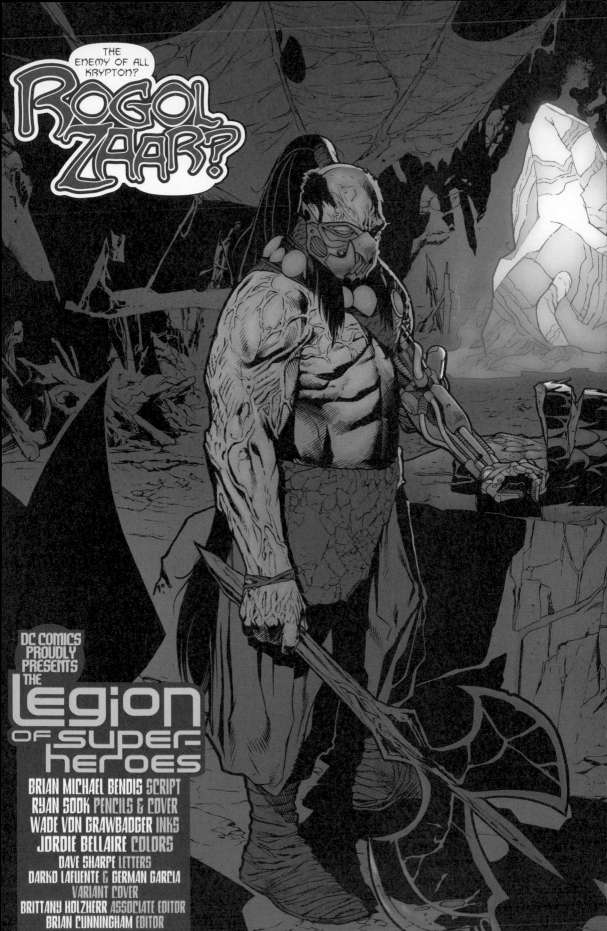

THE ENEMY OF ALL KRYPTON?

ROGOL ZAAR?

DC COMICS PROUDLY PRESENTS THE

LEGION OF SUPER-HEROES

BRIAN MICHAEL BENDIS SCRIPT

RYAN SOOK PENCILS & COVER

WADE VON GRAWBADGER INKS

JORDIE BELLAIRE COLORS

DAVE SHARPE LETTERS

DARKO LAFUENTE & GERMAN GARCIA
VARIANT COVER

BRITTANY HOLZHERR ASSOCIATE EDITOR

BRIAN CUNNINGHAM EDITOR

SUPERBOY CREATED BY JERRY SIEGEL.
BY SPECIAL ARRANGEMENT WITH
THE JERRY SIEGEL FAMILY.

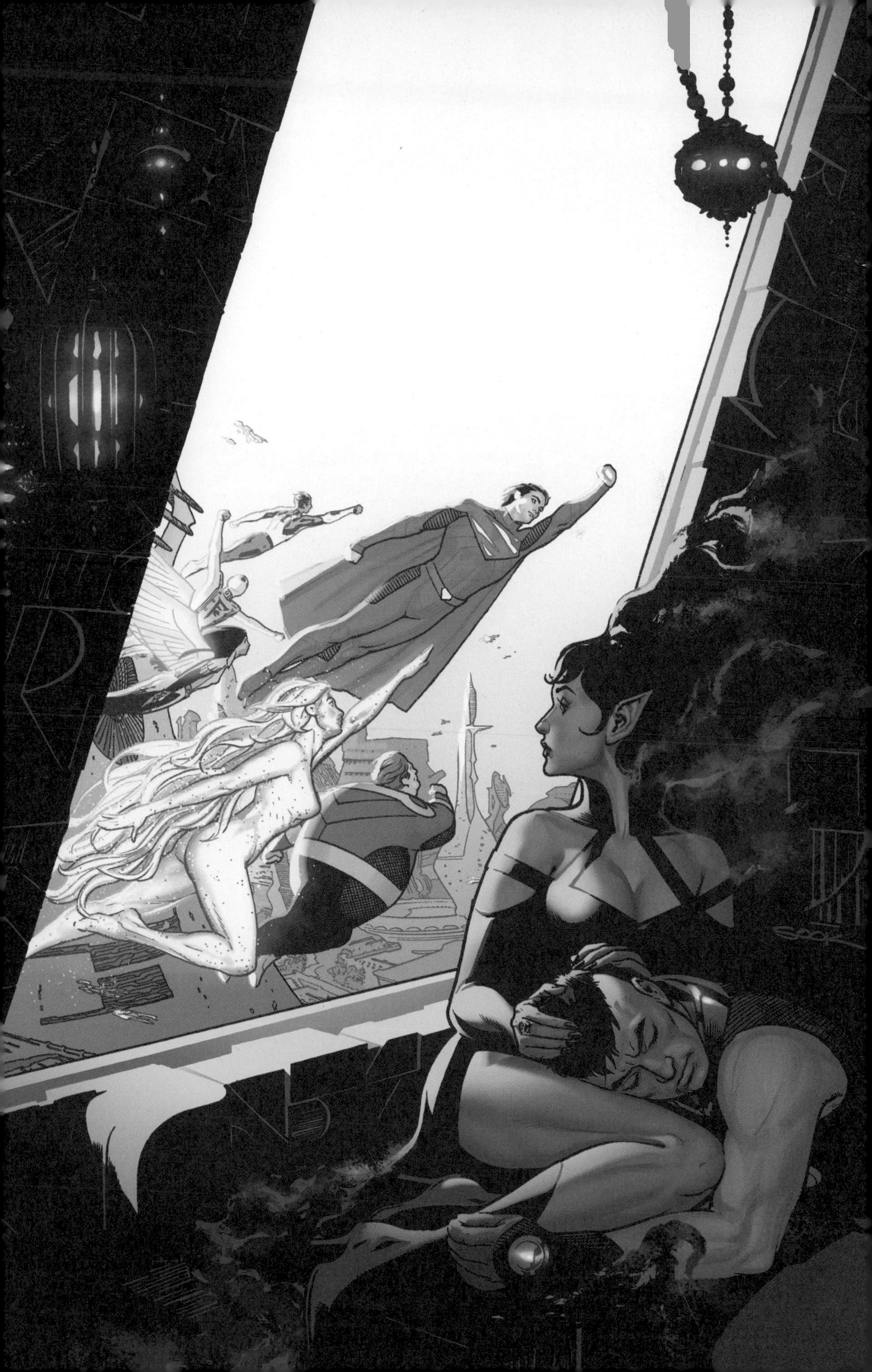

RYAN SOOK
Cover Artist

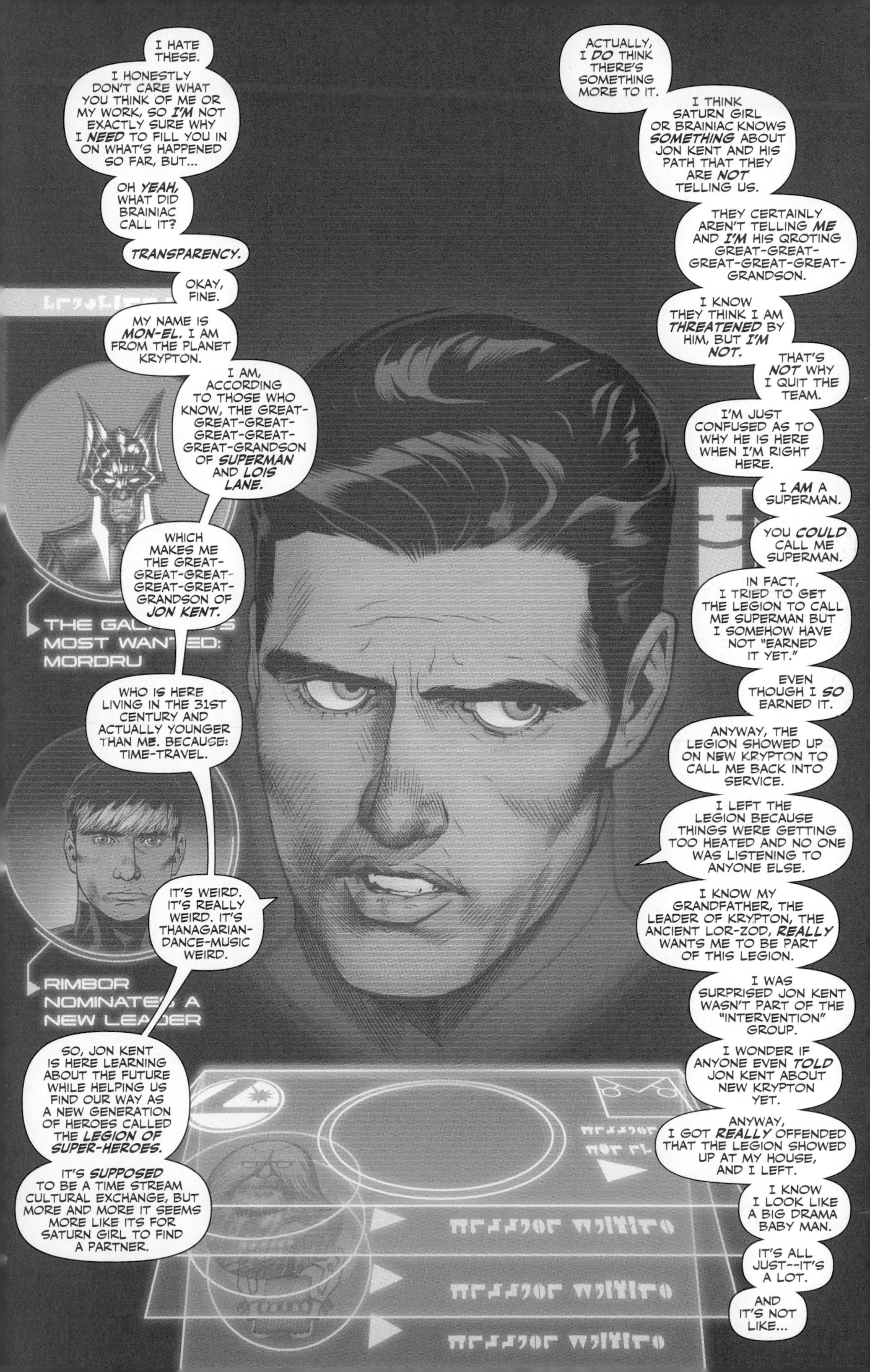
I HATE THESE.
I HONESTLY DON'T CARE WHAT YOU THINK OF ME OR MY WORK, SO I'M NOT EXACTLY SURE WHY I NEED TO FILL YOU IN ON WHAT'S HAPPENED SO FAR, BUT...
OH YEAH, WHAT DID BRAINIAC CALL IT?
TRANSPARENCY.
OKAY, FINE.
MY NAME IS MON-EL. I AM FROM THE PLANET KRYPTON.
I AM, ACCORDING TO THOSE WHO KNOW, THE GREAT-GREAT-GREAT-GREAT-GREAT-GREAT-GRANDSON OF SUPERMAN AND LOIS LANE.
WHICH MAKES ME THE GREAT-GREAT-GREAT-GREAT-GREAT-GRANDSON OF JON KENT.
WHO IS HERE LIVING IN THE 31ST CENTURY AND ACTUALLY YOUNGER THAN ME. BECAUSE: TIME-TRAVEL.
IT'S WEIRD. IT'S REALLY WEIRD. IT'S THANAGARIAN-DANCE-MUSIC WEIRD.
SO, JON KENT IS HERE LEARNING ABOUT THE FUTURE WHILE HELPING US FIND OUR WAY AS A NEW GENERATION OF HEROES CALLED THE LEGION OF SUPER-HEROES.
IT'S SUPPOSED TO BE A TIME STREAM CULTURAL EXCHANGE, BUT MORE AND MORE IT SEEMS MORE LIKE ITS FOR SATURN GIRL TO FIND A PARTNER.
ACTUALLY, I DO THINK THERE'S SOMETHING MORE TO IT.
I THINK SATURN GIRL OR BRAINIAC KNOWS SOMETHING ABOUT JON KENT AND HIS PATH THAT THEY ARE NOT TELLING US.
THEY CERTAINLY AREN'T TELLING ME AND I'M HIS QROTING GREAT-GREAT-GREAT-GREAT-GREAT-GRANDSON.
I KNOW THEY THINK I AM THREATENED BY HIM, BUT I'M NOT.
THAT'S NOT WHY I QUIT THE TEAM.
I'M JUST CONFUSED AS TO WHY HE IS HERE WHEN I'M RIGHT HERE.
I AM A SUPERMAN.
YOU COULD CALL ME SUPERMAN.
IN FACT, I TRIED TO GET THE LEGION TO CALL ME SUPERMAN BUT I SOMEHOW HAVE NOT "EARNED IT YET."
EVEN THOUGH I SO EARNED IT.
ANYWAY, THE LEGION SHOWED UP ON NEW KRYPTON TO CALL ME BACK INTO SERVICE.
I LEFT THE LEGION BECAUSE THINGS WERE GETTING TOO HEATED AND NO ONE WAS LISTENING TO ANYONE ELSE.
I KNOW MY GRANDFATHER, THE LEADER OF KRYPTON, THE ANCIENT LOR-ZOD, REALLY WANTS ME TO BE PART OF THIS LEGION.
I WAS SURPRISED JON KENT WASN'T PART OF THE "INTERVENTION" GROUP.
I WONDER IF ANYONE EVEN TOLD JON KENT ABOUT NEW KRYPTON YET.
ANYWAY, I GOT REALLY OFFENDED THAT THE LEGION SHOWED UP AT MY HOUSE, AND I LEFT.
I KNOW I LOOK LIKE A BIG DRAMA BABY MAN.
IT'S ALL JUST--IT'S A LOT.
AND IT'S NOT LIKE...
MORDRU
RIMBOR
NEW LEADER

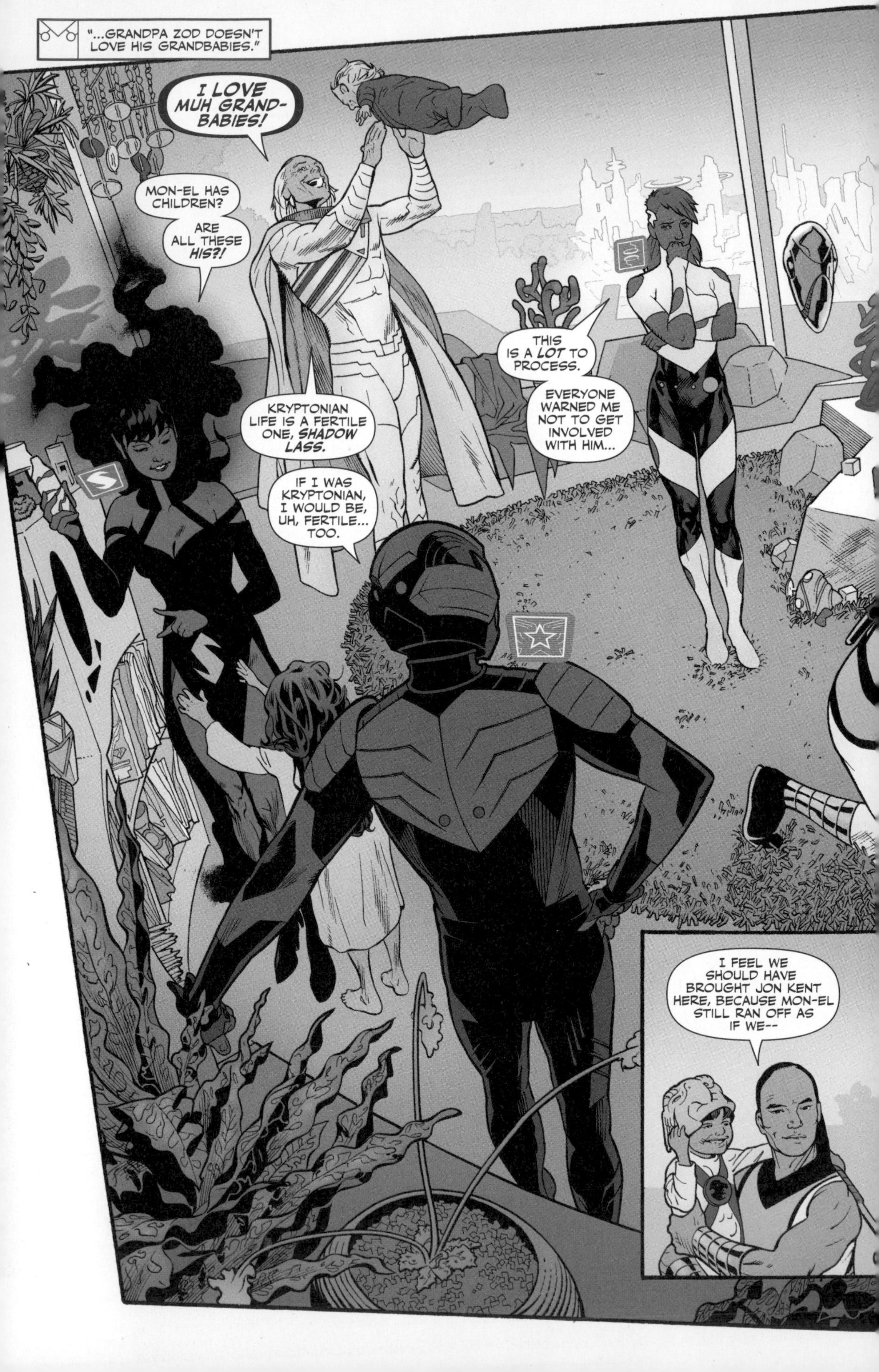

"...GRANDPA ZOD DOESN'T LOVE HIS GRANDBABIES."
I LOVE MUH GRAND-BABIES!
MON-EL HAS CHILDREN?
ARE ALL THESE HIS?!
KRYPTONIAN LIFE IS A FERTILE ONE, SHADOW LASS.
IF I WAS KRYPTONIAN, I WOULD BE, UH, FERTILE... TOO.
THIS IS A LOT TO PROCESS.
EVERYONE WARNED ME NOT TO GET INVOLVED WITH HIM...
I FEEL WE SHOULD HAVE BROUGHT JON KENT HERE, BECAUSE MON-EL STILL RAN OFF AS IF WE--

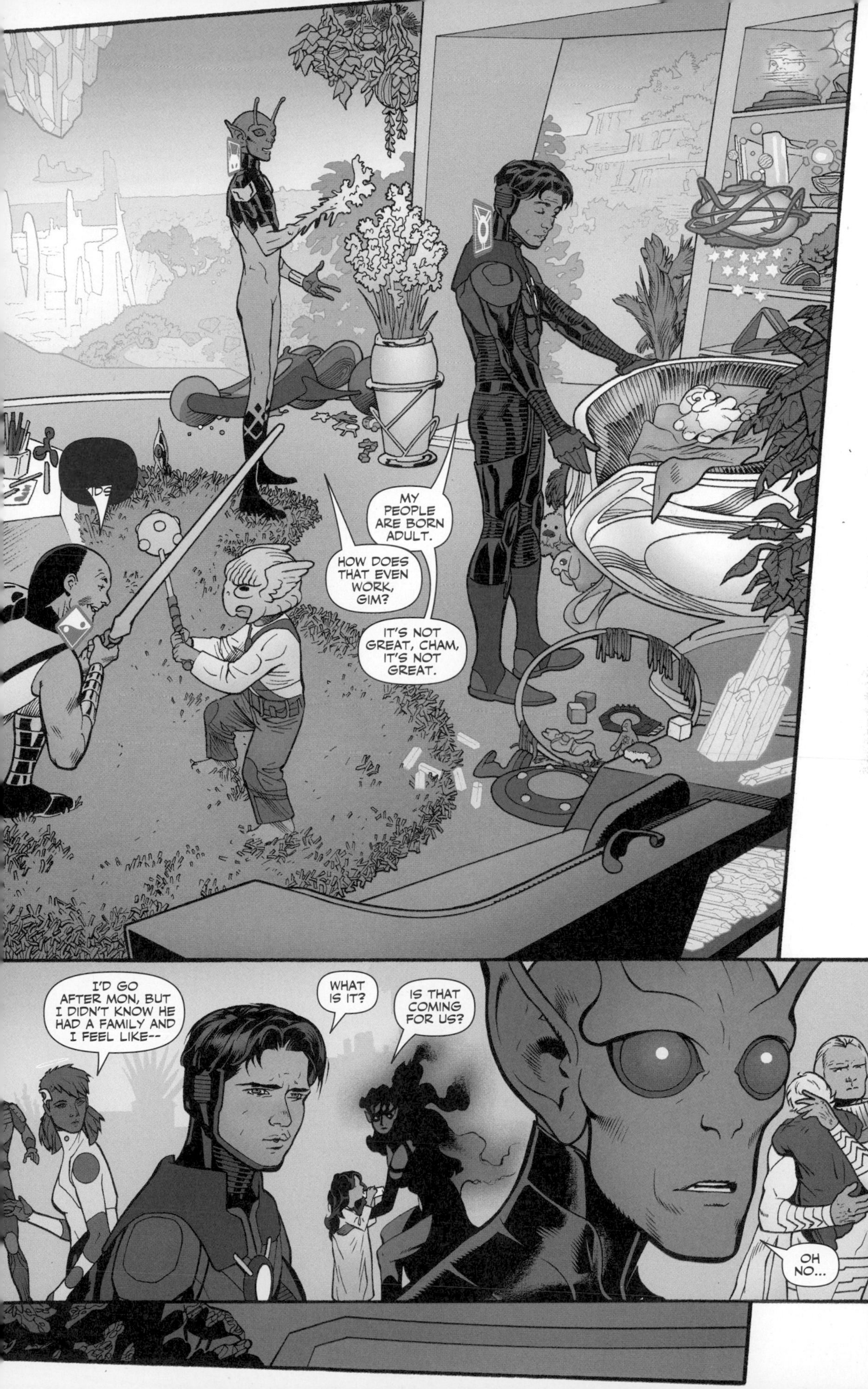
MY PEOPLE ARE BORN ADULT.
HOW DOES THAT EVEN WORK, GIM?
IT'S NOT GREAT, CHAM, IT'S NOT GREAT.
I'D GO AFTER MON, BUT I DIDN'T KNOW HE HAD A FAMILY AND I FEEL LIKE--
WHAT IS IT?
IS THAT COMING FOR US?
OH NO...

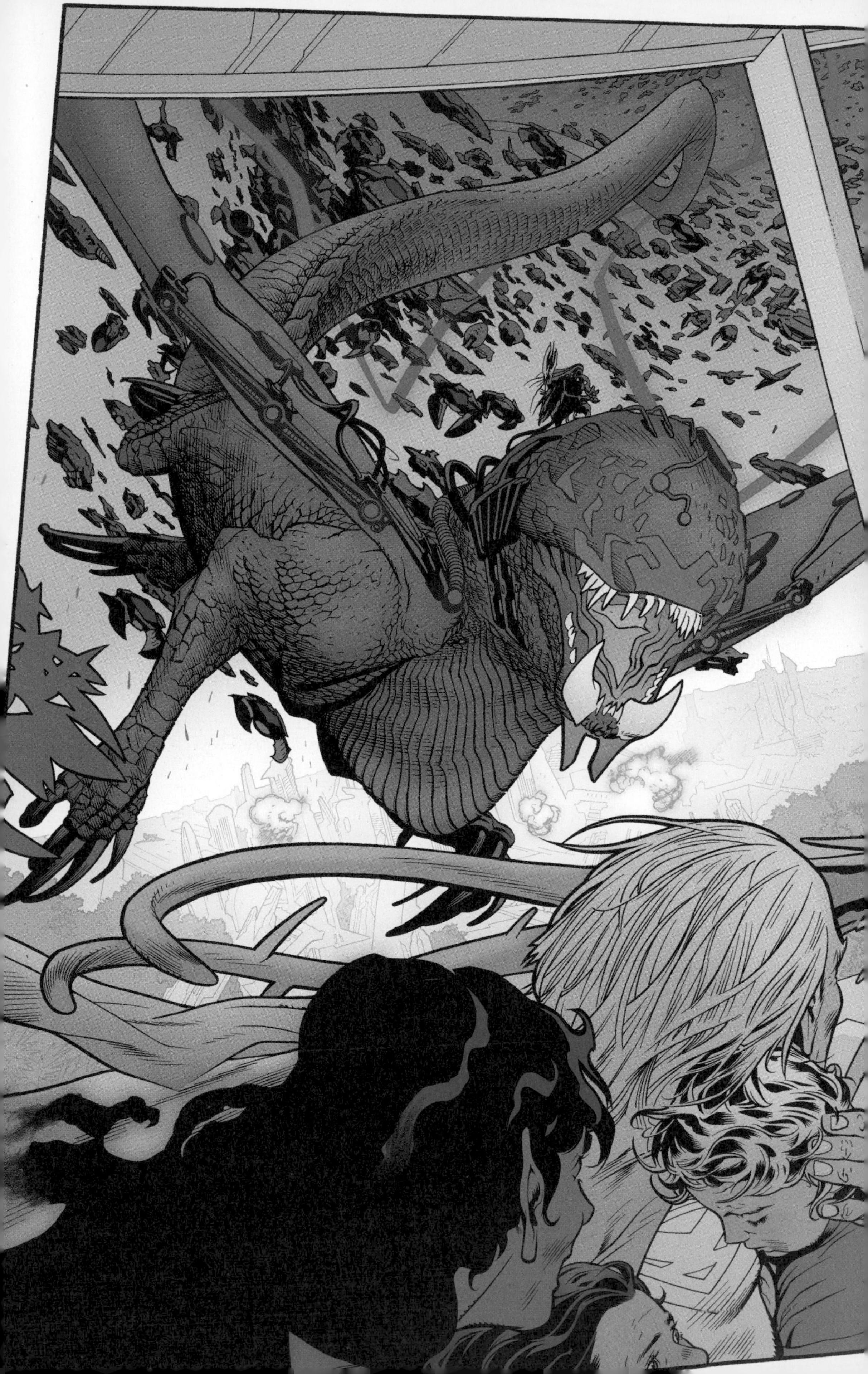

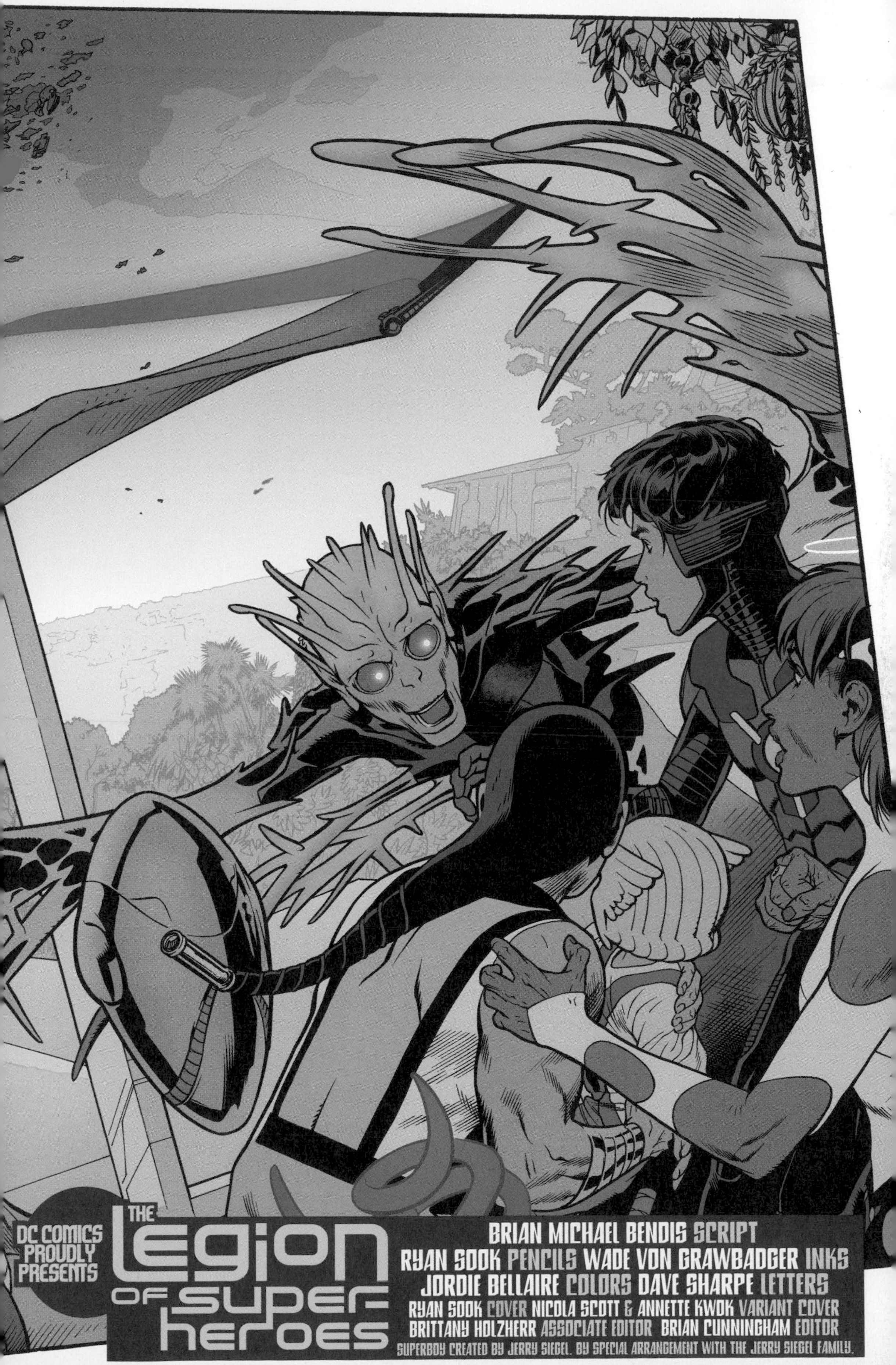
DC COMICS PROUDLY PRESENTS
THE LEGION OF SUPER-HEROES
BRIAN MICHAEL BENDIS SCRIPT
RYAN SOOK PENCILS WADE VON GRAWBADGER INKS
JORDIE BELLAIRE COLORS DAVE SHARPE LETTERS
RYAN SOOK COVER NICOLA SCOTT & ANNETTE KWOK VARIANT COVER
BRITTANY HOLZHERR ASSOCIATE EDITOR BRIAN CUNNINGHAM EDITOR
SUPERBOY CREATED BY JERRY SIEGEL. BY SPECIAL ARRANGEMENT WITH THE JERRY SIEGEL FAMILY.

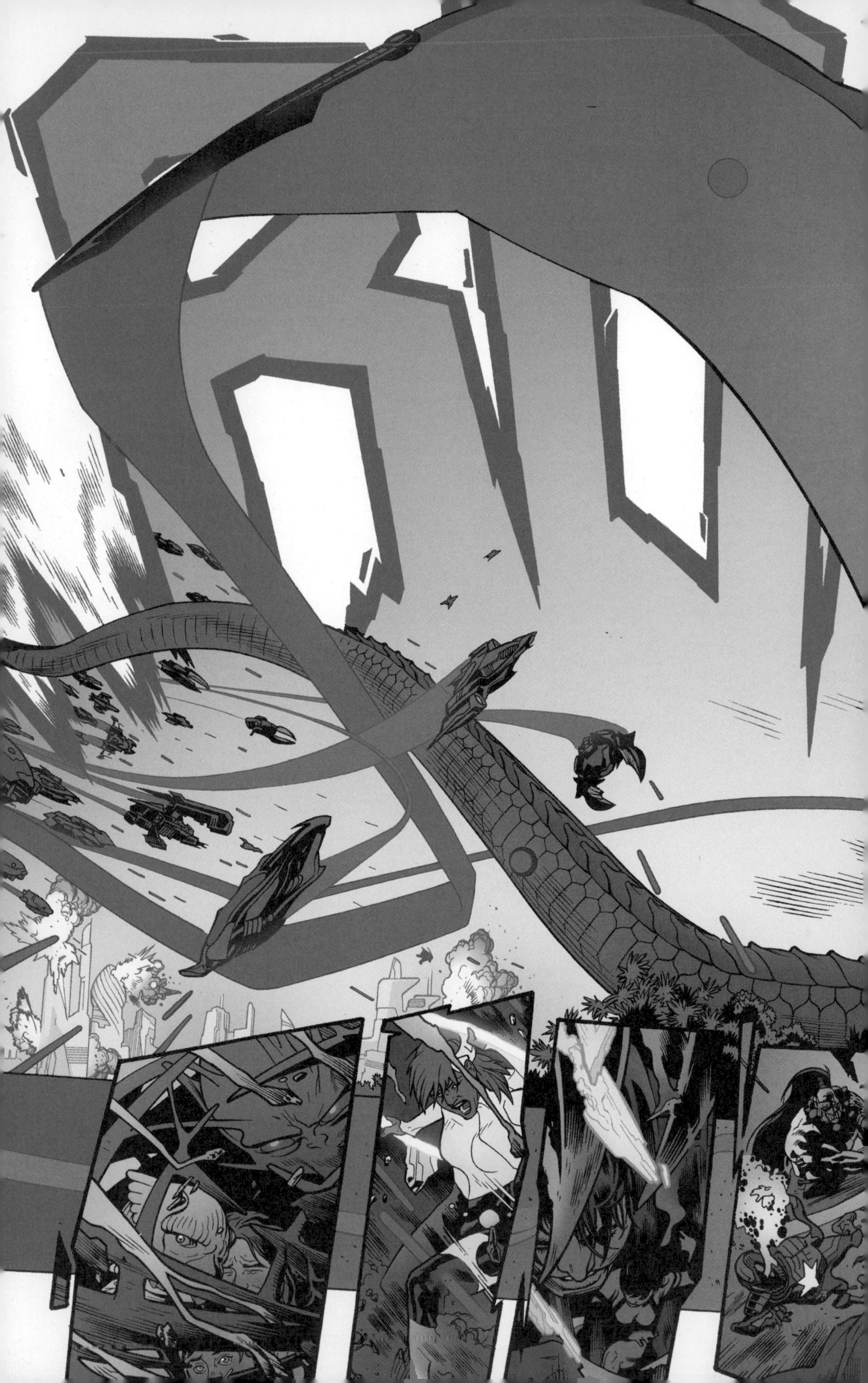

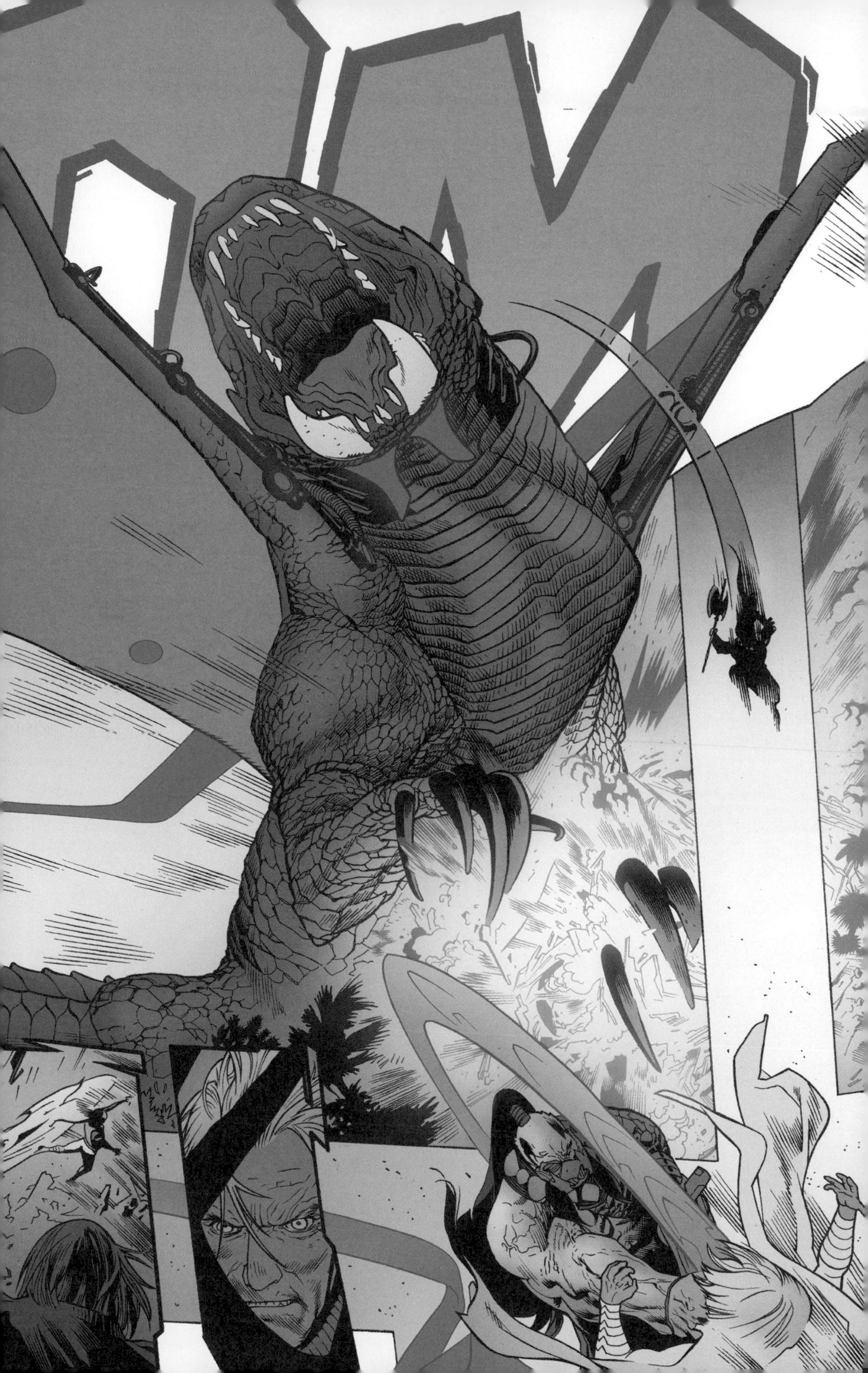

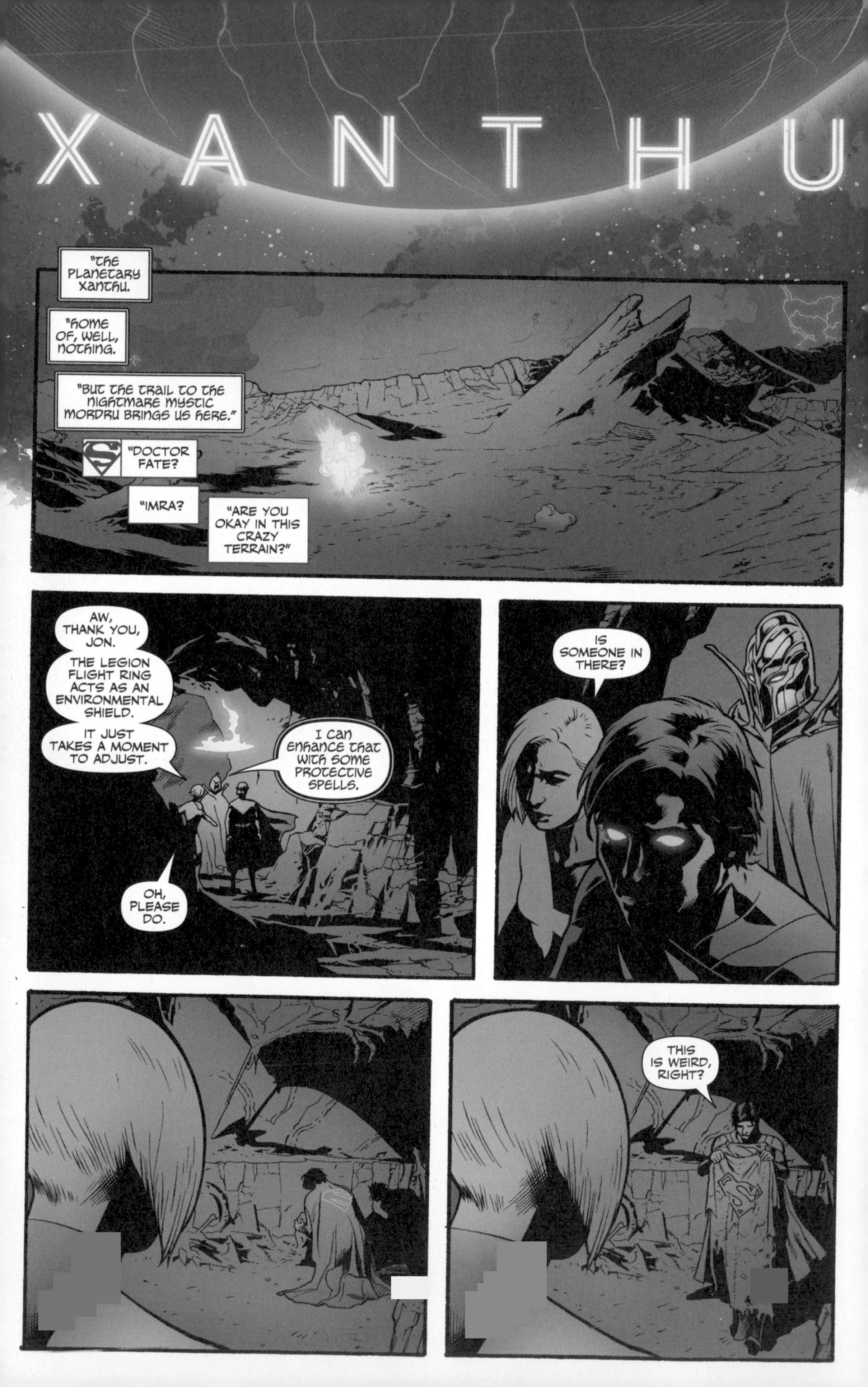
XANTHU
"THE PLANETARY XANTHU.
"HOME OF, WELL, NOTHING.
"BUT THE TRAIL TO THE NIGHTMARE MYSTIC MORDRU BRINGS US HERE."
"DOCTOR FATE?
"IMRA?
"ARE YOU OKAY IN THIS CRAZY TERRAIN?"
AW, THANK YOU, JON.
THE LEGION FLIGHT RING ACTS AS AN ENVIRONMENTAL SHIELD.
IT JUST TAKES A MOMENT TO ADJUST.
I CAN ENHANCE THAT WITH SOME PROTECTIVE SPELLS.
OH, PLEASE DO.
IS SOMEONE IN THERE?
THIS IS WEIRD, RIGHT?

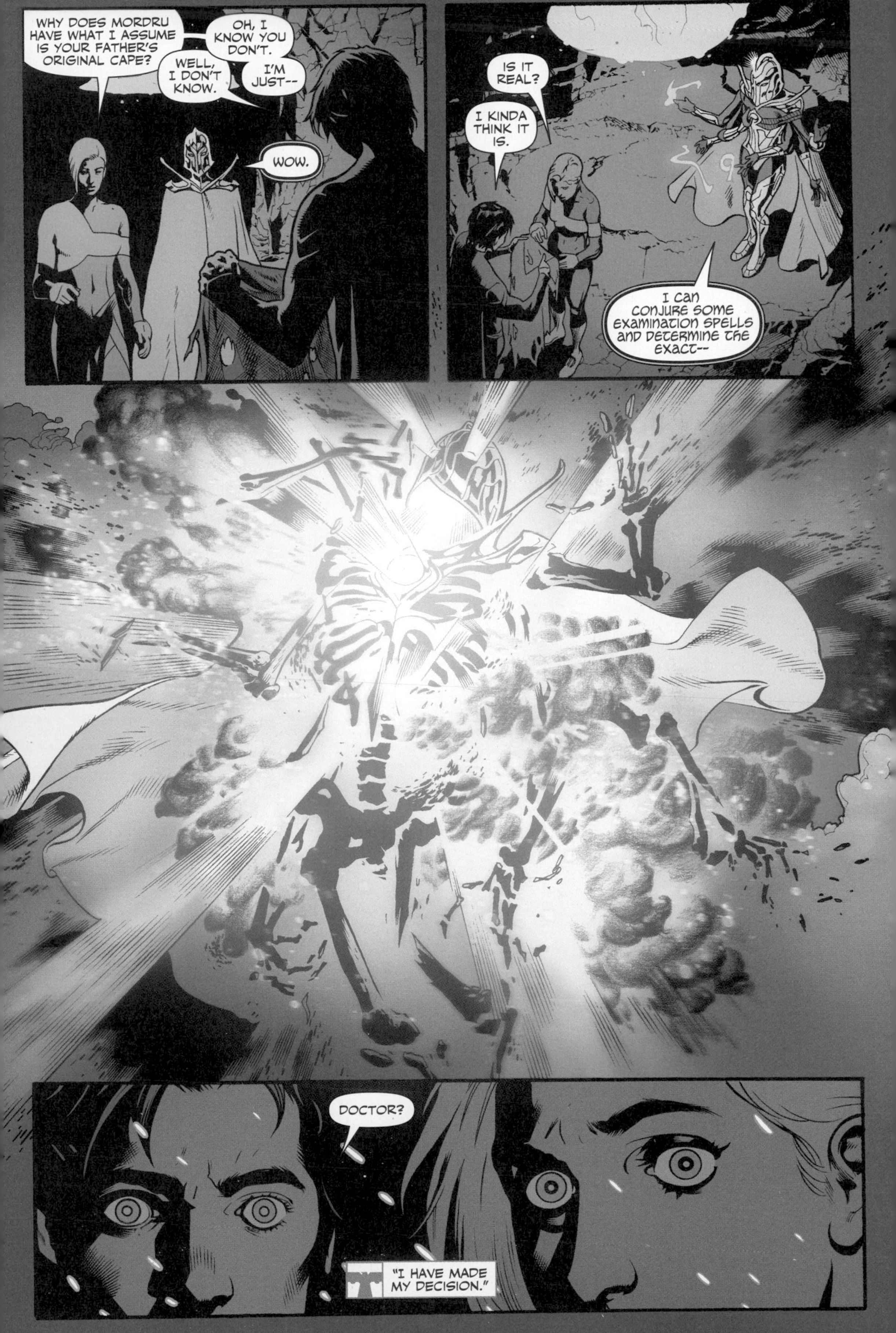
WHY DOES MORDRU HAVE WHAT I ASSUME IS YOUR FATHER'S ORIGINAL CAPE?
WELL, I DON'T KNOW.
OH, I KNOW YOU DON'T.
I'M JUST--
WOW.
IS IT REAL?
I KINDA THINK IT IS.
I CAN CONJURE SOME EXAMINATION SPELLS AND DETERMINE THE EXACT--
DOCTOR?
"I HAVE MADE MY DECISION."

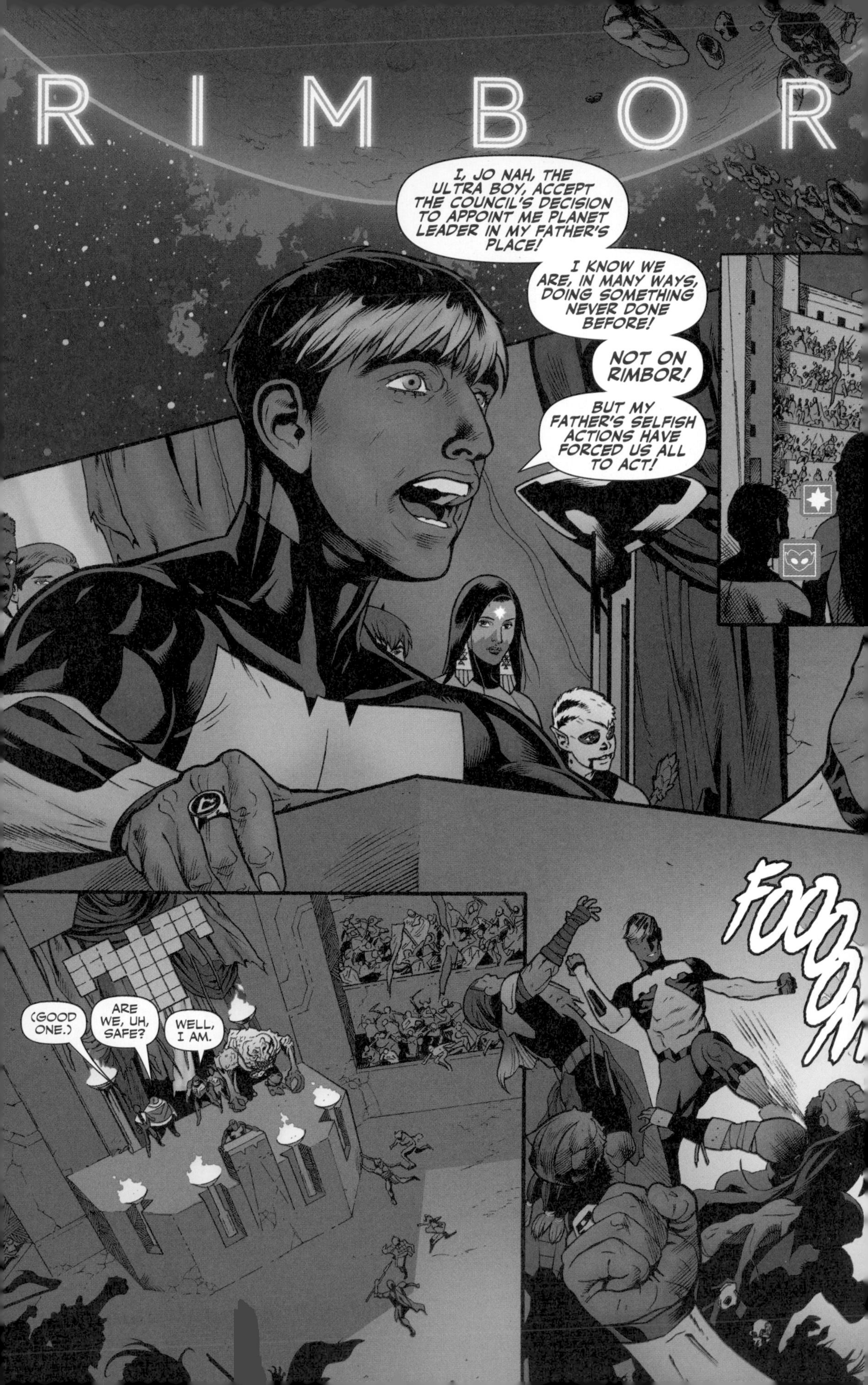
RIMBOR
I, JO NAH, THE ULTRA BOY, ACCEPT THE COUNCIL'S DECISION TO APPOINT ME PLANET LEADER IN MY FATHER'S PLACE!
I KNOW WE ARE, IN MANY WAYS, DOING SOMETHING NEVER DONE BEFORE!
NOT ON RIMBOR!
BUT MY FATHER'S SELFISH ACTIONS HAVE FORCED US ALL TO ACT!
FOOOOOM
(GOOD ONE.)
ARE WE, UH, SAFE?
WELL, I AM.

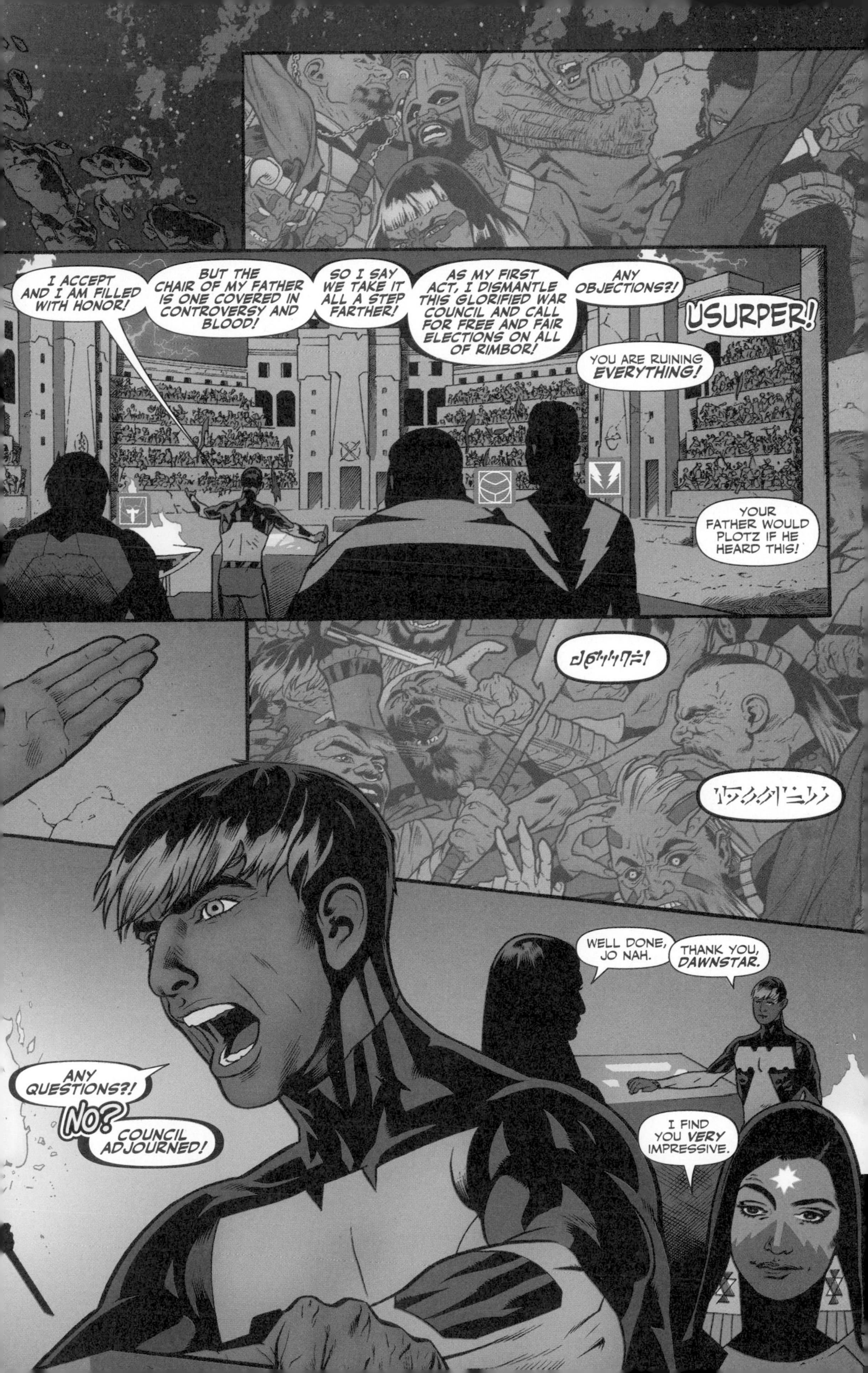
I ACCEPT AND I AM FILLED WITH HONOR!
BUT THE CHAIR OF MY FATHER IS ONE COVERED IN CONTROVERSY AND BLOOD!
SO I SAY WE TAKE IT ALL A STEP FARTHER!
AS MY FIRST ACT, I DISMANTLE THIS GLORIFIED WAR COUNCIL AND CALL FOR FREE AND FAIR ELECTIONS ON ALL OF RIMBOR!
ANY OBJECTIONS?!
USURPER!
YOU ARE RUINING EVERYTHING!
YOUR FATHER WOULD PLOTZ IF HE HEARD THIS!
ANY QUESTIONS?!
NO?
COUNCIL ADJOURNED!
WELL DONE, JO NAH.
THANK YOU, DAWNSTAR.
I FIND YOU VERY IMPRESSIVE.

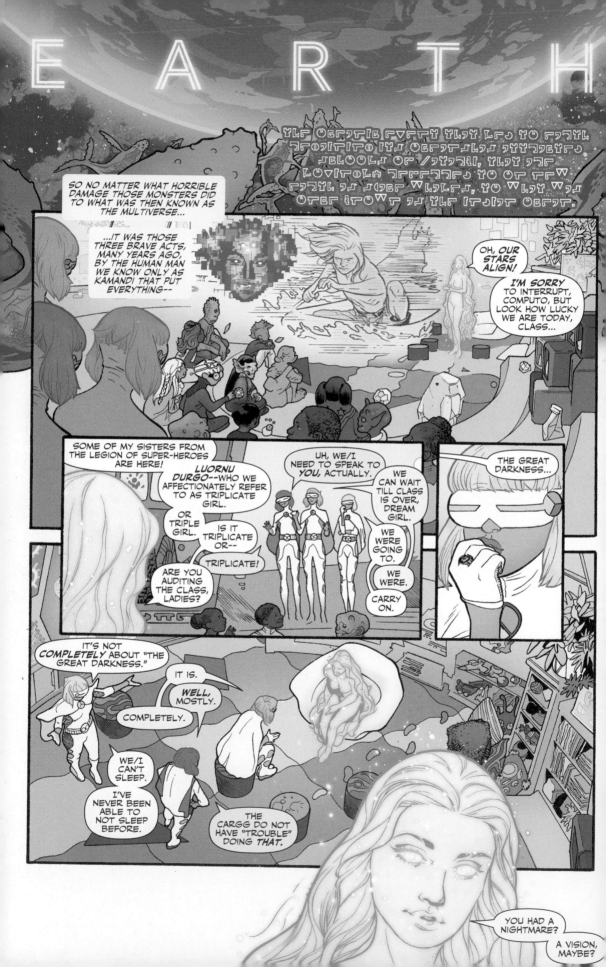

ᛏᛁᚠ ᚢᛖᚱᛏᛁᚠ ᚱᚢᛖᚱᛐ ᛐᛏᚠᛐ ᛐᛖᛐ ᛐᛟ ᚱᛐᛐᛁᛐ
ᛐᚱᛟᛁᛐᛁᛐᛟ ᛁᛐᛐ ᚢᛖᚱᛐᛁᛐᛐ ᛐᛐᛐᛐᛐᛖᛐᛐᛟ
ᛌᛖᛐᛟᛟᛐᛐ ᛟᚱ /ᛐᛐᛐᛐᛁ, ᛐᛐᛐᛐ ᛐᛐᚱ
ᛐᛟᛐᛁᛐᛟᛐᛐ ᛐᛐᛐᛐᛐᛐᛐ ᛐᛟ ᛟᚱ ᚱᚱᛐ
ᚱᛐᛐᛐ ᛐᛐ ᛐᛟᚱ ᛐᛐᛐᚱᛐ, ᛐᛟ ᛐᛐᛐ ᛐᛐ
ᛟᚱᚱ ᛁᚱᛟᛐᚱ ᛐᛐ ᛐᛏᚠ ᛁᚱᛐᛟᛏ ᚢᚱᛖᚱᛐ.

SO NO MATTER WHAT HORRIBLE DAMAGE THOSE MONSTERS DID TO WHAT WAS THEN KNOWN AS THE MULTIVERSE...

...IT WAS THOSE THREE BRAVE ACTS, MANY YEARS AGO, BY THE HUMAN MAN WE KNOW ONLY AS KAMANDI THAT PUT EVERYTHING--

OH, *OUR STARS ALIGN!*

I'M SORRY TO INTERRUPT, COMPUTO, BUT LOOK HOW LUCKY WE ARE TODAY, CLASS...

SOME OF MY SISTERS FROM THE LEGION OF SUPER-HEROES ARE HERE!

LUORNU DURGO--WHO WE AFFECTIONATELY REFER TO AS TRIPLICATE GIRL.

OR TRIPLE GIRL.

IS IT TRIPLICATE OR--

TRIPLICATE!

ARE YOU AUDITING THE CLASS, LADIES?

UH, WE/I NEED TO SPEAK TO *YOU*, ACTUALLY.

WE CAN WAIT TILL CLASS IS OVER, DREAM GIRL.

WE WERE GOING TO.

WE WERE.

CARRY ON.

THE GREAT DARKNESS...

IT'S NOT *COMPLETELY* ABOUT "THE GREAT DARKNESS."

IT IS.

WELL, MOSTLY.

COMPLETELY.

WE/I CAN'T SLEEP.

I'VE NEVER BEEN ABLE TO NOT SLEEP BEFORE.

THE CARGG DO NOT HAVE "TROUBLE" DOING *THAT*.

YOU HAD A NIGHTMARE?

A VISION, MAYBE?

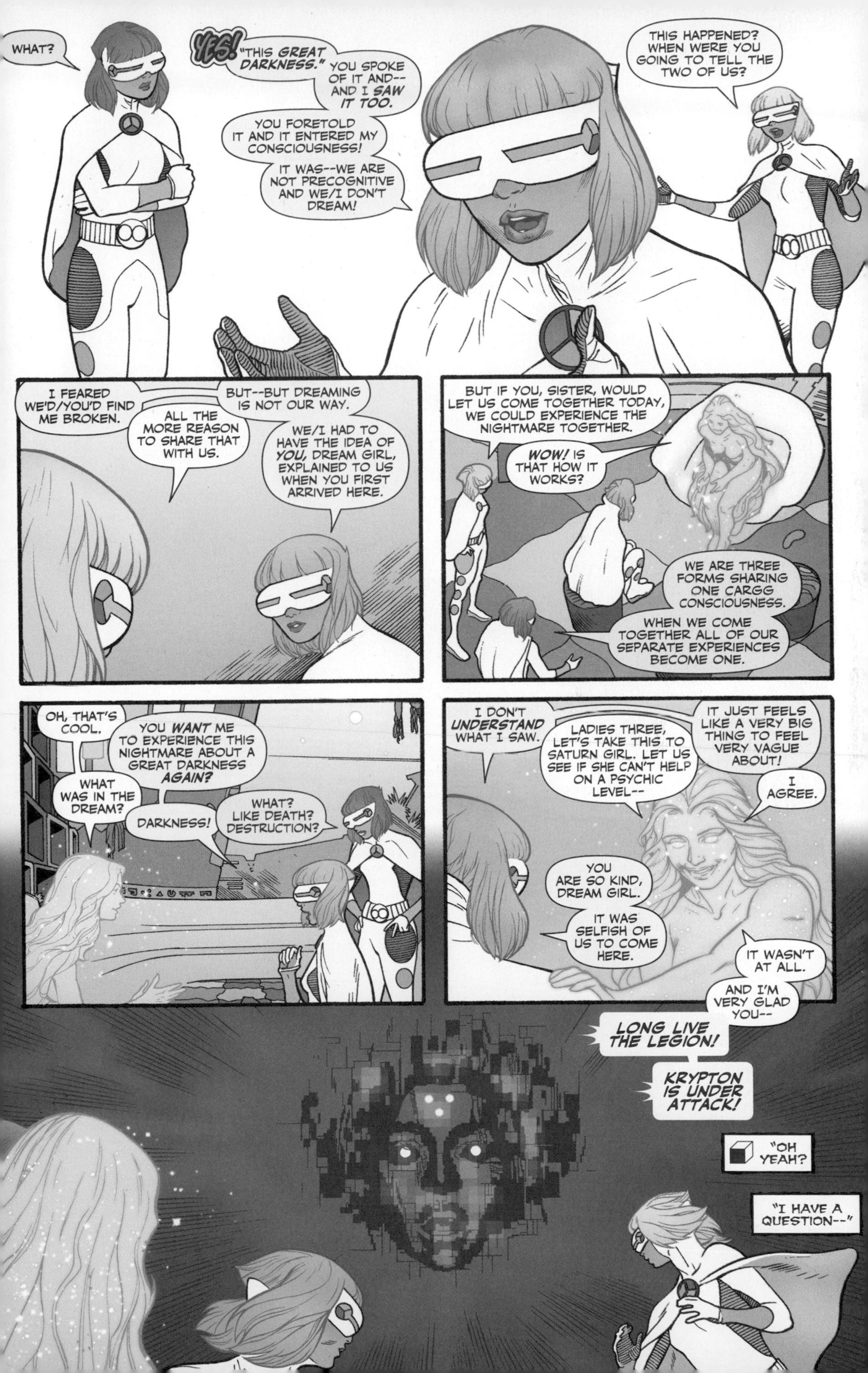
WHAT?
YES!
"THIS GREAT DARKNESS." YOU SPOKE OF IT AND-- AND I SAW IT TOO.
YOU FORETOLD IT AND IT ENTERED MY CONSCIOUSNESS!
IT WAS--WE ARE NOT PRECOGNITIVE AND WE/I DON'T DREAM!
THIS HAPPENED? WHEN WERE YOU GOING TO TELL THE TWO OF US?
I FEARED WE'D/YOU'D FIND ME BROKEN.
BUT--BUT DREAMING IS NOT OUR WAY.
ALL THE MORE REASON TO SHARE THAT WITH US.
WE/I HAD TO HAVE THE IDEA OF YOU, DREAM GIRL, EXPLAINED TO US WHEN YOU FIRST ARRIVED HERE.
BUT IF YOU, SISTER, WOULD LET US COME TOGETHER TODAY, WE COULD EXPERIENCE THE NIGHTMARE TOGETHER.
WOW! IS THAT HOW IT WORKS?
WE ARE THREE FORMS SHARING ONE CARGG CONSCIOUSNESS.
WHEN WE COME TOGETHER ALL OF OUR SEPARATE EXPERIENCES BECOME ONE.
OH, THAT'S COOL.
YOU WANT ME TO EXPERIENCE THIS NIGHTMARE ABOUT A GREAT DARKNESS AGAIN?
WHAT WAS IN THE DREAM?
DARKNESS!
WHAT? LIKE DEATH? DESTRUCTION?
I DON'T UNDERSTAND WHAT I SAW.
LADIES THREE, LET'S TAKE THIS TO SATURN GIRL. LET US SEE IF SHE CAN'T HELP ON A PSYCHIC LEVEL--
IT JUST FEELS LIKE A VERY BIG THING TO FEEL VERY VAGUE ABOUT!
I AGREE.
YOU ARE SO KIND, DREAM GIRL.
IT WAS SELFISH OF US TO COME HERE.
IT WASN'T AT ALL.
AND I'M VERY GLAD YOU--
LONG LIVE THE LEGION!
KRYPTON IS UNDER ATTACK!
"OH YEAH?
"I HAVE A QUESTION--"

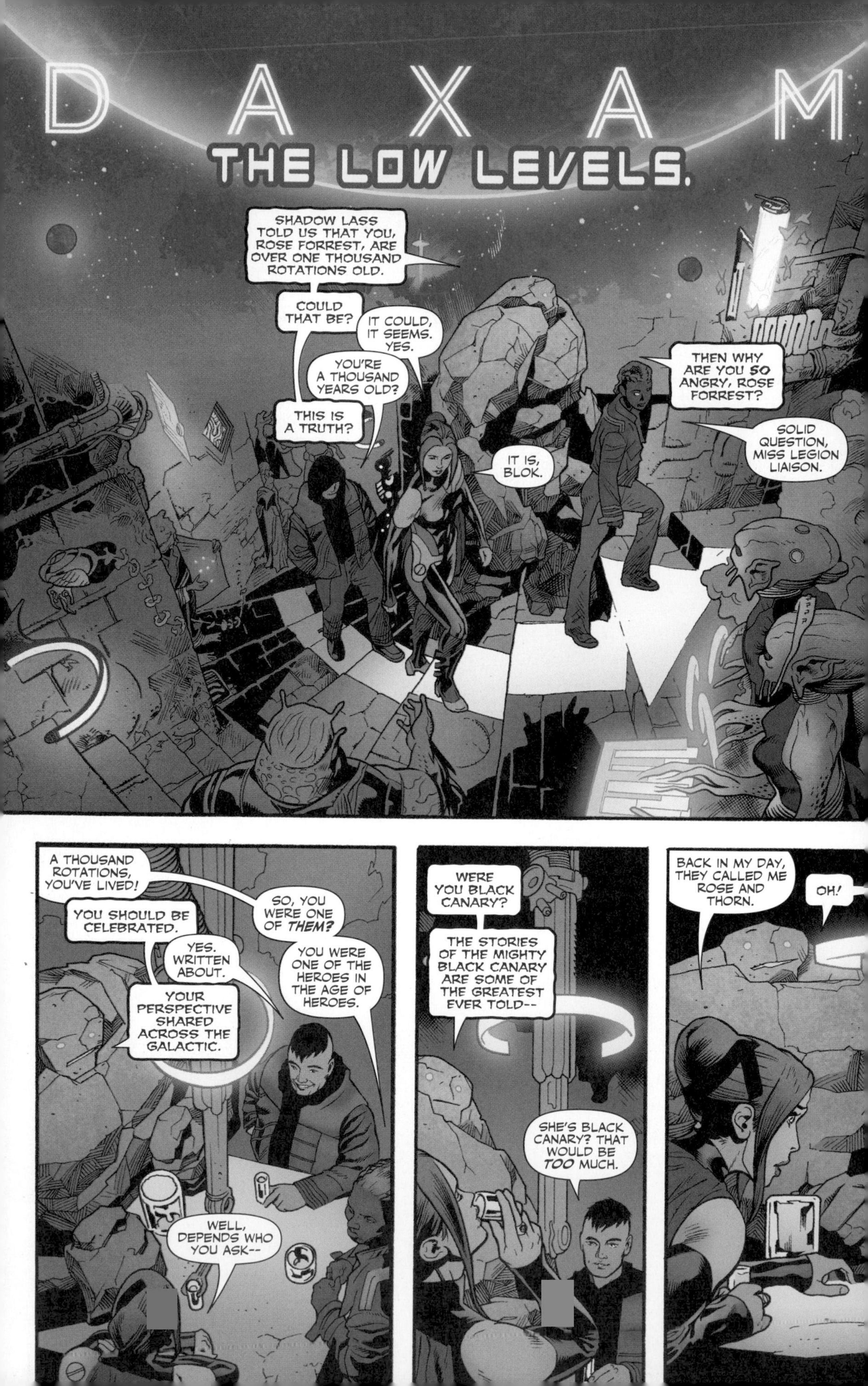
DAXAM
THE LOW LEVELS.
SHADOW LASS TOLD US THAT YOU, ROSE FORREST, ARE OVER ONE THOUSAND ROTATIONS OLD.
COULD THAT BE?
IT COULD, IT SEEMS. YES.
YOU'RE A THOUSAND YEARS OLD?
THIS IS A TRUTH?
IT IS, BLOK.
THEN WHY ARE YOU **SO** ANGRY, ROSE FORREST?
SOLID QUESTION, MISS LEGION LIAISON.
A THOUSAND ROTATIONS, YOU'VE LIVED!
YOU SHOULD BE CELEBRATED.
YES. WRITTEN ABOUT.
YOUR PERSPECTIVE SHARED ACROSS THE GALACTIC.
SO, YOU WERE ONE OF ***THEM?***
YOU WERE ONE OF THE HEROES IN THE AGE OF HEROES.
WELL, DEPENDS WHO YOU ASK--
WERE YOU BLACK CANARY?
THE STORIES OF THE MIGHTY BLACK CANARY ARE SOME OF THE GREATEST EVER TOLD--
SHE'S BLACK CANARY? THAT WOULD BE ***TOO*** MUCH.
BACK IN MY DAY, THEY CALLED ME ROSE AND THORN.
OH!

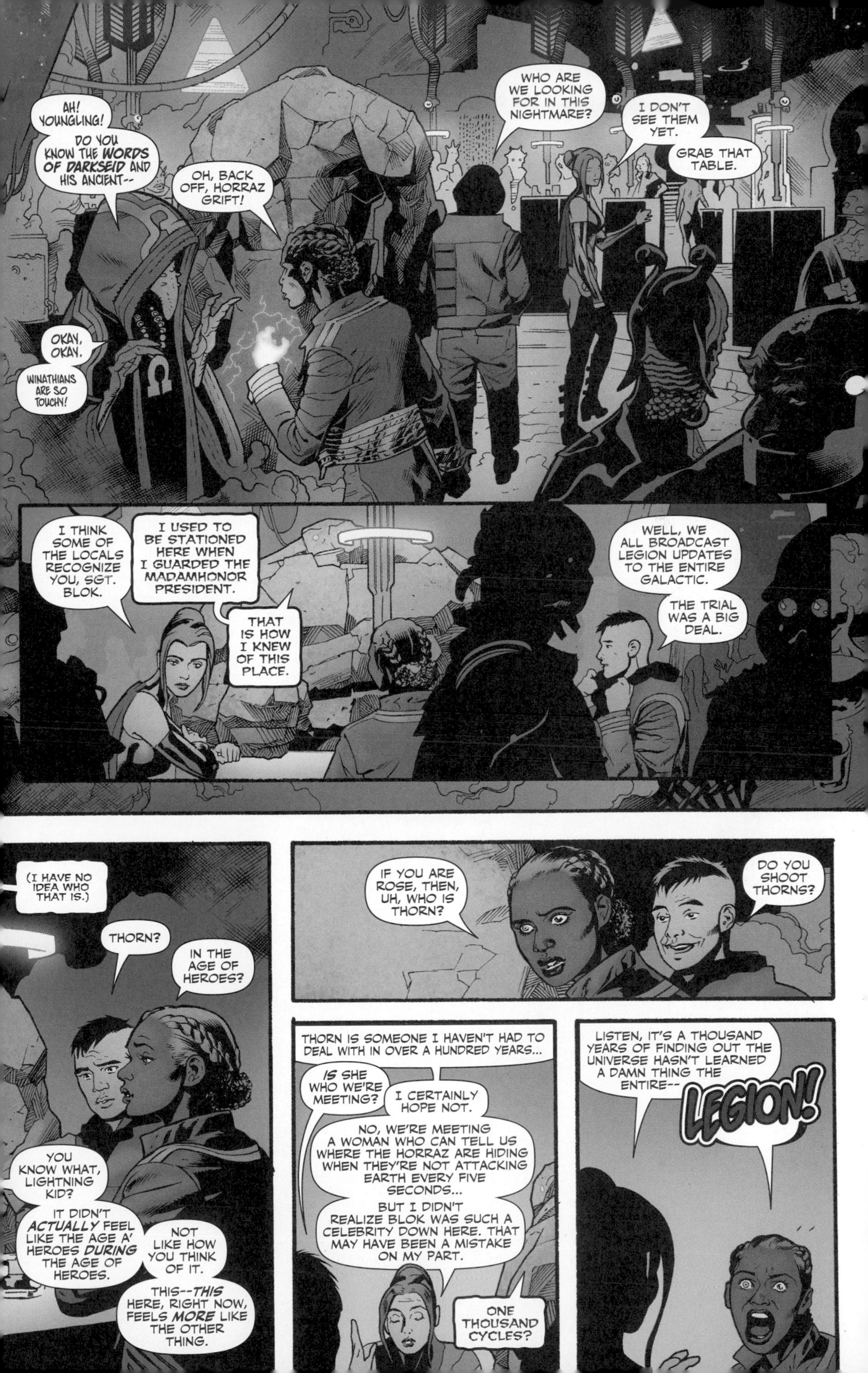
AH! YOUNGLING!
DO YOU KNOW THE WORDS OF DARKSEID AND HIS ANCIENT--
OH, BACK OFF, HORRAZ GRIFT!
OKAY, OKAY.
WINATHIANS ARE SO TOUCHY!
WHO ARE WE LOOKING FOR IN THIS NIGHTMARE?
I DON'T SEE THEM YET.
GRAB THAT TABLE.
I THINK SOME OF THE LOCALS RECOGNIZE YOU, SGT. BLOK.
I USED TO BE STATIONED HERE WHEN I GUARDED THE MADAMHONOR PRESIDENT.
THAT IS HOW I KNEW OF THIS PLACE.
WELL, WE ALL BROADCAST LEGION UPDATES TO THE ENTIRE GALACTIC.
THE TRIAL WAS A BIG DEAL.
IF YOU ARE ROSE, THEN, UH, WHO IS THORN?
DO YOU SHOOT THORNS?
(I HAVE NO IDEA WHO THAT IS.)
THORN?
IN THE AGE OF HEROES?
YOU KNOW WHAT, LIGHTNING KID?
IT DIDN'T ACTUALLY FEEL LIKE THE AGE A' HEROES DURING THE AGE OF HEROES.
NOT LIKE HOW YOU THINK OF IT.
THIS--THIS HERE, RIGHT NOW, FEELS MORE LIKE THE OTHER THING.
THORN IS SOMEONE I HAVEN'T HAD TO DEAL WITH IN OVER A HUNDRED YEARS...
IS SHE WHO WE'RE MEETING?
I CERTAINLY HOPE NOT.
NO, WE'RE MEETING A WOMAN WHO CAN TELL US WHERE THE HORRAZ ARE HIDING WHEN THEY'RE NOT ATTACKING EARTH EVERY FIVE SECONDS...
BUT I DIDN'T REALIZE BLOK WAS SUCH A CELEBRITY DOWN HERE. THAT MAY HAVE BEEN A MISTAKE ON MY PART.
ONE THOUSAND CYCLES?
LISTEN, IT'S A THOUSAND YEARS OF FINDING OUT THE UNIVERSE HASN'T LEARNED A DAMN THING THE ENTIRE--
LEGION!

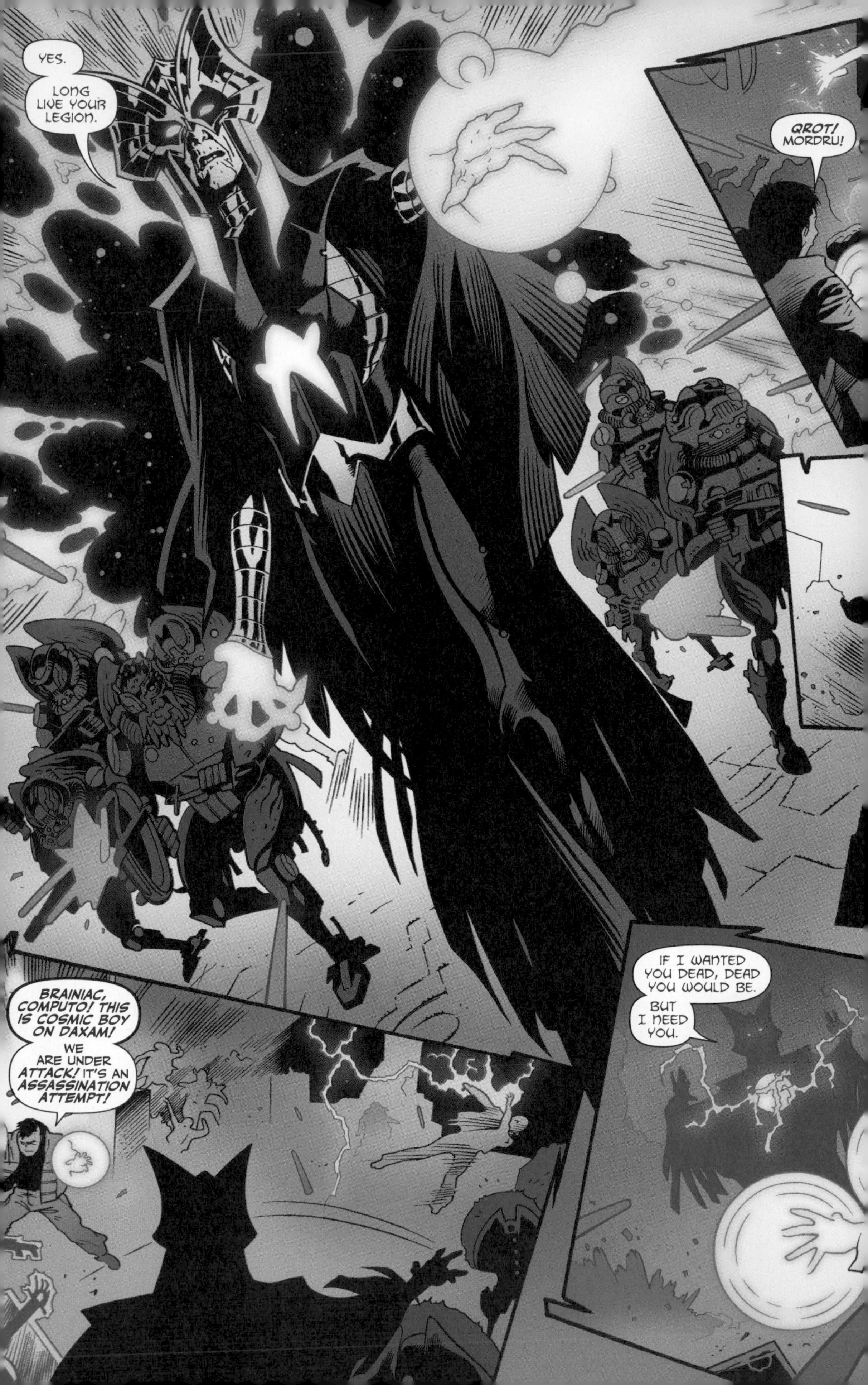
YES.
LONG LIVE YOUR LEGION.
QROT! MORDRU!
BRAINIAC, COMPUTO! THIS IS COSMIC BOY ON DAXAM!
WE ARE UNDER ATTACK! IT'S AN ASSASSINATION ATTEMPT!
IF I WANTED YOU DEAD, DEAD YOU WOULD BE.
BUT I NEED YOU.

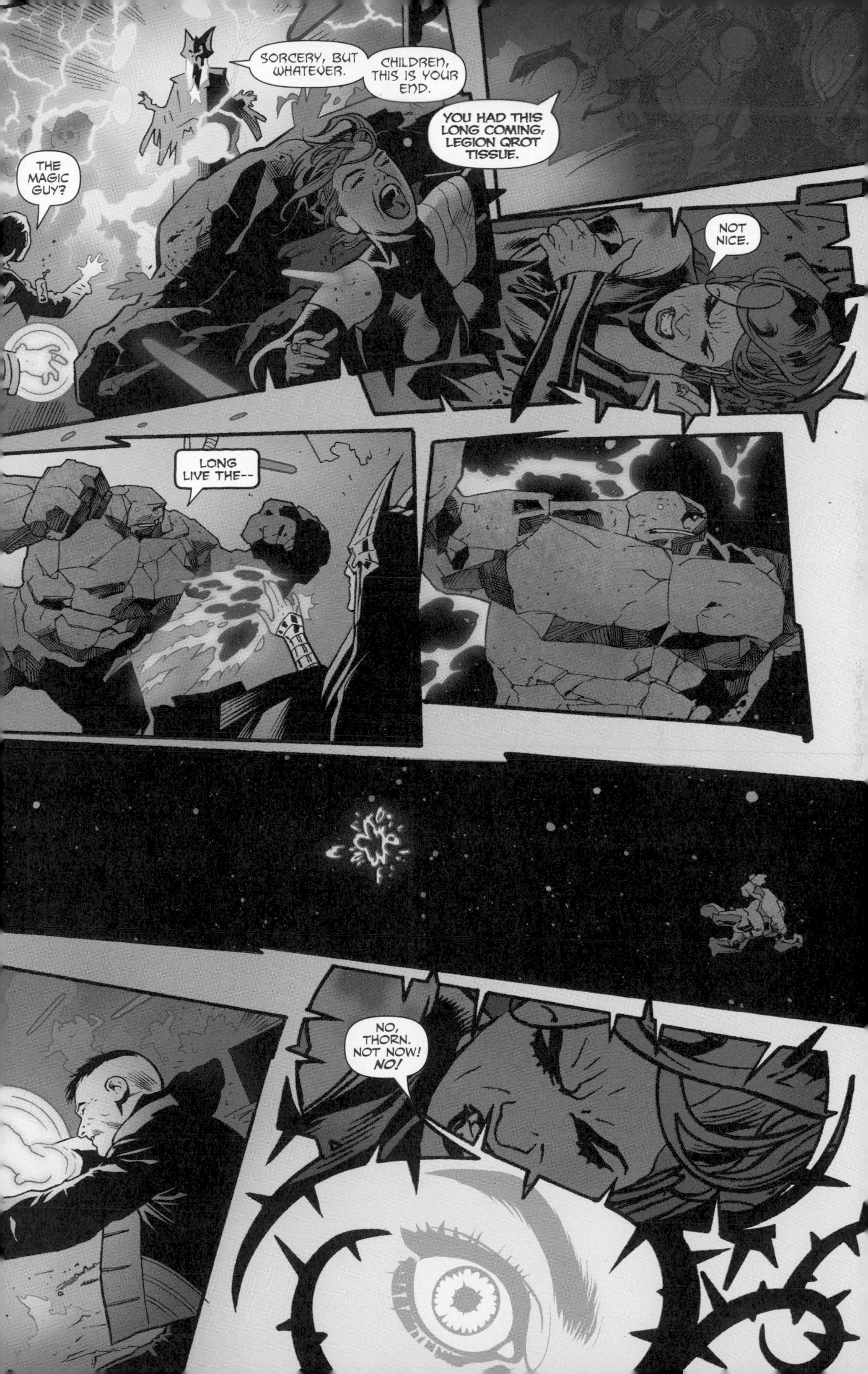
SORCERY, BUT WHATEVER.
CHILDREN, THIS IS YOUR END.
YOU HAD THIS LONG COMING, LEGION QROT TISSUE.
THE MAGIC GUY?
NOT NICE.
LONG LIVE THE--
NO, THORN. NOT NOW! NO!

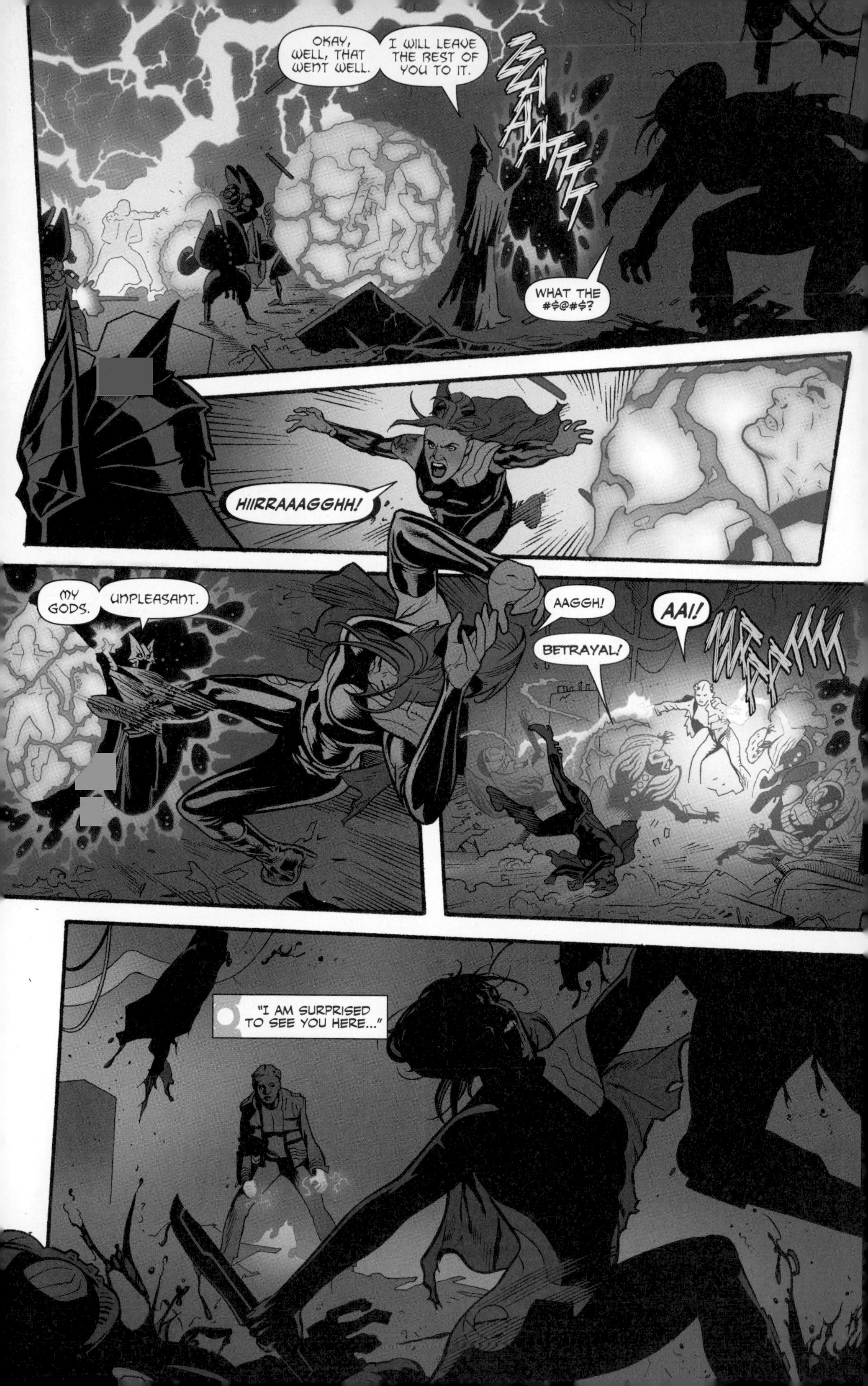
OKAY, WELL, THAT WENT WELL.
I WILL LEAVE THE REST OF YOU TO IT.
WHAT THE #$@#$?
HIIRRAAAGGHH!
MY GODS.
UNPLEASANT.
AAGGH!
BETRAYAL!
AAI!
"I AM SURPRISED TO SEE YOU HERE..."

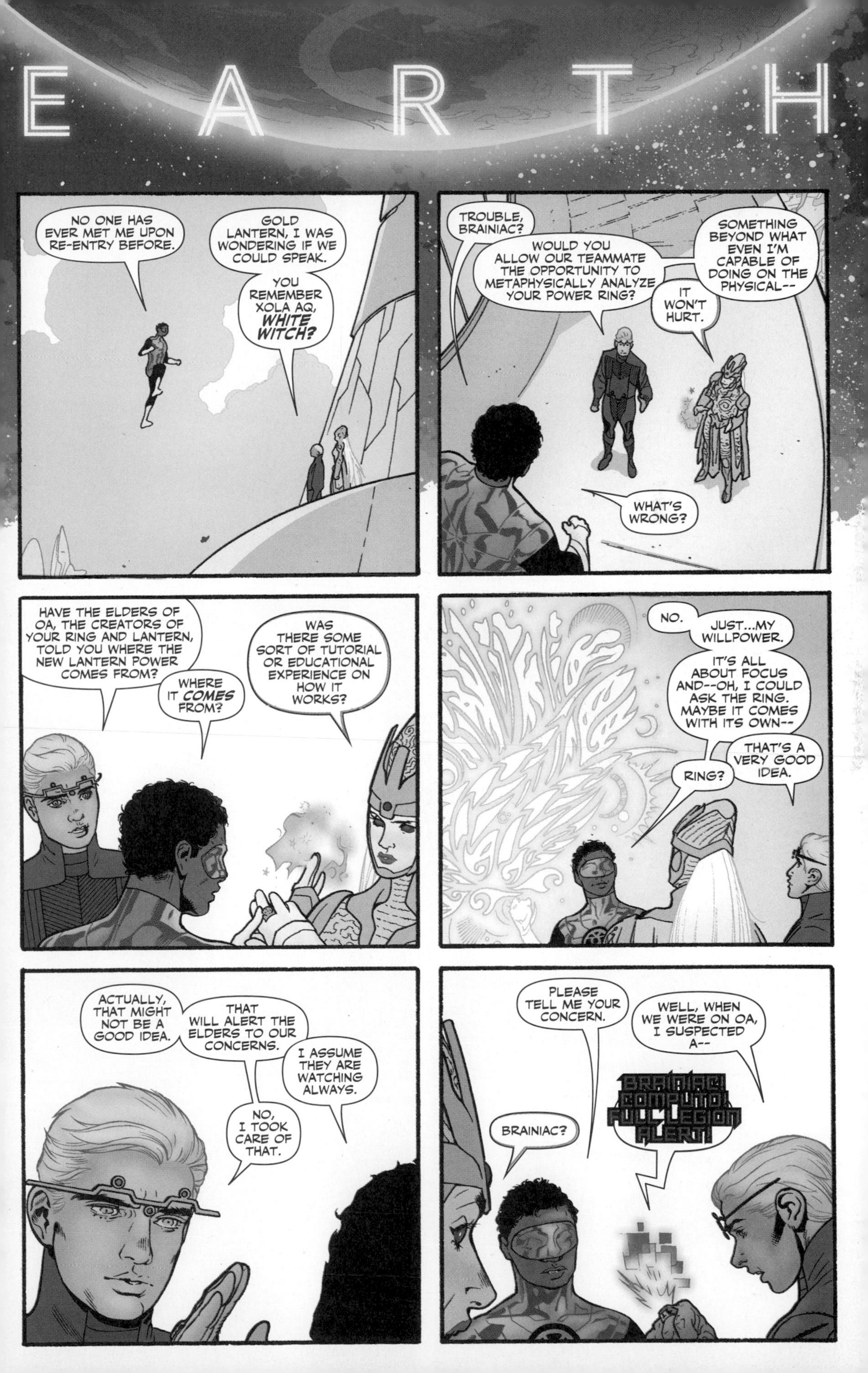
EARTH
NO ONE HAS EVER MET ME UPON RE-ENTRY BEFORE.
GOLD LANTERN, I WAS WONDERING IF WE COULD SPEAK.
YOU REMEMBER XOLA AQ, *WHITE WITCH?*
TROUBLE, BRAINIAC?
WOULD YOU ALLOW OUR TEAMMATE THE OPPORTUNITY TO METAPHYSICALLY ANALYZE YOUR POWER RING?
SOMETHING BEYOND WHAT EVEN I'M CAPABLE OF DOING ON THE PHYSICAL--
IT WON'T HURT.
WHAT'S WRONG?
HAVE THE ELDERS OF OA, THE CREATORS OF YOUR RING AND LANTERN, TOLD YOU WHERE THE NEW LANTERN POWER COMES FROM?
WHERE IT *COMES* FROM?
WAS THERE SOME SORT OF TUTORIAL OR EDUCATIONAL EXPERIENCE ON HOW IT WORKS?
NO.
JUST...MY WILLPOWER.
IT'S ALL ABOUT FOCUS AND--OH, I COULD ASK THE RING. MAYBE IT COMES WITH ITS OWN--
RING?
THAT'S A VERY GOOD IDEA.
ACTUALLY, THAT MIGHT NOT BE A GOOD IDEA.
THAT WILL ALERT THE ELDERS TO OUR CONCERNS.
I ASSUME THEY ARE WATCHING ALWAYS.
NO, I TOOK CARE OF THAT.
PLEASE TELL ME YOUR CONCERN.
WELL, WHEN WE WERE ON OA, I SUSPECTED A--
BRAINIAC?
BRAINIAC! COMPUTO! FULL LEGION ALERT!

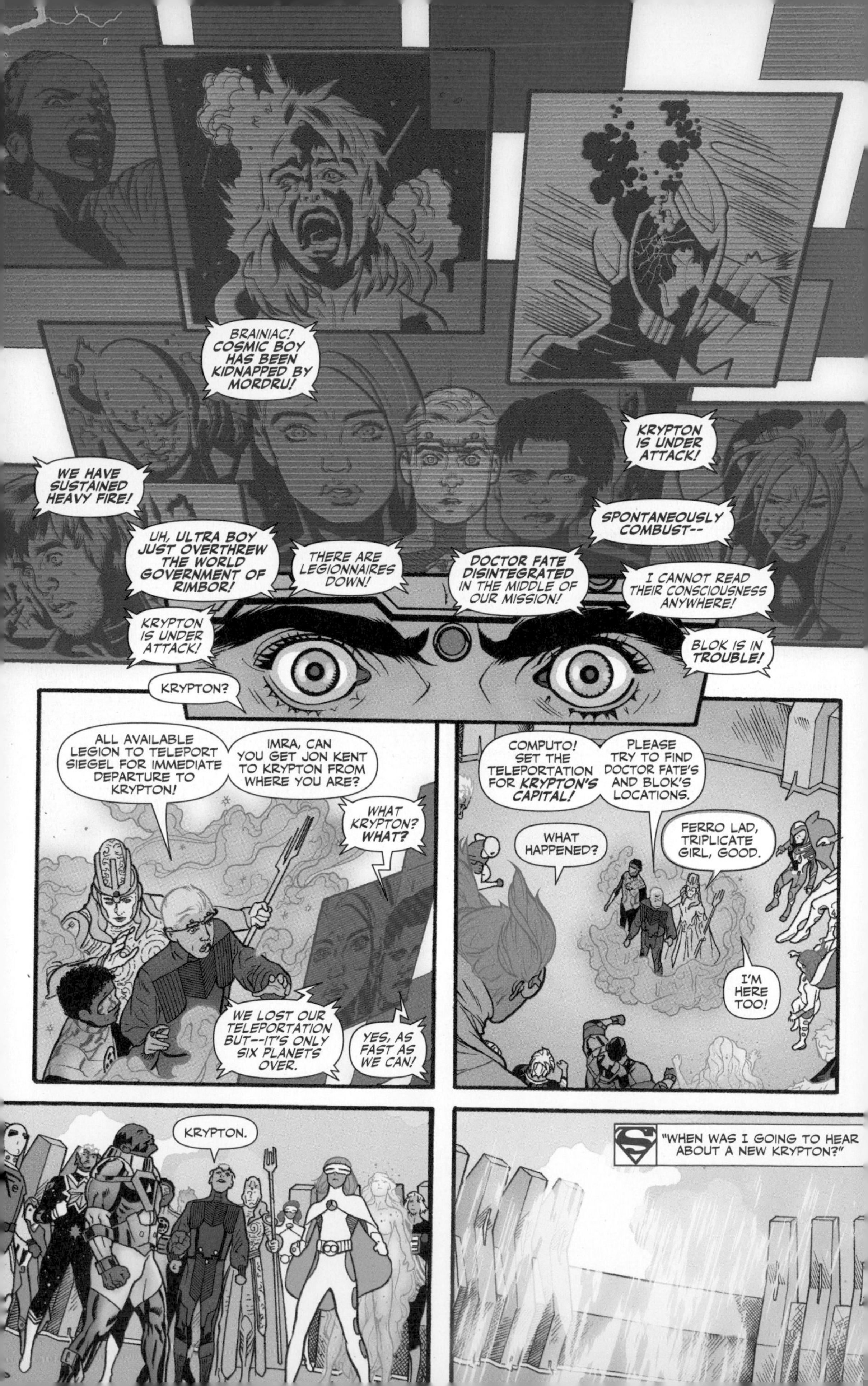
BRAINIAC! COSMIC BOY HAS BEEN KIDNAPPED BY MORDRU!
KRYPTON IS UNDER ATTACK!
WE HAVE SUSTAINED HEAVY FIRE!
SPONTANEOUSLY COMBUST--
UH, ULTRA BOY JUST OVERTHREW THE WORLD GOVERNMENT OF RIMBOR!
THERE ARE LEGIONNAIRES DOWN!
DOCTOR FATE DISINTEGRATED IN THE MIDDLE OF OUR MISSION!
I CANNOT READ THEIR CONSCIOUSNESS ANYWHERE!
KRYPTON IS UNDER ATTACK!
BLOK IS IN TROUBLE!
KRYPTON?
ALL AVAILABLE LEGION TO TELEPORT SIEGEL FOR IMMEDIATE DEPARTURE TO KRYPTON!
IMRA, CAN YOU GET JON KENT TO KRYPTON FROM WHERE YOU ARE?
WHAT KRYPTON? WHAT?
WE LOST OUR TELEPORTATION BUT--IT'S ONLY SIX PLANETS OVER.
YES, AS FAST AS WE CAN!
COMPUTO! SET THE TELEPORTATION FOR KRYPTON'S CAPITAL!
PLEASE TRY TO FIND DOCTOR FATE'S AND BLOK'S LOCATIONS.
WHAT HAPPENED?
FERRO LAD, TRIPLICATE GIRL, GOOD.
I'M HERE TOO!
KRYPTON.
"WHEN WAS I GOING TO HEAR ABOUT A NEW KRYPTON?"

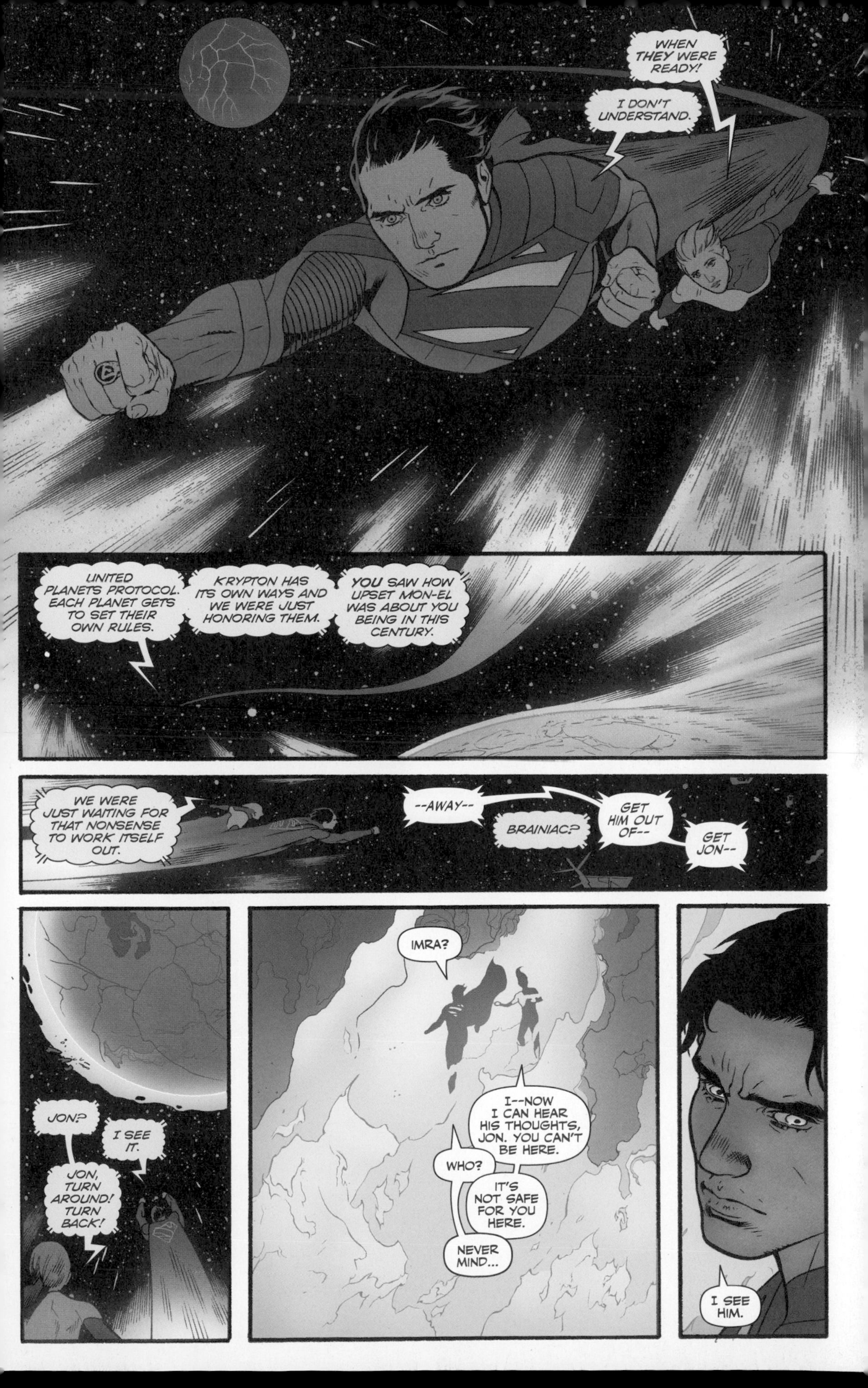
WHEN THEY WERE READY!
I DON'T UNDERSTAND.
UNITED PLANETS PROTOCOL. EACH PLANET GETS TO SET THEIR OWN RULES.
KRYPTON HAS ITS OWN WAYS AND WE WERE JUST HONORING THEM.
YOU SAW HOW UPSET MON-EL WAS ABOUT YOU BEING IN THIS CENTURY.
WE WERE JUST WAITING FOR THAT NONSENSE TO WORK ITSELF OUT.
--AWAY--
BRAINIAC?
GET HIM OUT OF--
GET JON--
JON?
I SEE IT.
JON, TURN AROUND! TURN BACK!
IMRA?
I--NOW I CAN HEAR HIS THOUGHTS, JON. YOU CAN'T BE HERE.
WHO?
IT'S NOT SAFE FOR YOU HERE.
NEVER MIND...
I SEE HIM.

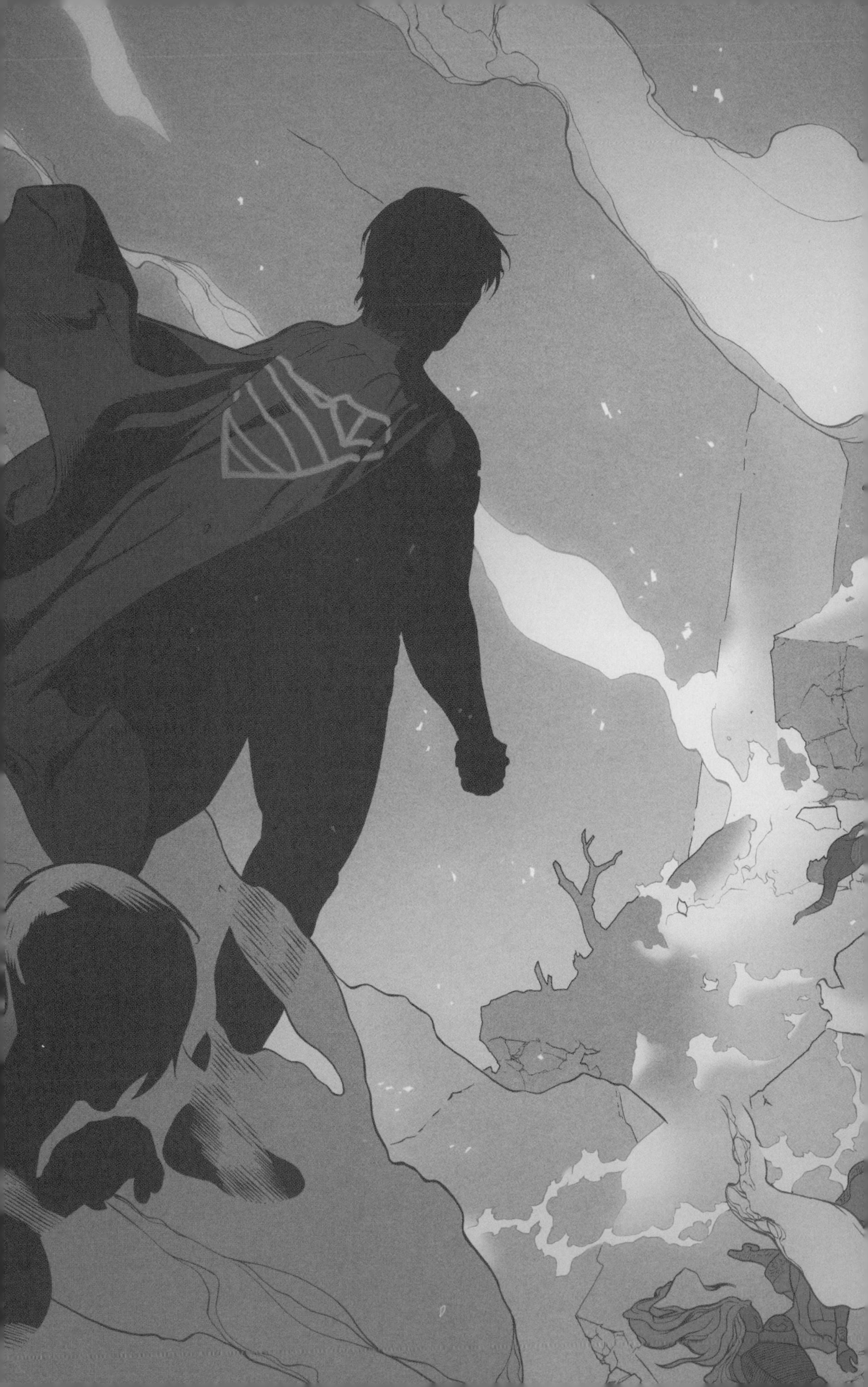

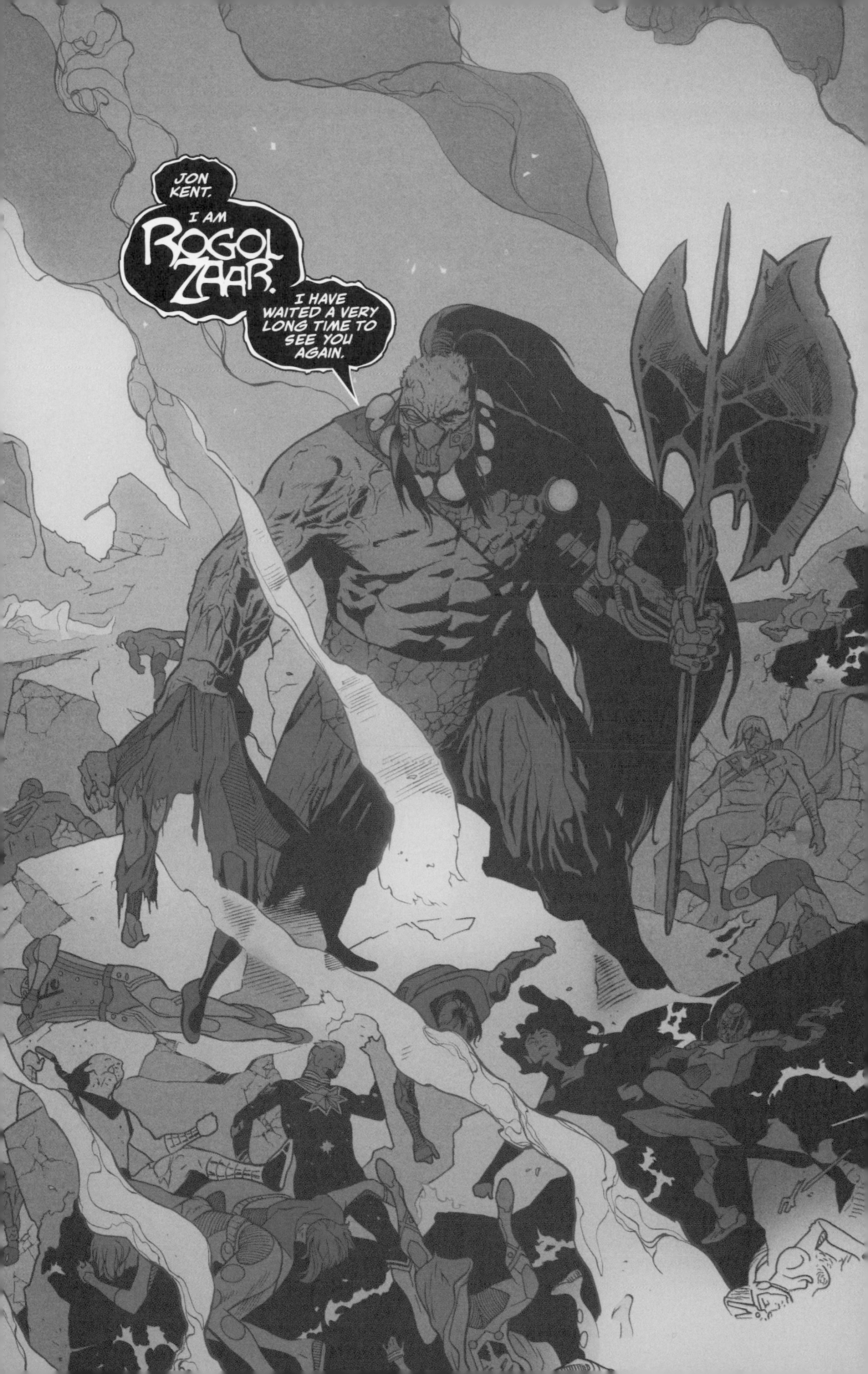
JON KENT.
I AM ROGOL ZAAR.
I HAVE WAITED A VERY LONG TIME TO SEE YOU AGAIN.

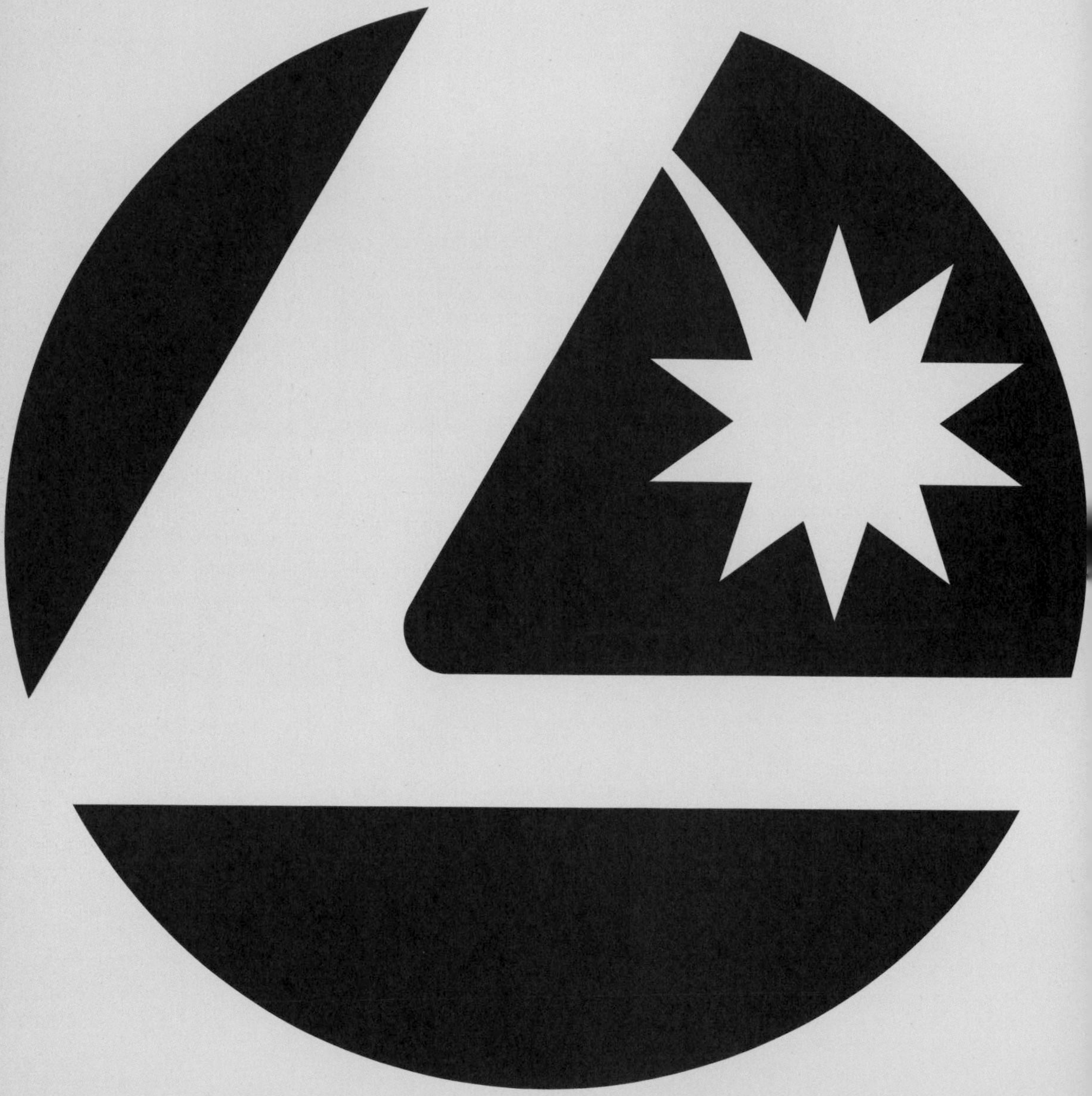

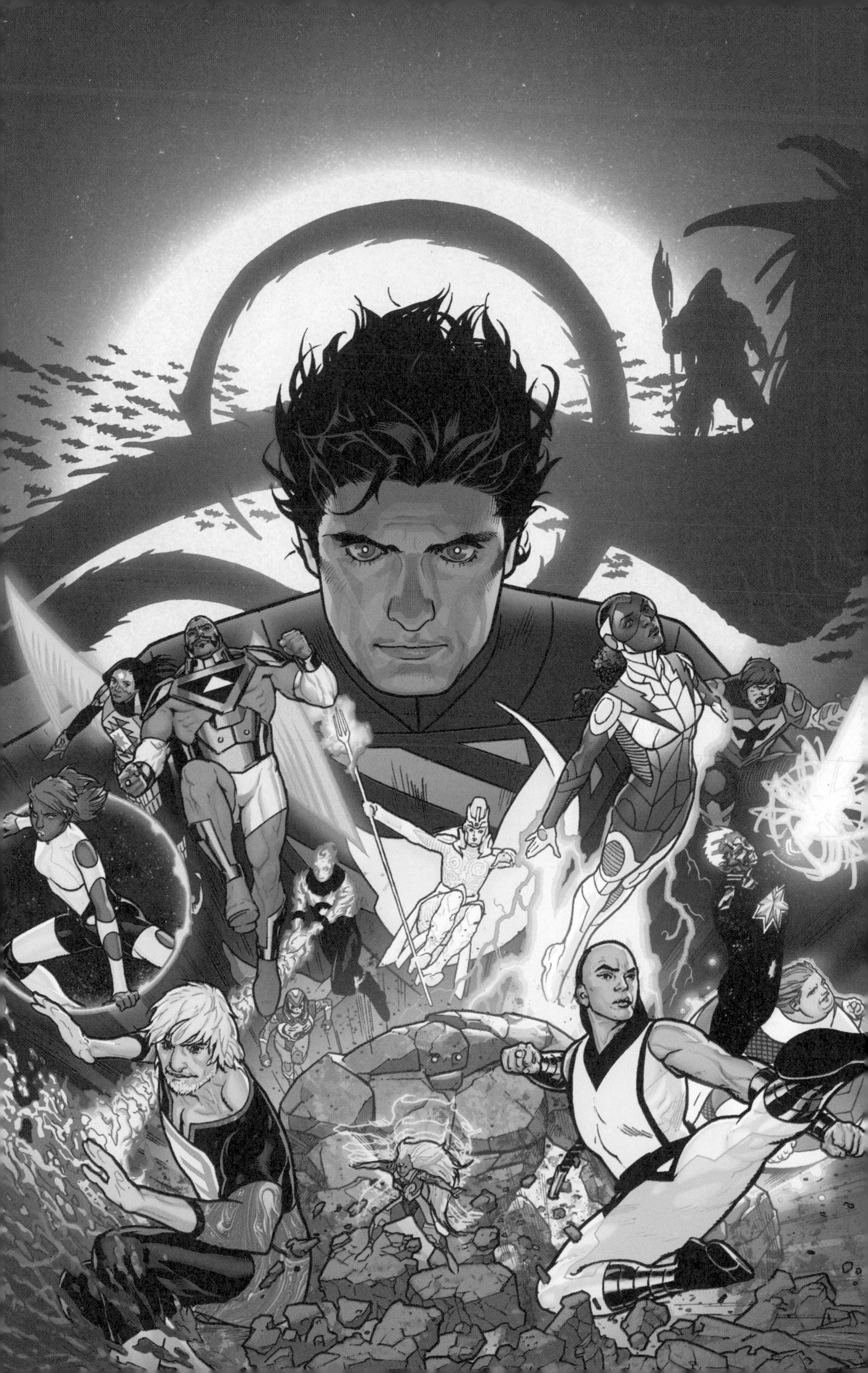

RYAN SOOK
Cover Artist

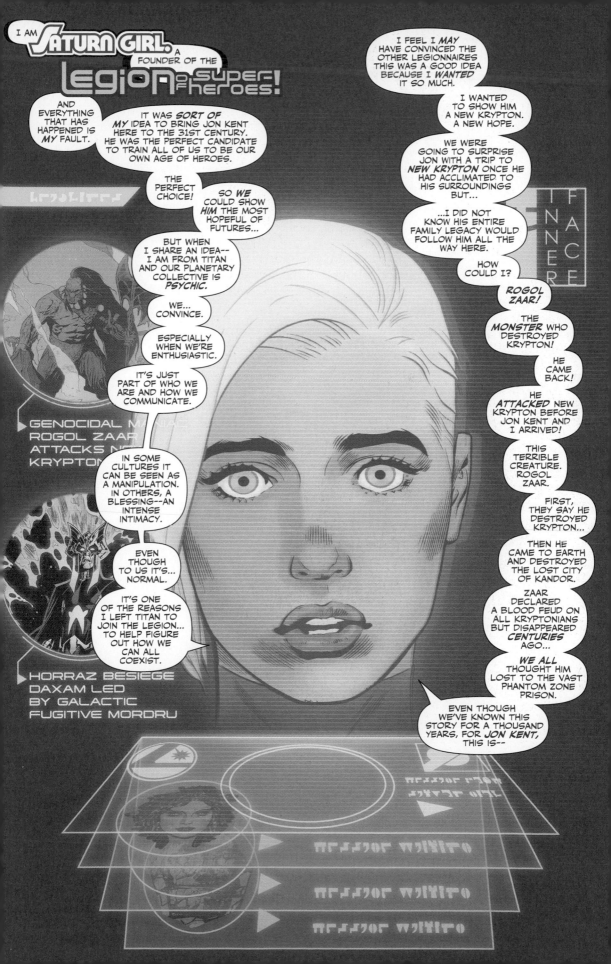

I AM **SATURN GIRL**, A FOUNDER OF THE **LEGION** OF **SUPER HEROES!**

AND EVERYTHING THAT HAS HAPPENED IS **MY** FAULT.

IT WAS **SORT OF MY** IDEA TO BRING JON KENT HERE TO THE 31ST CENTURY. HE WAS THE PERFECT CANDIDATE TO TRAIN ALL OF US TO BE OUR OWN AGE OF HEROES.

THE PERFECT CHOICE!

SO **WE** COULD SHOW **HIM** THE MOST HOPEFUL OF FUTURES...

BUT WHEN I SHARE AN IDEA-- I AM FROM TITAN AND OUR PLANETARY COLLECTIVE IS **PSYCHIC.**

WE... CONVINCE.

ESPECIALLY WHEN WE'RE ENTHUSIASTIC.

IT'S JUST PART OF WHO WE ARE AND HOW WE COMMUNICATE.

IN SOME CULTURES IT CAN BE SEEN AS A MANIPULATION. IN OTHERS, A BLESSING--AN INTENSE INTIMACY.

EVEN THOUGH TO US IT'S... NORMAL.

IT'S ONE OF THE REASONS I LEFT TITAN TO JOIN THE LEGION... TO HELP FIGURE OUT HOW WE CAN ALL COEXIST.

▶ GENOCIDAL MANIAC ROGOL ZAAR ATTACKS NEW KRYPTON

▶ HORRAZ BESIEGE DAXAM LED BY GALACTIC FUGITIVE MORDRU

I FEEL I **MAY** HAVE CONVINCED THE OTHER LEGIONNAIRES THIS WAS A GOOD IDEA BECAUSE I **WANTED** IT SO MUCH.

I WANTED TO SHOW HIM A NEW KRYPTON. A NEW HOPE.

WE WERE GOING TO SURPRISE JON WITH A TRIP TO **NEW KRYPTON** ONCE HE HAD ACCLIMATED TO HIS SURROUNDINGS BUT...

...I DID NOT KNOW HIS ENTIRE FAMILY LEGACY WOULD FOLLOW HIM ALL THE WAY HERE.

HOW COULD I?

ROGOL ZAAR!

THE **MONSTER** WHO DESTROYED KRYPTON!

HE CAME BACK!

HE **ATTACKED** NEW KRYPTON BEFORE JON KENT AND I ARRIVED!

THIS TERRIBLE CREATURE. ROGOL ZAAR.

FIRST, THEY SAY HE DESTROYED KRYPTON...

THEN HE CAME TO EARTH AND DESTROYED THE LOST CITY OF KANDOR.

ZAAR DECLARED A BLOOD FEUD ON ALL KRYPTONIANS BUT DISAPPEARED **CENTURIES** AGO...

WE ALL THOUGHT HIM LOST TO THE VAST PHANTOM ZONE PRISON.

EVEN THOUGH WE'VE KNOWN THIS STORY FOR A THOUSAND YEARS, FOR **JON KENT,** THIS IS--

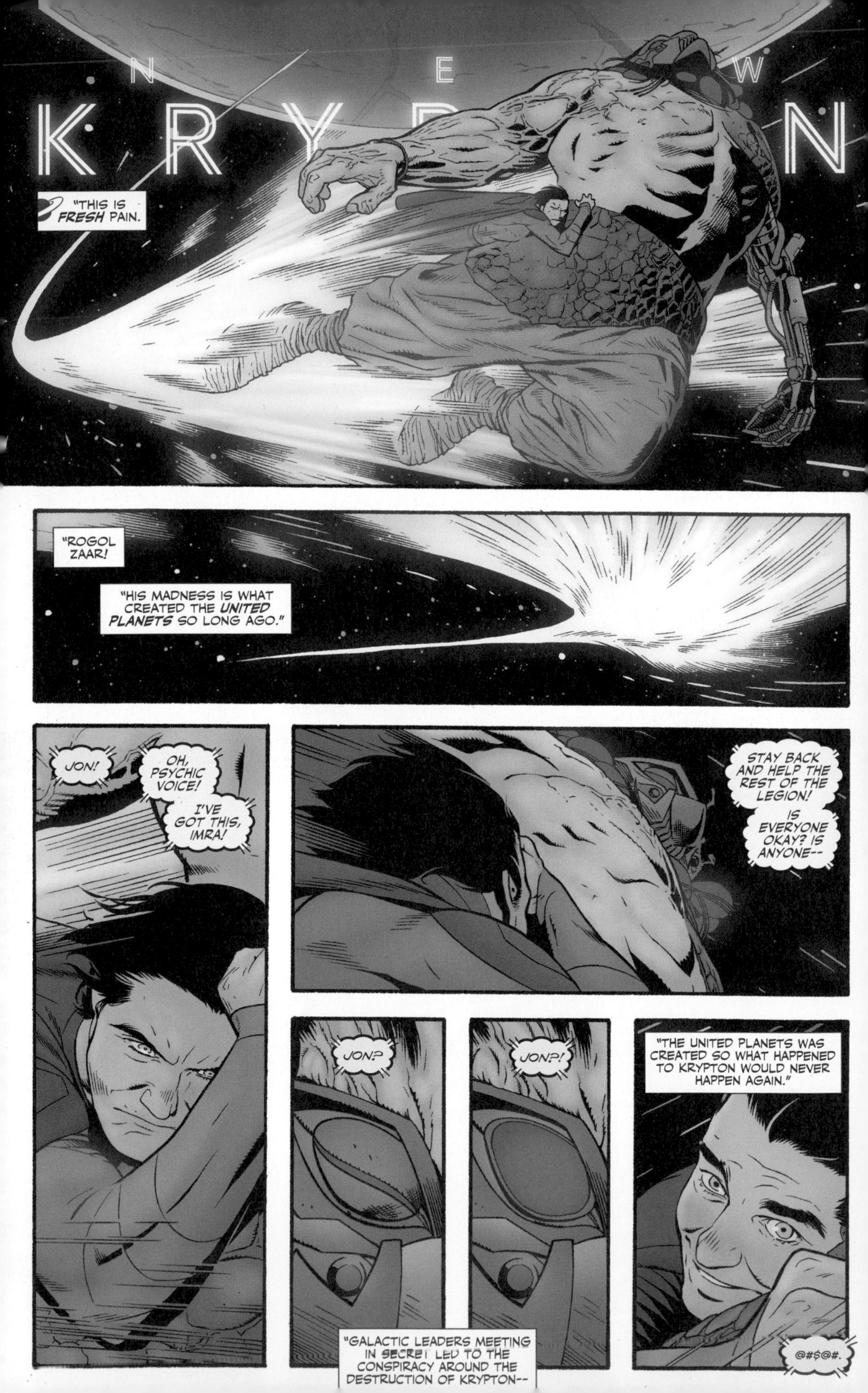
NEW
KRYPTON
"THIS IS FRESH PAIN.
"ROGOL ZAAR!
"HIS MADNESS IS WHAT CREATED THE UNITED PLANETS SO LONG AGO."
JON!
OH, PSYCHIC VOICE!
I'VE GOT THIS, IMRA!
STAY BACK AND HELP THE REST OF THE LEGION!
IS EVERYONE OKAY? IS ANYONE--
JON?
JON?!
"THE UNITED PLANETS WAS CREATED SO WHAT HAPPENED TO KRYPTON WOULD NEVER HAPPEN AGAIN."
"GALACTIC LEADERS MEETING IN SECRET LED TO THE CONSPIRACY AROUND THE DESTRUCTION OF KRYPTON--
@#$@#.

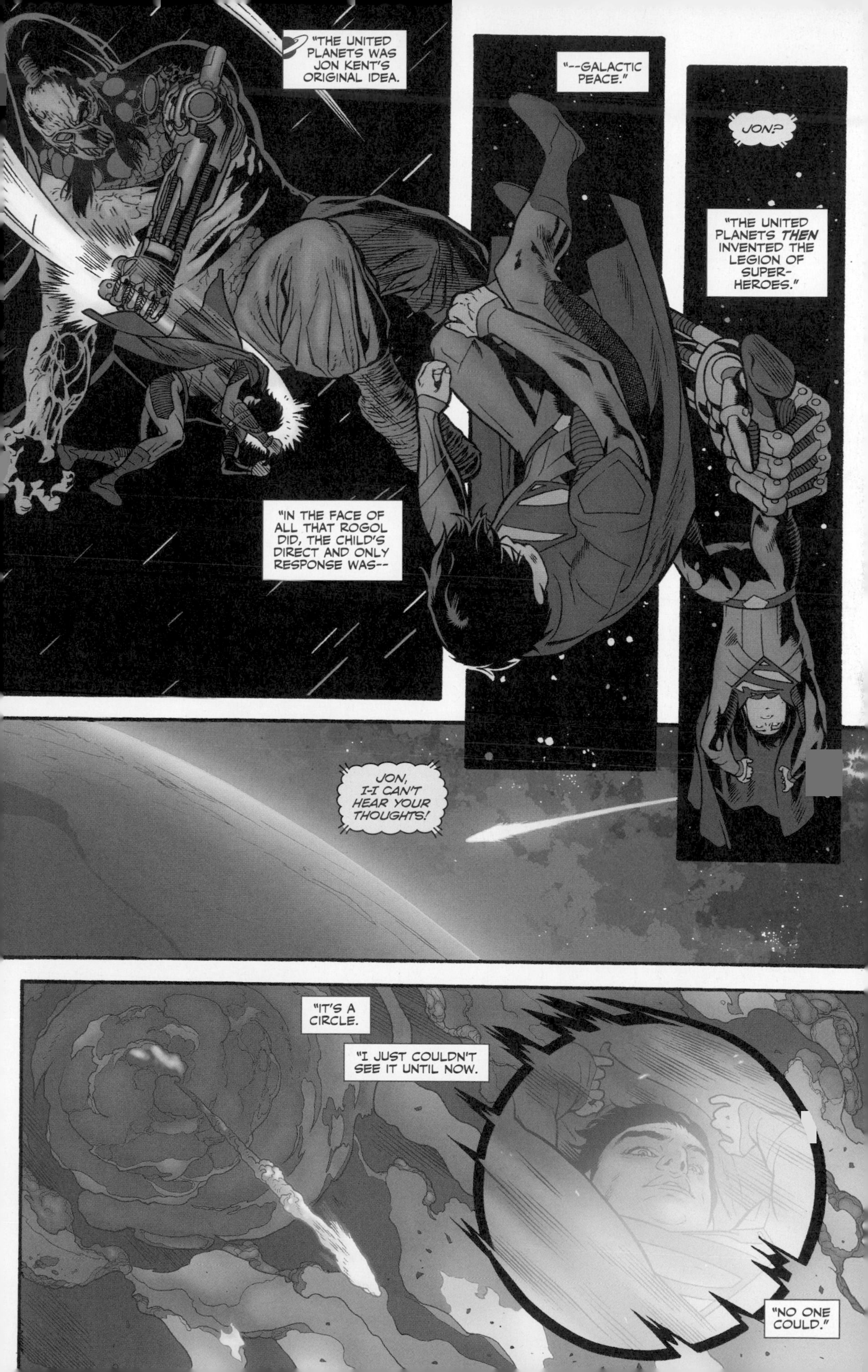
"THE UNITED PLANETS WAS JON KENT'S ORIGINAL IDEA.
"--GALACTIC PEACE."
JON?
"THE UNITED PLANETS *THEN* INVENTED THE LEGION OF SUPER-HEROES."
"IN THE FACE OF ALL THAT ROGOL DID, THE CHILD'S DIRECT AND ONLY RESPONSE WAS--
JON, I-I CAN'T HEAR YOUR THOUGHTS!
"IT'S A CIRCLE.
"I JUST COULDN'T SEE IT UNTIL NOW.
"NO ONE COULD."

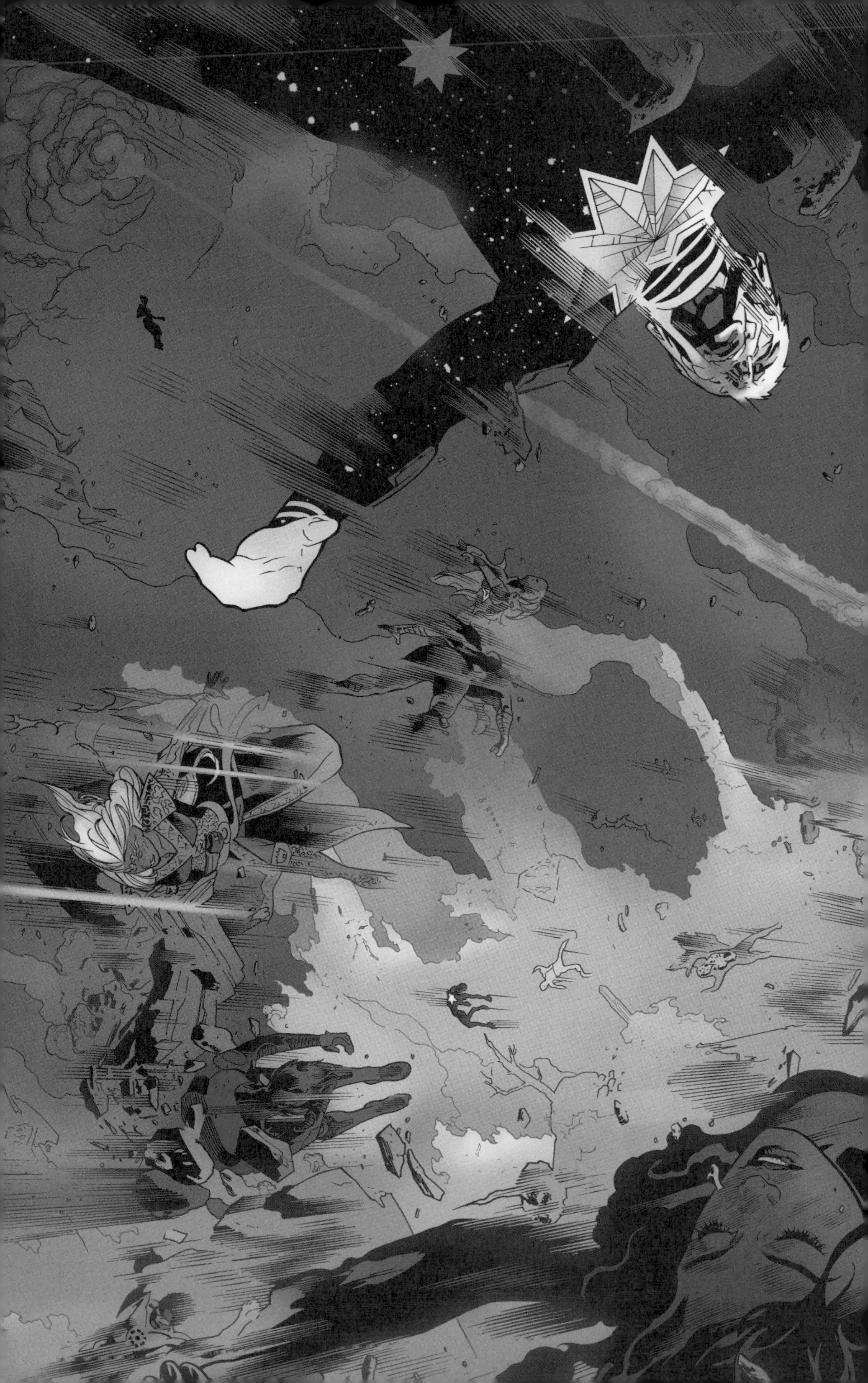

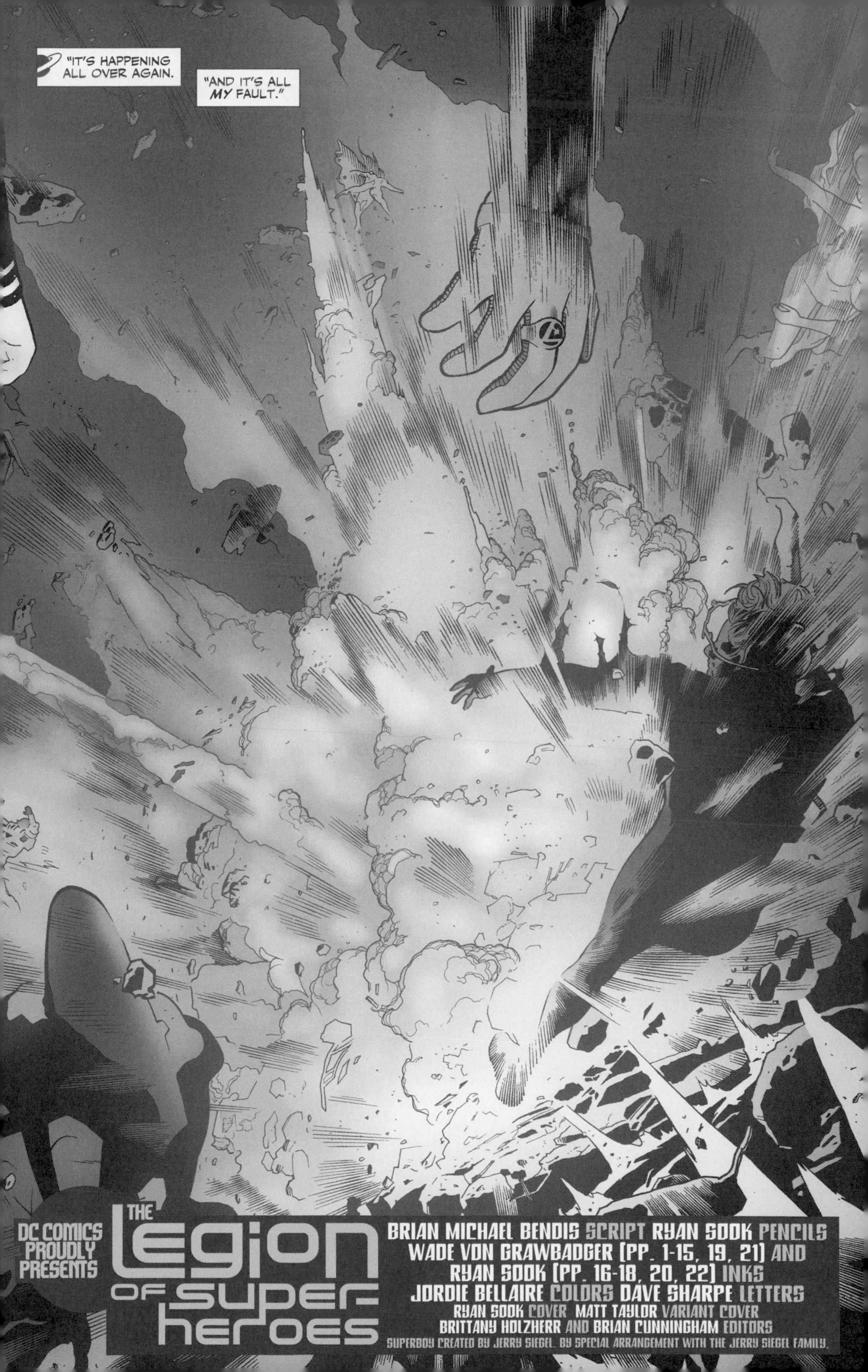

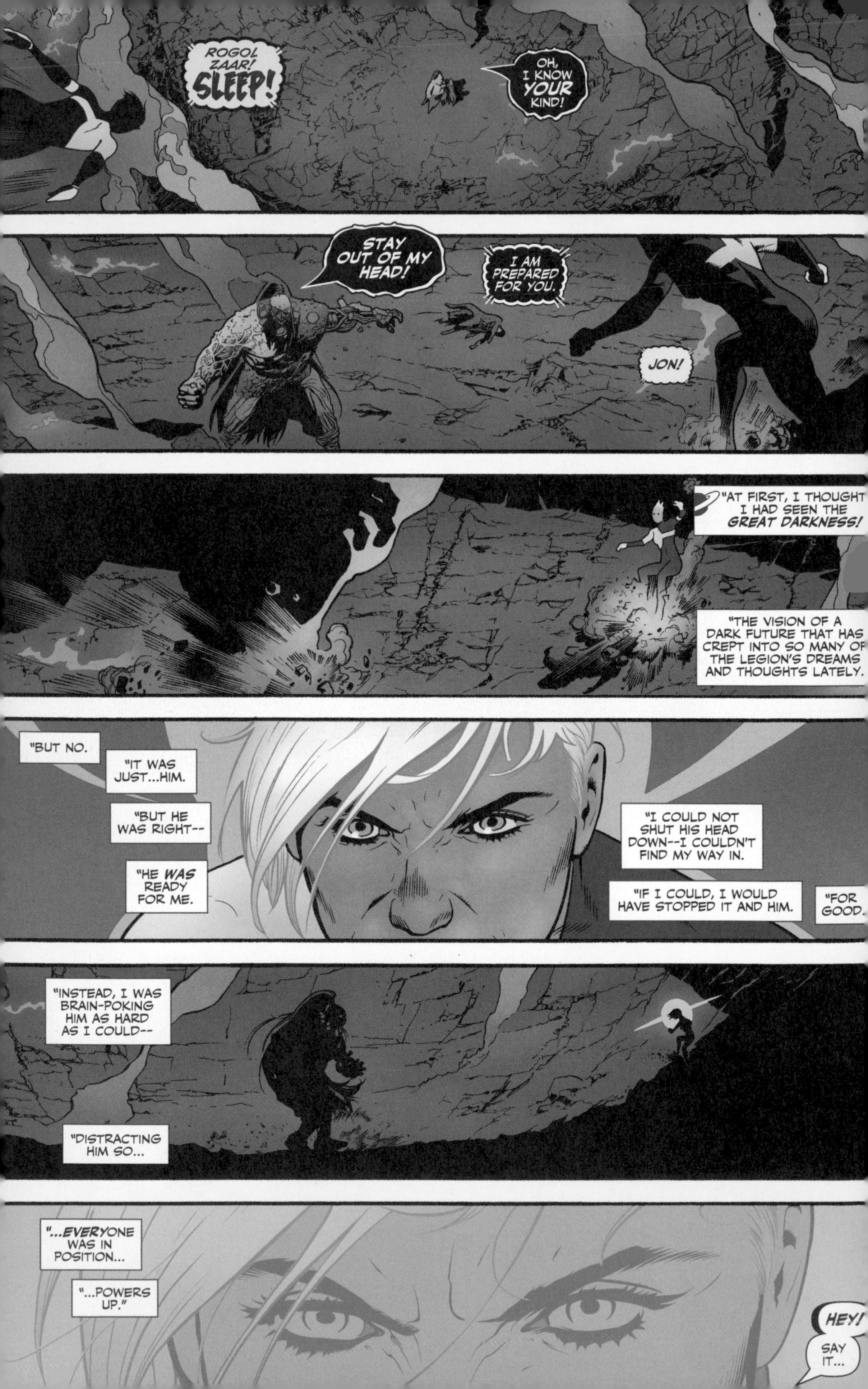
ROGOL ZAAR! SLEEP!
OH, I KNOW YOUR KIND!
STAY OUT OF MY HEAD!
I AM PREPARED FOR YOU.
JON!
"AT FIRST, I THOUGHT I HAD SEEN THE GREAT DARKNESS!
"THE VISION OF A DARK FUTURE THAT HAS CREPT INTO SO MANY OF THE LEGION'S DREAMS AND THOUGHTS LATELY.
"BUT NO.
"IT WAS JUST...HIM.
"BUT HE WAS RIGHT--
"HE WAS READY FOR ME.
"I COULD NOT SHUT HIS HEAD DOWN--I COULDN'T FIND MY WAY IN.
"IF I COULD, I WOULD HAVE STOPPED IT AND HIM.
"FOR GOOD.
"INSTEAD, I WAS BRAIN-POKING HIM AS HARD AS I COULD--
"DISTRACTING HIM SO...
"...EVERYONE WAS IN POSITION...
"...POWERS UP."
HEY!
SAY IT...

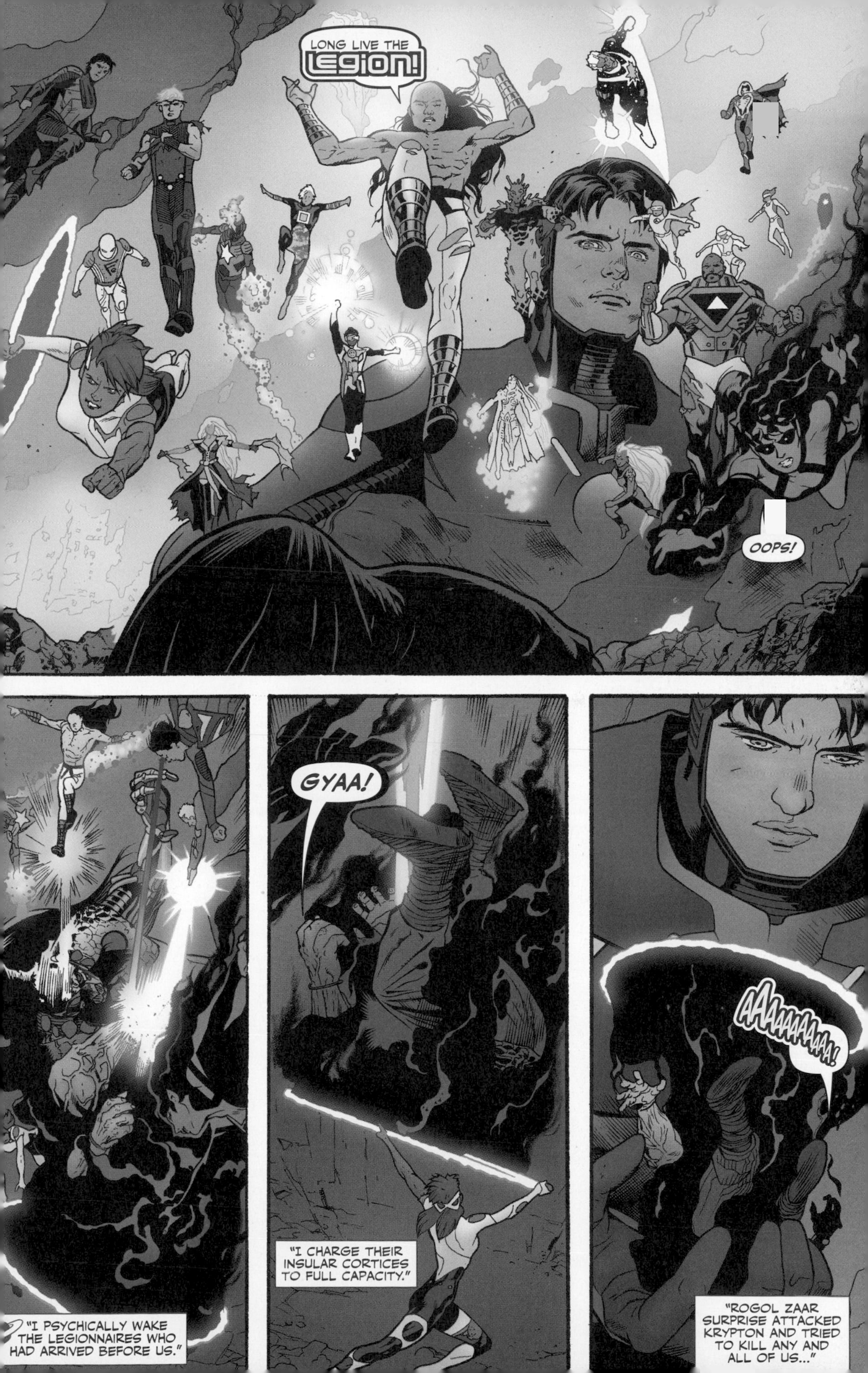

LONG LIVE THE LEGION!
OOPS!
"I PSYCHICALLY WAKE THE LEGIONNAIRES WHO HAD ARRIVED BEFORE US."
GYAA!
"I CHARGE THEIR INSULAR CORTICES TO FULL CAPACITY."
AAAAAAAAAA!
"ROGOL ZAAR SURPRISE ATTACKED KRYPTON AND TRIED TO KILL ANY AND ALL OF US..."

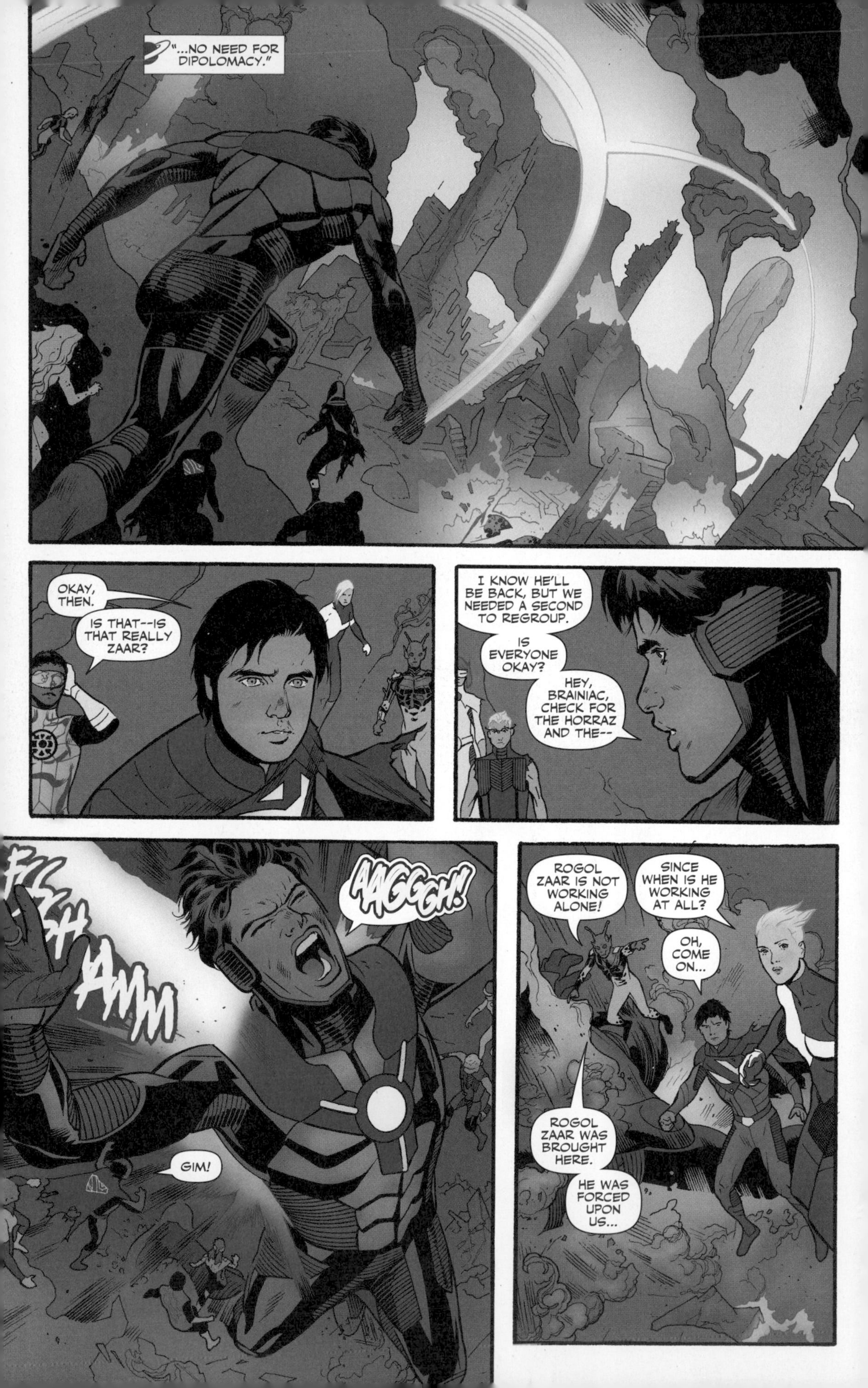
"...NO NEED FOR DIPOLOMACY."
OKAY, THEN.
IS THAT--IS THAT REALLY ZAAR?
I KNOW HE'LL BE BACK, BUT WE NEEDED A SECOND TO REGROUP.
IS EVERYONE OKAY?
HEY, BRAINIAC, CHECK FOR THE HORRAZ AND THE--
AAGGGH!
GIM!
ROGOL ZAAR IS NOT WORKING ALONE!
SINCE WHEN IS HE WORKING AT ALL?
OH, COME ON...
ROGOL ZAAR WAS BROUGHT HERE.
HE WAS FORCED UPON US...

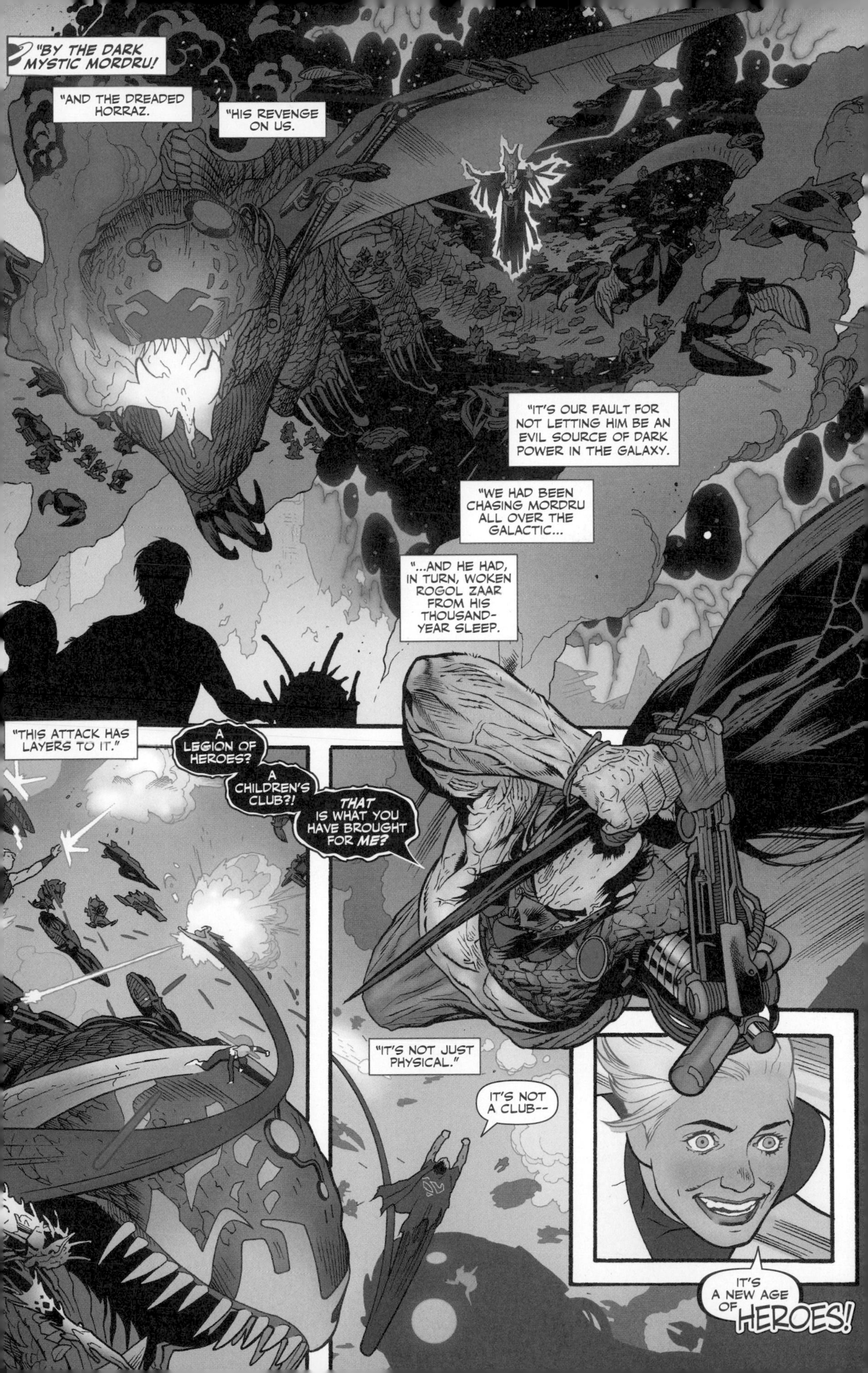
"BY THE DARK MYSTIC MORDRU!
"AND THE DREADED HORRAZ.
"HIS REVENGE ON US.
"IT'S OUR FAULT FOR NOT LETTING HIM BE AN EVIL SOURCE OF DARK POWER IN THE GALAXY.
"WE HAD BEEN CHASING MORDRU ALL OVER THE GALACTIC...
"...AND HE HAD, IN TURN, WOKEN ROGOL ZAAR FROM HIS THOUSAND-YEAR SLEEP.
"THIS ATTACK HAS LAYERS TO IT."
A LEGION OF HEROES?
A CHILDREN'S CLUB?!
THAT IS WHAT YOU HAVE BROUGHT FOR ME?
"IT'S NOT JUST PHYSICAL."
IT'S NOT A CLUB--
IT'S A NEW AGE OF HEROES!

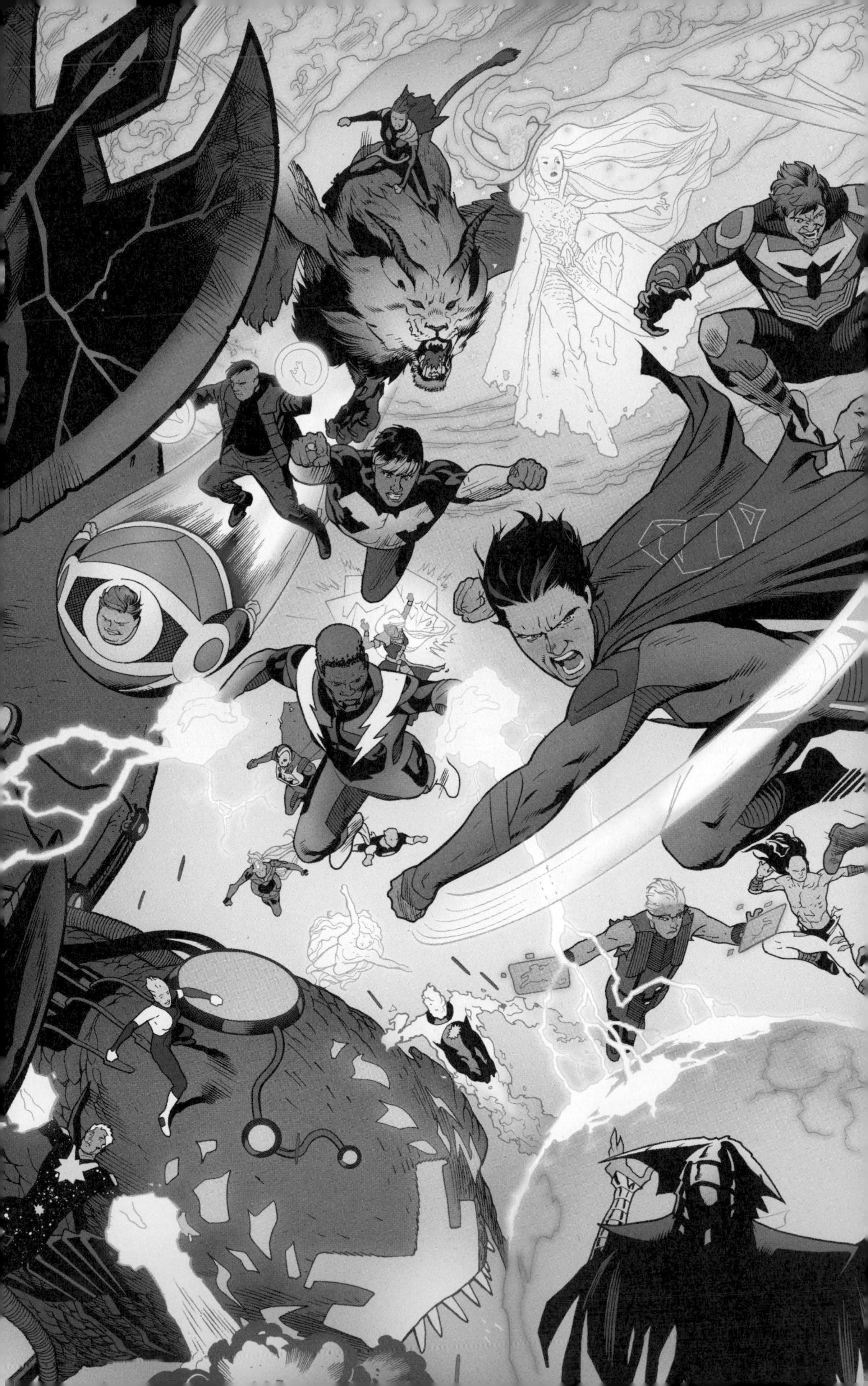

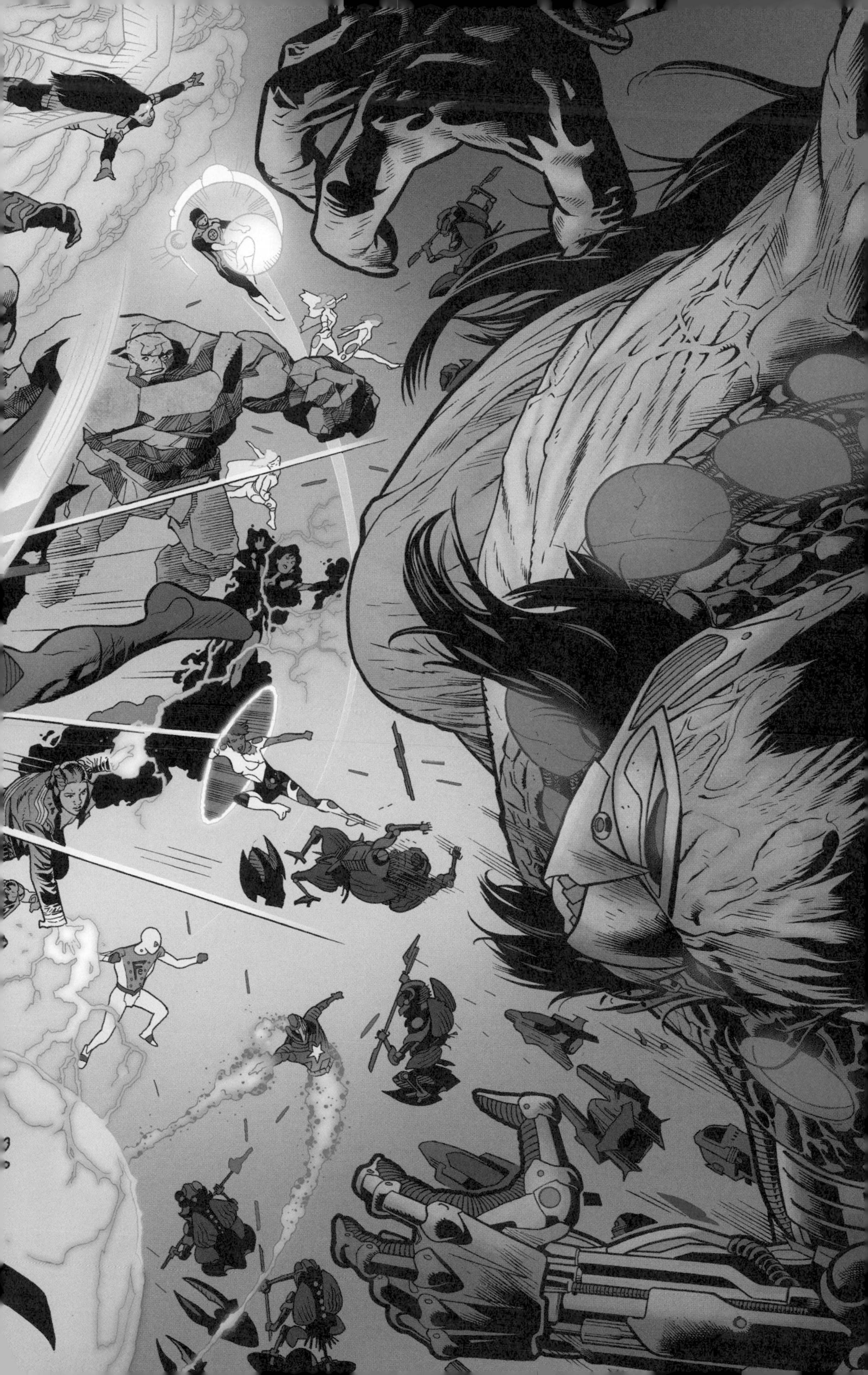

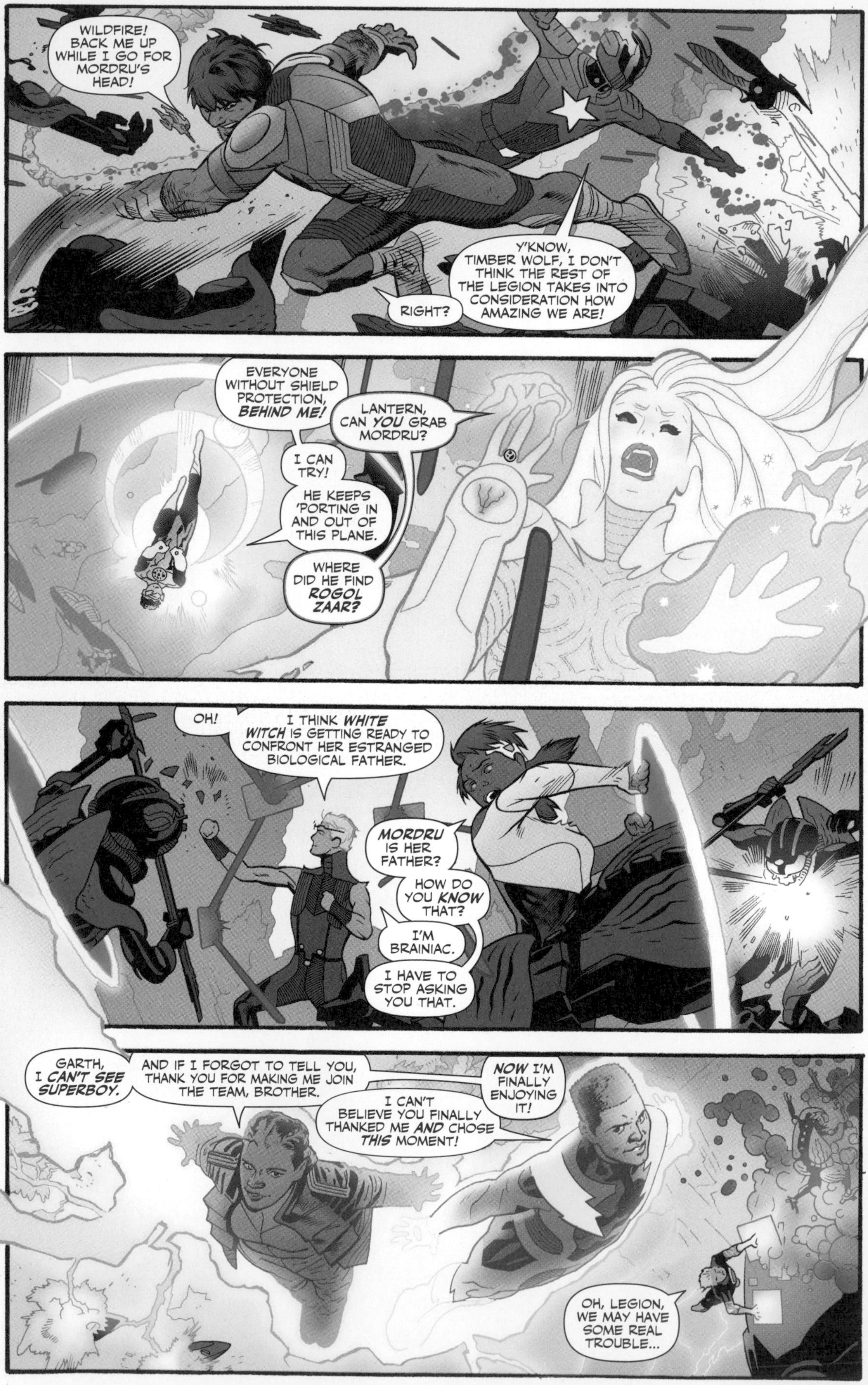
WILDFIRE! BACK ME UP WHILE I GO FOR MORDRU'S HEAD!
Y'KNOW, TIMBER WOLF, I DON'T THINK THE REST OF THE LEGION TAKES INTO CONSIDERATION HOW AMAZING WE ARE!
RIGHT?
EVERYONE WITHOUT SHIELD PROTECTION, BEHIND ME!
LANTERN, CAN YOU GRAB MORDRU?
I CAN TRY!
HE KEEPS 'PORTING IN AND OUT OF THIS PLANE.
WHERE DID HE FIND ROGOL ZAAR?
OH!
I THINK WHITE WITCH IS GETTING READY TO CONFRONT HER ESTRANGED BIOLOGICAL FATHER.
MORDRU IS HER FATHER?
HOW DO YOU KNOW THAT?
I'M BRAINIAC.
I HAVE TO STOP ASKING YOU THAT.
GARTH, I CAN'T SEE SUPERBOY.
AND IF I FORGOT TO TELL YOU, THANK YOU FOR MAKING ME JOIN THE TEAM, BROTHER.
NOW I'M FINALLY ENJOYING IT!
I CAN'T BELIEVE YOU FINALLY THANKED ME AND CHOSE THIS MOMENT!
OH, LEGION, WE MAY HAVE SOME REAL TROUBLE...

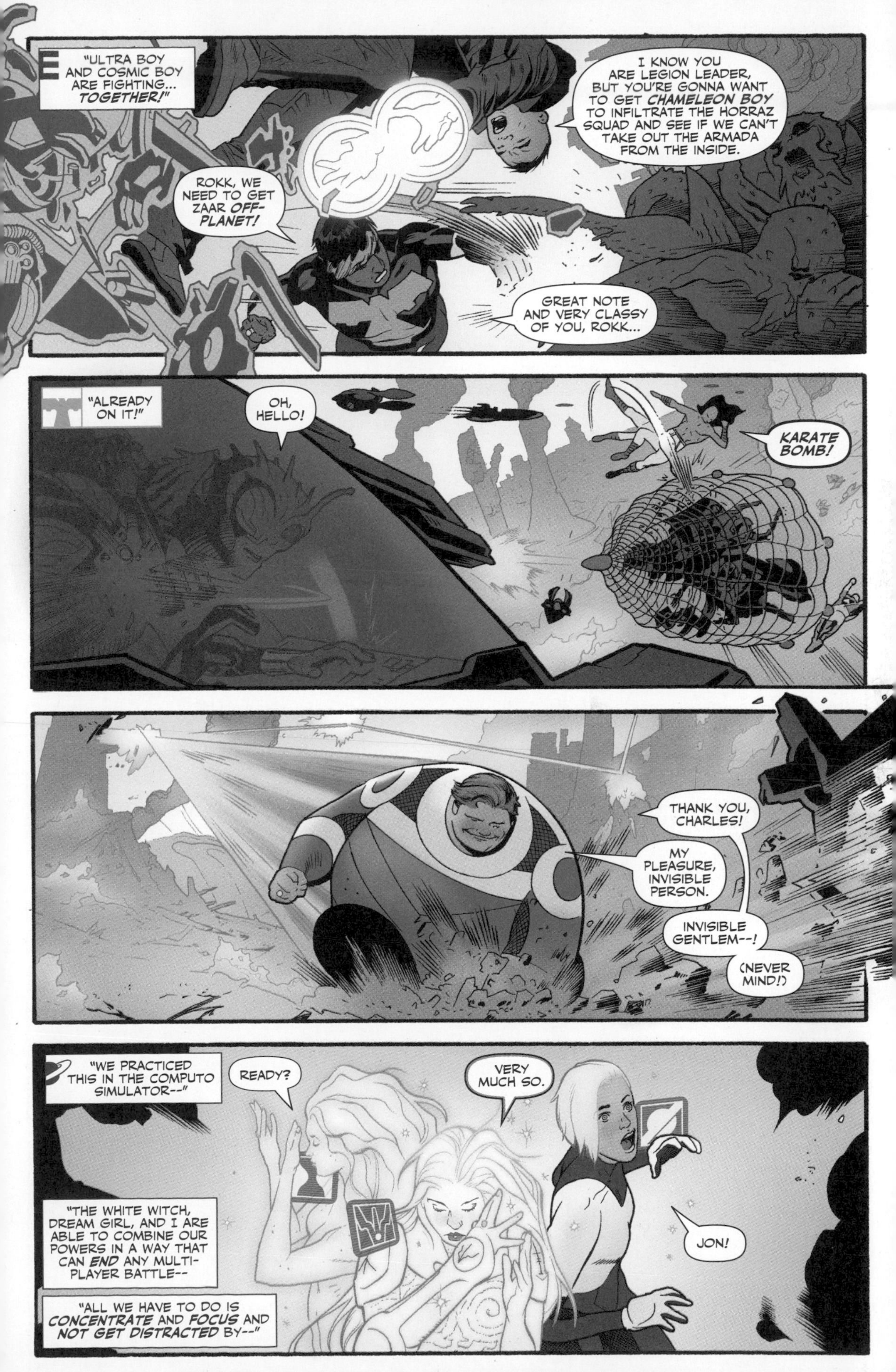
"ULTRA BOY AND COSMIC BOY ARE FIGHTING... *TOGETHER!*"
I KNOW YOU ARE LEGION LEADER, BUT YOU'RE GONNA WANT TO GET *CHAMELEON BOY* TO INFILTRATE THE HORRAZ SQUAD AND SEE IF WE CAN'T TAKE OUT THE ARMADA FROM THE INSIDE.
ROKK, WE NEED TO GET ZAAR *OFF-PLANET!*
GREAT NOTE AND VERY CLASSY OF YOU, ROKK...
"ALREADY ON IT!"
OH, HELLO!
KARATE BOMB!
THANK YOU, CHARLES!
MY PLEASURE, INVISIBLE PERSON.
INVISIBLE GENTLEM--!
(NEVER MIND!)
"WE PRACTICED THIS IN THE COMPUTO SIMULATOR--"
READY?
VERY MUCH SO.
"THE WHITE WITCH, DREAM GIRL, AND I ARE ABLE TO COMBINE OUR POWERS IN A WAY THAT CAN *END* ANY MULTI-PLAYER BATTLE--
JON!
"ALL WE HAVE TO DO IS *CONCENTRATE* AND *FOCUS* AND *NOT GET DISTRACTED* BY--"

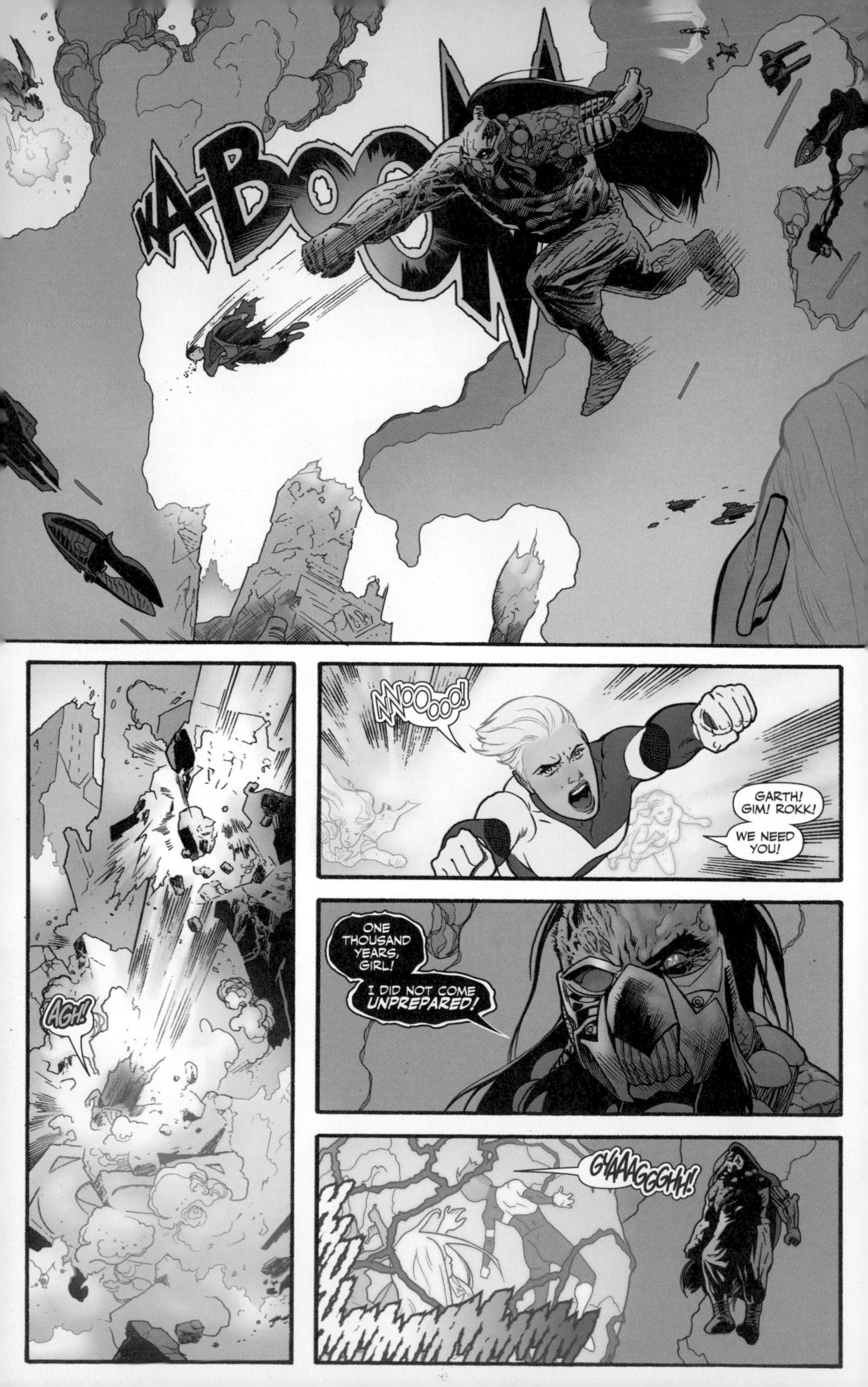
KA-BOOM
NNOOOOO!
GARTH! GIM! ROKK!
WE NEED YOU!
AGH!
ONE THOUSAND YEARS, GIRL!
I DID NOT COME *UNPREPARED!*
GYAAAGGGHH!

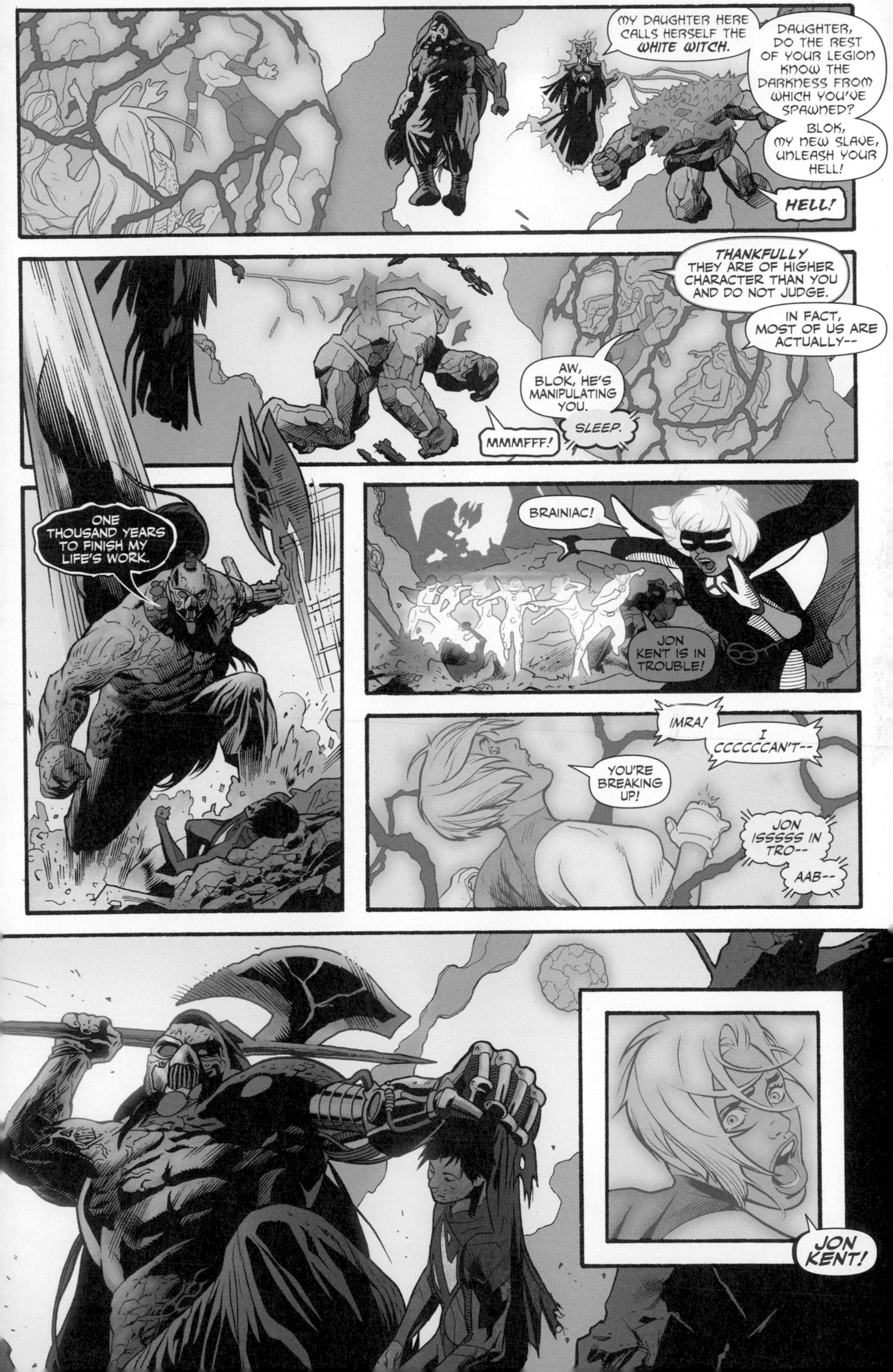
MY DAUGHTER HERE CALLS HERSELF THE WHITE WITCH.
DAUGHTER, DO THE REST OF YOUR LEGION KNOW THE DARKNESS FROM WHICH YOU'VE SPAWNED?
BLOK, MY NEW SLAVE, UNLEASH YOUR HELL!
HELL!
THANKFULLY THEY ARE OF HIGHER CHARACTER THAN YOU AND DO NOT JUDGE.
IN FACT, MOST OF US ARE ACTUALLY--
AW, BLOK, HE'S MANIPULATING YOU.
SLEEP.
MMMFFF!
ONE THOUSAND YEARS TO FINISH MY LIFE'S WORK.
BRAINIAC!
JON KENT IS IN TROUBLE!
IMRA!
I CCCCCCAN'T--
YOU'RE BREAKING UP!
JON ISSSSS IN TRO--
AAB--
JON KENT!

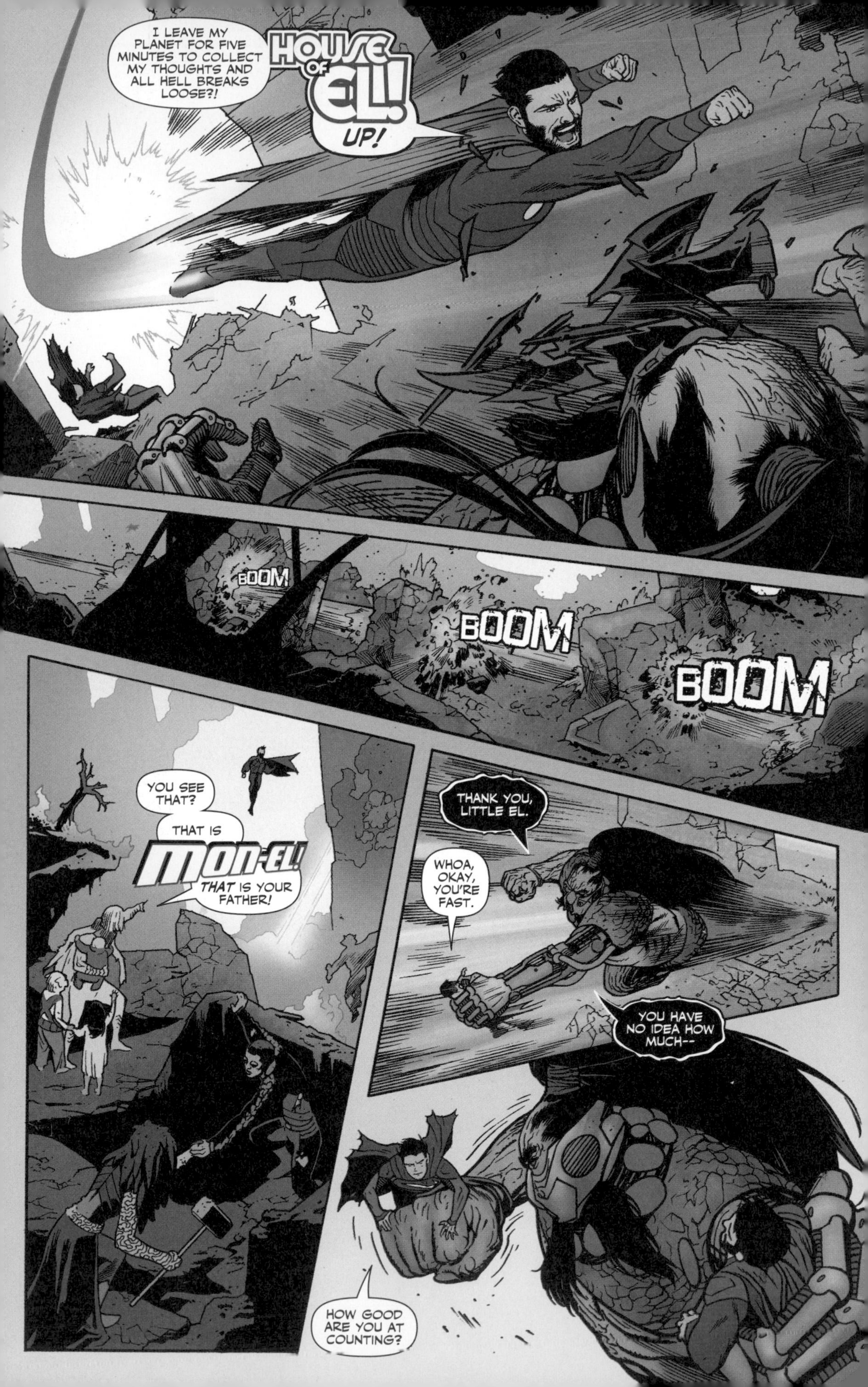
I LEAVE MY PLANET FOR FIVE MINUTES TO COLLECT MY THOUGHTS AND ALL HELL BREAKS LOOSE?!
HOUSE OF EL! UP!
BOOM
BOOM
BOOM
YOU SEE THAT?
THAT IS
MON-EL!
THAT IS YOUR FATHER!
THANK YOU, LITTLE EL.
WHOA, OKAY, YOU'RE FAST.
YOU HAVE NO IDEA HOW MUCH--
HOW GOOD ARE YOU AT COUNTING?

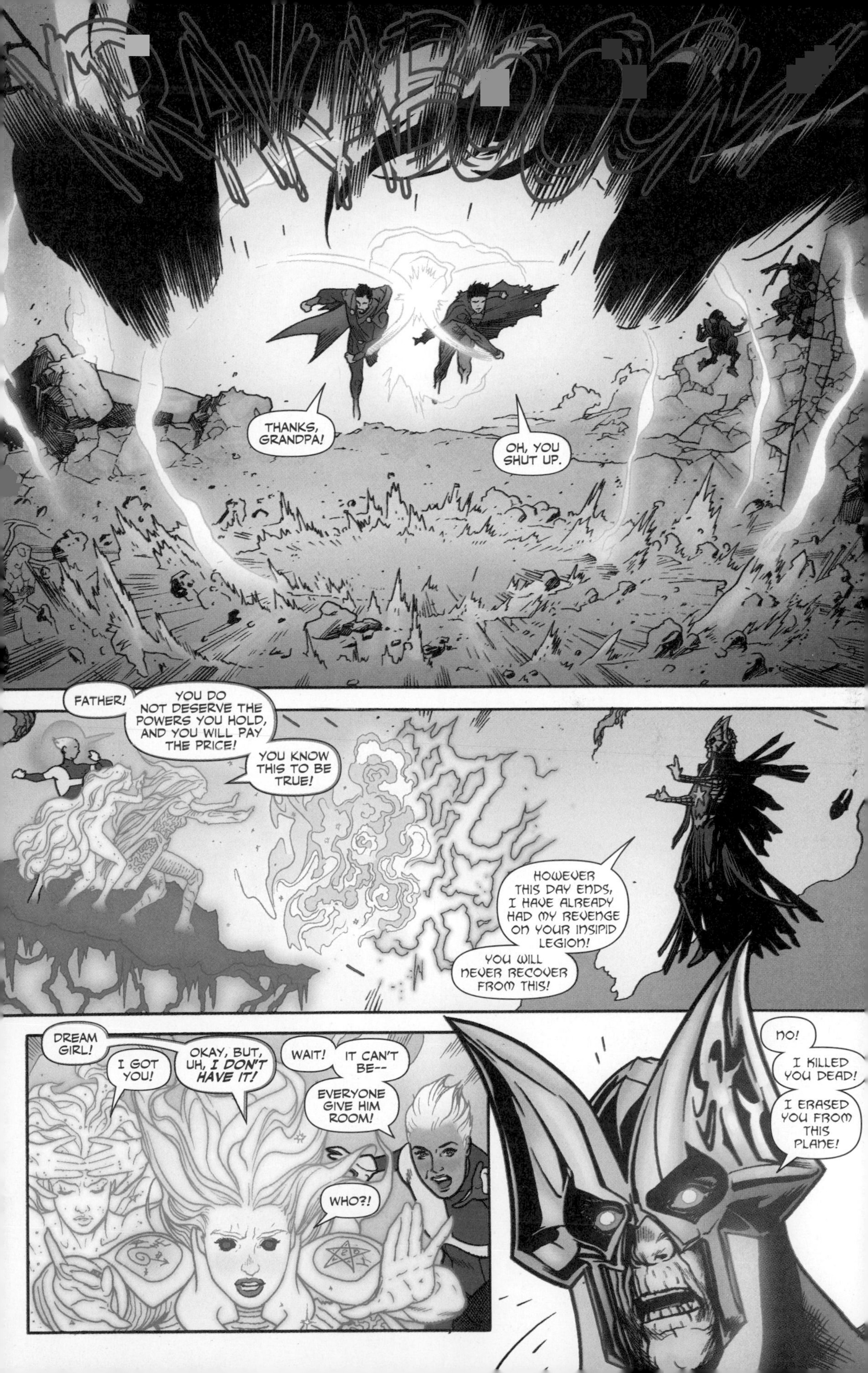
KRAKABOOOM
THANKS, GRANDPA!
OH, YOU SHUT UP.
FATHER!
YOU DO NOT DESERVE THE POWERS YOU HOLD, AND YOU WILL PAY THE PRICE!
YOU KNOW THIS TO BE TRUE!
HOWEVER THIS DAY ENDS, I HAVE ALREADY HAD MY REVENGE ON YOUR INSIPID LEGION!
YOU WILL NEVER RECOVER FROM THIS!
DREAM GIRL!
I GOT YOU!
OKAY, BUT, UH, I DON'T HAVE IT!
WAIT!
IT CAN'T BE--
EVERYONE GIVE HIM ROOM!
WHO?!
NO!
I KILLED YOU DEAD!
I ERASED YOU FROM THIS PLANE!

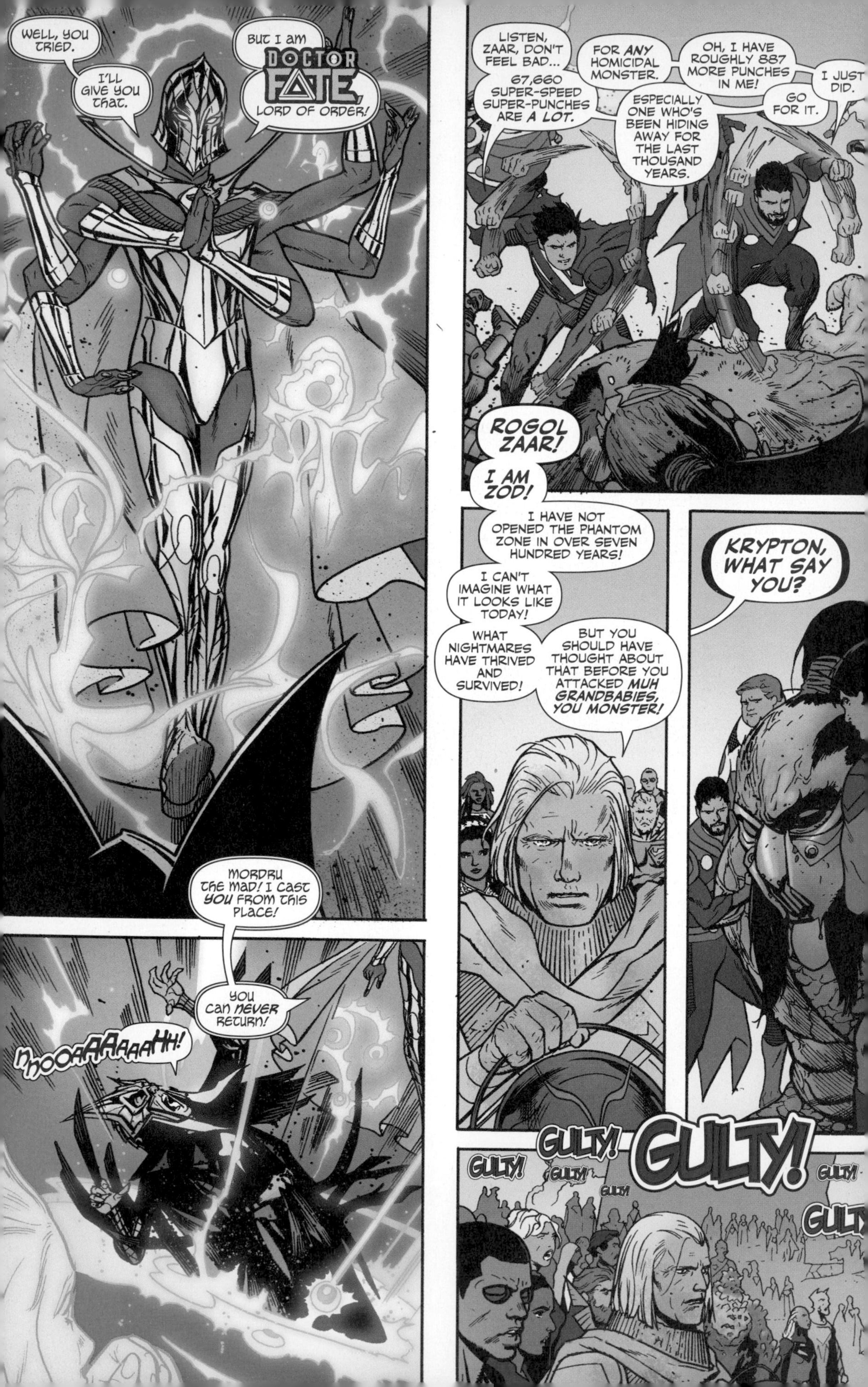
WELL, YOU TRIED.
I'LL GIVE YOU THAT.
BUT I AM DOCTOR FATE, LORD OF ORDER!
MORDRU THE MAD! I CAST YOU FROM THIS PLACE!
YOU CAN NEVER RETURN!
NNOOAAAAAAAHH!
LISTEN, ZAAR, DON'T FEEL BAD...
67,660 SUPER-SPEED SUPER-PUNCHES ARE A LOT.
FOR ANY HOMICIDAL MONSTER.
ESPECIALLY ONE WHO'S BEEN HIDING AWAY FOR THE LAST THOUSAND YEARS.
OH, I HAVE ROUGHLY 887 MORE PUNCHES IN ME!
GO FOR IT.
I JUST DID.
ROGOL ZAAR!
I AM ZOD!
I HAVE NOT OPENED THE PHANTOM ZONE IN OVER SEVEN HUNDRED YEARS!
I CAN'T IMAGINE WHAT IT LOOKS LIKE TODAY!
WHAT NIGHTMARES HAVE THRIVED AND SURVIVED!
BUT YOU SHOULD HAVE THOUGHT ABOUT THAT BEFORE YOU ATTACKED MUH GRANDBABIES, YOU MONSTER!
KRYPTON, WHAT SAY YOU?
GUILTY! GUILTY!
GUILTY! GUILTY! GUILTY! GUILTY! GUILTY!

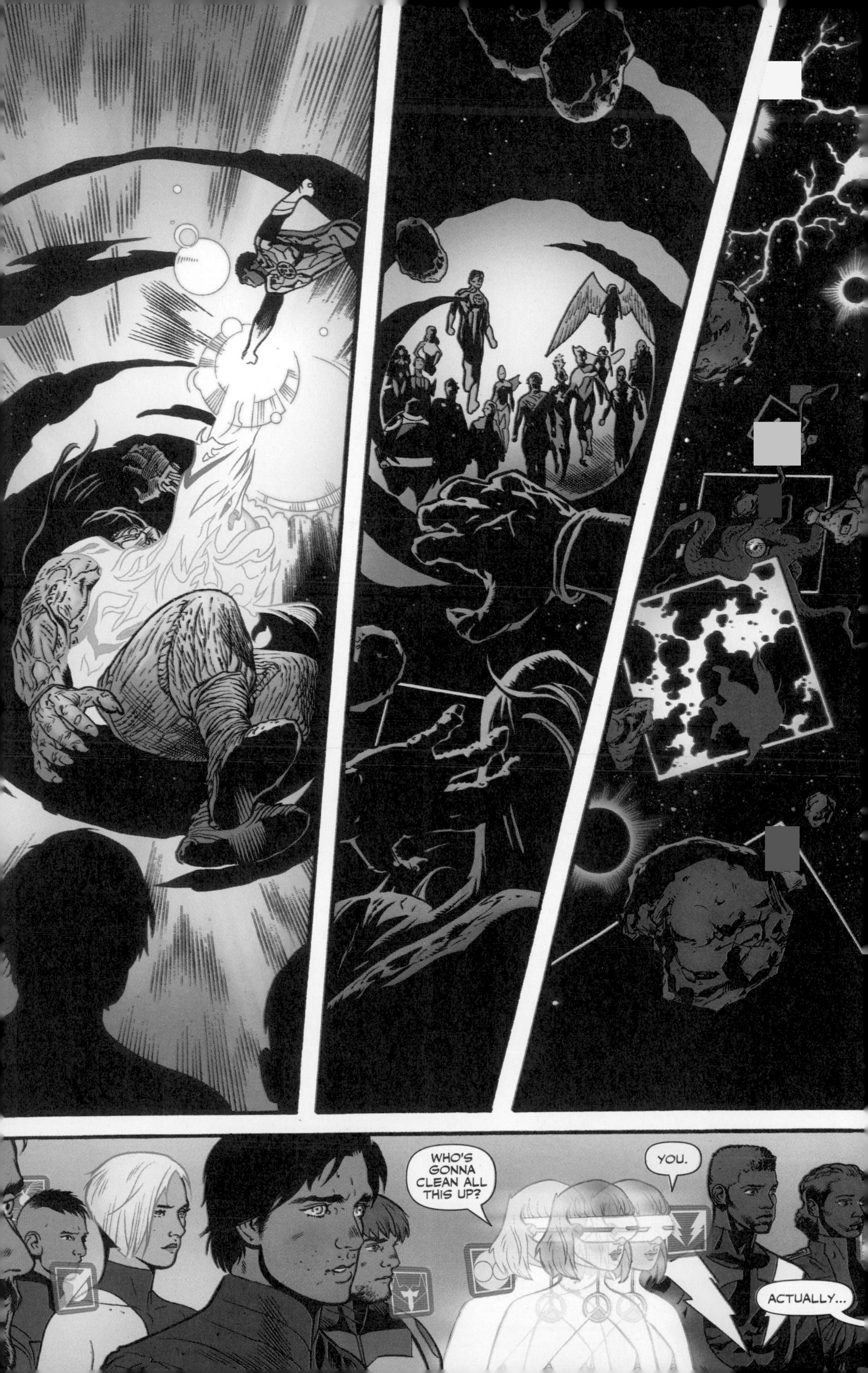
WHO'S GONNA CLEAN ALL THIS UP?
YOU.
ACTUALLY...

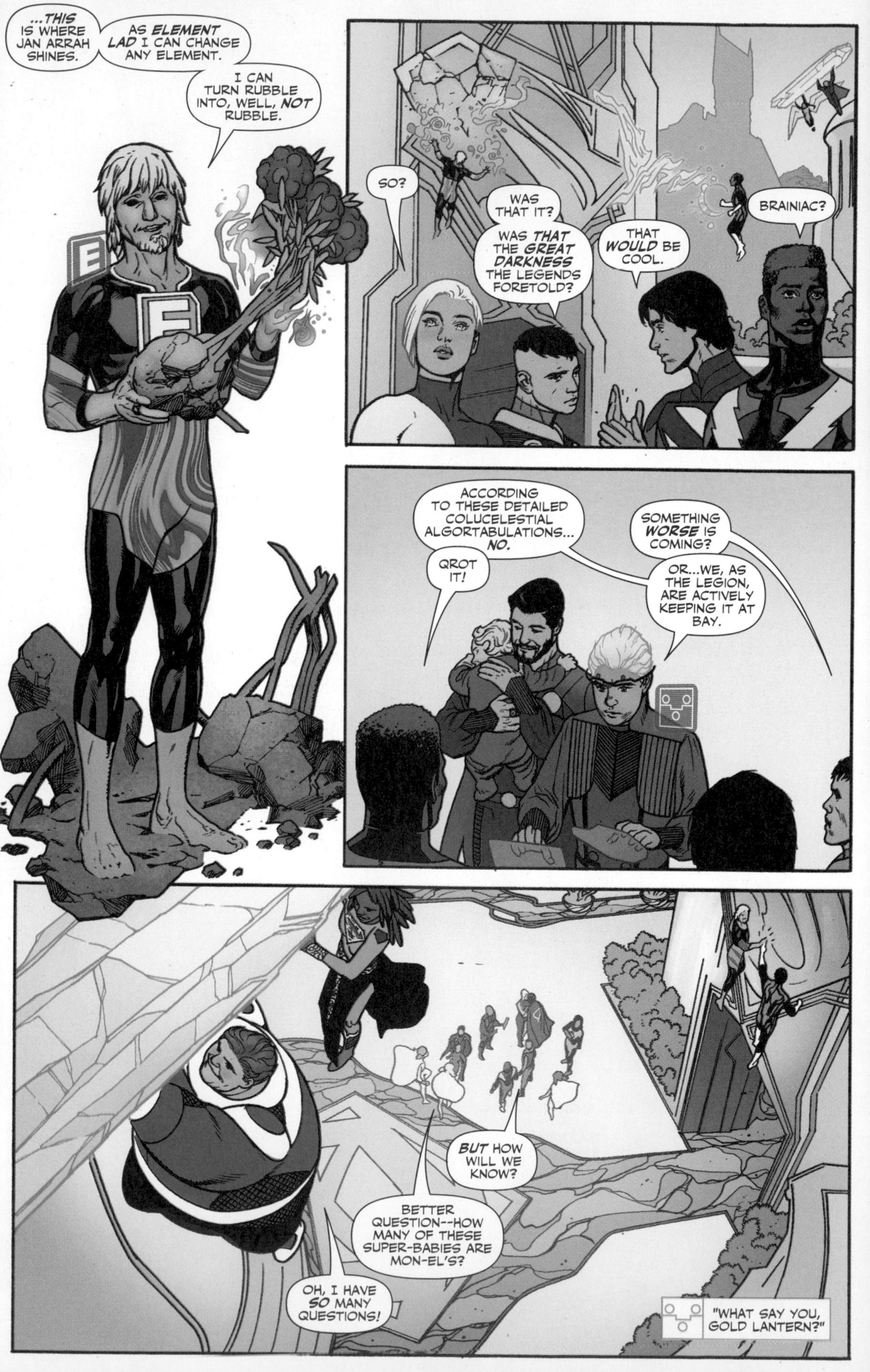

...THIS IS WHERE JAN ARRAH SHINES.
AS ELEMENT LAD I CAN CHANGE ANY ELEMENT.
I CAN TURN RUBBLE INTO, WELL, NOT RUBBLE.
SO?
WAS THAT IT?
WAS THAT THE GREAT DARKNESS THE LEGENDS FORETOLD?
THAT WOULD BE COOL.
BRAINIAC?
ACCORDING TO THESE DETAILED COLUCELESTIAL ALGORTABULATIONS... NO.
QROT IT!
SOMETHING WORSE IS COMING?
OR...WE, AS THE LEGION, ARE ACTIVELY KEEPING IT AT BAY.
BUT HOW WILL WE KNOW?
BETTER QUESTION--HOW MANY OF THESE SUPER-BABIES ARE MON-EL'S?
OH, I HAVE SO MANY QUESTIONS!
"WHAT SAY YOU, GOLD LANTERN?"

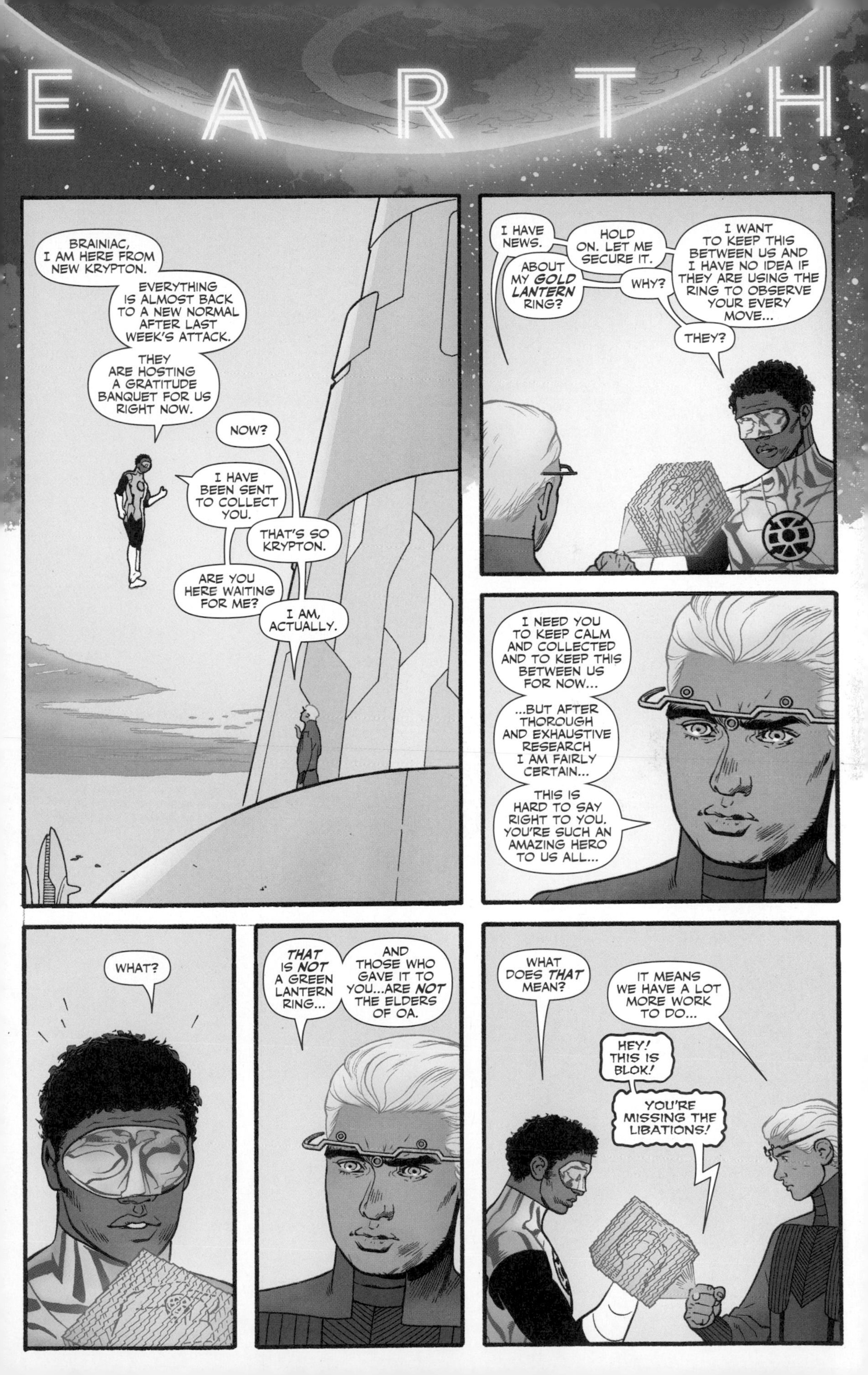
EARTH
BRAINIAC, I AM HERE FROM NEW KRYPTON.
EVERYTHING IS ALMOST BACK TO A NEW NORMAL AFTER LAST WEEK'S ATTACK.
THEY ARE HOSTING A GRATITUDE BANQUET FOR US RIGHT NOW.
NOW?
I HAVE BEEN SENT TO COLLECT YOU.
THAT'S SO KRYPTON.
ARE YOU HERE WAITING FOR ME?
I AM, ACTUALLY.
I HAVE NEWS.
HOLD ON. LET ME SECURE IT.
I WANT TO KEEP THIS BETWEEN US AND I HAVE NO IDEA IF THEY ARE USING THE RING TO OBSERVE YOUR EVERY MOVE...
ABOUT MY GOLD LANTERN RING?
WHY?
THEY?
I NEED YOU TO KEEP CALM AND COLLECTED AND TO KEEP THIS BETWEEN US FOR NOW...
...BUT AFTER THOROUGH AND EXHAUSTIVE RESEARCH I AM FAIRLY CERTAIN...
THIS IS HARD TO SAY RIGHT TO YOU. YOU'RE SUCH AN AMAZING HERO TO US ALL...
WHAT?
THAT IS NOT A GREEN LANTERN RING...
AND THOSE WHO GAVE IT TO YOU...ARE NOT THE ELDERS OF OA.
WHAT DOES THAT MEAN?
IT MEANS WE HAVE A LOT MORE WORK TO DO...
HEY! THIS IS BLOK!
YOU'RE MISSING THE LIBATIONS!

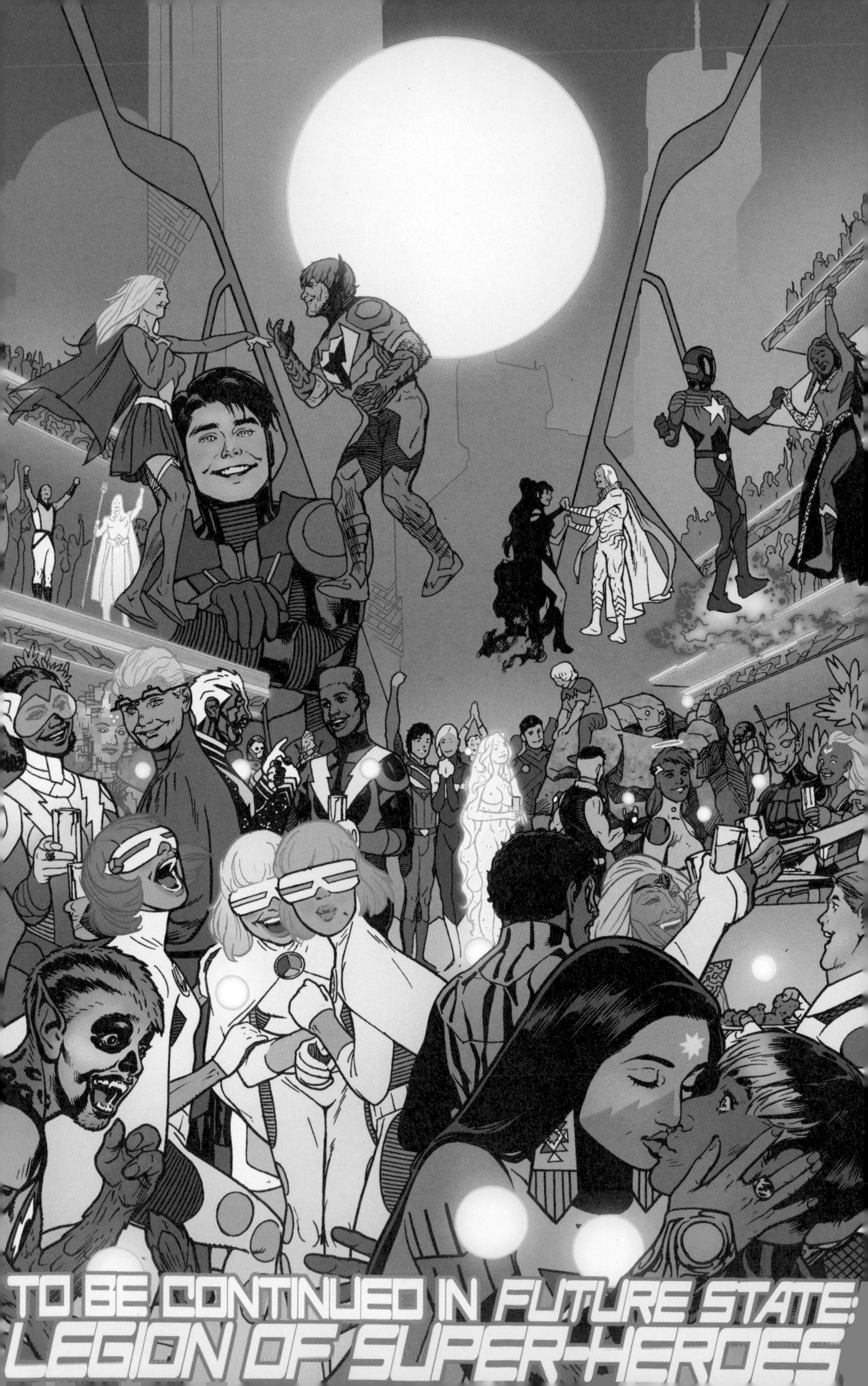
TO BE CONTINUED IN FUTURE STATE:
LEGION OF SUPER-HEROES

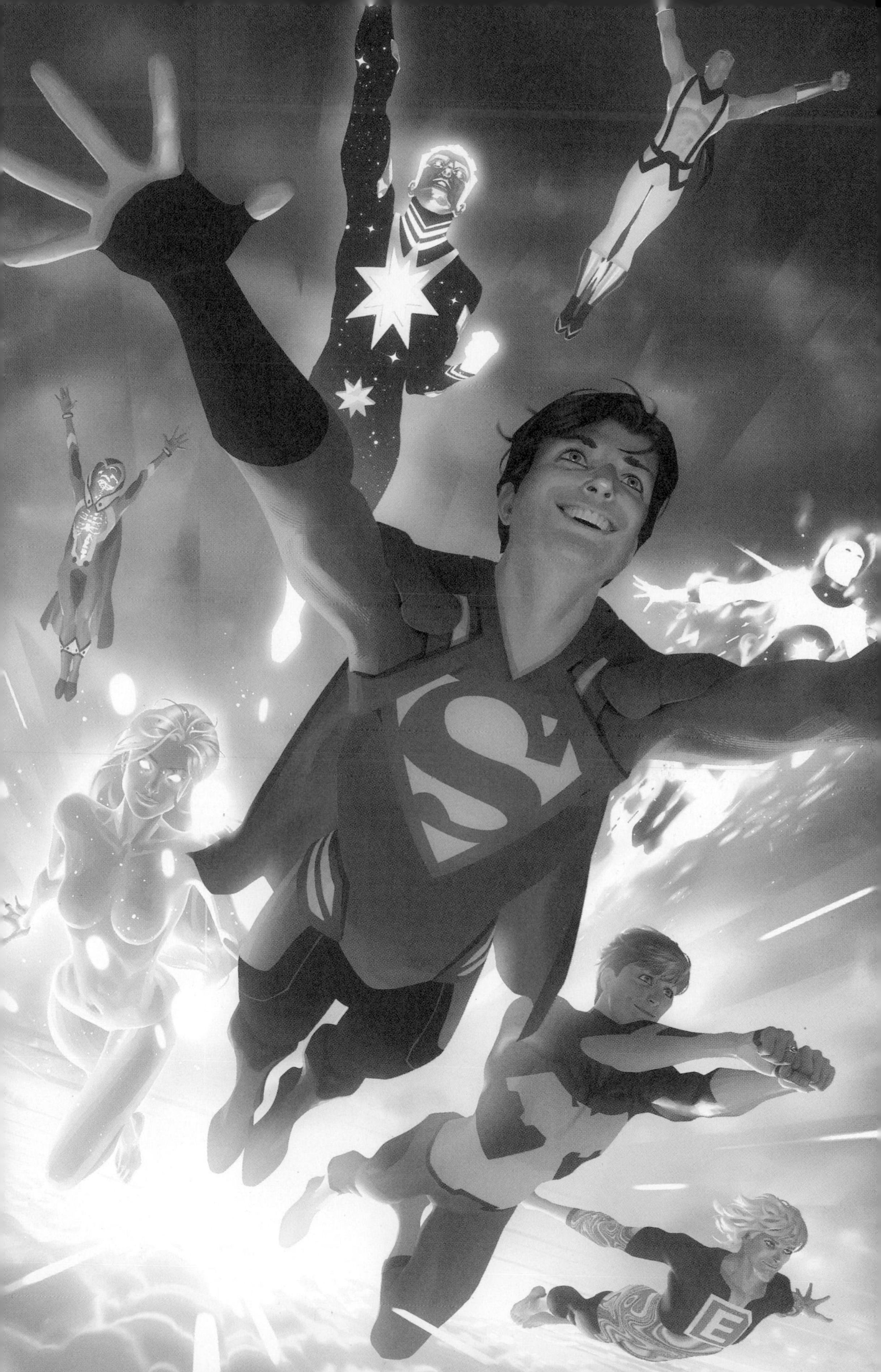

Legion of Super-Heroes **#7** variant cover by **ALEX GARNER**

***Legion of Super-Heroes* issue #7** Gold Lantern design variant cover by **RYAN SOOK**

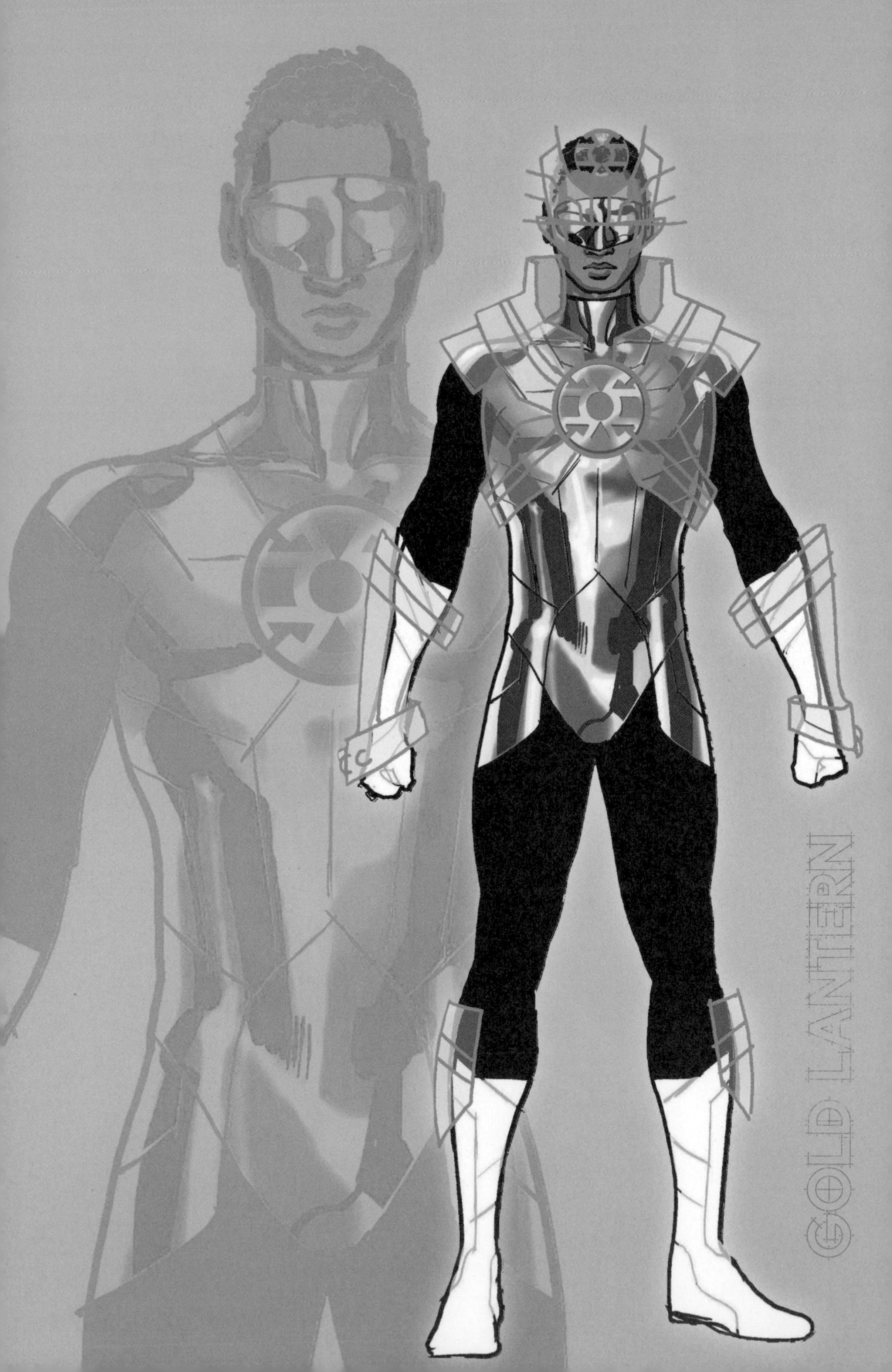
GOLD LANTERN

Legion of Super-Heroes **#8** variant cover by **DUSTIN NGUYEN**

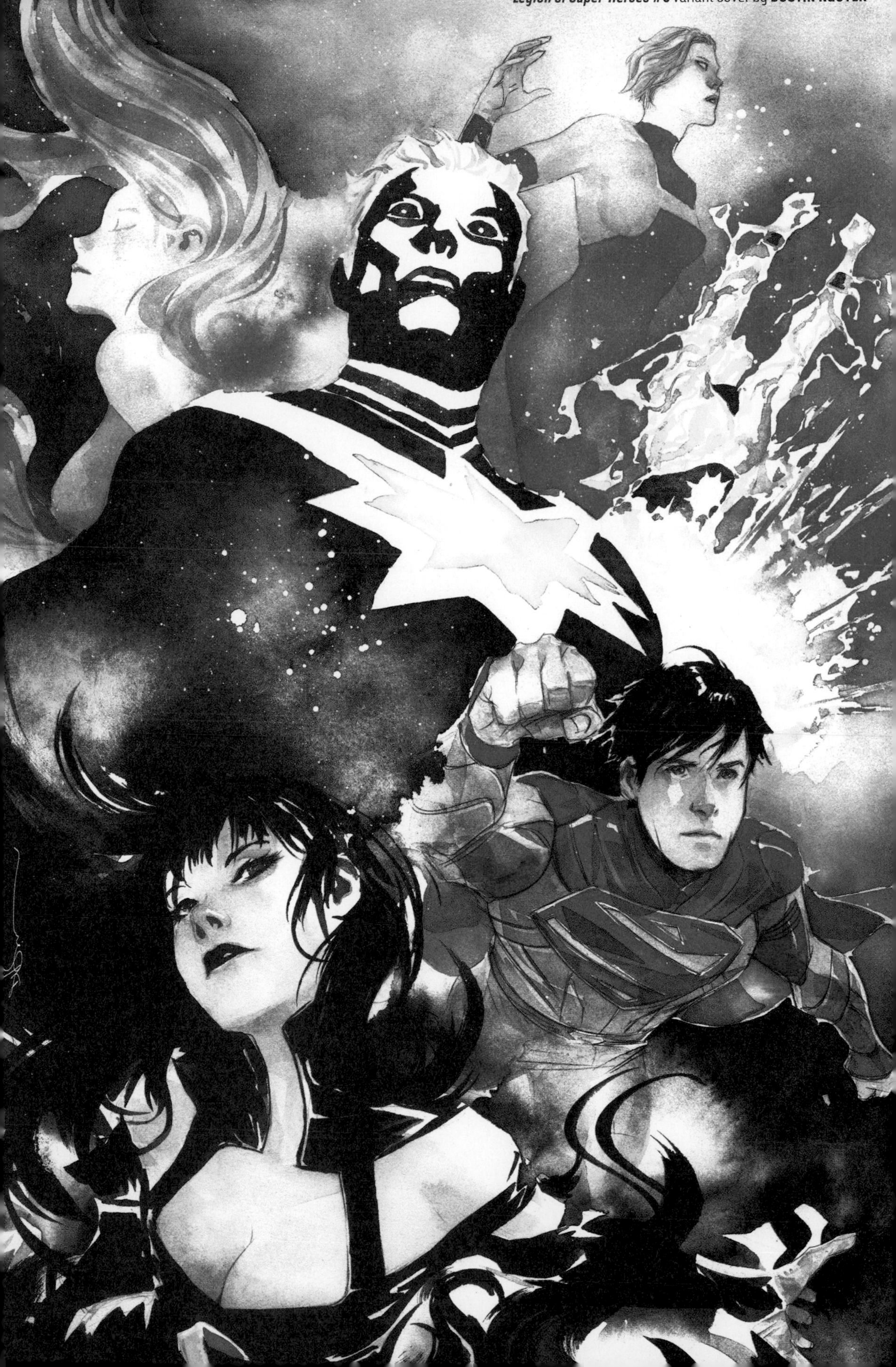

Legion of Super-Heroes **#9** variant cover by **ANDRÉ LIMA ARAÚJO** and **CHRIS O'HALLORAN**

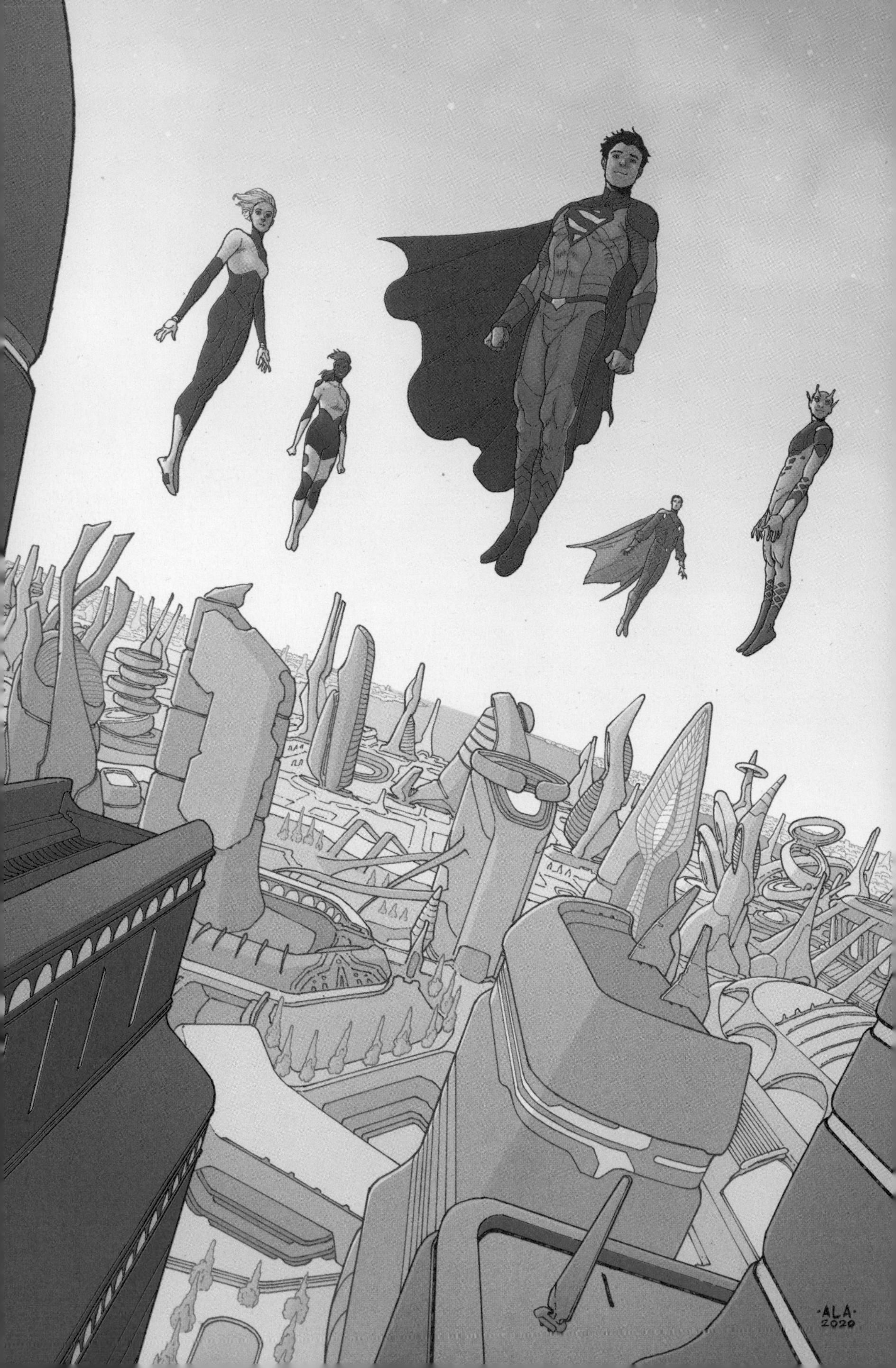

·ALA·
2020

Legion of Super-Heroes **#10** variant cover by
DARKO LAFUENTE and **GERMAN GARCIA**

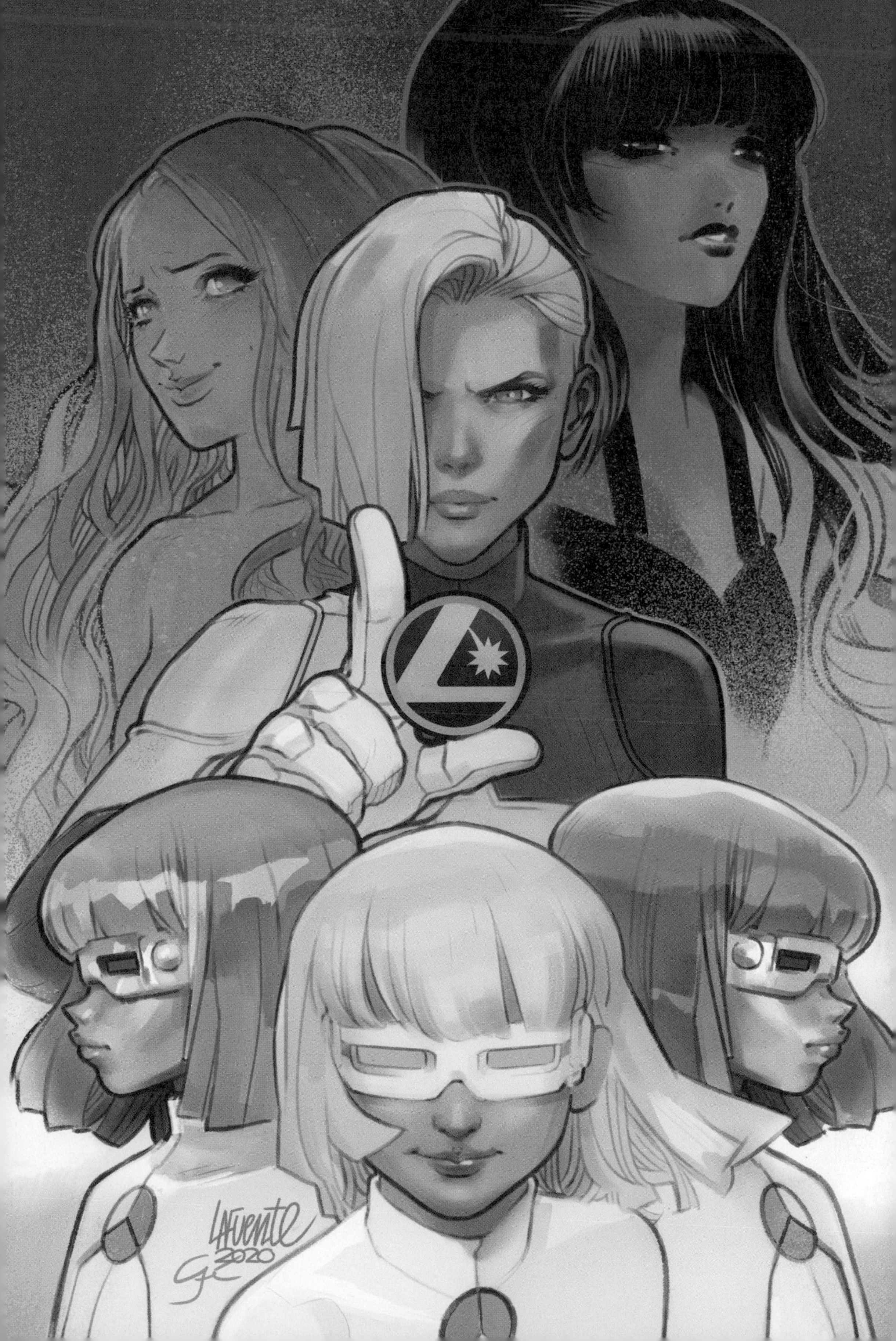

Legion of Super-Heroes **#11** variant cover by
NICOLA SCOTT and **ANNETTE KWOK**

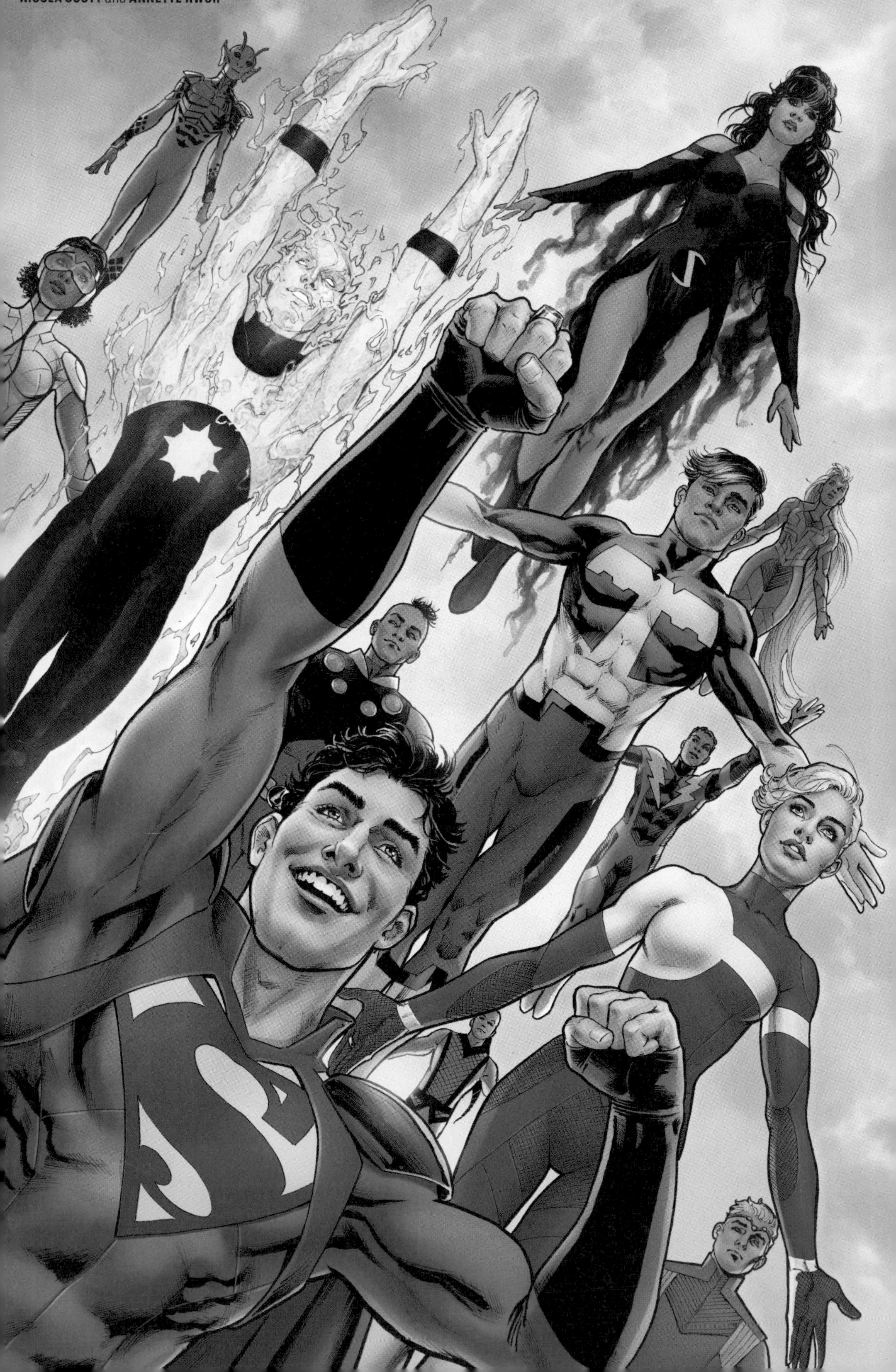

Legion of Super-Heroes **#12** variant cover by **MATT TAYLOR**

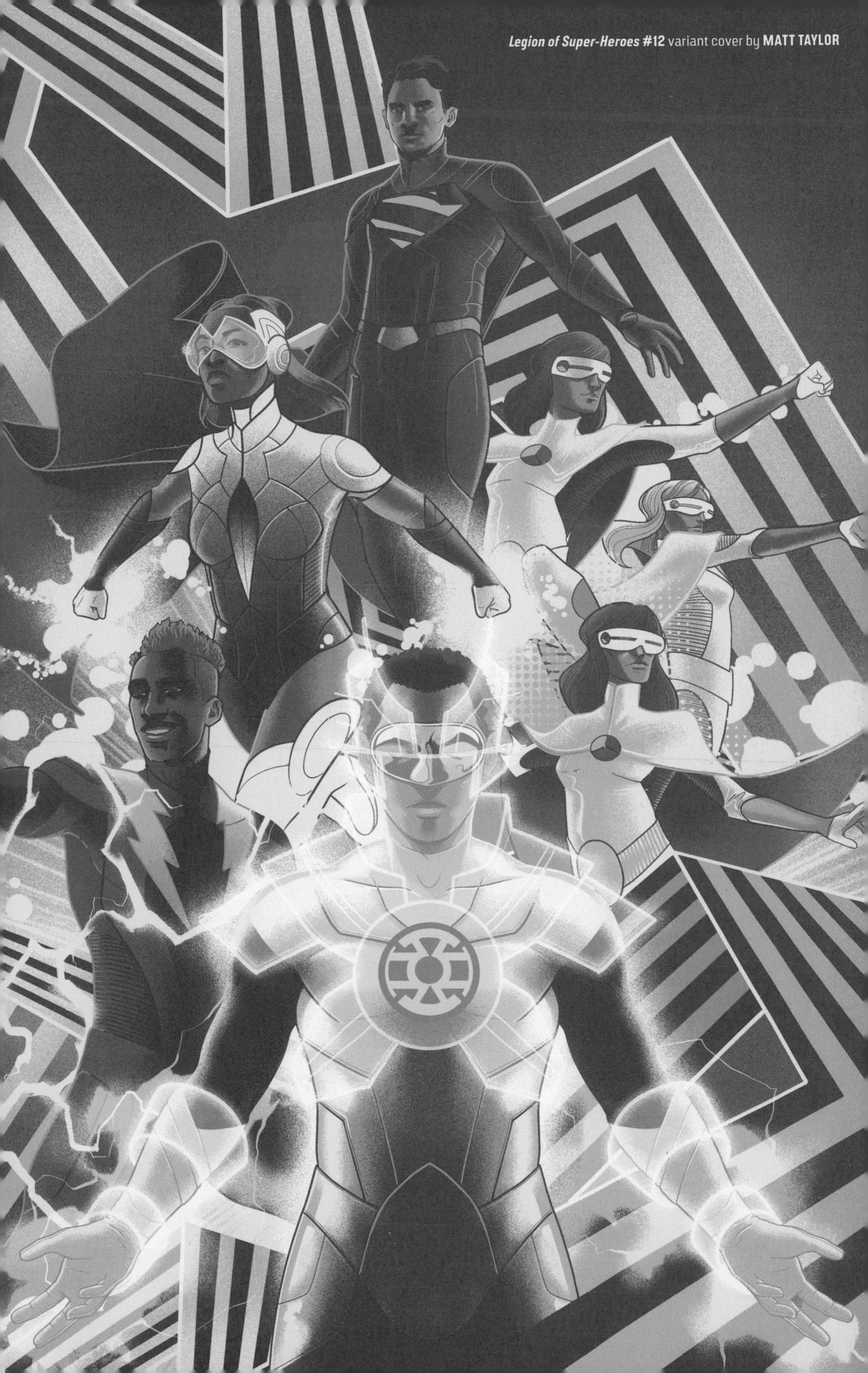

Concept Art by RYAN SOOK

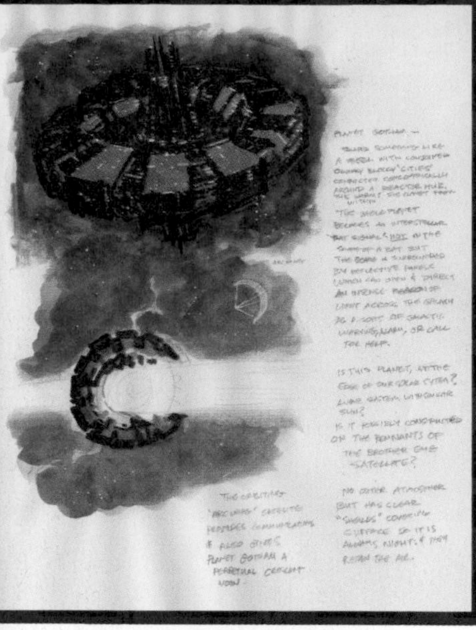
PLANET GOTHAM —
IS THIS PLANET, AT THE EDGE OF OUR SOLAR SYSTEM?
IS IT POSSIBLY CONSTRUCTED ON THE REMNANTS OF THE BROTHER EYE SATELLITE?
NO OUTER ATMOSPHERE BUT HAS CLEAR "SHIELDS" COVERING SURFACE SO IT IS ALWAYS NIGHT & THEY RETAIN THE AIR.

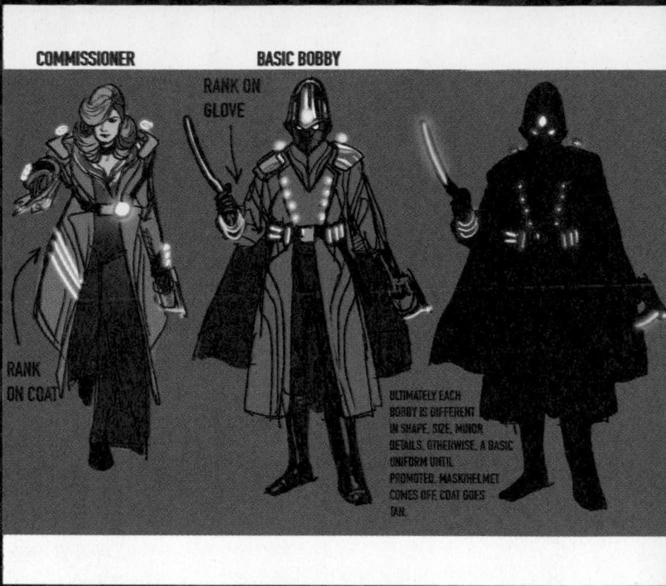
COMMISSIONER
BASIC BOBBY
RANK ON GLOVE
RANK ON COAT
ULTIMATELY EACH BOBBY IS DIFFERENT IN SHAPE, SIZE, MINOR DETAILS. OTHERWISE, A BASIC UNIFORM UNTIL PROMOTED. MASK/HELMET COMES OFF, COAT GOES TAN.

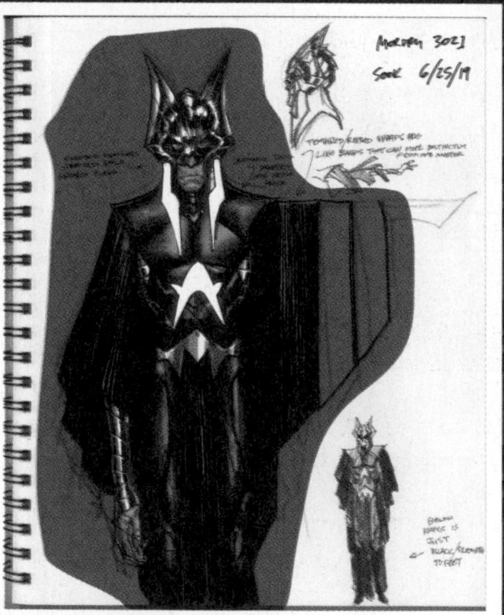
MORDRU 3021
SOOK 6/25/19

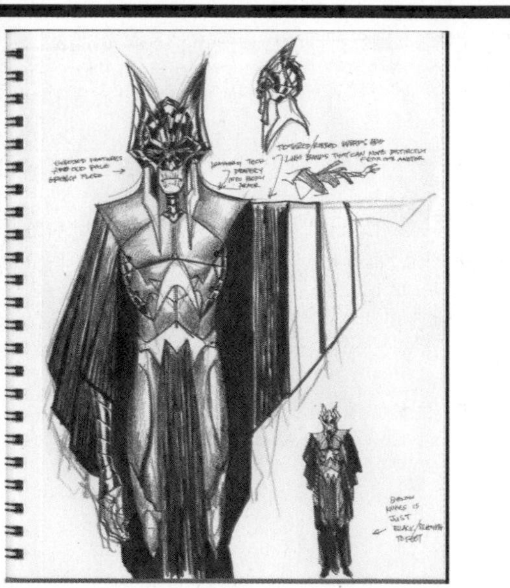

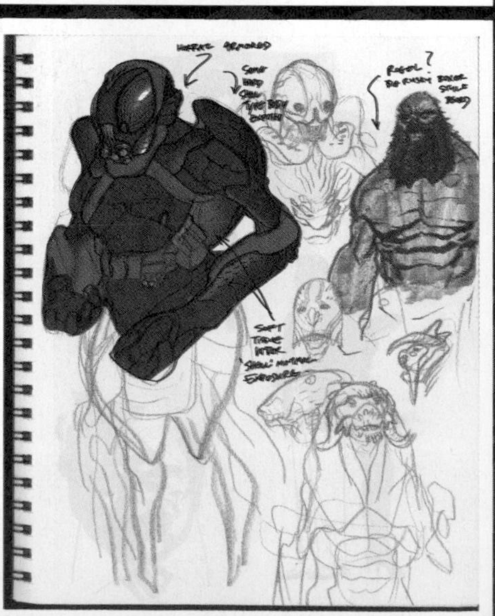

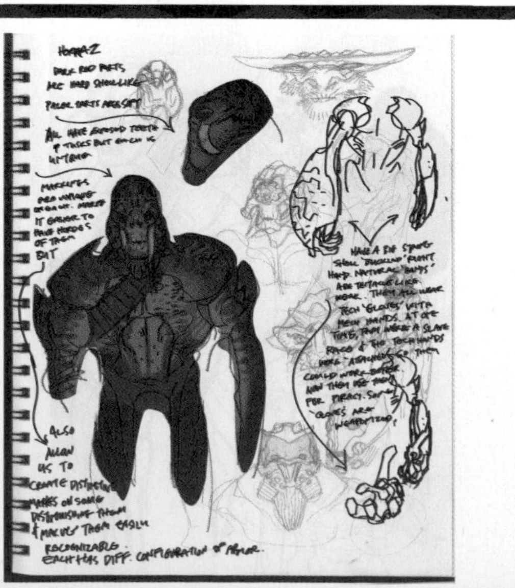
EACH HAS DIFF. CONFIGURATION OF ARMOR.

DAXAM

DAXAM IS A SYSTEM MADE UP OF THREE PLANETS ORBITING THE UNITED PLANETS BLDG. OR HUB WHICH IS AN ANCIENT STRUCTURE WITH UNKNOWN ORIGIN WHICH HANGS OVER A "SUSPENDED" BLACK HOLE KNOWN AS THE FOUNTAIN AND FURNACE. IT IS CONSIDERED TO BE THE BIRTHPLACE OF OUR UNIVERSE. IT IS IN A STATE OF PERPETUAL CREATION/DESTRUCTION SO NORMAL BLACK HOLE PROPERTIES DON'T APPLY. THE PLANETS AND CENTRAL STRUCTURE ARE IN SYMBOTIC BALANCE WITH THE FOUNT ALLOWING FOR INCOMING AND OUTGOING SHIPS TO REMAIN UNAFFECTED BY THE INTENSE COSMIS FORCES AT THEIR CENTER. THESE FORCES PROVIDE A CONSTANT LIGHT DISPLAY OF BRILLIANT MAGNITUDE WHICH LEAVE ALL THREE PLANETS TO HAVE PERPETUAL DAYLIGHT, BOTH DIRECTLY ON ONE SIDE AND AMBIENTLY FROM THE "DARK" SIDE. EACH PLANET IS PERFECTLY SPLIT INTO TWO EXTREME CLIMATES. HALF DESERT, HALF TROPICAL. ALL THE PLANETS AND THE U.P. STRUCTURE ARE MADE OF THE PRIMARY ELEMENT DAXAMITE. A BLACK ANGULAR CRYSTALINE STRUCTURE WHIC HAS BEEN CARVED BY THE INHABITANTS INTO DWELLING PLACES. THESE BLACKISH CRYSTALS EXTRUDE AT SHARP ANGLES FROM THE OTHERWISE VERY ORGANIC ELEMENTS SURROUNDING THEM. GLOWING ORBS ARE THE LIGHT SOURCE INSIDE THE DWELLINGS AND ALSO LIGHT THE GREAT HALL. THE RING AROUND THE GREAT HALL HAS SMALL HALF DOMED ORBS WHICH ARE ACTUALLY THE OFFICES OF THE REPS FROM EACH PLANET IN THE GALACTIC. DAXAM IS THE HOME OF CHAMELEON BOY AND HIS MOTHER PRESIDENT BRANDE. DAXAMITE, LIKE IT'S INHABITANTS HAS UNUSUAL CAMOUFLAGING AND SHAPE CHANGING ABILITIES. THE WHOLE SYSTEM, LIKE CHAMELEON BOY, IS REPRESENTED MAINLY BY A TRIADIC PALETTE OF GREENISH/ORANGES/DARK PURPLES.

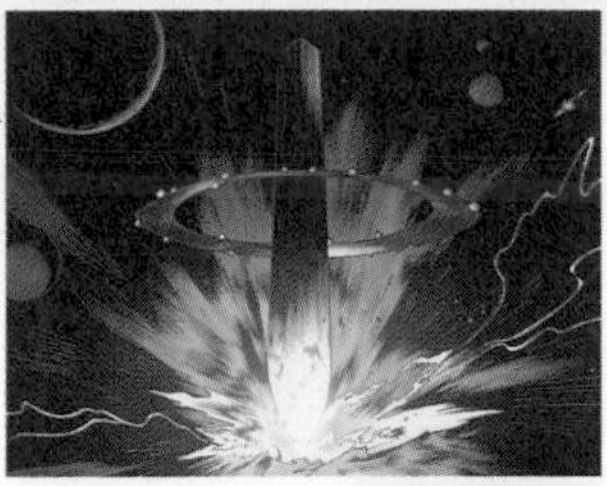

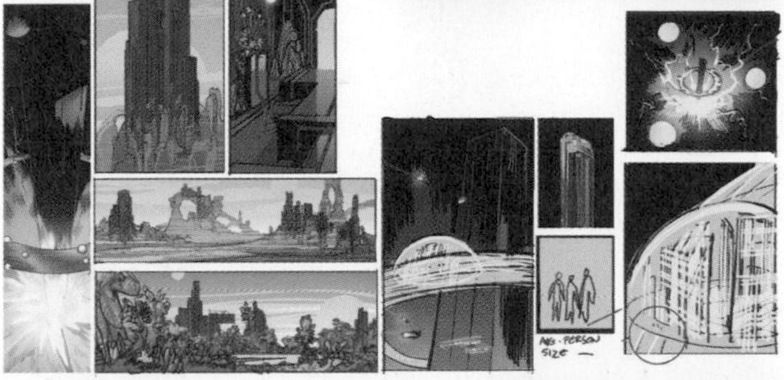

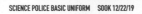

SCIENCE POLICE BASIC UNIFORM SOOK 12/22/19

FIVE GLOWING EYE LENSES ON HELMET ALLOW FOR MULTI SPECTRUM VISUALS. SMALL SCREEN SHOWS IDENTITY OF OFFICER WHEN NEEDED. OTHERWISE IT'S DARK. GREY BULKY TACTICAL GEAR IS DESIGNED TO DE-GENDER AND DE-RACE/SPECIES OFFICERS. GRAY UPPER BODY GARMENT IS "FLASH-FABRIC" AND CAN ACT LIKE A FLASH GRENADE LIGHTING UP WHEN NEEDED TO BLIND OPONENTS WITHOUT AFFECTING THE OFFICER. MOST WEAPONRY IS NON LETHAL BUT HIGHLY DEBILITATING. FIREARM HOWEVER CAN BE SET TO LETHAL FORCE.

FOR OUR PURPOSES, THE FLAT GRAY TONES SET THESE GUYS OFF FROM THE HIGHLY COLORFUL SETTINGS AND CHARACTERS OF THE FUTURE AND SPEAK TO THE UNIFORMITY/CONFORMITY OF GOVT. "SOLDIERS". THE PUNCH OF YELLOW BEING SOMETHING WE CAN USE ARTISTICALLY AS WELL AS HARKENING TO PRESENT DAY POLICE UNIFORMS.

EMBLEM ON BREAST IS INTERLAC "S" AND "P".

EACH HELMET HAS A NUMERICAL OFFICER NUMBER SCRIBED IN INTERLAC.

AS WITH REGULAR SOLDIERS, POLICE INDIVIDUAL UNIFORMS MAY BE DISTINGUISHED BY VARIATIONS OF WEAPONS AND PLACEMENTS, ETC.

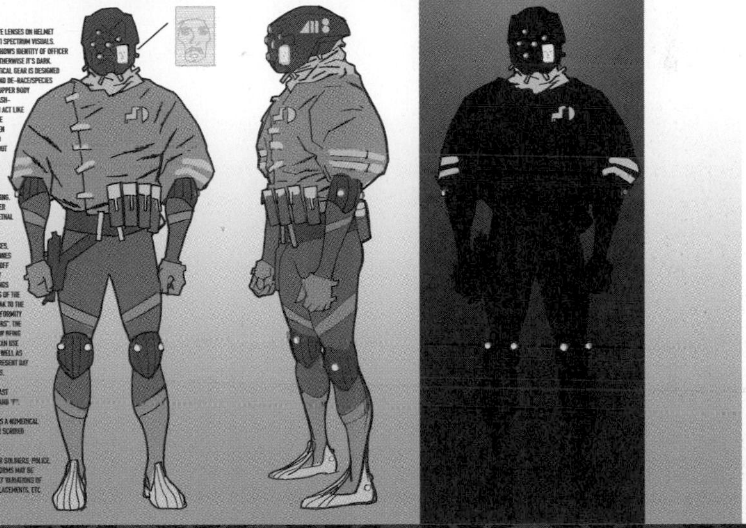

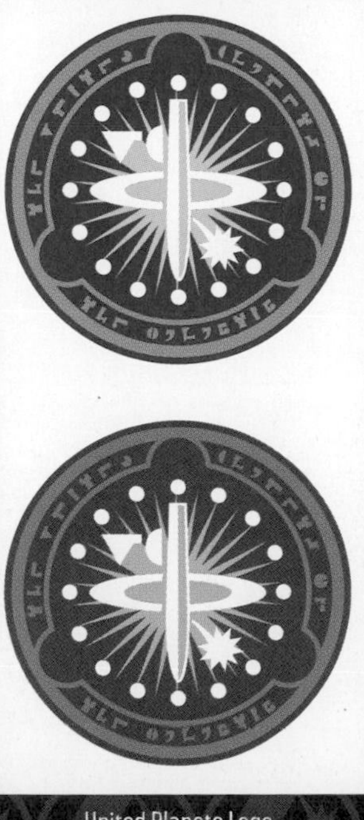

United Planets Logo

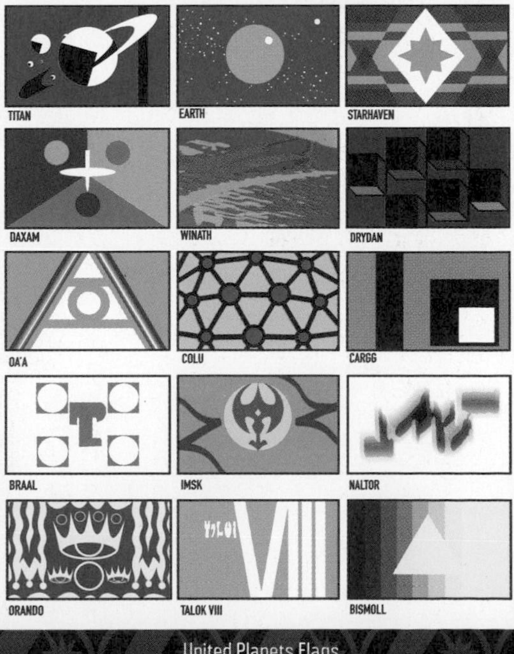
TITAN
EARTH
STARHAVEN
DAXAM
WINATH
DRYDAN
OA'A
COLU
CARGG
BRAAL
IMSK
NALTOR
ORANDO
TALOK VIII
BISMOLL

United Planets Flags

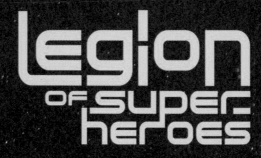

INTERLAC TRANSLATION GUIDE

Legion of Super Heroes

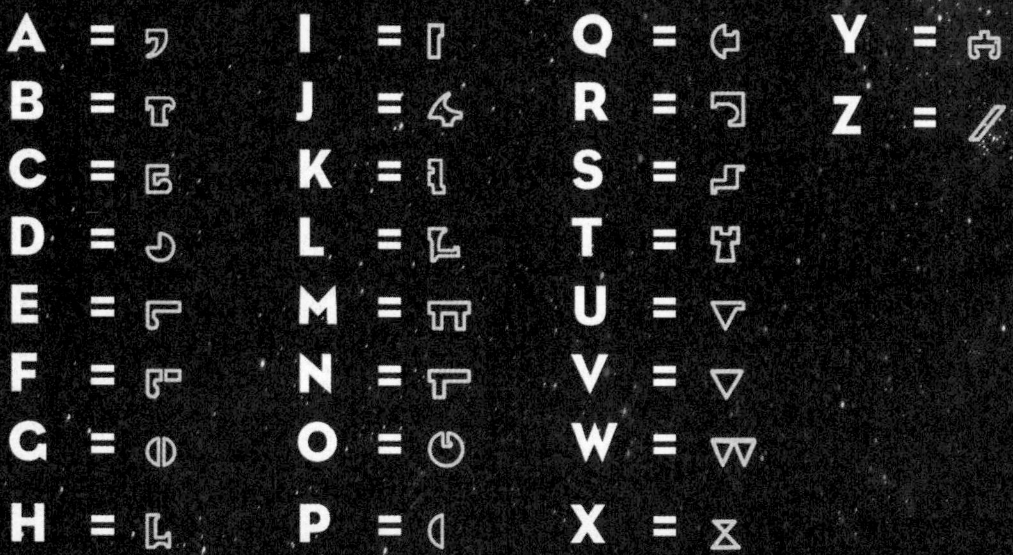
A =
B =
C =
D =
E =
F =
G =
H =
I =
J =
K =
L =
M =
N =
O =
P =
Q =
R =
S =
T =
U =
V =
W =
X =
Y =
Z =